Mastering AWS Serverless

Architecting, developing, and deploying serverless solutions on AWS

Miguel A. Calles

www.bpbonline.com

First Edtion 2024

ISBN: 978-93-55516-114

Distributors:

BPB PUBLICATIONS
20, Ansari Road, Darya Ganj
New Delhi-110002
Ph: 23254990/23254991

DECCAN AGENCIES
4-3-329, Bank Street,
Hyderabad-500195
Ph: 24756967/24756400

MICRO MEDIA
Shop No. 5, Mahendra Chambers,
150 DN Rd. Next to Capital Cinema,
V.T. (C.S.T.) Station, MUMBAI-400 001
Ph: 22078296/22078297

To View Complete BPB Publications Catalogue Scan the QR Code:

Published by Manish Jain for BPB Publications, 20 Ansari Road, Darya Ganj, New Delhi-110002 and Printed by him at Manipal Technologies, Manipal

www.bpbonline.com

Dedicated to

My wife and children

About the Author

Miguel A. Calles is an AWS Community Builder with a focus on serverless and a published author on serverless security. Miguel works on cloud computing and cybersecurity projects and has been writing on both topics since 2016. He has worked on multiple serverless projects since 2018 as a developer and security engineer. Miguel is currently a Senior Systems Engineer and Security Analyst at Iris Technology and was formerly the Chief Technology Officer at VeriToll building serverless solutions. Miguel has a Bachelor of Science degree in Material Science and Engineering from the Massachusetts Institute of Technology, a Master of Business Administrator degree from the University of Florida, a Cloud Security Alliance's Certificate of Cloud Security Knowledge certification, and an AWS Certified Solution Architect Associate certification. For fun, Miguel enjoys bowling with his family.

About the Reviewer

Syed is a pioneer and **subject matter expert** (**SME**) in application modernization and cloud computing. He is a holder of multiple industry certifications in Azure, AWS, GCP, Oracle, PMP, CSM. With more than a decade of expertise in product development, architecture, scalability, and modernization, Syed has held positions with Oracle, the Big 4 technology advisory companies like PwC and Ernst & Young, as well as other contemporary application enterprises. Syed has also published articles in leading Journal of Cloud Computing. Syed is a skilled and devoted technology management executive who employs his more than 15 years of expertise in the design and development of high-demand On Premise / Commercial of the Shelf Software / SaaS solutions. He possesses specialized knowledge in designing and constructing highly scalable and highly available systems. In order to assist them in establishing and managing their businesses by taking control of their frequently cumbersome applications, Syed has provided consulting services to some of the world's top corporations. Syed assists businesses in modernizing their applications by emphasizing scale and availability, aiding cloud migration, DevOps transformations, and risk-based problem identification. Syed offers expert guidance, strategy, and thought leadership to assist you in solving application modernization issues. Syed promotes change by collaborating with enterprises of all sizes and executive team

Acknowledgement

I thank my wife and children for supporting and believing in me. Writing a book takes time and energy; sometimes it meant having less family time with you. Thank you for supporting me even when it meant I was sometimes unavailable.

I am grateful to BPB Publications for presenting the opportunity to write on serverless, a topic I enjoy. Their team has been professional and diligent from start to finish. Their review processes provided me with valuable feedback that shaped this book well.

Thank you to my colleagues at Raytheon and Secjuice, who guided me along my writing journey, and my colleagues at Transurban, VeriToll, and Iris Technology, who provided me with opportunities to work on serverless to create solutions for their missions. Thank you to the staff at AWS for building great solutions and providing me with resources to create serverless solutions and accepting me into the AWS Community Builders program.

Thank you to my readers who took an interest in this book. Thank you to the audience of my blog posts who took the time to read my content, share it on social media, and provide feedback. This support encourages me to continue writing more and sharing what I know and learn.

I appreciate my parents, sister, and in-laws for being there for me.

Last but not least, I thank my Creator for another opportunity to continue writing and growing.

Preface

When I pondered the title, **Mastering AWS Serverless**, I tried to determine what it takes to become a master at anything. I envisioned a master wearing a martial arts suit with black belts and teaching a group of young learners. The master would be telling me to execute one single motion repeatedly. The repetition taught by the master would shape these learners to perform those motions with perfection. Over time, the exercises would eventually shape those learners into masters if they continued. Therefore, this book needed to have exercises.

The martial arts dojo is not easily translated into a book, and repeated reading exercises several times can become incredibly dull. Yet, repetition is a crucial activity to master any skill. Thus, I provided as many hands-on exercises as possible. To keep the book interesting, I created a variety of exercises. Yet, there was some inherent repetition: modifying the serverless function settings and defining security permissions. By the end of the book, you will have created a basic serverless application and have done some "repetition exercises" to help you start your journey to become a master in AWS serverless.

Another reason for writing this book is to help you understand AWS serverless. Even with its popularity, only a minority of developers know about it and understand how to use it. This book aims to bridge the gap by explaining concepts and building an application. Understanding concepts is fundamental, but many developers (including myself) learn best with hands-on work. Watching a presentation and reading a book helps to understand why something works. However, *real learning* happens after writing code, running it, and seeing it work. By the end of the book, you will understand how to use serverless. Here is an overview of the book.

Chapter 1: Introduction to AWS Serverless– We will lay the foundation of AWS serverless. We will start with an overview of cloud computing and how that enabled serverless computing. After that, we will learn about the different services used in serverless architectures and designs, including serverless computing, serverless storage, and other services.

Chapter 2: Overview of Serverless Applications– We will provide an overview of different types of serverless applications. There are many ways to use serverless. We will cover the most common ways to build applications using AWS serverless, which include website development, application programming interfaces, mobile app development, data processing, and notifications.

Chapter 3: Designing Serverless Architectures– We will provide an overview of how to design serverless architectures and design topics to consider. We will review monolithic and client-server architectures and how they can migrate to the AWS cloud and transition to AWS serverless. We will discuss using event-driven, microservices, and ad hoc architectures serverless.

Chapter 4: Launching a Website– We will provide hands-on exercises to create a serverless website. The hands-on exercises will cover setting up an AWS account, registering a new domain with Route 53, enabling and disabling S3 website hosting, creating a record in Route 53, requesting a certificate from AWS Certificate Manager (ACM), creating a CloudFront distribution, and create aliases for the distribution in Route 53.

Chapter 5: Creating an API– We will create and manage an API, send requests to a serverless function, and learn about its OpenAPI specification. The hands-on exercise will cover adding a new web page to use the API, invalidating the distribution to clear CloudFront cache, creating an API with API Gateway, integrating a Lambda function with the API, and exporting the API integration.

Chapter 6: Saving and Using Data– We will focus on saving and using data using object storage and serverless databases. The hands-on exercises will cover creating an S3 bucket for object storage, getting the object contents from a Lambda function, creating a DynamoDB database table, and getting the table data from a Lambda function. You will modify the function setting and security permissions multiple times in this chapter and throughout the rest of the book.

Chapter 7: Adding Authentication and Authorization– We will demonstrate how a website could add authentication and authorization to restrict certain pages to logged-in users. We will conduct hands-on exercises to add authentication and authorization using Amazon Cognito by creating a new Cognito user pool, customizing its hosted user interface, and updating the website. We will update the website by adding the login and logout buttons, the auth callback page, the logout page, and the account page.

Chapter 8: Processing Data Using Automation and Machine Learning– We will focus on how to use serverless computing to process data. The hands-on exercises will cover tracking authentication callbacks with an API and transforming that data using a Lambda function and an EventBridge schedule rule. We explore analyzing the transformed data with machine learning.

Chapter 9: Sending Notifications– We will send notifications using email, text messaging, and mobile push notifications. The hands-on exercises will cover configuring SES for emails, sending an email from a Lambda function, setting up an SNS topic to trigger a

Lambda function, sending a topic message from a Lambda function, setting up SNS for text messages, and sending a text message from a Lambda function.

Chapter 10: Additional Automation Topics– We discuss automation tasks that a serverless architecture can support. We will explore automation tasks that include setting up backups, analyzing text using Amazon Comprehend, performing text-to-speech using Amazon Polly, analyzing images using Amazon Rekognition, and auditing security settings using AWS Config.

Chapter 11: Architecture Best Practices– We will focus on architecture best practices when using serverless computing. We will walk through the AWS Well-Architected Framework and apply its Serverless Applications Lens. The Framework and Lens provide various best practices. We will review them to help you better architect and design your serverless applications.

Chapters 12: Next Steps– We will focus on the next steps you can explore to continue mastering AWS serverless. We only covered a few topics in-depth but explored them since it was necessary to gain exposure to them. Some of the following steps will include advanced topics such as attaching layers to Lambda functions, orchestrating function execution using AWS Step Functions, automatically creating resources using infrastructure as code with AWS CloudFormation, AWS Serverless Application Model, and AWS Cloud Development Kit, creating repeatable deployment processes using AWS CodeBuild and AWS CodePipeline, and testing serverless applications.

Code Bundle and Coloured Images

Please follow the link to download the
Code Bundle and the *Coloured Images* of the book:

https://rebrand.ly/j2hb61w

The code bundle for the book is also hosted on GitHub at
https://github.com/bpbpublications/Mastering-AWS-Serverless.
In case there's an update to the code, it will be updated on the existing GitHub repository.

We have code bundles from our rich catalogue of books and videos available at **https://github.com/bpbpublications**. Check them out!

Errata

We take immense pride in our work at BPB Publications and follow best practices to ensure the accuracy of our content to provide with an indulging reading experience to our subscribers. Our readers are our mirrors, and we use their inputs to reflect and improve upon human errors, if any, that may have occurred during the publishing processes involved. To let us maintain the quality and help us reach out to any readers who might be having difficulties due to any unforeseen errors, please write to us at :

errata@bpbonline.com

Your support, suggestions and feedbacks are highly appreciated by the BPB Publications' Family.

Piracy

If you come across any illegal copies of our works in any form on the internet, we would be grateful if you would provide us with the location address or website name. Please contact us at **business@bpbonline.com** with a link to the material.

If you are interested in becoming an author

If there is a topic that you have expertise in, and you are interested in either writing or contributing to a book, please visit **www.bpbonline.com**. We have worked with thousands of developers and tech professionals, just like you, to help them share their insights with the global tech community. You can make a general application, apply for a specific hot topic that we are recruiting an author for, or submit your own idea.

Reviews

Please leave a review. Once you have read and used this book, why not leave a review on the site that you purchased it from? Potential readers can then see and use your unbiased opinion to make purchase decisions. We at BPB can understand what you think about our products, and our authors can see your feedback on their book. Thank you!

For more information about BPB, please visit **www.bpbonline.com**.

Join our book's Discord space

Join the book's Discord Workspace for Latest updates, Offers, Tech happenings around the world, New Release and Sessions with the Authors:

https://discord.bpbonline.com

Table of Contents

Chapter 1
Introduction to AWS Serverless

Introduction

This book aims to help you master serverless on **Amazon Web Services** (**AWS**).[1] As a master, you will have the skill, knowledge, and proficiency to build serverless applications in the AWS cloud. With the master knowledge, you will be on your road to becoming a serverless expert.

This chapter will lay the foundation of AWS serverless. We will start with an overview of cloud computing and how that enabled serverless computing. After that, we will learn about the different services used in serverless architectures and designs.

Structure

We will cover the following topics in this chapter:

- Introduction to cloud computing
- Introduction to serverless computing
- Introduction to serverless storage
- Introduction to serverless services
- Reviewing AWS serverless services

1 Amazon, Amazon Web Services and AWS are registered trademarks of Amazon Web Services, Inc.

Objectives

At the end of the chapter, you will understand AWS's services. You can apply that knowledge when we discuss a serverless application built on AWS.

Introduction to cloud computing

In the early days of computing, organizations hosted equipment in buildings they managed. An organization would buy servers, data storage, router, switches, and racks. They dedicated a room (or sometimes an entire building) to having multiple equipment racks. Cables interconnect connected the equipment to switches and routers that provided network connectivity. Some networks provided local networks that interconnected a select number of devices. Other networks provided connectivity to the organization's Intranet so their staff could connect to their equipment and network services. Some networks provided Internet connectivity where internet-connected devices could connect. These network configurations enabled the *on-premises* hosting and computing in the organization's data warehouse. See *Figure 1.1* for an example of an organization's on-premises infrastructure:

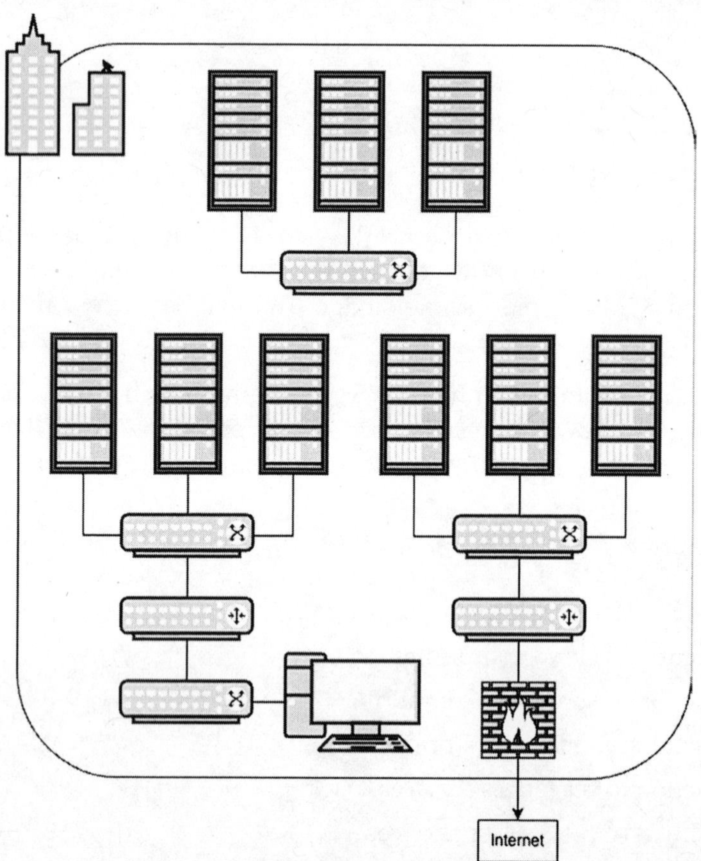

Figure 1.1: *An example infrastructure diagram showing on-premises hosting and computing*

As Internet speeds and connectivity improved, service providers created data warehouses to provide hosting and computing as a service. For example, an organization would pay a service fee for a web server to be made available. An organization could perform a make-or-buy analysis. It would host the web server when it made sense from business, financial, and legal standpoints. Otherwise, they would *rent* a web server to save on costs (for example, operational, labor costs, and maintenance) and possibly offload some legal, compliance, and security implications to the service provider.

The organization's infrastructure diagrams became simpler as it rented hosting from service providers. Some diagrams started showing a cloud to abstract all the servers and services that were no longer on-premises but provided by a service provider. See *Figure 1.2* for an example of an organization's infrastructure that uses a service provider. In this example figure, a computer that accessed servers using internal networking now accesses them from the service provider, which is depicted as a cloud:

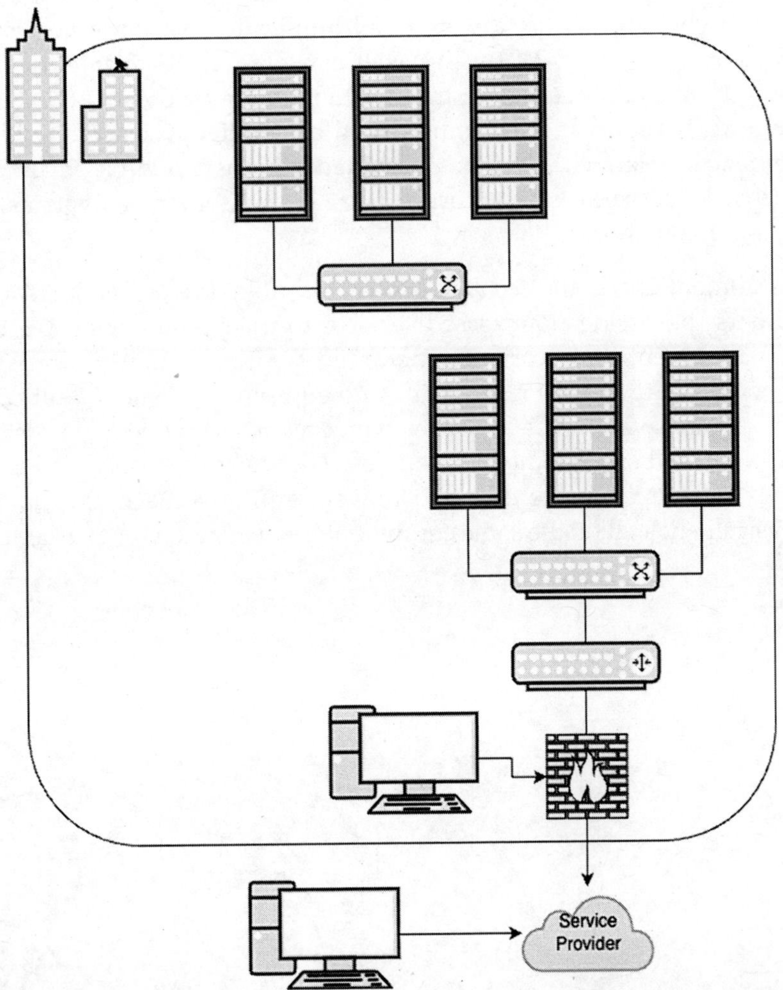

Figure 1.2: *An example infrastructure diagram that shows a service provider as a cloud*

The term *cloud computing* was eventually accepted. We will refer to cloud computing as a set of services and resources provided by a third-party service provider that is accessed via the Internet and are not physically hosted inside an organization's building. This working definition is essential because some serverless solutions allow an organization to perform serverless computing using on-premises hardware. We are focusing on AWS serverless, which is a set of serverless services that AWS, a cloud computing provider (or cloud provider for short), offers.

Cloud providers became popular because their prices became more cost-effective, and service offerings were more powerful. These improvements were fueled by more affordable equipment, higher capacity data storage, faster Internet speeds, and higher bandwidth. Furthermore, companies created new technologies that allowed multiple servers to run within one physical server. These innovations enabled new cloud providers to emerge.

AWS launched its services to the public in 2006 by offering Internet-based services that customers could configure using a web-based application.[2] A customer could sign up for an AWS account, use the **AWS web-based console** (**AWS console** for short), create a server, configure the networking, set up the **Domain Name System** (**DNS**), and get an **Internet Protocol** (**IP**) address. A customer could have a live web server within minutes, for example. Since its launch, AWS has provided various cloud-based products: cloud computing (that is, servers), cloud storage (that is, file server equivalents), databases, networking, and many more.

As previously mentioned, the virtual server technologies enabled AWS and other service providers to provide cloud-based services to their customers. AWS created data warehouses (or data centers) in various geographical regions within a country and around the world. They configured their networking and equipment to allow multiple customers to create servers and save their data, so they were *logically* separated. No customer would be able to access another customer's resources. They were logically separated because the software would separate the data and prevent authorized access even though they might be physically hosted on the same equipment. See *Figure 1.3* for an example of logical separation:

2 "Overview of Amazon Web Services." Amazon Web Services, Inc. **https://docs.aws.amazon.com/whitepapers/latest/aws-overview/introduction.html**

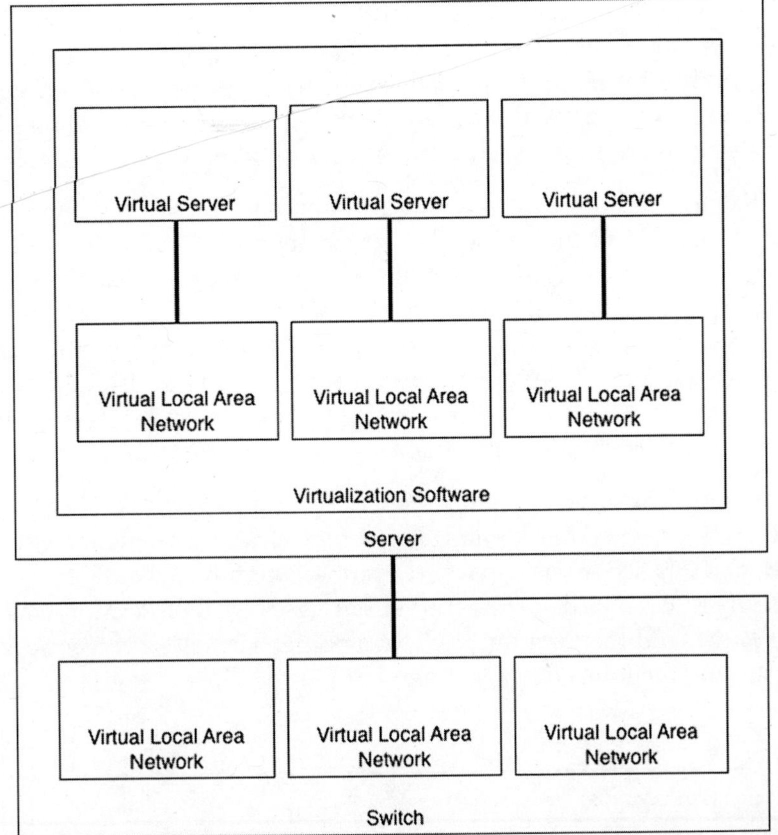

Figure 1.3: An example of logical separation that a cloud provider might implement

With virtualization technologies, AWS can support several customers with the equipment in their data centers. Furthermore, it allows customers to choose:

- The number, speed and type of **central processing unit** (**CPU**) processors
- The **random access memory** (**RAM**) size
- The size of the disk space
- The number, speed and type of graphical processing units
- Other specifications to meet their needs.

How the CPU, RAM, and disk space are provisioned on the physical hardware is done for us.

AWS follows the shared responsibility model to ensure our data is stored and accessed safely.[3] AWS is committed to the *Security of the Cloud*, and they believe it is the customer's responsibility for the *Security in the Cloud*. This means that AWS will ensure the cloud

3 "Shared Responsibility Model." Amazon Web Services. **https://aws.amazon.com/compliance/shared-responsibility-model/**

services and infrastructure is secure. Any hardware, software, data storage, networking, building, staff, operations, and so on, involved in providing cloud services is secured and maintained securely. This also means that how the customer uses the AWS cloud is their responsibility to secure. Like with any software and service, there are best practices for using them. The customer must know how to and be willing to implement them.

Secure virtualization technologies advanced to another level of virtualization. Initially, the technology provided virtual networks, servers, and disk space. This allowed for the introduction of containers. A container is like a virtual server but extremely lightweight. The container's operating system has a minimum set of libraries and dependencies and no graphical display. The container has no resources but shares them with the server running the container orchestration software. A virtual server needs a virtual CPU, RAM, disk drive, network interfaces, and other resources, whereas a container *borrows* the resources from the physical server when it needs them.

For example, a physical server may have 4 CPUs, 16 **gigabytes** (**GB**) of RAM, and one **terabyte** (**TB**) of disk space. That server can host four virtual servers that each have 1 CPU, 4 GB of RAM, and 250 MB of disk space. We cannot add a fifth virtual server because we are out of resources. Even if the virtual server only uses 2 GB of RAM, it was provisioned with 4 GB of RAM, and they are unusable by another virtual server. See *Figure 1.4* for a drawing illustrating the four virtual servers:

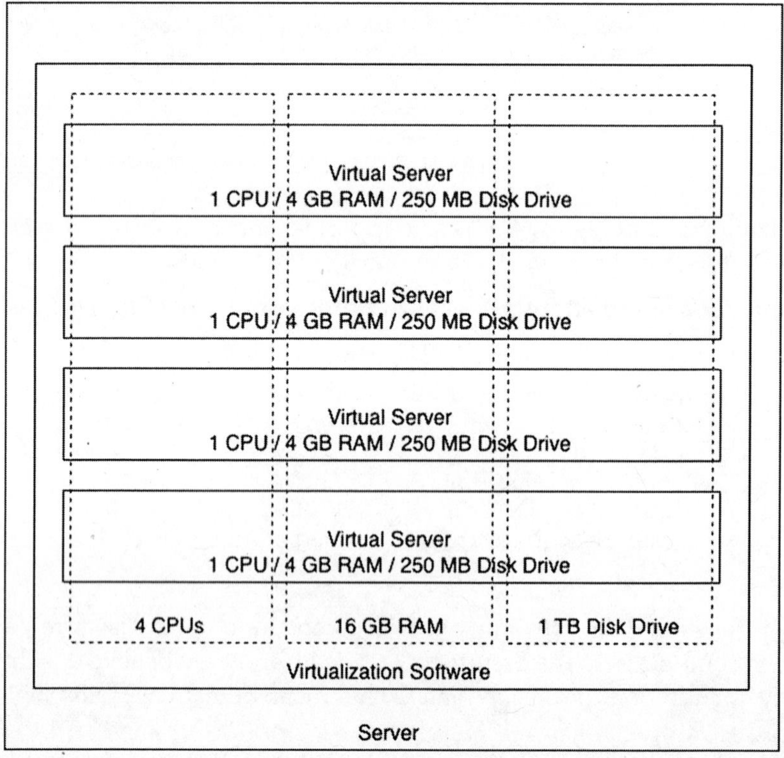

Figure 1.4: *An example of four virtual servers running on a physical server*

Containers use resources differently. Suppose we create four containers on the physical server. The containers only use 0.5 CPUs and 1 GB of RAM. The containers will use an *image* that has the operating system, and they all share the same image. Any runtime files are stored in a temporary container disk drive that grows as needed and is deleted when the container is stopped. The container can use a volume to store files on the drive permanently. These four containers share resources and use up a total of 2 CPUs, 1 GB of RAM, the size of the container image, and the size of the new files. As long as there are still available resources on the physical server, we can continue creating containers. See *Figure 1.5* for a drawing illustrating the containers:

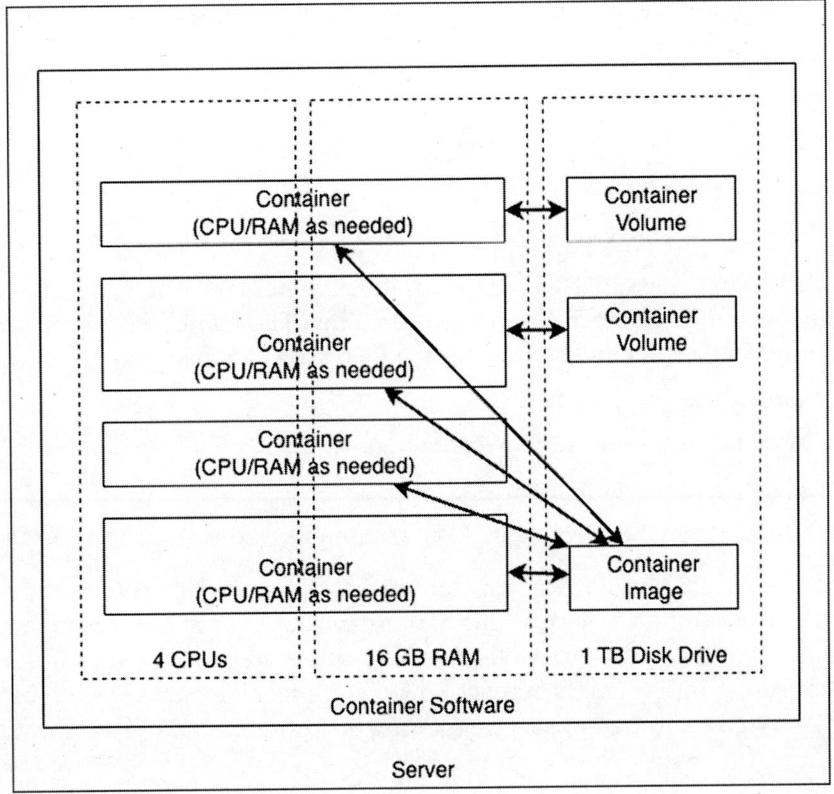

Figure 1.5: *An example of containers running on a physical server*

Cloud providers were able to improve their service offerings because they maximized the utilization of the physical server resources. Furthermore, it allowed organizations to design their applications to use smaller *servers* that used fewer resources and could be less expensive. The ability to potentially run an application in a single container resulted in the next level of innovation: serverless computing.

Introduction to serverless computing

In 2014, AWS introduced AWS **Lambda**, which is their serverless computing service.[4] Lambda allows us to upload and run code as a function without configuring a server or a container. The service uses containers to run the code. When we upload the code to the Lambda service, it is stored as a compressed file inside AWS. When the Lambda function needs to run the code, the service will create a new container, create a volume using the compressed file, execute the code, and delete the container after a period of inactivity. How the Lambda service manages that process is beyond our control. We specify the parameters we would like our Lambda function to have:

- Amount of RAM
- Maximum execution time
- Trigger(s) that starts the code execution
- Function code compressed file
- Security permissions

There are other parameters that we will learn in later chapters. The Lambda service uses the Lambda function parameters to create a container. The Lambda service is considered serverless instead of a container service for the following reasons:

- The purpose is to run code
- We cannot directly manage the containers
- The containers are short-lived
- AWS may choose to move away from containers as the underlying technology

Other serverless providers do not use containers for serverless computing, and how AWS operates the Lambda service is out of our control. A container service assumes the containers are running for long periods. Containers are often used as small servers, and the container configuration might impact how the application runs. As a result, defining the Lambda service as a different service offering makes sense.

Moving to a serverless offering provided many benefits to AWS and its customers. In the previous examples, a physical server could host four virtual servers and more than four containers. The physical server can host many more containers because they are created when they are needed and deleted when they are not. Using the previous example, we can potentially host 100s over Lambda function configurations because the underlying containers only exist when they are needed. The likelihood that all the Lambda functions need to exist simultaneously is low. This is a benefit for AWS customers because they can define as many Lambda functions as needed and only pay when they are used, which can be significantly less than provisioning a server or container.

4 "AWS Lambda Releases." Amazon Web Services. **https://docs.aws.amazon.com/lambda/latest/dg/lambda-releases.html**

The serverless computing model provides the following benefits:

- On-demand usage
- Elasticity
- Scalability
- Rapid development
- Reduced infrastructure
- Reduced maintenance
- Lower costs
- Smaller attack surfaces

The success of serverless computing resulted in cloud providers creating new serverless services and updating existing services to work with serverless applications.

Introduction to serverless storage

In 2006, AWS introduced Amazon **Simple Storage Service** (**S3**), which is their object storage service.[5] S3 was one of AWS's early service offerings.[6] S3 is an object storage where we can store any type of data as an object associated with a key name. We store data in buckets which allows us to create logical groups for our objects. We cannot access objects like files in an operating system or file share server. We access the S3 data using the following AWS capabilities:

- The web-based console
- The **application programming interface** (**API**)
- The **command line interface** (**CLI**)
- The **software development kit** (**SDK**)

AWS and many developers consider S3 as part of the AWS serverless offering. Much like how we do not need to worry about how a Lambda function is created and managed, AWS will manage how we save data to S3. With S3, we can:

- Save an object as big as 5 TB.[7]
- Have no limit on how many objects we can save to a bucket.[8]
- Create up to 1000 buckets

5 "Document history." Amazon Web Services. **https://docs.aws.amazon.com/AmazonS3/latest/userguide/WhatsNew.html**

6 "What is Amazon S3?" Amazon Simple Storage Service User Guide. Amazon Web Services. **https://docs.aws.amazon.com/AmazonS3/latest/userguide/Welcome.html**

7 "Amazon Simple Storage Service endpoints and quotas." Reference Guide. Amazon Web Services. **https://docs.aws.amazon.com/general/latest/gr/s3.html**

8 "Bucket restrictions and limitations." Amazon Simple Storage Service User Guide. Amazon Web Services. **https://docs.aws.amazon.com/AmazonS3/latest/userguide/BucketRestrictions.html**

S3 provides flexibility and scalability in storage, similarly to how Lambda provides that for computing.

Since then, AWS has introduced serverless databases or serverless versions of non-serverless databases. Object storage is beneficial for storing large amounts of data but can be inefficient for querying and searching. Services exist that enable querying and searching for object storage, but that can result in a more complex design and increased costs. Rather, we can use serverless databases. A popular serverless database is Amazon DynamoDB.

DynamoDB is a key-value or **Non-Structured Query Language (NoSQL)** database.[9] Unlike other SQL or NoSQL database services, DynamoDB does not require us to have a dedicated server. AWS fully manages DynamoDB, using multiple servers and disk drives to handle the traffic and store our database table. When we use DynamoDB, we can focus on tables and their data without worrying about configuring and managing the database servers. We work with the tables and data using the AWS console, API, CLI, or SDK.

DynamoDB allows us to configure how much data we can read and write per second (that is, read and write capacity). There are two capacity modes:

- **Provisioned capacity:** We can specify how much *read capacity* and *write capacity* we want as available for our application to use. This provides us with predictability in performance and costs. This mode is best for when we have a consistent number of reads and writes to our table.
- **On-demand capacity:** We can use a pay-per-use mode where we do not need to specify how much capacity we need. This gives us the most flexibility, but we pay higher prices per read and write. This mode is best when we have unpredictable or spikey traffic or when our data sits idle most of the time.

Furthermore, DynamoDB has no limits to the amount of data a table can store. This unlimited storage provides the benefits of object storage with the added features of database operations.[10]

Introduction to serverless services

Data storage and application interfaces were the next logical areas to introduce a serverless solution.

9 "What is DynamoDB?" Amazon DynamoDB Developer Guide. Amazon Web Services. **https://docs.aws.amazon.com/amazondynamodb/latest/developerguide/Introduction.html**

10 "Service, account, and table quotas in Amazon DynamoDB." Amazon DynamoDB Developer Guide. Amazon Web Services. **https://docs.aws.amazon.com/amazondynamodb/latest/developerguide/ServiceQuotas.html**

Serverless data storage services were designed to have the following key benefits:

- Elastic capacities
- Scalable resources

Many serverless data storage services provide *virtually unlimited* or very high data storage. These services do not require provisioning for a specific amount of data storage. Instead, data is stored as needed.

There are different serverless data storage service options which include:

- Object storage
- File systems
- Relational databases
- Non-relational / key-value / document databases

We will explore these services in more detail when we explore the AWS serverless services.

The application interface services can be serverless or not. These services are often categorized as serverless because they work well with serverless computing and provide on-demand, elastic, and scalable characteristics. These application interfaces include:

- API gateways, management, and services
- Messaging and notifications
- Workflow and business logic orchestration
- Event buses and management

We will explore these services in more detail when we explore the AWS serverless services.

Reviewing AWS serverless services

AWS has a web page dedicated to its serverless capabilities.[11] See *Figure 1.6*, which has a screen capture of a section of the AWS serverless web page showing some serverless services:

11 "Serverless on AWS." Amazon Web Services. **https://aws.amazon.com/serverless/**

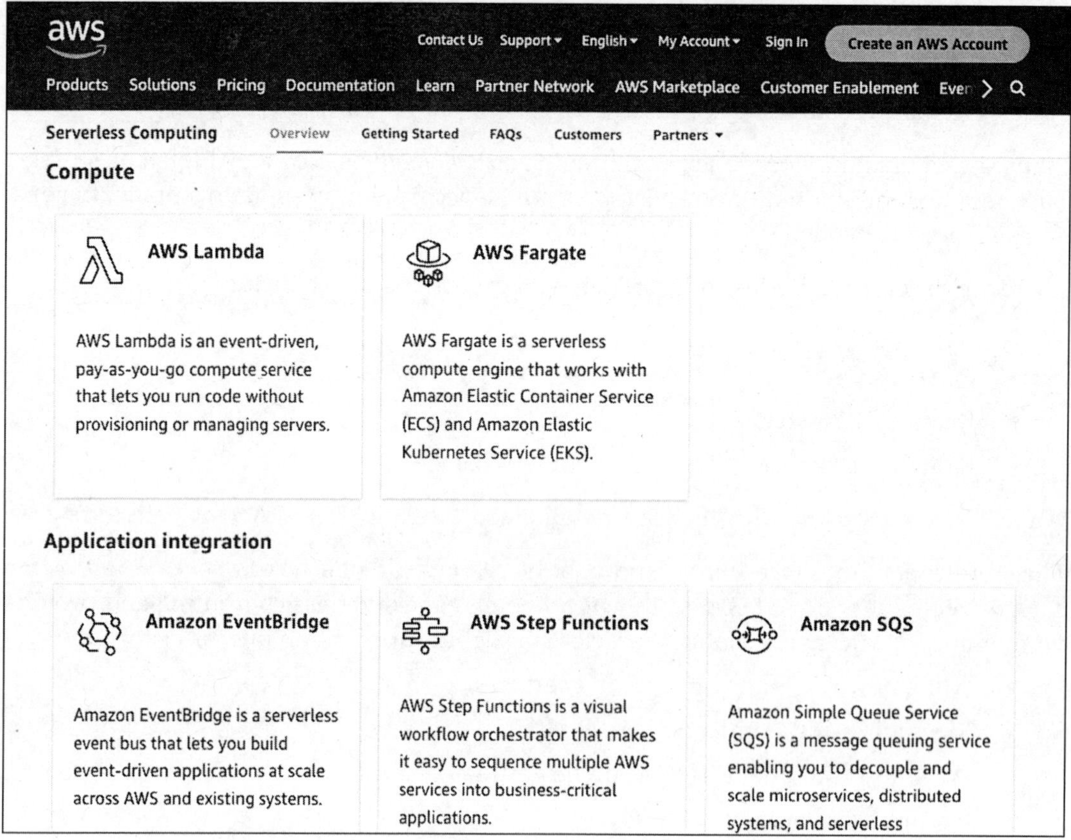

Figure 1.6: *A screen capture of the AWS serverless computing web page*

AWS provides the following serverless services and services that work well with serverless computing:

- Amazon Aurora Serverless
- Amazon API Gateway
- Amazon CloudFront
- Amazon CloudWatch
- Amazon Cognito
- Amazon DynamoDB (Database)
- Amazon EventBridge
- Amazon **Elastic File System (EFS)**

- Amazon Lambda
- Amazon Neptune Serverless
- Amazon OpenSearch Serverless
- Amazon RedShift Serverless
- Amazon **Relational Database Service** (**RDS**) Proxy
- Amazon **Simple Email Service (SES)**
- Amazon **Simple Notification Service (SNS)**
- Amazon **Simple Storage Service (S3)**
- Amazon **Simple Queue Service** (**SQS**)
- AWS AppSync
- AWS Fargate
- AWS Step Functions

These services are well documented in the AWS website and documentation, but we will review some of these services that we will use in this book.

Amazon Lambda

We reviewed Lambda earlier in the chapter. (See the Amazon Lambda icon in *Figure 1.7*.)

Figure 1.7: *Amazon Lambda icon*

To summarize this service, Lambda allows us to execute functions (code) without configuring physical servers, virtual servers, and containers. We specify the Lambda functions configuration, upload the code, and define what events will start (trigger) the code execution.

We will use Lambda functions as our compute and website backend. See *Figure 1.8* for an example of a Lambda function resource:

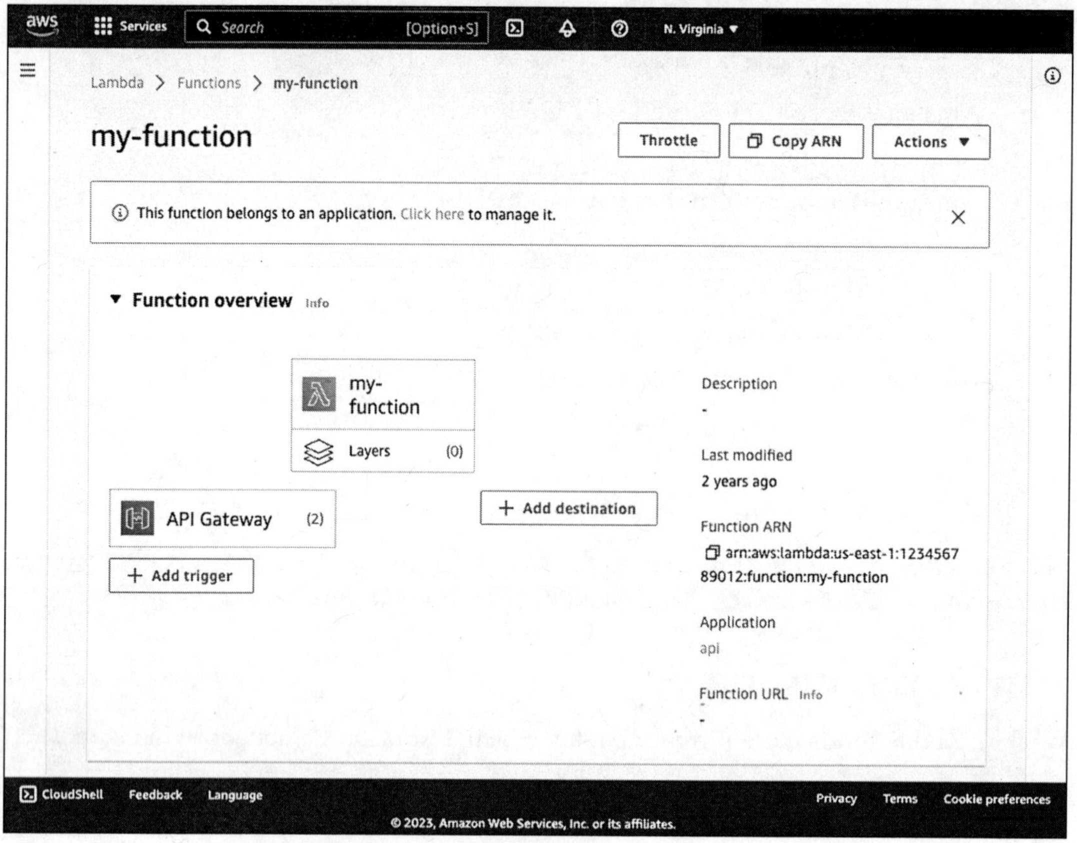

Figure 1.8: *An example of a Lambda function resource*

Amazon API Gateway

API Gateways allows us to create and manage an API for our applications.[12] (See the Amazon API Gateway icon in *Figure 1.9*.)

Figure 1.9: *Amazon API Gateway icon*

We can create APIs that follow the **Representational State Transfer** (**REST**) designs and WebSocket communications protocol. There are two flavors of RESTful APIs:

12 "What is Amazon API Gateway?" Amazon API Gateway Developer Guide. Amazon Web Services. **https://docs.aws.amazon.com/apigateway/latest/developerguide/welcome.html**

- **REST APIs:** They provide rich API endpoints that support the **HTTP** (**Hyper-Text Transfer Protocols**) (for example, **`GET`**, **`POST`**, **`PUT`**, **`DELETE OPTIONS`**). They use the request-response, where an HTTP request is made to an API endpoint, and it sends a response.
- **HTTP (Hyper-Text Transfer Protocols) APIs:** They provide simpler RESTful APIs and natively support OpenID Connect and **OAuth** (**Open Authorization**) 2.0 protocol.

We can manually create the API or use the OpenAPI[13] Specification.

We will use API Gateway to create the API endpoints for our application. See *Figure 1.10* for an example of an API:

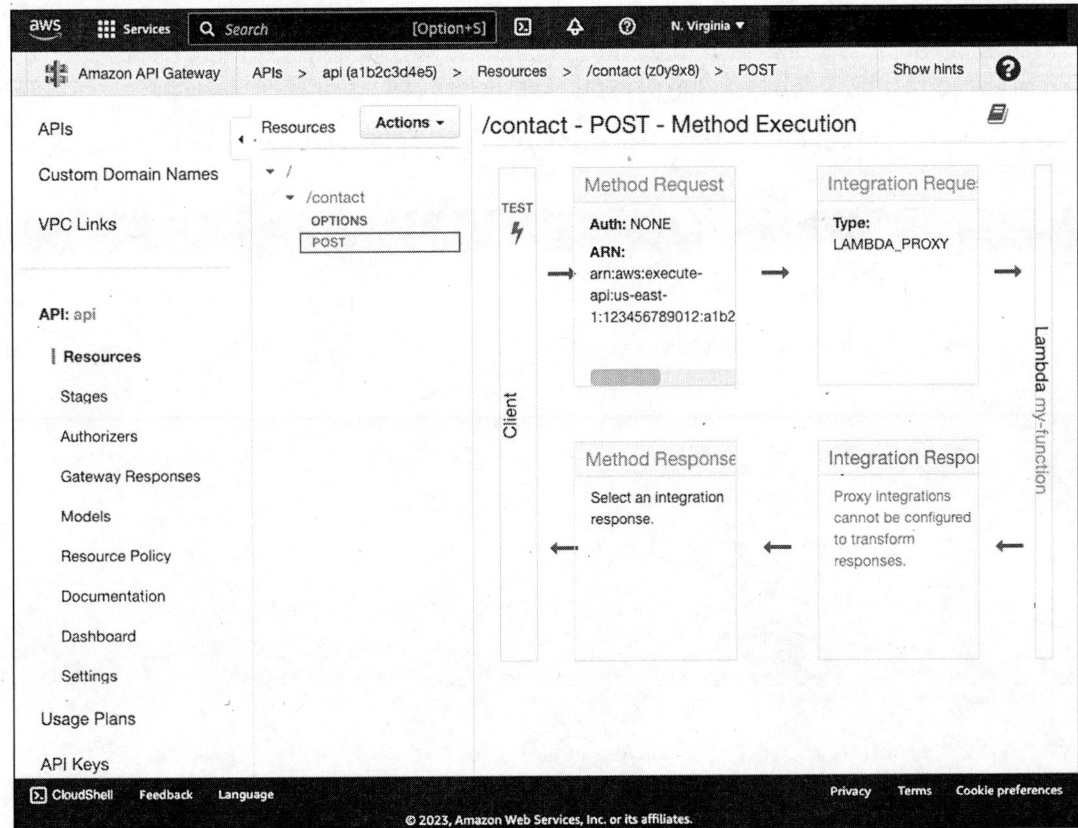

Figure 1.10: *An example of an API Gateway API resource*

13 OpenAPI is a trademark of The Linux Foundation.

Amazon Simple Storage Service

We reviewed the Amazon **Simple Storage Service** (**S3**) earlier in the chapter. (See the Amazon S3 icon in *Figure 1.11*)

***Figure 1.11**: Amazon S3 icon*

To summarize this service, S3 allows us to upload various data types as objects. We associate an object with a key name and upload it to the bucket. An object can be up to 5 TB in size, and a bucket has no limit on the number of objects or total disk space.

We will use S3 to host our website files and save our application data. See *Figure 1.12* for an example of a bucket:

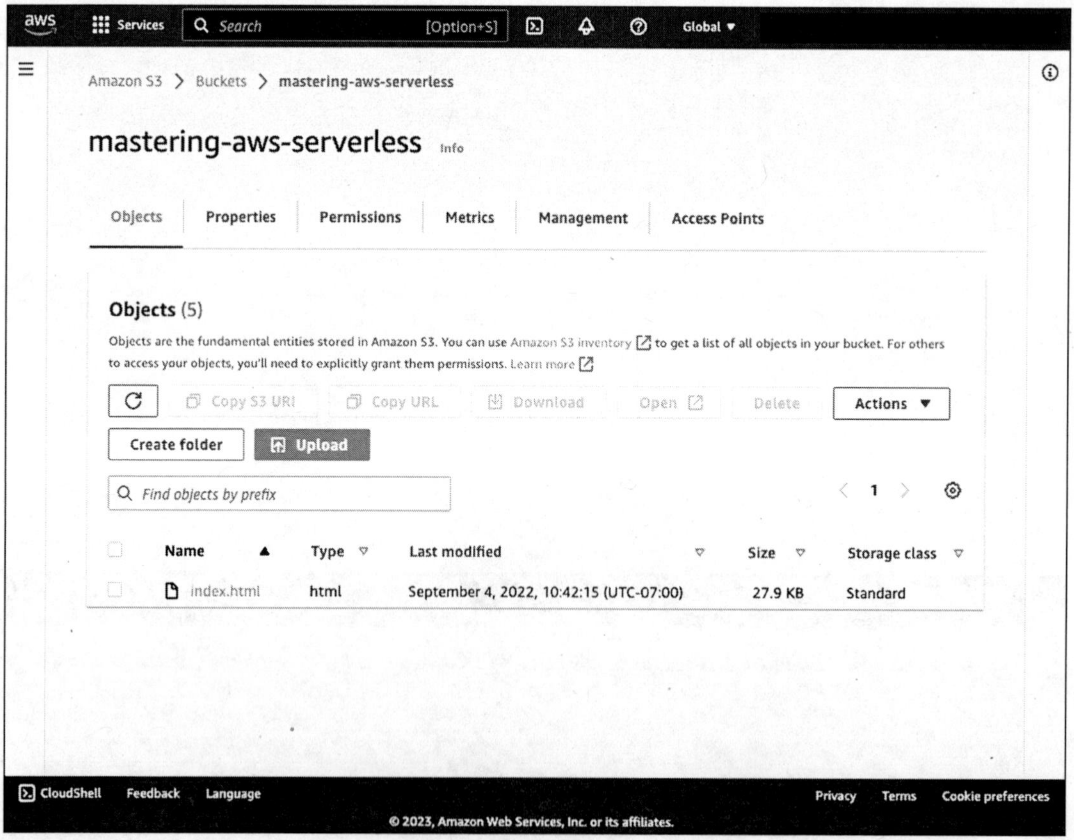

aws Services Search [Option+S] Global

Amazon S3 > Buckets > mastering-aws-serverless

mastering-aws-serverless Info

Objects | Properties | Permissions | Metrics | Management | Access Points

Objects (5)

Objects are the fundamental entities stored in Amazon S3. You can use Amazon S3 inventory to get a list of all objects in your bucket. For others to access your objects, you'll need to explicitly grant them permissions. Learn more

Copy S3 URI | Copy URL | Download | Open | Delete | Actions

Create folder | Upload

Find objects by prefix

Name	Type	Last modified	Size	Storage class
index.html	html	September 4, 2022, 10:42:15 (UTC-07:00)	27.9 KB	Standard

CloudShell Feedback Language Privacy Terms Cookie preferences

© 2023, Amazon Web Services, Inc. or its affiliates.

***Figure 1.12**: An example of an S3 bucket resource*

Amazon CloudFront

CloudFront provides a **Content Delivery Network (CDN)** that caches copies of website files at locations that are geographically closers to the client.[14] See the Amazon CloudFront icon in *Figure 1.13*:

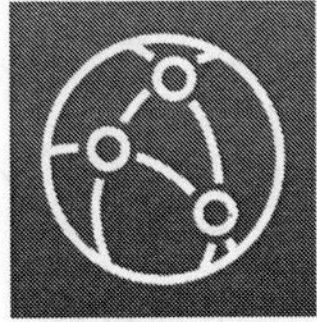

Figure 1.13: *Amazon CloudFront icon*

The client can get the website files faster since the data has to travel a shorter distance. Also, it is faster to deliver cached copies rather than asking a server or AWS service to look up and respond to the data.

CloudFront works well with serverless applications because it can deliver cached copies of the data rather than using serverless resources to respond to HTTP requests.

We will use CloudFront to provide a CDN distribution for the HTML files stored in an S3 bucket. See *Figure 1.14* for an example of a CloudFront distribution:

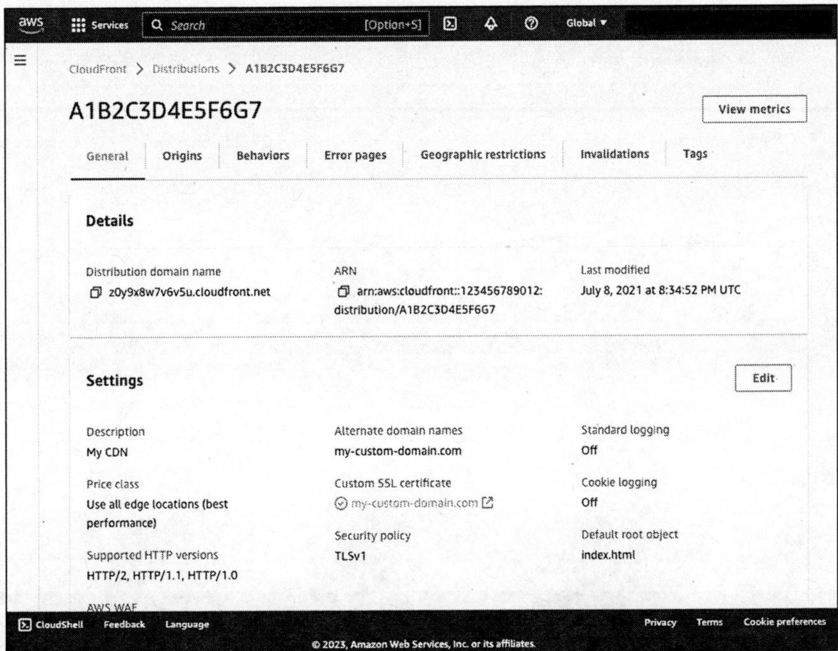

Figure 1.14: *An example of a CloudFront distribution resource*

14 "What is Amazon CloudFront?" Amazon CloudFront Developer Guide. Amazon Web Services. **https://docs.aws.amazon.com/AmazonCloudFront/latest/DeveloperGuide/Introduction.html**

Amazon DynamoDB

We reviewed the Amazon **Simple Storage Service** (**S3**) earlier in the chapter. See the Amazon DynamoDB icon in *Figure 1.15*:

***Figure 1.15**: Amazon DynamoDB icon*

To summarize this service, **DynamoDB** provides key-value storage, database operations, and provisioned or on-demand read-write capacity.

We will use **DynamoDB** to save our website data. See *Figure 1.16* for an example of a table:

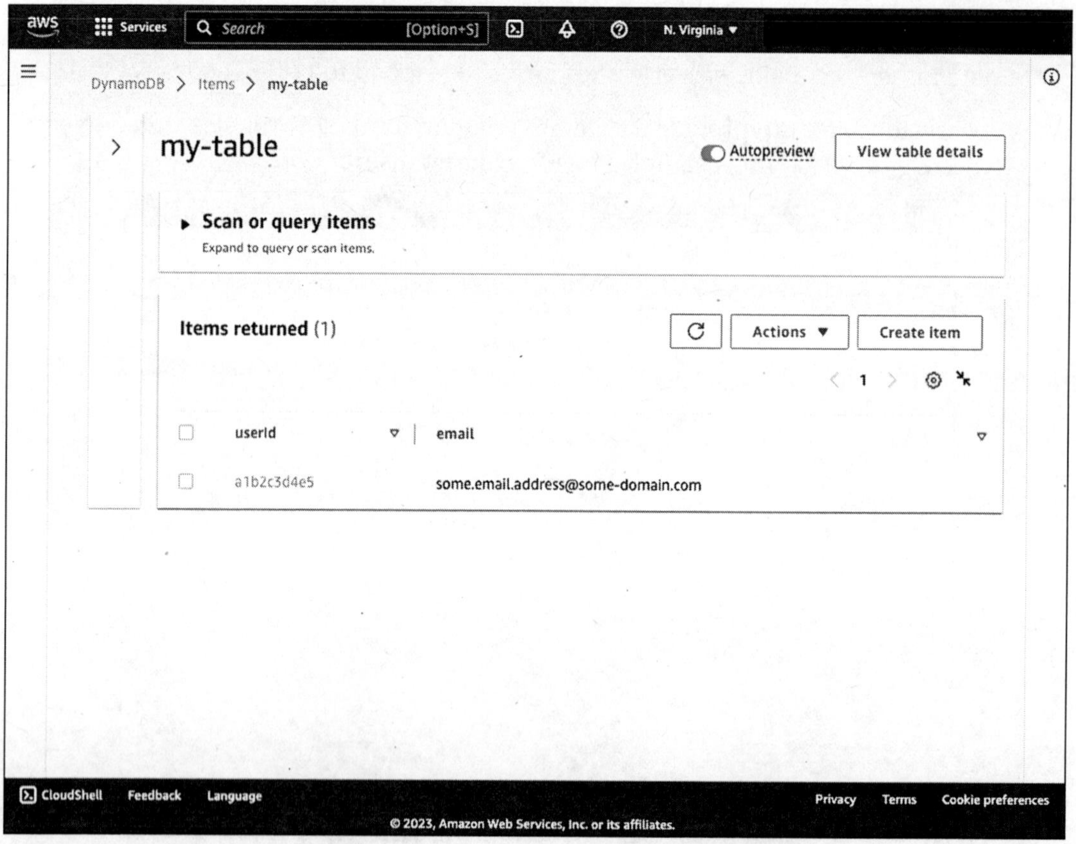

aws Services Search [Option+S] N. Virginia

DynamoDB > Items > my-table

my-table

Autopreview

View table details

Scan or query items

Expand to query or scan items.

Items returned (1)

Actions

Create item

userId	email
a1b2c3d4e5	some.email.address@some-domain.com

CloudShell Feedback Language

Privacy Terms Cookie preferences

© 2023, Amazon Web Services, Inc. or its affiliates.

***Figure 1.16:** An example of a DynamoDB table resource*

Amazon CloudWatch

CloudWatch allows us to monitor our serverless applications using its metrics, alarms, and logs features.[15] See the Amazon CloudWatch icon in *Figure 1.17*:

***Figure 1.17**: Amazon CloudWatch icon*

CloudWatch will automatically create logs and some metrics. We can do the following with CloudWatch:

- Create a dashboard.
- Enable detailed monitoring and anomaly detection.
- Enable application monitoring.
- View application logs.
- Create alarms.

We will use **CloudWatch** for application logging. See *Figure 1.18* for an example of logs:

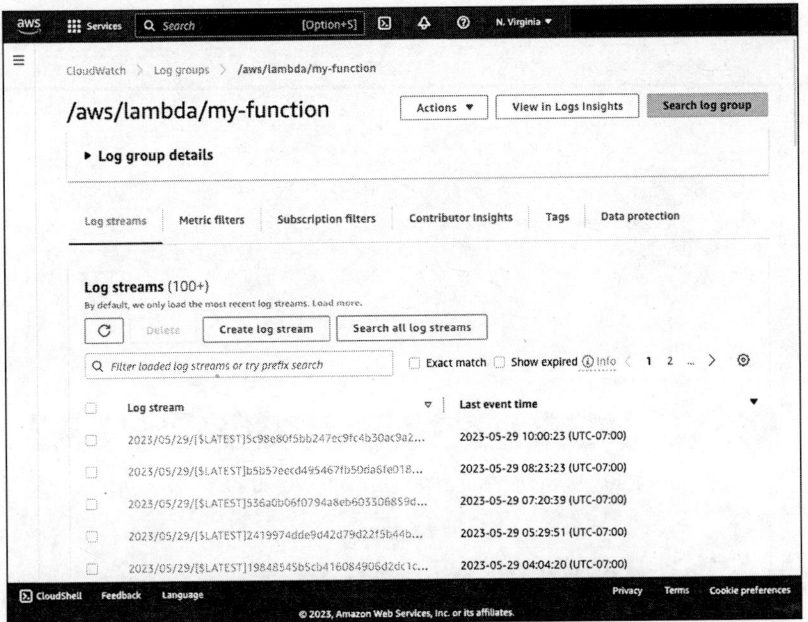

***Figure 1.18:** An example of CloudWatch logs*

15 "What is Amazon CloudWatch?" Amazon CloudWatch User Guide. Amazon Web Services. **https://docs.aws.amazon.com/AmazonCloudWatch/latest/monitoring/WhatIsCloudWatch.html**

Amazon EventBridge

EventBridge allows us to route events using a bus.[16] See the Amazon EventBridge icon in *Figure 1.19*:

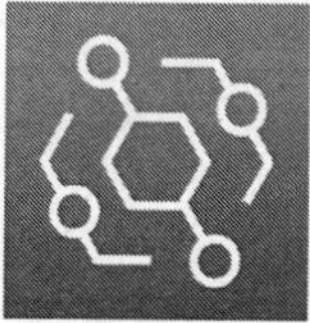

Figure 1.19: Amazon EventBridge icon

We can route events between AWS services and third-party services. It enables us to create rules to schedule events to send to our application. It is serverless and allows us to expand our event-driven designs for our serverless applications.

We will use **EventBridge** to schedule events that trigger Lambda functions to process data. See *Figure 1.20* for an example of an **EventBridge** scheduled event:

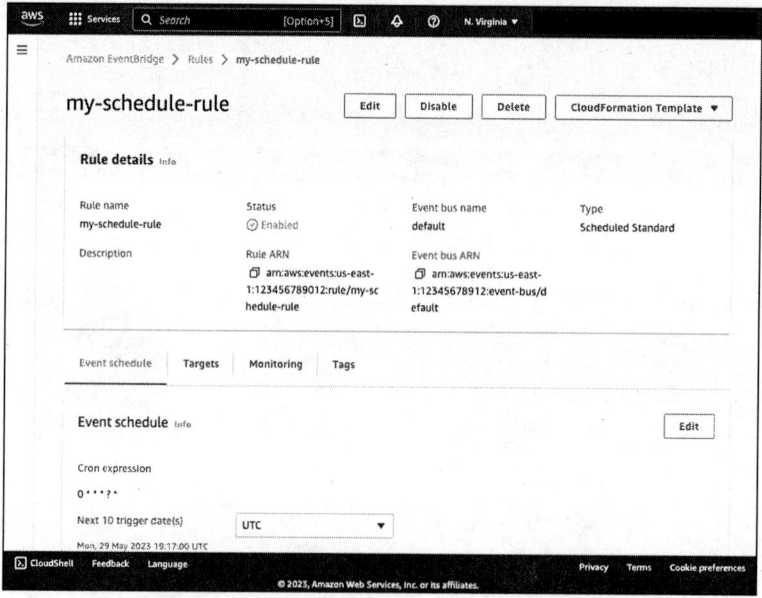

***Figure 1.20:** An example of an EventBridge schedule rule resource*

Amazon Simple Email Service

Simple Email Service (SES) provides us with a way to send and receive emails. (See the Amazon SES icon in *Figure 1.21*.)

16 "What is Amazon EventBridge?" Amazon EventBridge User Guide. Amazon Web Services. **https://docs.aws.amazon.com/eventbridge/latest/userguide/eb-what-is.html**

Figure 1.21: Amazon SES icon

SES provides us with a **Simple Mail Transfer Protocol** (**SMTP**) service which allows us to send and receive email from a verified domain or identity. We can read and send emails using the AWS APIs and SDKs.

We will use SES to send emails from our application. See *Figure 1.22* for an example of a verified identity:

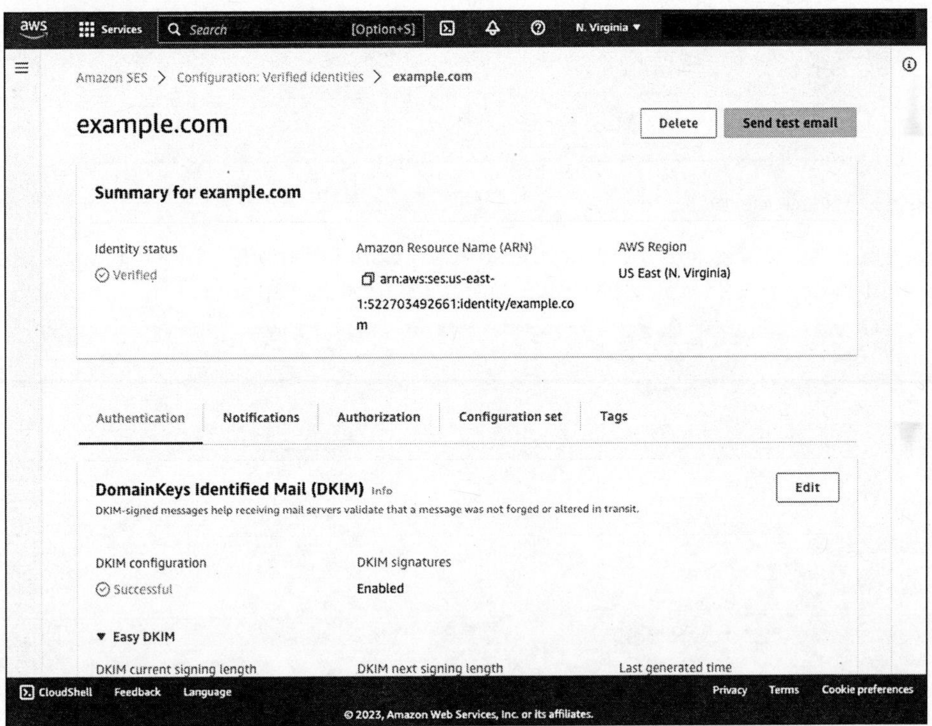

Figure 1.22: An example of an SES verified identity

Amazon Simple Notification Service

Simple Notification Service (**SNS**) provides us with a way to send notifications. See the Amazon SNS icon in *Figure 1.23*:

Figure 1.23: Amazon SNS icon

We can send text messages using the **Simple Messaging Service** (**SMS**), mobile push notifications, and send messages between Lambda functions. We use topics to organize our notifications. We use subscriptions to add:

- Phone numbers for SMS
- Platform application endpoints for push notifications
- Amazon Kinesis Data Firehose endpoints
- Amazon SQS endpoints
- AWS Lambda endpoints
- Email addresses
- HTTP endpoints

When we publish a message to a topic, the subscription endpoints will receive the message. See *Figure 1.24* for an example of an SNS topic and its subscriptions:

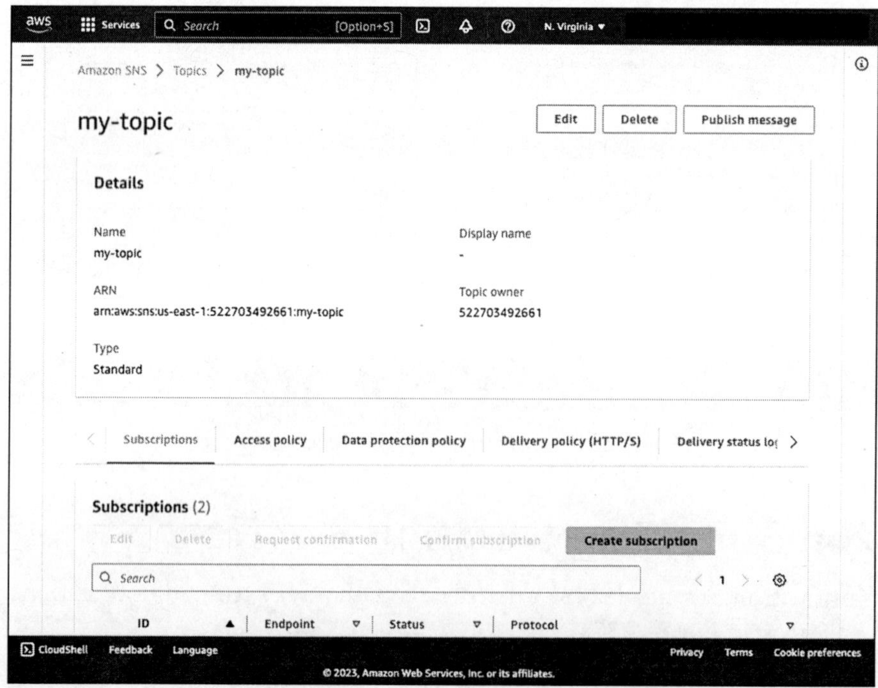

Figure 1.24: An example of an SNS topic and its subscriptions

Amazon Cognito

Cognito provides us with an **identity provider** (**IdP**) service.[17] See the Amazon Cognito icon in *Figure 1.25*:

Figure 1.25: *Amazon Cognito icon*

We can allow users to create accounts and sign into (authenticate) our application using User Pools. We can also enable users to use popular social logins and other IdP services to sign into our application using Identity Pools. Cognito supports the following external IdPs:

- Facebook[18]
- Login with Amazon
- Google[19]
- Sign in with Apple[20]
- OpenID[21] Connect IdPs
- **Security Assertion Markup Language** (**SAML**)[22] IdPs

Cognito allows us to verify what web pages and data a user is authorized to access.

We will use Cognito to provide authentication and authorization for our web application. See *Figure 1.26* for an example of a Cognito **User Pool** resource:

---

17 "What is Amazon Cognito?" Amazon Cognito Developer Guide. Amazon Web Services. **https://docs.aws.amazon.com/cognito/latest/developerguide/what-is-amazon-cognito.html**

18 Facebook is a registered trademark of Facebook, Inc.

19 Google is a registered trademark of Google LLC

20 Apple is a registered trademark of Apple, Inc.

21 OpenID is a registered trademark of the OpenID Foundation.

22 SAML and Security Assertion Markup Language are trademarks of OASIS, the open standards consortium where the [SAML] specification is owned and developed. SAML is a copyrighted work of OASIS Open. All rights reserved.

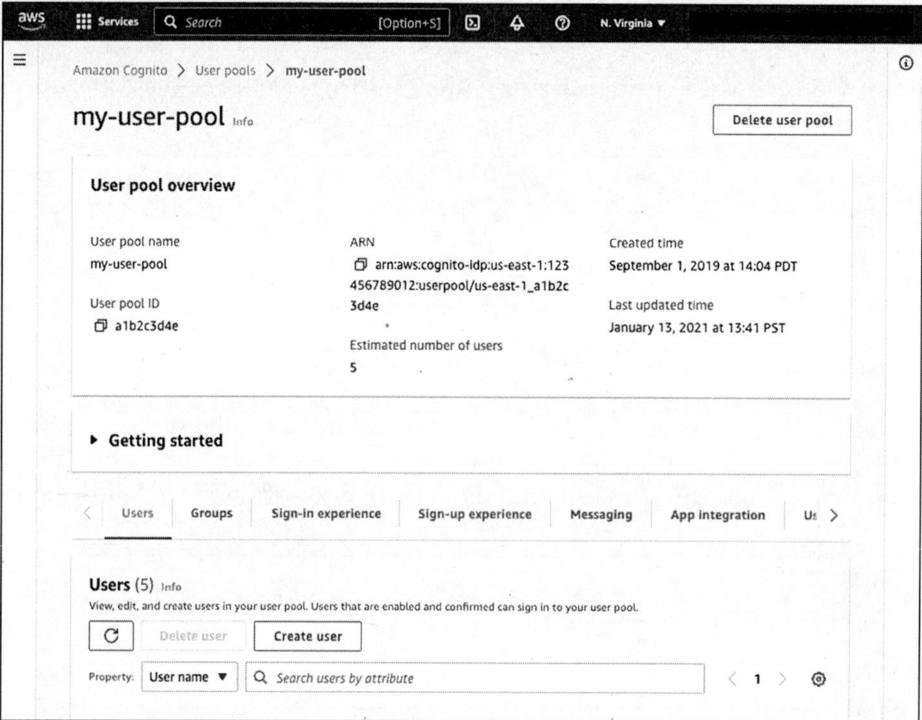

Figure 1.26: An example of a Cognito User Pool resource

AWS Identity and Access Management

The **Identity and Access Management (IAM)** allows us to manage IAM users and access AWS cloud resources.[23] See the AWS IAM icon in *Figure 1.27*:

Figure 1.27: AWS IAM icon

We did not list the IAM service earlier because it is not considered serverless. IAM is a foundational service that we will use to secure access to our AWS account and the resources used in our application.

We will use IAM to create policies and roles for our application. See *Figure 1.28* for an example of an IAM role:

23 "What is IAM?" AWS Identity and Access Management User Guide. Amazon Web Services. **https://docs.aws.amazon.com/IAM/latest/UserGuide/introduction.html**

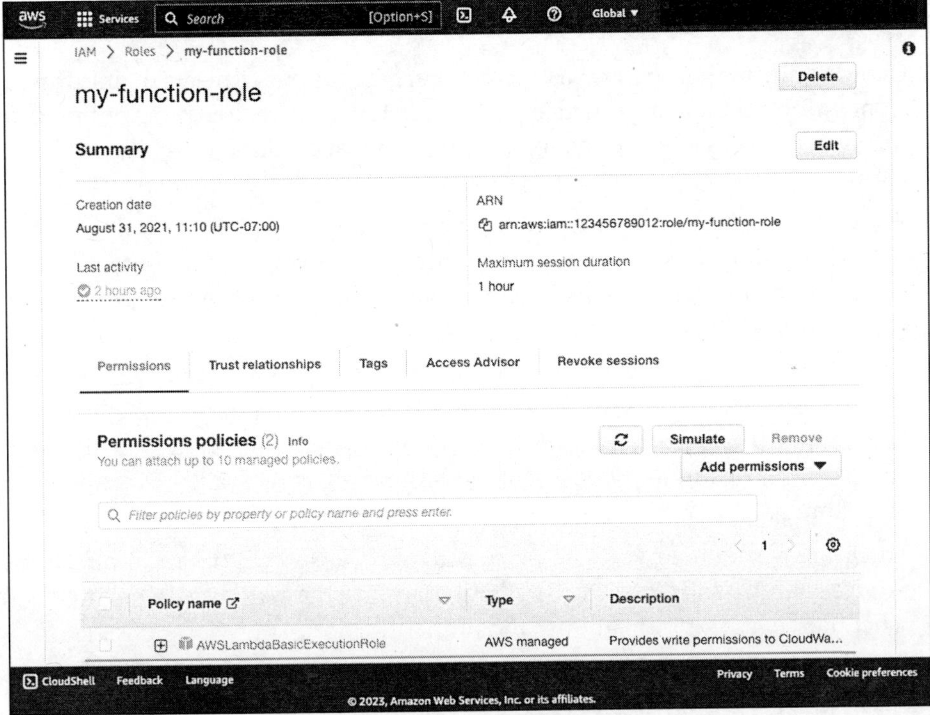

Figure 1.28: An example of an IAM role resource

Conclusion

In this chapter, we explained how organizations started with on-premises computing. As the Internet improved, service providers created Internet-based solutions for providing servers, storage, networking, and other services. These types of offerings became known as cloud computing.

Technologies were created to provide virtual servers where one physical server could host multiple virtual servers. The next evolution was the invention of containers which allowed physical servers to host even more lightweight *virtual servers* as containers. Container technology enabled the creation of serverless computing where AWS creates and deletes containers as needed to execute code.

The success of serverless computing enabled AWS and other cloud service providers to apply the concept to data storage, databases, and other cloud services. We discussed the core serverless services we plan to use to build our application. We will touch on the AWS serverless and related services later in the book. The goal of this chapter was to introduce AWS serverless. Explaining every service at this time might get overwhelming. Hopefully, the services we explained help you see how we can use AWS serverless to create an application.

Points to remember

- Cloud computing initially was a way for organizations to move their infrastructure from on-premises to a third-party provider. Over time, cloud computing provided managed services, such as computing, storage, databases, networking, and software.
- Serverless computing with AWS Lambda allows running code as functions without having to worry about configuring, securing and maintaining a server. The developer is still responsible for securing the code, data, and processes per the shared responsibility model.
- Serverless storage allows us to save data with virtually unlimited data storage using object storage (S3) and serverless databases (for example, DynamoDB). Furthermore, storage costs vary based on the service and how quickly the data is accessed. For example, S3 data storage is typically less expensive than DynamoDB data storage.
- There are various serverless services available to use in our applications. The services allow configuring various use cases, such as APIs, caching, orchestration, scheduled events, notifications, and authentication.

Multiple choice questions

1. **Which of these items is not a benefit of serverless computing with AWS Lambda?**
   a. On-demand usage
   b. Elasticity
   c. Scalability
   d. Rapid development
   e. Reduced infrastructure
   f. Direct maintenance
   g. Lower costs
   h. Smaller attack surfaces

   Answer: f

   AWS does not allow us to access or maintain the operating system or underlying infrastructure that runs Lambda functions.

2. **Which of these items is a benefit of serverless storage with Amazon S3?**
   a. File system access
   b. Unlimited number of objects
   c. Unlimited object size
   d. Unlimited number of buckets

Answer: b

Amazon S3 can store unlimited objects in a bucket, but it has limits on the object size and the number of buckets. It does not provide file system access since it is object storage.

3. **Which of these AWS services is not a serverless service?**
   a. Amazon Aurora Serverless
   b. Amazon CloudFront
   c. Amazon CloudWatch
   d. Amazon Cognito
   e. Amazon DynamoDB
   f. Amazon Lambda
   g. Amazon Neptune
   h. Amazon SNS
   i. Amazon S3
   j. Amazon SQS

   Answer: g

   Amazon Neptune Serverless is the serverless version of Amazon Neptune.

4. **Which feature does Amazon API Gateway not support?**
   a. REST APIs
   b. HTTP APIs
   c. Gateway APIs
   d. OpenAPI

   Answer: c

   Gateway APIs is not a valid term.

5. **Which service is used to view Lambda function logs?**
   a. Amazon CloudFront
   b. Amazon CloudWatch
   c. Amazon Cognito

   Answer: b

   Amazon CloudWatch stores logs among other features. Amazon CloudFront provides a content delivery network and Amazon Cognito provides authentication.

6. **Which services can be used to send events to Lambda functions?**
   a. Amazon API Gateway
   b. Amazon EventBridge

c. Amazon SES

d. Amazon SNS

Answer: c

Amazon SES is used to send emails and Lambda functions do not have email addresses.

Join our book's Discord space

Join the book's Discord Workspace for Latest updates, Offers, Tech happenings around the world, New Release and Sessions with the Authors:

https://discord.bpbonline.com

CHAPTER 2
Overview of Serverless Applications

Introduction

This chapter will provide an overview of different types of serverless applications. There are many ways to use serverless. We will cover what are the most common ways to build applications using AWS serverless.

Structure

We will cover the following topics in this chapter:

- Introduction to serverless applications
- Website development
- Application Programming Interfaces
- Mobile app development
- Data processing
- Notifications

Objectives

By the end of the chapter, you will understand applications that can be built using the AWS serverless services. You will understand how serverless computing can be used for websites, mobile apps, application programming interfaces, data processing, and notifications.

Introduction to serverless applications

We can define a serverless application as an application that was built as *serverless-first,* which means that an application was designed primarily to use serverless services and services that work well with serverless. A complementary term is *cloud native,* which means an application was designed to run in the cloud. A serverless-first application is also a cloud-native application. When referring to our serverless application, we should describe it as a *cloud native application that is serverless-first* because people will understand a cloud native application, but many may ask for an explanation of a serverless-first application.

Additionally, serverless services may be added to existing applications that are not serverless (for example, server-based applications and monoliths). Many organizations can adopt serverless services more effectively by adding them to existing applications rather than starting with a new serverless application. Creating a new serverless application may result in growing pains the organization may not be ready to handle. Starting by adding serverless services to an existing application will allow the organization to become familiar with and gain important lessons learned at a smaller scale.

In this book, we will start by creating a serverless application instead of adding serverless services to an existing application. We want to master AWS serverless by learning how to build an application that was designed to be serverless-first. This knowledge can be brought back to an organization to start applying serverless concepts to an existing application or start a new serverless application if appropriate.

We will cover the following use cases for a serverless application:

- Website development
- APIs
- Mobile app development
- Data processing
- Notifications

We can add these use cases to an existing application. For example, we may have APIs that have a server-based backend. We might need to add a new API to an upcoming project. We can implement that API with AWS serverless instead of modifying the existing server. For example, if we are adding new APIs for a new microservice among existing microservice APIs, we could choose to build the new microservice's API with AWS serverless without modifying the API code that runs on the server.

Let us explore these common use cases in more detail.

Website development

Websites are powered by web servers. When we visit a website, for example, **https://www.google.com**, there are many steps that happen.

The following list details the steps that happen when we visit a website:

1. The browser validates and accepts the web address.
2. The browser makes an HTTP request to the web address.
3. The operating systems' networking service will make a query to a **Domain Name System (DNS)** asking for information about the web address.
4. The DNS responds with an IP address or another web address. The previous steps are repeated when the DNS responds with another web address until an IP address is returned.
5. The HTTP request is forwarded to the IP address.
6. The web server receives the request.
7. The web server interprets and processes the request.
8. The web server sends a response.
9. The web browser receives the response.
10. The web browser interprets and processes the response.
11. The web browser visualizes the response as needed.

See *Figure 2.1* for a visualization of the steps above:

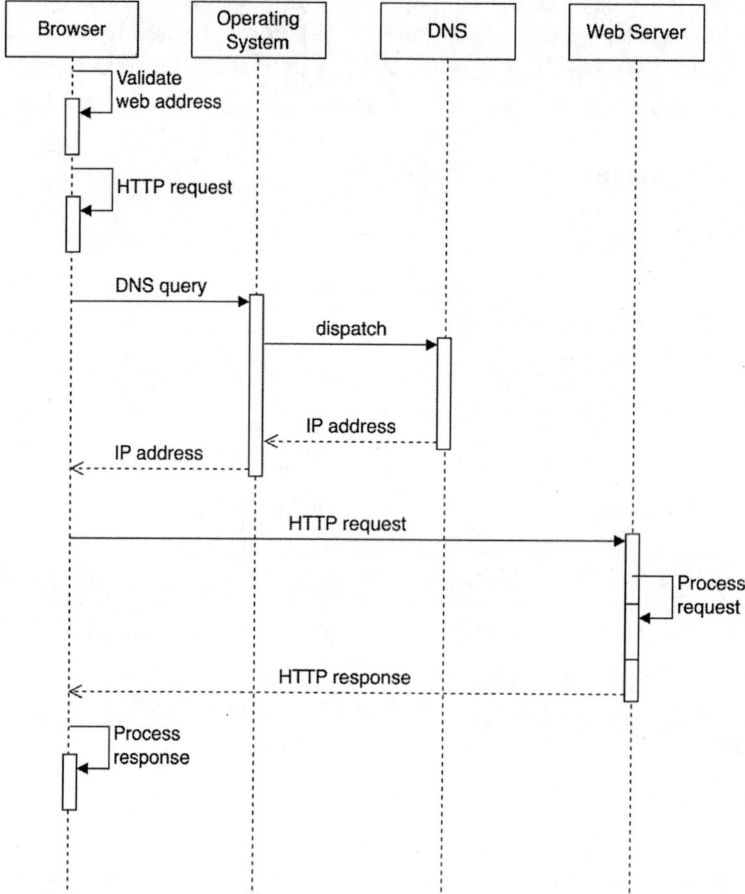

Figure 2.1: A visualization of an HTTP request

There are many components to the web server that allow it to process HTTP requests and send responses. A web server architecture typically has the following components:

- Internet service provider
- DNS records
- An operating system
- Networking services
- Web server software
- Web scripting language, developer platform
- Web pages
- Web application code
- Web application firewall
- **Content Delivery Network (CDN)**

See *Figure 2.2* for a visualization of the web server architecture components:

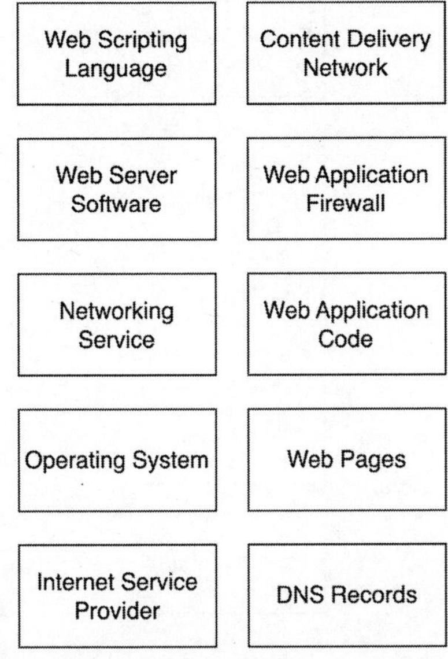

Figure 2.2: *A visualization of web server architecture components*

Websites are only served by web servers. Serverless websites are also served by web servers. It might be tempting to think that the *less* in serverless means *no*. Serverless does not mean *no servers* but *less servers*. Another way to say this would be that serverless allows us to focus *less* on servers, that is, *less focus on servers*. This means we can rely on AWS to maintain these facets of the web server.

The following includes the facets AWS maintains:

- Internet service provider
- DNS records (partly)
- An operating system
- Networking services
- Web server software
- Web scripting language or developer platform

We can then focus more of our attention and creativity on the following:

- DNS records (partly)
- Web pages
- Web application code
- Web application firewall
- CDN

See *Figure 2.3* for the serverless version of the web server architecture components:

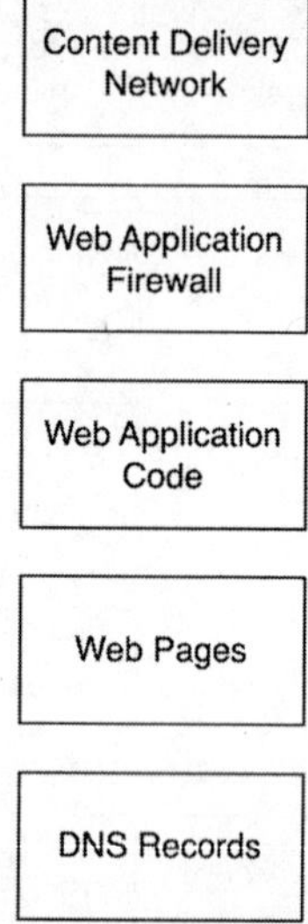

Figure 2.3: *A visualization of serverless website architecture components*

We will use the following AWS services to create a serverless website:

- **Amazon Route53** to manage our DNS records.
- **Amazon S3** to host our web pages or web application code.
- **Amazon CloudFront** to provide the CDN to cache our website files for faster delivery.
- **Amazon Certificate Manager** to provide **Secure Sockets Layer** (**SSL**) and **Transport Layer Security** (**TLS**) certificates for our custom domain names.
- **AWS WAF** to provide the web application firewall to protect our website.

These AWS services allow us to serve all the website files, which include:

- **HyperText Markup Language** (**HTML**) files
- **Cascading Style Sheets** (**CSS**) files
- **JavaScript** (**JS**) files
- **Joint Photographic Experts Group** (**JPEG** or **JPG**) files
- **Portable Network Graphics** (**PNG**) files
- **Scalable Vector Graphics** (**SVG**) files
- **Icon** (**ICO**) files
- **Text** (**TXT**) files
- Document files
- Archive files

The S3 service becomes our web server. It is designed to serve static files.

A web server might have a web scripting language or developer platform installed.

Some popular server-side script languages include:

- PHP
- ASP.NET
- Node.js
- Python
- Ruby
- Java
- GoLang

These languages run on a server. S3 serves static files and not dynamic files like those written in server-side scripting languages. As a result, a serverless website hosted on S3 cannot run server-side scripting language code. S3 will show the source code contents of the scripting file rather than interpreting it like a web server would.

The code written with server-side scripting languages is meant for the backend of the website. The front end of the website is the web pages that are displayed in the browser. The backend of the website is the processes and code that generate and provide the information to be shown in the front end.

A serverless website only provides the website's front end. If we need a backend, we will want to use the JAMstack comprising **JavaScript, APIs and Markup (JAM)**.

Let us explore each letter:

- **JavaScript**: The JavaScript code runs in the browser. We will use it to get the website data by making requests to an API.
- **APIs**: The API is our website's backend. We make HTTP requests to the API endpoint to send and receive data from our application. We will discuss how to build a serverless API later in this chapter.
- **Markup**: The markup is the content of our website. Typically, the markup is in HTML files. The HTML files contain the text and layout that is displayed to the user. The markup can also be written in other formats (for example, Markdown[1]). We can write our content using Markdown files and automatically convert them to HTML when updating the website.

Let us discuss how we will use the various AWS services to create our website.

1 Markdown is a registered trademark of The Markdown Foundation.

Amazon Route 53

Route 53 is a DNS service. See the Amazon Route 53 icon in *Figure 2.4*:

***Figure 2.4:** Amazon Route 53 icon*

We can use Route 53 to add the DNS records for a custom domain, for example, mydomain.com. We can choose not to use the service because other AWS services we will use (for example, API Gateway, S3, and CloudFront) will provide us with an AWS-provided domain name (one that does not use our custom domain). Also, we could buy and manage a custom domain name from a third-party DNS (that is, from another company) and add the DNS records to it. We will explore some reasons to use Route 53.

Some benefits of using Route 53 include:

- Buying and renewing domain names.
- Managing DNS records for a domain name.
- Allowing AWS to seamlessly work with DNS records for other AWS services.
- Using advanced DNS settings.
- Pay per usage.

We will use Route 53 to buy our domain. We want to ensure we can build a serverless application solely on AWS, including the domain. Furthermore, it reduces the possible confusion of explaining all the possible ways to buy a domain from a third-party provider.

We will also use Route 53 to manage our DNS records. We could put the DNS records in a third-party DNS, but we risk the confusion of the instructions working for some providers and not others.

Using Route 53 will allow AWS to seamlessly work with DNS records for the following services. Let us explore the related services:

- **Amazon API Gateway**: It allows us to create APIs. We can add a custom domain to an API and add the DNS records to Route 53.
- **Amazon CloudFront**: It allows us to create a distribution to provide us with CDN caching. We can add a custom domain to a distribution and add the DNS records to Route 53.
- **AWS Certificate Manager**: It allows us to create SSL/TLS certificates for our custom domains. We can validate that we own the custom domain by adding DNS

records to Route 53. Upon verification, the Certificate Manager will create the SSL/ TLS certificate.

- **AWS Web Application Firewall**: We can create a DNS firewall by using a Route 53 resolver.

We will use Route 53 throughout this book to create and add custom domains to our serverless application where appropriate.

S3

In the last chapter, we learned about S3. In this chapter, we will briefly touch on how to use S3 to serve static website files. S3 may be used in multiple ways. We will explain how S3 may be used.

S3 may be used to:

- Save private data
- Save public data and files
- Back up data
- Back up AWS resources
- Store log files
- Store audit data
- Static web hosting
- Send events to other AWS services

A serverless application may use S3 in all those ways, depending on the design of the system. As previously mentioned, our serverless application will use S3 for static web hosting (the front end), and we cannot use server-side scripting languages. We want to design our website to not rely on server-side scripting languages to update the HTML. Our website may use JavaScript in the browser to modify our HTML files as needed.

A website can use JavaScript for the following:

- **Interactive and dynamic websites**: There are various JavaScript plugins that make websites more interesting and fun to use.
- **API requests**: We can use JavaScript to make requests to an API to get information the website needs.
- **Modifying the browser's Document Object Model (DOM)**: JavaScript is allowed to modify the DOM, which is how the browser interprets the HTML data. This allows us to add, delete, and modify the HTML data in the browser without having to reload the web page.
- **Single Page Applications (SPA)**: JavaScript frameworks allow us to build an SPA that uses one HTML file. The SPA contains information about routes and various

pages. People may not realize they are using SPA since it appears to have multiple web pages as they browse the website.

Most browsers support JavaScript and have it enabled by default. We may run into an issue when a user disables JavaScript. The user will only be able to see the static content and not get the latest data. We can assume most users will have JavaScript enabled, and we can give them a warning when they have it disabled.

With this assumption, developers use an SPA framework for their serverless applications. Traditionally, a website was created with multiple HTML files, and users navigated to the HTML files that had the information they needed. With an SPA, we use one HTML file that has all the data from the various HTML files. The SPA uses JavaScript to show and hide the information. When a user clicks a link, it will hide the current *view* and show the desired view instead of loading another HTML page. This approach improves the website's **User Experience** (**UX**) and the developer's **Developer Experience** (**DX**).

There are various SPA frameworks like:

- Angular[2]
- Backbone.js[3]
- Ember[4]
- React[5]
- Vue[6]
- And many others

Using an SPA framework could improve our DX. We will not use one to create an application in this book though. This book aims to help you master AWS serverless and not a specific SPA framework. Instead, we will use HTML and JavaScript for our serverless website. We can use JavaScript get the data from the API and update the DOM.

CloudFront

In the last chapter, we learned about CloudFront. In this chapter, we will briefly touch on using CloudFront to provide a CDN for our website.

We should consider using a CDN for these types of files:

- HTML files
- CSS files
- JavaScript files

2 Angular is copyrighted by Google LLC under The MIT License.
3 Backbone.js is copyrighted by Jeremy Ashkenas, DocumentCloud.
4 Ember is a trademark of Tilde Inc.
5 React is copyrighted by Meta Platforms, Inc. and affiliates under The MIT License.
6 Vue.js is copyrighted by Evan You under The MIT License.

- Image files
- Document files
- Archive files
- Any other static files

Caching these files makes sense because they do not change often.

We can also cache dynamic data (like the data we get from our APIs). There are some things to consider when caching dynamic data from API responses.

The following describes some things to consider:

- **Outdated data**: When data changes very often, we run the risk that the cache responds with outdated data. This may be problematic depending on the criticality of the data and the sensitivity of the accuracy data.
- **Clearing cache**: We can request a distribution to invalidate cache. An invalidation will start clearing all the caches and start building a new cache. It may take several minutes for the cache to clear from all the cache locations around the world.
- **Costs**: We may begin to incur costs if we exceed the number of no-cost invalidation requests per month. If our API responses are verbose, we may incur additional costs to cache all that data.
- **Security**: We may run the risk of caching sensitive user data in a way that might result in an accidental disclosure.

We will explore using CloudFront for caching our S3 website files.

AWS Certificate Manager

AWS Certificate Manager (**ACM**) is an SSL and TLS certificate management service. See the AWS Certificate Manager icon in *Figure 2.5*:

Figure 2.5: *AWS Certificate Manager icon*

ACM allows us to create SSL and TLS certificates for our serverless websites and APIs. S3 websites, CloudFront distributions, and API Gateway APIs automatically have certificates when using the AWS-provided domain names. Using these domains is acceptable, but we will want to have custom domain names.

The following are some reasons to consider:

- **User experience**: Users will feel more comfortable visiting a website with a custom domain name.
- **Developer experience**: Writing code to send API requests to custom domain names is easier to manage than the AWS-provided domain names.
- **Consistency**: We will get new API endpoints when we recreate our AWS resources, but using a custom domain name ensures consistency.

We will need to validate that we own the custom domain name when we use it to customize the domain name for an AWS service. ACM provides us with two validation methods[7]:

- **Email validation**: AWS sends an email to the email addresses registered as contacts within Route 53. The email provides instructions for validating the domain name ownership.
- **DNS validation**: AWS will provide us with a **canonical name (CNAME)** record to add to Route 53. AWS will query the Route 53 DNS for the CNAME record and its value. It will validate the domain name ownership when the CNAME value matches the expected value.

We will use DNS validation in this book for the following reasons:

- **Developer experience**: As mentioned earlier, we can easily work with Route 53 to add the DNS records.
- **Simplified validation**: Email validation is a manual process and may result in a lapsed certificate if the email is lost or missed. Taking advantage of the automated DNS validation simplifies our setup.
- **Simplified renewals**: The certificates will automatically be renewed when AWS validates the CNAME record.

We will use an ACM certificate to create a certificate for the custom domain name we will use for our CloudFront distribution.

AWS Web Application Firewall

The AWS **Web Application Firewall (WAF)** is a security service to protect our web applications. See the AWS Firewall Manager icon in *Figure 2.6*:

Figure 2.6: *AWS Firewall Manager icon*

7 "Validating domain ownership." AWS Certificate Manager User Guide. Amazon Web Services. **https://docs.aws.amazon.com/acm/latest/userguide/domain-ownership-validation.html**

The AWS Firewall Manager manages all the WAFs. With WAF, we can protect our web applications and APIs from attacks. For example, websites can be vulnerable to **Cross Site Scripting (XSS)**[8] attacks where a user unintentionally loads a malicious script that can modify or steal the website data. We can configure a WAF rule to block scripts loading from untrusted sources.

We can create custom rule groups that are specific to our application and use AWS-managed rule groups. AWS provides the following managed rule groups[9]:

- **Core Rule Set (CRS)**: Protects websites against the OWASP Top 10[10] security risks.
- **Admin protection managed rule group**: Protects against external access to admin websites.
- **Known bad inputs managed rule group**: Protect websites and APIs by blocking request patterns used to exploit known vulnerabilities (for example, Log4j CVE-2021-44228[11]).
- **SQL database managed rule group**: Protects websites and APIs by blocking request patterns used to explore SQL database vulnerabilities. These may protect NoSQL databases (for example, DynamoDB) to some extent too.
- **Amazon IP reputation list managed rule group**: Protects websites and APIs by blocking known malicious IP addresses.
- **Anonymous IP list managed rule group**: Protect websites and APIs that are trying to hide their IP addresses by using a **Virtual Private Network (VPN)** and other obfuscation techniques.
- **Account creation fraud prevention rules listing**: Protects Amazon Cognito, websites, and APIs from common techniques used to create accounts using stolen account information and other techniques.
- **Account takeover prevention rules listing**: Protects Amazon Cognito, websites, and APIs from common techniques used to steal an account using stolen account information and other techniques.
- **Bot control rules listing**: Protects websites and APIs from undesired bot traffic.

Some rule groups were omitted because they are less likely to affect serverless applications.

Having a WAF is an important security practice to have in web applications and APIs. We will not be focusing on AWS WAF in this book. Creating and managing WAF rules is a web security practice and should be considered, but it is not specific to serverless applications.

8 "Cross Site Scripting (XSS)." KirstenS. OWASP Foundation. **https://owasp.org/www-community/attacks/xss/**

9 "AWS Managed Rules rule groups list." AWS WAF, AWS Firewall Manager, and AWS Shield Advanced Developer Guide. Amazon Web Services. **https://docs.aws.amazon.com/waf/latest/developerguide/aws-managed-rule-groups-list.html**

10 "OWASP Top Ten." OWASP Foundation. **https://owasp.org/www-project-top-ten/**

11 "CVE-2021-44228." The MITRE Corporation. **https://www.cve.org/CVERecord?id=CVE-2021-44228**

Instead, we will focus more on serverless security practices in this book to help you master AWS serverless.

Application Programming Interfaces

We have discussed that **Application Programming Interfaces (APIs)** are the backend for our website. As previously discussed, a serverless website running on S3 cannot run dynamic, server-side scripting languages. However, the website can use JavaScript to make requests to an API. We will explore in further detail what consists of an API.

An API consists of the following components:

- **Architecture**: The architecture is the way the API will connect. Arguably, the two most popular API architectures used in serverless applications are REST and GraphQL[12].
- **Endpoints**: The endpoint defines the HTTP address used to connect to the API. For example, **https://mydomain.com/api/catalog/**.
- **Parameters**: Parameters provide additional information to the endpoint but are not part of the endpoint. For example, **https://mydomain.com/api/catalog/boots/**. In this example, *boots* suffix was added to the path to filter the catalog. Sending an HTTP request with or without the *boots* parameter value will alter what data is returned.
- **Query**: Queries are similar to the parameters but do not modify the endpoint. For example, **https://mydomain.com/api/catalog?category=boots**. In this example, the endpoint is queried for a category with the value *boots*. Unlike parameters, there can be multiple queries in a request. For example, **https://mydomain.com/api/catalog?category=boots&price=low** will send both the category and price information values.
- **Request method**: The method uses the HTTP request methods[13] which include `GET`, `POST`, `PUT` and others. For example, the browser uses the `GET` method when we visit a website. When a web application tries to send data to an API, it will typically use the `POST` method.

Note: The method name can be written in lower case (for example, get) or upper case (for example, `GET`) but is typically written in upper case.

- **Request headers**: The request headers are part of the HTTP request format. Custom information about the request and requestor can be sent in a header. A common type of header used is the *Authorization* header, which contains the secret information that tells our application whether the user has authenticated and is a valid user to get data from the API.

---

12 GraphQL is a registered trademark of The Linux Foundation.

13 "HTTP request methods." MDN Web Docs. Mozilla Foundation. **https://developer.mozilla.org/en-US/docs/Web/HTTP/Methods**

- **Request body**: The request body contains information about data we want to send to our API. For example, we want to update our first name in our profile. We can send a request to **https://mydomain.com/api/user/** and include *first: Mike* in the request body. A common way to structure the request body data is to use the **JavaScript Object Notation** (**JSON**) format.
- **Response status codes**: The responses will send an HTTP response status code[14] indicating whether or not the request resulted in a successful response. For example, a successful request should return a *200 OK* status code, but a failed request might return a *500 Internal Server Error* status code.
- **Response body**: The response body contains information about data the API responded with. For example, a request to **https://mydomain.com/api/catalog/silly** might return `{}` (an empty JSON object) or `[]` (an empty JSON array) because no *silly* catalog items were found.

We will explore how to build an API using AWS serverless services.

API Gateway

As previously discussed, API Gateway allows us to create APIs that communicate HTTP using the REST architecture. When we create a REST API using API Gateway, we will configure various settings.

The following are the list of the settings we will configure:

- **Create an API**: We create an API, which is a group of endpoints. They will share the same base HTTP web address or **Uniform Resource Locator** (**URL**) or **Uniform Resource Identifier** (**URI**). For example, all endpoints within this API may use **https://mydomain.com/api** or **https://api.mydomain.com** as the base URL.
- **Define endpoints**: We define the endpoints we want in our API. For example, we may define `/catalog` and `/user` as our endpoints. We will be able to make HTTP requests to **https://mydomain.com/api/catalog** and **https://mydomain.com/api/user** assuming our base URL is **https://mydomain.com/api**.
- **Define the methods**: We need to define the method(s) each endpoint will respond to a request. For example, if we define the `GET` method for the `/catalog` endpoint, it will respond to HTTP `GET` requests but deny others (for example, HTTP `POST`).
- **Define the method request**: We can define the query and path parameters we expect for the request for each endpoint method. For example, we can define `/catalog/{categoryType}?color={color}` so the API can expect an HTTP request like `/catalog/boots?color=brown` as a valid request.

14 "HTTP response status codes." MDN Web Docs. Mozilla Foundation. **https://developer.mozilla.org/en-US/docs/Web/HTTP/Status**

Note: API Gateway uses the `{variableName}` syntax to define a variable within a string that will be replaced with the variable's value.

- **Define the integration request**: We will define what the endpoints will do when it receives a valid request. For example, we can integrate the request with a Lambda function. The function will receive the HTTP request information, run the code, and return the appropriate HTTP response.
- **Define the integration response**: Sometimes, we can modify the response from the integration. We cannot modify the response for integrations with Lambda functions.
- **Define the method response**: We can define what HTTP response status codes we expect to return. Furthermore, we can define the format of the response body (for example, specifying it is in JSON format.)

We will create an API using API Gateway to help you master AWS serverless.

AWS AppSync

We have not mentioned the AppSync service until now. See the AWS AppSync icon in *Figure 2.7*:

Figure 2.7: *AWS AppSync icon*

The AppSync services provide GraphQL APIs similarly to how API Gateway provides REST APIs. The following describes some of the differences:

- **Endpoints**: GraphQL uses one endpoint, whereas REST uses a collection of endpoints.
- **Definition**: GraphQL uses a schema written in Schema Definition Language, whereas REST leaves the definition up to the developer.
- **Request methods**: GraphQL relies on the operation types (for example, query) defined by the schema, whereas REST relies on HTTP methods to indicate what type of operations should occur.

When we create a GraphQL API using AppSync, we will perform the following:

- **Create a schema**: We will define the schema[15] that defines the API. The schema contains the schema root, types, and special object types. For example, we can define a root with a query and the related types as follows:

```
schema {
  query: Query
}
type Query {
  getCatalog(): [CatalogItem]
}
type CatalogItem {
  name: String
}
```

- **Attach a data source**: We will define from where to get data when an operation (for example, a query) occurs. For example, we might connect a query to a DynamoDB table to retrieve data and connect a mutation to a Lambda function to modify data.
- **Configure resolvers**: We will define how a request will work with a resolver. For example, the resolver for the query attached to a DynamoDB table data source will tell DynamoDB how to query the table and what data to return. The example below from the AWS AppSync Developer Guide[16] shows a resolver written using JavaScript:

```
import { util } from '@aws-appsync/utils';
export function request(ctx) {
  return { operation: 'Scan' };
}
export function response(ctx) {
  return ctx.result.items;
}
```

GraphQL is popular in serverless application development because it centralizes APIs into one endpoint and a single schema. Yet there are some drawbacks:

- **Learning curve**: Some consider learning GraphQL to be more difficult than learning REST API development. REST API development is consistent with how the browser uses HTTP to get and send data.

15 "Step 1: Designing your schema." AWS AppSync Developer Guide. Amazon Web Services. **https://docs.aws.amazon.com/appsync/latest/devguide/designing-your-schema.html**

16 "Configuring resolvers (JavaScript)." AWS AppSync Developer Guide. Amazon Web Services. **https://docs.aws.amazon.com/appsync/latest/devguide/configuring-resolvers-js.html**

- **Support**: GraphQL needs additional code libraries for it to work in the web application. JavaScript and other frontend frameworks support HTTP requests natively.
- **Flexibility**: The GraphQL schema is strict, and the interaction is limited to how it is defined. REST APIs provide flexibility. For example, one REST endpoint might return text data, and another might return JSON data. Sending a `POST` might be used to create new data, and sending a PUT might mean an update, or a `POST` might be used to both create and update data.

We will consider AppSync as an advanced topic for us to explore beyond this book. We will not use it to create a serverless application.

Mobile app development

Mobile apps are applications installed onto a mobile phone or smartphone. These apps run code that uses locally stored information.

Some data is not stored locally for various reasons:

- **Disk space**: Storing all the data the app may need may use a lot of disk space. Users may delete the app if they find it uses too much disk space.
- **Personalization**: Some data is specific to a user. It may not be feasible to store some or all the user data in the app.
- **Customization**: Some app features may only be available when the user enables it or enrolls into a subscription. It might be more efficient to only get the customization data when it is needed and when the user has the privileges to receive that data.
- **Security**: Some data may be sensitive and should not be stored within the app. Storing sensitive data on the phone increases the risk of the data being stolen by a virus or a malicious actor. If data needs to be stored on the phone, it is best to encrypt.

Mobile apps will need to use a method to get data from a remote source. These are some ways it can get remote data. The following is a list of some of the data strategies:

- **Load it from an external storage device**: Some applications are meant to read data from an external storage device, such as a **Universal Serial Bus (USB)** flash drive. A media player is an example of an app where a user can play their media files.
- **Download it from a website or CDN**: Some applications use static data they can easily download. They may also use an in-app browser where a popup window loads a website that shows the data.
- **Make an API request**: Some applications may send requests to an API to get data. They should use HTTPS to transmit the data securely. Furthermore, some APIs

may require authentication or authorization. Authentication and authorization are techniques to protect the API from getting data from untrusted sources. The authentication identifies the user while the authorization allows getting data specific to a user and a type of user (for example, an administrator). Some methods for authentication and authorization include JSON Web Tokens and OAuth 2.0.

- **Using a streaming protocol**: Some applications use a streaming protocol to get data. Media service apps (for example, music and video streaming services) allow users to listen to a song or watch a video without downloading the data onto their smartphone. Some streaming protocols include **HTTP Live Streaming** (**HLS**) and **Moving Picture Experts Group-Dynamic Adaptive Streaming** (**MPEG-DASH**).

A mobile app may want to use a serverless application to get its data. The serverless application may be designed similarly to one for a website. Rather than the request coming from a web browser, it will come from a mobile application using an API or web request.

If our app is meant to stream media, we can take advantage of the AWS media services[17]. We will not focus on building a streaming media application in this book. Although adding streaming media to a serverless application is possible, the complexity of uploading, converting, storing, and servicing the media might become a distraction to mastering the foundational elements in an AWS serverless. Instead, we will build a serverless application that will support a mobile app that gets its data from API and web requests. The S3, DynamoDB, Lambda, CloudFront, and many other serverless services used to build a serverless website can also be used for mobile apps. Furthermore, the scalability and cost efficiency benefits typically gained for a serverless website will also apply to a serverless mobile application backend.

API Gateway

We can use API Gateway to create REST API endpoints for a mobile app. A mobile app is a client that runs on a mobile operating system, similar to our serverless website which is a client that runs on a web browser. Many mobile app development frameworks support making HTTP requests from the mobile app. Therefore, it is very likely that you can create a mobile app that interacts with APIs hosted by API Gateway.

AppSync

We can use AppSync to create an GraphQL API endpoint for a mobile app. Support for GraphQL may not come natively in mobile app development frameworks. Many can support GraphQL by installing and configuring an extension. AWS provides AWS Amplify that brings AppSync support to many frontend frameworks.[18]

17 "AWS Media Services." Amazon Web Services. **https://aws.amazon.com/media-services/**

18 "Amplify Documentation." Amplify Dev Center. **https://docs.amplify.aws/**

Data processing

Data processing involves working with data. There are four types of data operations. The data operations include:

- **Create**: This operation creates or adds new data to our data source(s).
- **Read**: This operation reads existing data from our data source(s).
- **Update**: This operation updates existing data from our data source(s).
- **Delete**: This operation deletes or removes existing data from our data source(s).

These are often referred to as **Create Read Update Delete** (**CRUD**). We will use CRUD operations when working with our data. Furthermore, these operations align nicely with REST APIs. For example:

- **Create**: We can define an API endpoint that uses the `POST` HTTP request method to create data.
- **Read**: We can define an API endpoint that uses the `GET` HTTP request method to read data.
- **Update**: We can define an API endpoint that uses the `PUT` HTTP request method to update data.
- **Delete**: We can define an API endpoint that uses the `DELETE` HTTP request method to delete data.

This way of defining API endpoints that match our data processing operations is commonly used. Sometimes we need to move data from one data source to another. For example, we might want to move older data from a DynamoDB table to an S3 bucket for archiving. Another example is getting data from various sensors saved to an S3 bucket and moving it to a data warehouse where it can be processed for machine learning.

There are two main techniques:

- **Extract, Transform, and Load (ETL)**: This consists of extracting the data from one data source, transforming it to a different format, and loading it into the target data source. The ETL approach results in the data being in the correct format in the target data source. The data processing is done before the data is moved.
- **Extract, Load, and Transform (ELT)**: Consists of extracting the data from one data source, loading it into the target data source, and transforming it into a different format. The ELT approach results in the data being in the same format as the target data source. The data processing happens after the data is moved.

According to AWS, it has been found that ELT is more common in the cloud compared to ETL.[19] We will explore both methods in our serverless application when working with our data sources.

19 "What is ETL (Extract Transform Load)?" Amazon Web Services. **https://aws.amazon.com/what-is/etl/**

S3

Our application will also use S3 buckets as data sources for saving, using, and processing data. A serverless application may use S3 for the following:

- **Image files**: In addition to the website image files, S3 can store images from our application data. For example, pictures for a product catalog saved in various dimensions (for example, thumbnails, small, medium, and large sizes).
- **User data uploads**: Users might need to upload documents and pictures to our application. S3 can store these user uploads.
- **Database backups**: We can replicate or backup our database data to S3.
- **Data processing**: We might want to modify and process our data to support various business logic and integrations to other systems.
- **Data analysis**: We might want to analyze data to understand user behaviors, purchase patterns, or any other insights to help improve business and website operations. We could use custom analysis tools, business intelligence software, statistical analysis, machine learning, or artificial intelligence to analyze our data.
- **Other ways**: A serverless application may use S3 in various other ways depending on the business needs and technical requirements.

We could use a database to save, use, and process these data types. Although a database is an option, we might want to use S3 for other reasons.

The following are the three main reasons:

- **Cost**: S3 typically has lower read / write costs than DynamoDB or other databases.
- **Speed**: S3 is a good choice when our data does need fast read and write times.
- **Caching**: We can add a CDN to S3 to cache our data for faster read times by the browser.

Next, we will explore using DynamoDB tables for our database.

DynamoDB

Our application will use DynamoDB tables as data sources to save, use, and process data. A serverless application may use DynamoDB for the following:

- **Data processing**: The same data processing mentioned for S3 could be done with DynamoDB when speed is important, and we need to query our data.
- **Data analysis**: The same analysis data mentioned can be done with DynamoDB, when there are lower volumes of data.

- **User-specific data**: Storing user specific data is best stored in DynamoDB. The faster read times will improve the user experience. Furthermore, storing more sensitive data could be more secure in DynamoDB than in S3 since S3 buckets were designed to be public.

A serverless application can be built using all S3 buckets or all DynamoDB tables. These are design decisions that the development team will need to make for each serverless application project. We will use a mix of S3 buckets and DynamoDB buckets to help you master AWS serverless.

Notifications

Our application will use internal and external notifications. Let us explore these two main types of notifications:

- **Internal**: These are notifications that stay within the application, that is, a user does not receive them.
- **External**: These are notifications that are sent from the application, for example, to a user or an external service.

We will use the term *event* when referring to an *internal notification* to avoid confusion with the term *notification*. When we refer to a *notification*, we are referring to *external notifications*. The terms *event* for internal and *notification* for external is commonly understood by the AWS community.

We will use events to perform business logic in our application backend. We will use notifications to send information to a user or external service. There are multiple services involved in sending events and notifications.

Simple Notification Service

As mentioned in the previous chapter, **Simple Notification Service** (**SNS**) allows us to send notifications via email, text message or push notification or events to a Lambda function, SQS queue or an HTTP endpoint. SNS can be used in the following ways:

- Sending notifications to multiple recipients.
- Sending events from one AWS service to another.
- Sending events to an external service.

See *Figure 2.8* for an example of an SNS message being sent to multiple destinations:

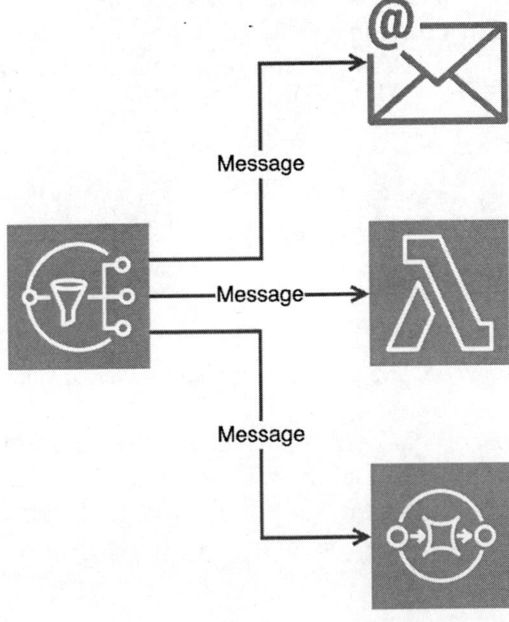

Figure 2.8: An example of an SNS message being sent to multiple destinations

An event or notification sent by SNS is a one-time delivery. The recipient will not receive the information if it is not available at the time it was sent.

Amazon Simple Queue Service

Amazon Simple Queue Service (**SQS**) allows us to queue messages. See the Amazon SQS icon in *Figure 2.9*:

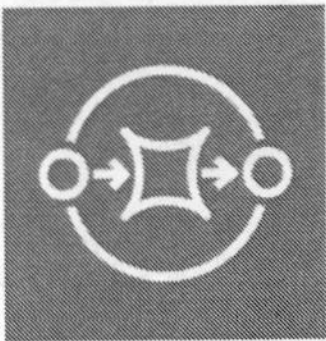

Figure 2.9: Amazon SQS icon

Unlike SNS, messages put in the queue stay in the queue until they are deleted, or they expire. For example, we can send an event to an SQS queue and store it as a message in the queue. The message contains information about a user requesting account deletion. We want to ensure that the account is deleted. A Lambda function can poll the queue to look for messages. When it finds a message, it will process the account deletion request. After it is done, it will delete the message from the queue.

Let us explore the different scenarios.

For example, it is possible that an account delete request may be lost if the SNS topic sends the event to a Lambda function and the function has a bug where it keeps failing. See *Figure 2.10*. which depicts the message being sent once and the Lambda function having an error:

Figure 2.10: *Example of an SNS message being sent to a Lambda function with an error*

Eventually, the development team will discover the bug in the Lambda function code, but any account deletion requests will be lost. Instead, the topic can send the message to a queue, and the Lambda function can poll the queue. If the Lambda function keeps failing, the message will stay in the queue until it expires. See *Figure 2.11*. which depicts the message being sent to a queue:

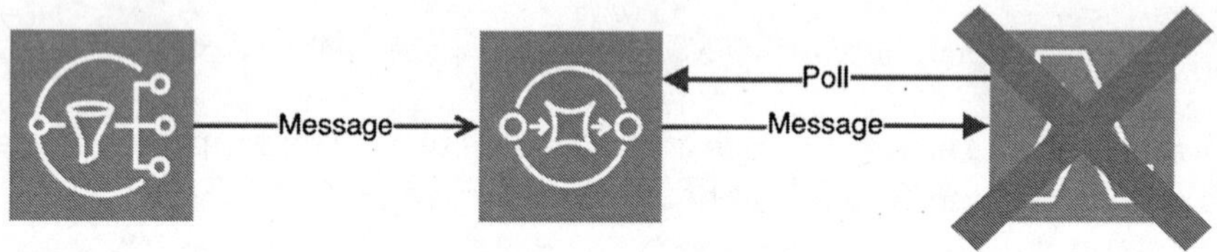

Figure 2.11: *Example of an SNS message being sent to a queue*

Hopefully, the developers will have fixed the bug before the message expires; the retention period can be configured to be up to 14 days. When function code is fixed, the function will process the account deletion request and delete it from the queue. See *Figure 2.12*, which depicts the function deleting the message from the queue:

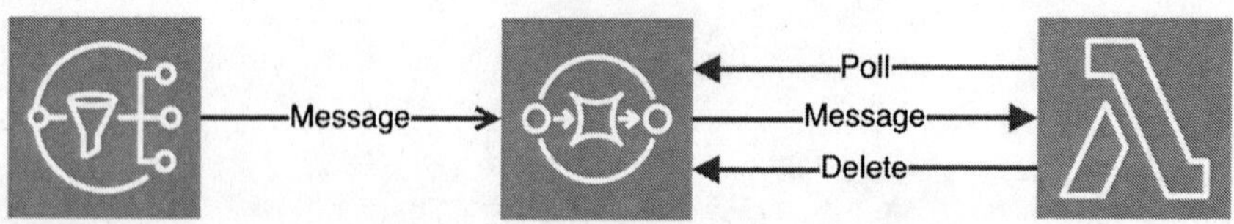

Figure 2.12: *Example of a Lambda function deleting a message from a queue*

When events from an SNS topic cannot be lost, we can have the topic send the events to an SQS queue instead of the intended target (for example, a Lambda function).

CloudWatch

As mentioned in the previous chapter, we can create CloudWatch alarms to monitor metrics and billing. For example, we can create a billing alarm that will notify us when the AWS billing amount has exceeded a threshold.[20] Alarms can send an event to an SNS topic.

EventBridge

As mentioned in the previous chapter, we can use EventBridge to create one-time or recurring scheduled events. Recurring scheduled events can follow a rate-based schedule[21] (for example, once every five minutes) or a cron-based schedule[22] (for example, 12:00 am every day). We will use recurring scheduled events to send events to Lambda functions that will process data and perform other periodic processes.

Simple Email Service

As mentioned in the previous chapter, we can use **Simple Email Service** (**SES**) to send emails. We will create lambda functions that use the AWS SDK to send emails to email addresses on a list.

S3 event notification

We had discussed S3 buckets but not the S3 event notification. S3 can send an event notification to SQS, SNS, EventBridge and Lambda[23] when certain actions occur.

The following describes the actions that result in S3 event notifications:

- **Objects created, restored or removed**: This allows our serverless application to be alerted when objects in our buckets were updated.
- **Reduced Redundancy Storage (RRS) object lost**: Our application can be alerted an object using the RRS class is lost. RRS is used when the S3 Standard storage class is not needed.

20 "Scenario: Monitor your estimated charges using CloudWatch." Amazon CloudWatch User Guide. Amazon Web Services. **https://docs.aws.amazon.com/AmazonCloudWatch/latest/monitoring/gs_monitor_estimated_charges_with_cloudwatch.html**

21 "Rate expressions reference." Amazon EventBridge User Guide. Amazon Web Services. **https://docs.aws.amazon.com/eventbridge/latest/userguide/eb-rate-expressions.html**

22 "Cron expressions reference." Amazon EventBridge User Guide. Amazon Web Services. **https://docs.aws.amazon.com/eventbridge/latest/userguide/eb-cron-expressions.html**

23 "Amazon S3 Event Notifications." Amazon Simple Storage Service User Guide. Amazon Web Services. **https://docs.aws.amazon.com/AmazonS3/latest/userguide/EventNotifications.html**

Note: AWS recommends avoiding using the RRS class since the S3 Standard storage class is more cost-effective.[24]

- **Replication**: Our application can be alerted when there are failures when replicating our bucket objects to another bucket.
- **S3 lifecycle transition and expiration**: Our application can be alerted when an object transitions from one class to another or expires based on the S3 Lifecycle rules that define when an object makes those transitions.
- **S3 intelligent-tiering automatic archival**: Our application can be alerted when an object in the S3 Intelligent-Tiering class transitions to the Archive Access tier or Deep Archive Access tier.
- **Object tagging**: Our application can be alerted when an object is tagged or untagged.
- **Object Access Control List (ACL) changes**: Our application can be alerted when an object ACL is created or modified.

We will use S3 event notifications to notify our serverless application when objects are created to start data processing activities.

DynamoDB Streams

We had discussed DynamoDB tables but not the DynamoDB streams. See the Amazon DynamoDB stream icon in *Figure 2.13*:

Figure 2.13: *Amazon DynamoDB stream icon*

DynamoDB can send an event to a lambda function[25] when the data in the table is created, updated or deleted. We will use DynamoDB streams to notify our serverless application when tables are modified to start data processing activities.

24 "Using Amazon S3 storage classes." Amazon Simple Storage Service User Guide. Amazon Web Services. **https://docs.aws.amazon.com/AmazonS3/latest/userguide/storage-class-intro.html**

25 "Change data capture for DynamoDB Streams." Amazon DynamoDB Developer Guide. Amazon Web Services. **https://docs.aws.amazon.com/amazondynamodb/latest/developerguide/Streams.html**

Conclusion

In this chapter, we introduced serverless applications. We explored AWS serverless, which may be used for website development, APIs, mobile app development, data processing, and notifications. We covered some of the AWS services that are used for each category.

AWS serverless focuses less on web servers but the website features only provide front-end functionality. The backend functionality in a web server moved to APIs. Moving to APIs allows us to build serverless backends that support serverless websites and mobile apps. Both API and mobile app development remain similar, but instead of the APIs are powered by AWS serverless instead of a server-based backend. Furthermore, the data processing and notification functions no longer need to be done on a web server and can be done using AWS serverless. Events provide internal notifications within our serverless application to support data processing, and notifications send emails, text messages, and push notifications to users.

Points to remember

- S3 cannot run server-side scripting languages like a web server. Additional services like Lambda and CloudFront can provide "server-side" functionality.
- Serverless websites must rely on HTML, JavaScript and CSS files to display the website and use JavaScript to send and retrieve data from an API.
- JAMstack stands for JavaScript, APIs and Markup and is a modern web development approach that pre-renders the site into static pages, which then interact with APIs using JavaScript.
- Single Page Application frameworks can help with creating a serverless website.
- There is typically a lower learning curve with REST APIs than GraphQL APIs.
- Events typically trigger Lambda functions to run. These events include HTTP requests, EventBridge rules, CloudWatch alarms, SNS topic messages, S3 event notifications, and DynamoDB streams. They may also be triggered using the AWS management console and AWS SDKs.
- Notifications are used for sending external messages and internal messages within the application. To avoid overloading the term *notifications*, we will refer to internal system-level notifications as *events* and external user-facing notifications as *notifications*.
- An SNS topic will send the message when it is published and can send it to multiple subscribers. An SQS queue keeps a message in its queue until a subscriber deletes it from the queue or the message reaches its expiration.

Multiple choice questions

1. **What types of files would not make sense to use in S3 for a serverless website?**
    a. PNG
    b. JavaScript
    c. Node.js
    d. JPEG
    e. CSS
    f. HTML
    g. Document files
    h. Archive files

    Answer: c

    Node.js is a server-side scripting language. S3 cannot run Node.js. Loading a Node.js file will show the code, but not run it.

2. **Which AWS service allows us to create a custom domain name for our application?**
    a. CloudFront
    b. ACM
    c. WAF
    d. CloudWatch
    e. Route 53
    f. AppSync
    g. SNS

    Answer: e

    Route 53 is a domain name service provider that allows us to register custom domain names.

3. **What AWS product or service provides GraphQL support to front-end frameworks?**
    a. AppSync
    b. Amplify
    c. API Gateway
    d. ACM
    e. Angular

    Answer: b

    Amplify brings GraphQL support to many frontend frameworks for the AppSync service.

4. **Which terms do not apply to API Gateway?**

   a. HTTP

   b. REST

   c. Method

   d. Schema

   e. Resolver

   f. Request

   Answer: e

   Resolver is a GraphQL term.

5. **Which of the following CRUD data processing operations is incorrect?**

   a. Create

   b. Read

   c. Update

   d. Destroy

   Answer: d

   The D in CRUD stands for Delete.

6. **Which service is best to ensure events are processed and not lost?**

   a. SNS

   b. SQS

   c. S3

   d. DynamoDB

   e. SES

   Answer: b

   SQS will keep a message in the queue until it is deleted, or it expires.

7. **Which service sends both (external) notifications and (internal) events?**

   a. SES

   b. SNS

   c. SQS

   d. S3

   Answer: b

   SNS can send email, text messages, push notifications and events to SQS, Lambda and HTTP endpoints.

8. **Which service protects a web site from attacks?**
   a. Amazon Route 53
   b. AWS WAF
   c. AWS AppSync
   d. Amazon CloudWatch
   e. Amazon API Gateway

   Answer: b

   The AWS WAF provides a web application firewall to protect against web-based attacks. Amazon API Gateway has built-in protections for API endpoints.

9. **Which data processing technique is preferred in cloud?**
   a. ELT
   b. ETL
   c. CRUD

   Answer: a

   According to AWS, ELT is preferred in the cloud because it provides the processing power needed to transform the data loaded into the cloud.

CHAPTER 3
Designing Serverless Architectures

Introduction

This chapter will provide an overview of how to design serverless architectures and design topics to consider.

Structure

We will cover the following topics in this chapter:

- Introduction to serverless architectures
- Principles in serverless architectures
- Design considerations and potential drawbacks

Objectives

By the end of the chapter, you will understand how to design serverless architectures. Since serverless architectures are typically based on event-driven architectures, the chapter will describe how events are used to integrate serverless services together. You will be able to design a serverless architecture for a new or existing product.

Introduction to serverless architectures

So far, we have discussed the following:

- Traditional on-premises infrastructure
- Cloud infrastructure
- Virtual servers
- Containers
- Serverless applications

Next, we will discuss how to design the architecture for a serverless application. We are going to start from traditional web server architectures and move our way up to serverless architectures. Making the jump from a web server architecture to a serverless architecture might be difficult for some of us. There is some fundamental knowledge about the AWS cloud that might not be obvious at first. Therefore, it would be best if we started with a single web server and updated the architecture step-by-step to explain how the web server and the web application evolve to become fully serverless.

Reviewing the monolithic architecture

In this section, we will review monolithic architectures which have a standalone web server in the architecture. Though many of us know this well, it would be good to review it, so we are on the same page and to benefit us who are new to web development.

A monolithic architecture consists of the following:

- **Hosting**: The hosting can be on-premises or in the cloud.
- **Server**: The server runs a physical server or a virtual server in the hosting. The host assigns an IP address.
- **Domain name**: The domain name is registered on a DNS server or service and points to the IP address of the server.

The server consists of the following elements:

- Web server software
- Web scripting language
- Database
- Web pages
- Web application code
- Static files

See *Figure 3.1* for an illustration of a monolithic architecture. We reviewed a similar view of a web server in the previous chapter:

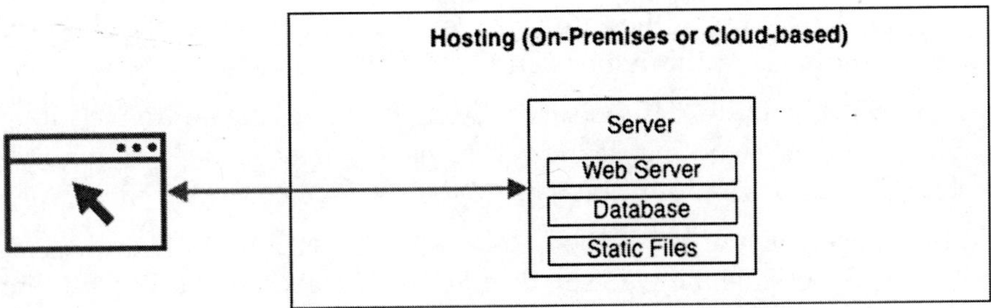

Figure 3.1: An example of a monolithic architecture

This architecture relies on one server performing all aspects of the application. When a browser visits an URL (for example, **https://mydomain.com**), there is a series of steps that take place.

The following describes those steps:

1. HTTP request is sent to the IP address of the server.
2. The server is running web server software that knows how to process the HTTP request.
3. The web server software processes the HTTP request to return the HTML data.
4. The web server software also returns other static files that are requested.

The web server software can run web application code using the web script language.

The web server software does the following:

- Determines whether the URL is targeting an HTML file, static file, or web application code.
- If the target is an HTML file or static file, it returns the contents of that file.
- If the target is web application code, it will execute the code and return the response, which is HTML data or the data of a static file.

The web application code is written to achieve an expected outcome. For example, it can return HTML data showing catalog items, including their names, prices, and image URLs. The code might need to retrieve data.

The code can retrieve data from the following sources:

- A file saved on the server's file system.
- Data stored in a database.
- Data from an API endpoint.
- Data stored in another URL (for example, another web server or a CDN).

For simplicity, we will assume this architecture will only retrieve information from a file on the server's file system and a database running on the server.

The server is a one-stop shop for the entire web application. This approach has limitations. The following describes some limitations and concerns:

- **Single point of failure**: If the server stops working, the entire website and web application stops working. If the server has a malfunction, it is possible all the website files and web application are lost if they were not backed up.
- **Performance constraints**: If there are many requests to the website (or website traffic), it is possible the web server might be overwhelmed. When there are too many requests, the web server might take much longer to respond, or it might stop responding.
- **File storage constraints**: Our website and web application might be media rich. It might have large numbers of images and videos, which consume a lot of disk space on the file storage. There might not be enough file storage to contain all the media files needed to make the website a success. Furthermore, when the disk space gets too low, it might affect the web server's performance.
- **Over provisioning**: We might have a server with multiple CPUs and large amounts of RAM to be ready for a large website traffic. We might be paying extra for greater capacity during the times when there is little website traffic. Furthermore, we might have a large disk space size to provide ample amounts of file storage. We might be paying extra for additional disk space that may not be used for a long time.
- **Under provisioning**: We might have a server with an insufficient number of CPUs and RAM to meet the demand of the website traffic. When the demand exceeds the provisioning, the web server will start responding slowly or stop responding.
- **Security**: With all the code and data storage in a single server, there is a higher importance to securing the server to avoid a data breach and data loss.

Using one web server works well when there is low website traffic and it is not media-rich. A successful website should result in more website traffic over time. We could continue upgrading our web server, but at some point, it would benefit us to explore a different architecture. We will discuss alternate architectures in this chapter, such as client-server, microservices, and event driven.

Reviewing the client-server architecture

We can start modifying the monolithic architecture to separate the components that interact with the client (that is, the web browser).

These components include:

- **Web pages (that is, HTML files):** The web browser gets the HTML data and renders a web page.
- **Static (for example, CSS and JavaScript) files:** The web browser gets the content of the static files and uses them to render the web pages.

- **Media (that is, picture and movie) files:** The web browser will display the images and videos on the web page.
- **Web application code:** The web browser will run the code that returns the HTML data (and other data) needed to render the web page.

The web application code needs the web scripting language and web server software to run. This leaves the database not directly interacting with the client. This means we can move the database to another server. We now have two servers:

- **Web server**: This server runs the website files and web application code.
- **Database server**: This server runs the database.

See *Figure 3.2* for an illustration of a basic client-server architecture:

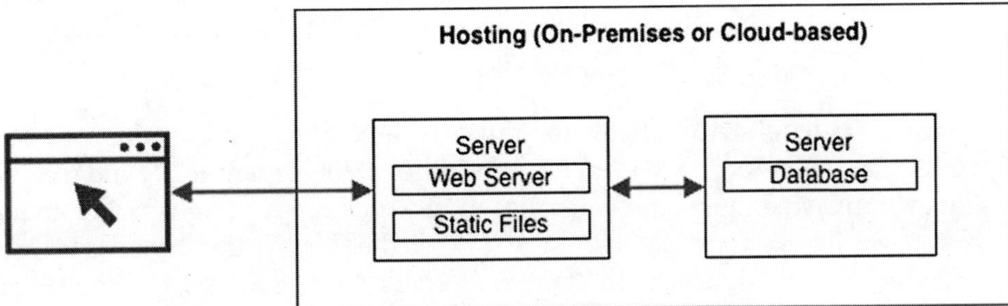

Figure 3.2: An example of a client-server architecture

Using this architecture provides the following benefits:

- **Reduces the single point of failure**: In the event the web server has an issue, the database remains unaffected. In the event the database has an issue, the web server still runs.
- **Improves performance**: The web server and database server will be able to focus on one purpose, which typically improves performance. If the web server experiences high traffic, the web server might be overloaded, but the database might be unaffected or affected less.
- **Improves file storage**: The web server file system can be sized to provide sufficient storage for the web pages, static files, and media. The database file system can be sized to store sufficient data.
- **Enables elasticity**: We can add additional servers when the website traffic exceeds the capabilities of one web server and remove them when the traffic drops.
- **Enables high availability**: We can add backup web servers and database servers to keep the website functional. When one server fails, we can switch to its backup. See *Figure 3.3* for an example of a high-availability design:

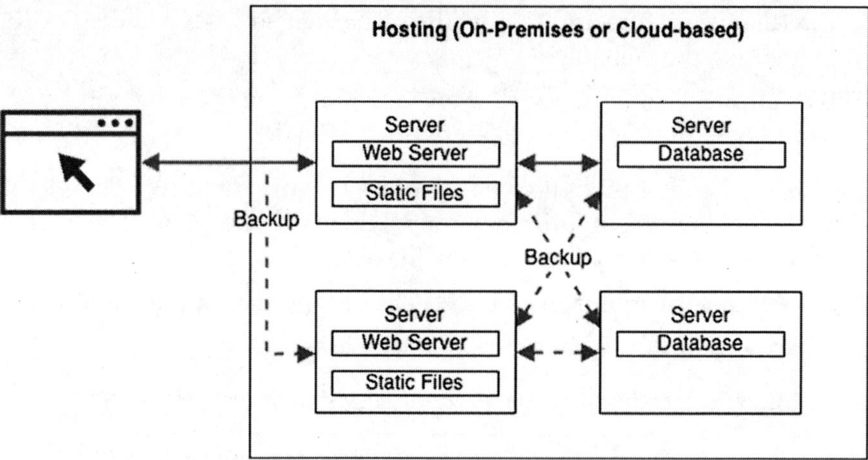

Figure 3.3: An example of a high availability design

- **Enables fault tolerance**: Fault tolerance is similar to high availability, but the additional servers are not backups. The additional servers are active and redundant. For example, in a high availability design, the web server might switch to a read-only backup copy of the database server when the primary database server crashes. In a fault-tolerant design, both database servers copy data to each other. When one database server crashes, the web server can continue reading and writing data to the other database server. Furthermore, the website can sustain multiple failures. Oftentimes a fault tolerance design uses multiple hosting locations to sustain a failure in one location. See *Figure 3.4* for an example of a fault tolerant design:

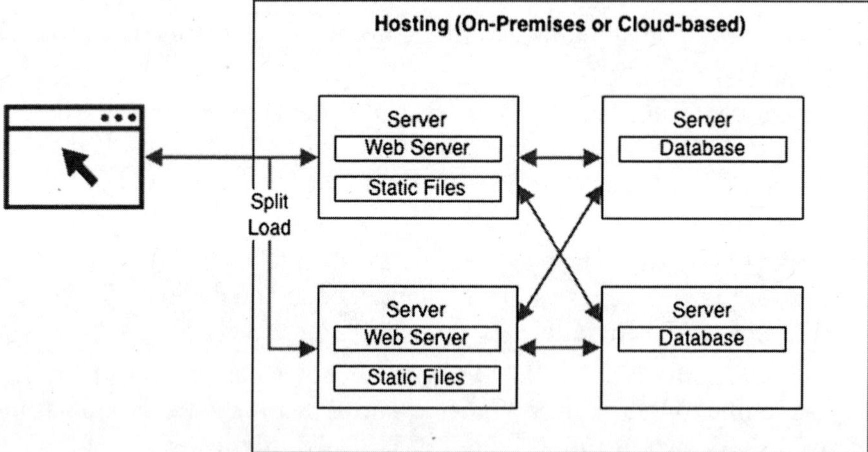

Figure 3.4: An example of a fault tolerant design

Now that we have separated the web server and database server, we can explore other enhancements to our architecture. We can explore the following changes:

- **Separate media files**: We might want to move media files to a separate server to reduce the burden on the web server running the web application code. Transferring large media files uses large amounts of network bandwidth and may affect the CPU and RAM. Having these files in a separate server allows it to focus on delivering high bandwidth content and allows the webserver to focus on running the web application code.
- **Separate web pages and static files**: We might want to move these files to a separate server when they rarely change. For example, the home page is an HTML file that stays the same. The home page has a login button that sends the user to a different URL that runs the web application code. Furthermore, there are certain images that are used for the web page design, and they rarely change. These images can be moved too. Moving these files to a new server allows that server to optimize the delivery of these files (possibly by enabling caching).

See *Figure 3.5* for an example of our updated client-server architecture:

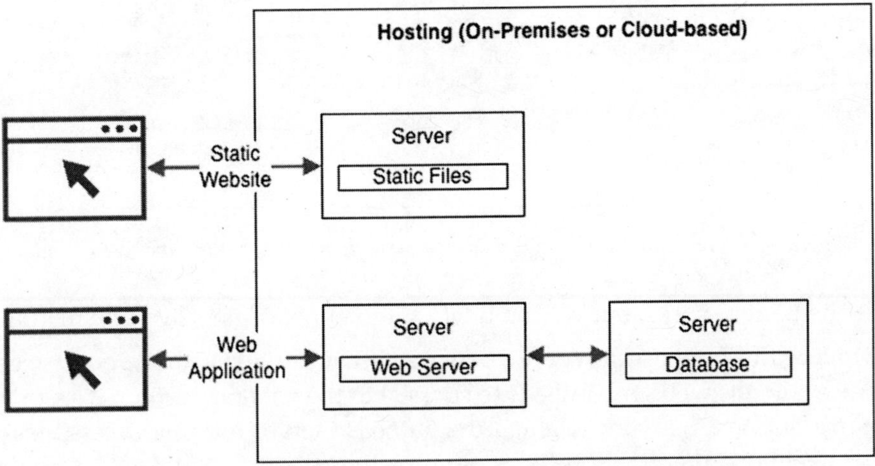

Figure 3.5. An example of an updated client-server architecture

Now that we have a more flexible architecture, we can explore using the AWS cloud to implement our architecture and make additional enhancements.

Migrating our architecture to the AWS cloud

The previous architectures could have been built on the AWS cloud, another cloud, or a web hosting service. We will focus on implementing our updated client-server architecture on the AWS cloud using the AWS services. We will use the following AWS services:

- **Route 53**: We will use Route 53 as the DNS for our domain name.
- **Amazon Virtual Private Cloud (VPC)**: We will use a VPC to create networks for our servers.

- **Amazon Elastic Cloud Compute (EC2)**: We will use EC2 to create virtual servers.

We will start by replicating the client-server architecture without any enhancements. See *Figure 3.6* for an example of our updated client-server architecture built in the AWS cloud using an EC2 instance for each server:

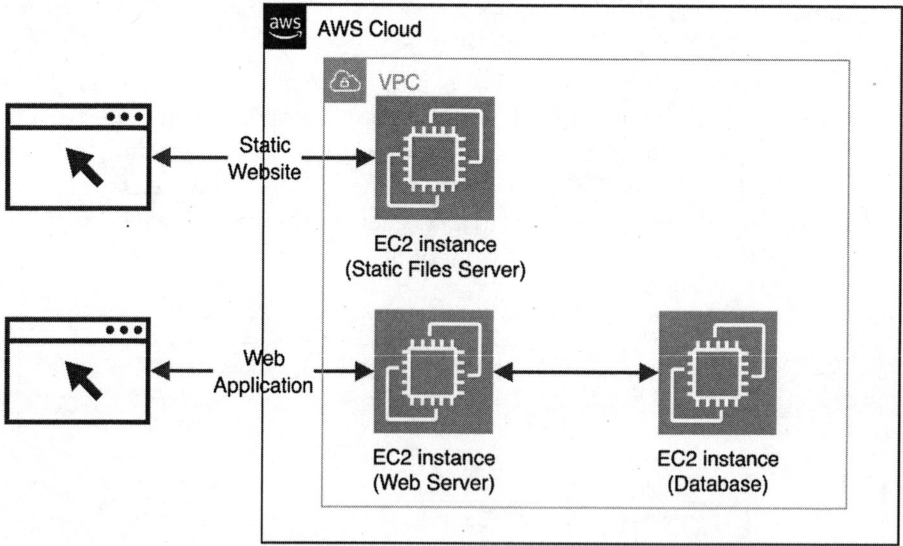

Figure 3.6: *An example of an updated client-server architecture built in the AWS cloud*

This implementation works, but we can make some improvements which include:

- **Moving the database server to a private network (that is, not Internet accessible)**: Since only the web server needs to connect to the database server, we should move it to a different network. Making the database server Internet-accessible increases the likelihood that it will be attacked directly.
- **Adding a Content Delivery Network (CDN)**: The static files that rarely change can be cached. We might have enabled caching in the static files web server, but it is typically limited to caching in the client and the server. A CDN will cache these static files at the routers closest to the client. When a client requests these static files, it can get a cached copy from the closest router (managed by the CDN) instead of the web server. We will use CloudFront as our CDN.

See *Figure 3.7* for an example of our updated client-server architecture built in the AWS cloud:

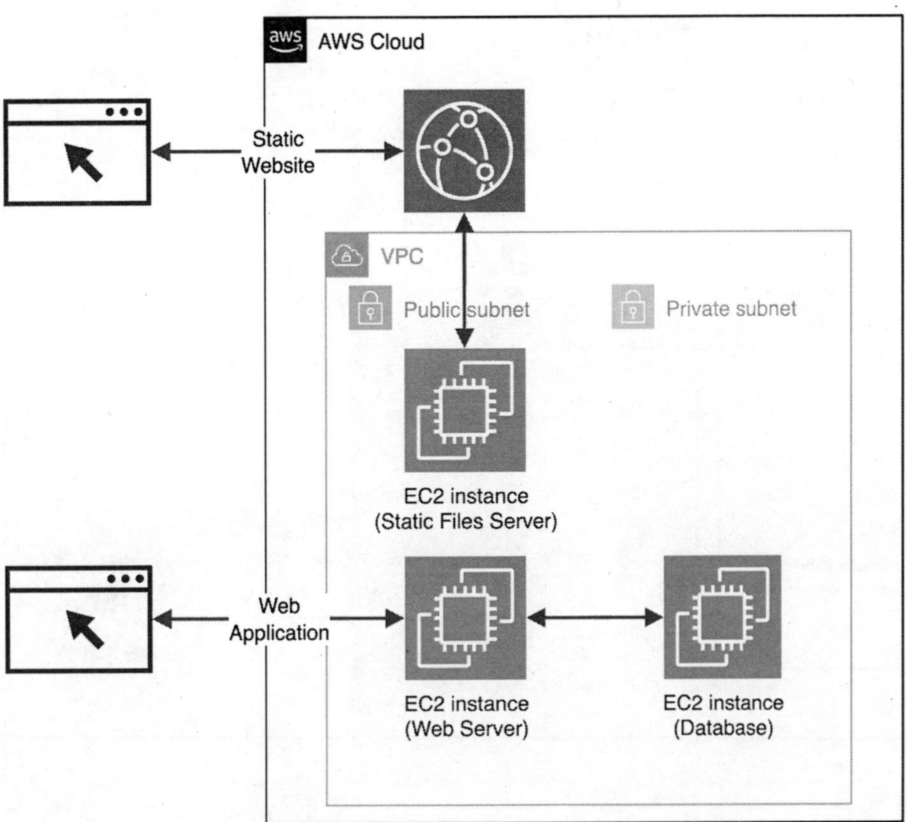

***Figure 3.7:** An example of an updated client-server architecture built in the AWS cloud*

In this update, we introduced an AWS service that was previously not part of the architecture. Adding CloudFront did not alter our design, but it did augment our design. Moving the database server to a different network did alter our design.

We can explore other AWS services to modify our design. We will explore using the following AWS services:

- **Amazon Relational Database Service (RDS)**: We can use RDS or another database service to host our database instead of having to maintain our own database server.
- **Amazon Elastic File System (EFS)**: We can move static files and media files to EFS which provides scalable and highly available storage capacity. EFS provides a **Network File System** (**NFS**) that may be easier for developers to adopt.
- **S3**: We can move static files and media files to S3, which provides highly available and virtually unlimited storage capacity. S3 is not an NFS and requires API calls to upload and modify our files.

See *Figure 3.8* for an example of our updated client-server architecture built in the AWS cloud:

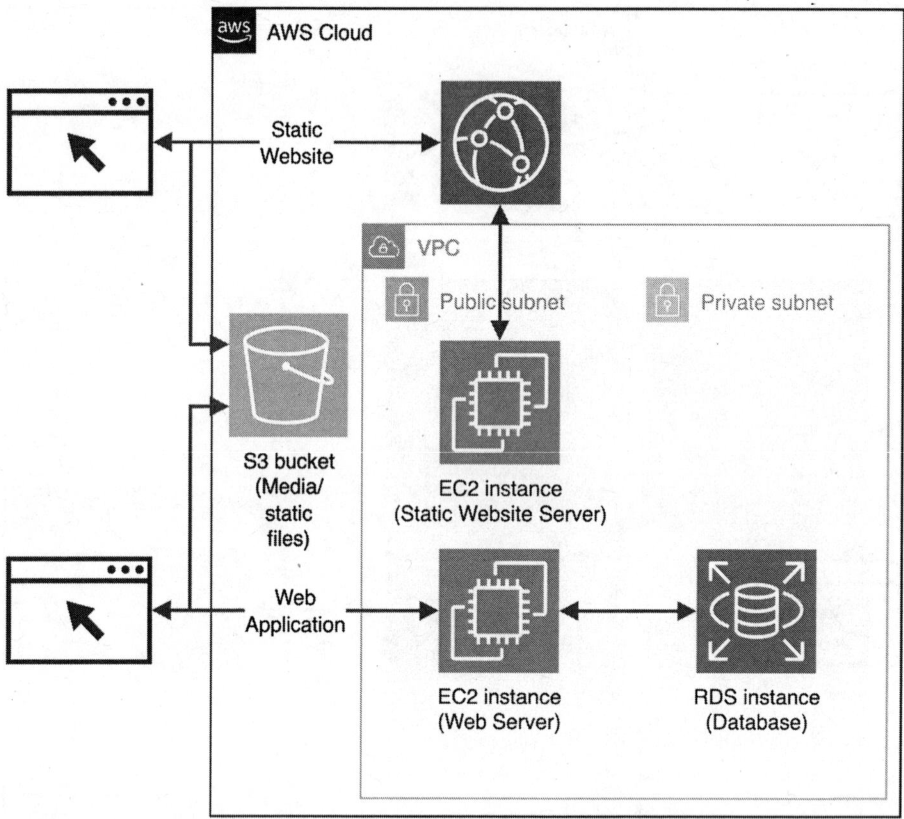

***Figure 3.8:** An example of an updated client-server architecture built in the AWS cloud*

We can update our architecture to make it highly available by doing the following:

- **Additional EC2 servers**: We can add additional EC2 servers to provide redundancy.
- **Adding an elastic load balancer**: We can add a load balancer to distribute the traffic among the servers.
- **Adding RDS standby replicas**: We can add a replica that becomes the primary database server if the primary server goes down.
- **Adding RDS read replicas**: We can add replicas to distribute the load among the servers.

See *Figure 3.9* for an example of our updated client-server architecture built in the AWS cloud:

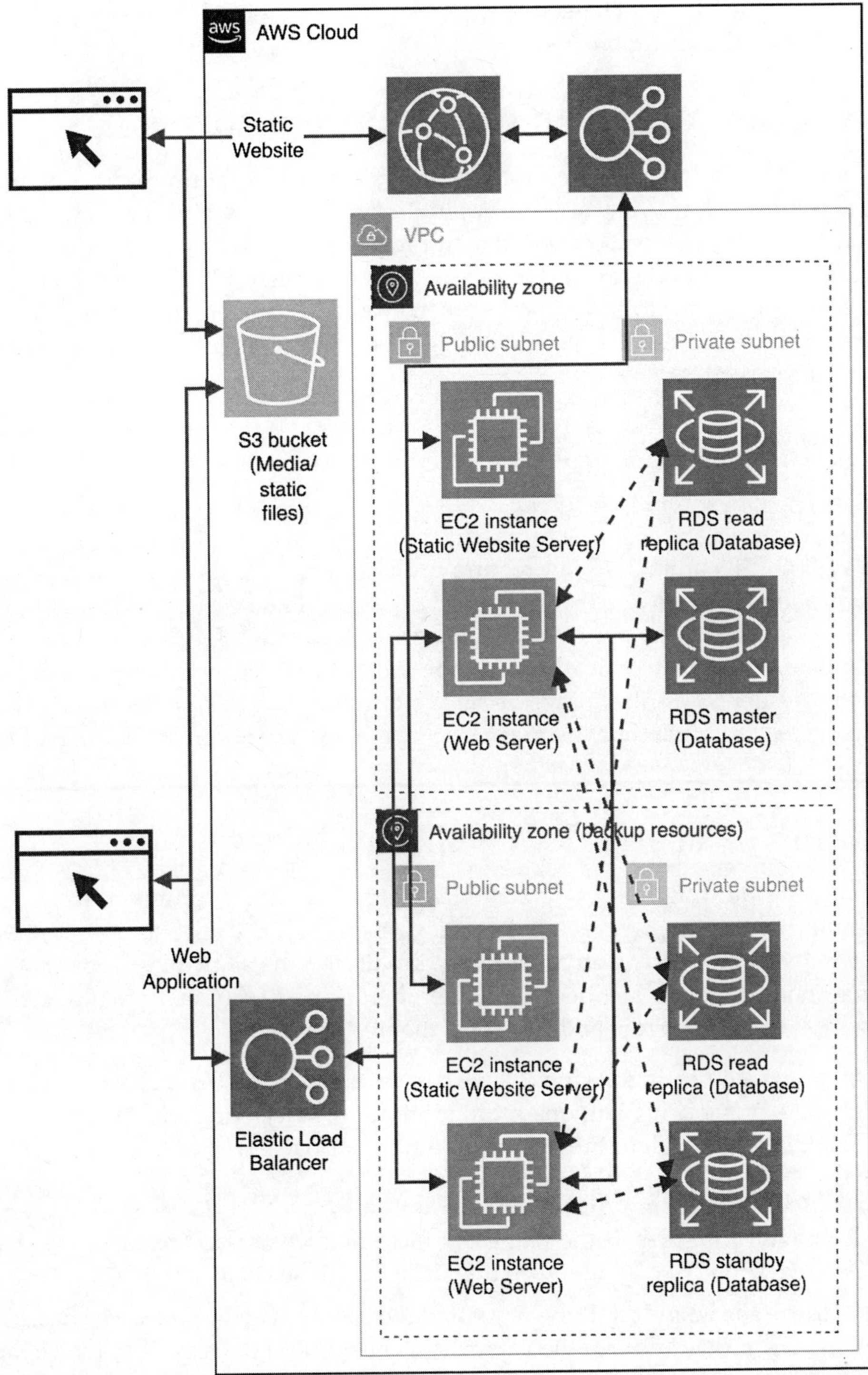

Figure 3.9: An example of an updated client-server architecture built in the AWS cloud

Now that we updated our architecture, we are leveraging more AWS services, we can start introducing serverless components.

Adding serverless to our architecture

We are going to add serverless services to our existing architecture. Some organizations may be uncomfortable moving an entire application to serverless. For some, it was probably a big transition moving their servers from on-premises to the AWS cloud. Adding another way of designing architecture could be overwhelming. As a result, it is good to know how to modify an existing one to add serverless to it. When we have proven to our organization that we have mastered AWS serverless, it might be more willing to adopt an architecture that only uses serverless services.

Recognizing serverless storage

We can help make the case for serverless services by highlighting the architecture already has serverless services. By moving the media file storage to EFS and / or S3, we have added serverless. Both EFS and S3 do not require provisioning a server to use it. It is possible the organization was unaware it adopted serverless services because it saw both EFS and S3 as file storage. This is an appropriate perspective, especially for EFS, since it is an NFS that resembles file storage on a web server. S3 is object storage and not file storage. Yet, some will consider S3 as file storage because entire files can be uploaded and retrieved. Recognizing the use of serverless storage might ease the transition into adding additional serverless components to the architecture.

Migrating to a serverless website

We should consider migrating to a serverless website as the first serverless project. In the example architecture, we have been using a web server for the static website and a different web server for the web application. Modifying the static files web server has a low impact on the existing architecture. Rather than using a web server to host static web pages, we can use CloudFront and S3 to host them.

S3 has built-in web hosting. Using it will suffice, but for the best UX, we should add CloudFront. As previously mentioned, CloudFront provides our CDN. We can configure our domain to go to the CloudFront distribution to retrieve our static website.

CloudFront will do the following:

- **Retrieve cache files**: If the requested file already exists in the cache and has not expired, CloudFront will return the cache file to the client.
- **Retrieve the S3 object**: If the requested file is not cached or the cache has expired, CloudFront will retrieve the contents of the S3 object, return it to the client, and cache it.

By adopting the S3 and CloudFront design for hosting our static website, we can eliminate the static files server from the architecture. See *Figure 3.10* for an example of our updated AWS architecture with a serverless website:

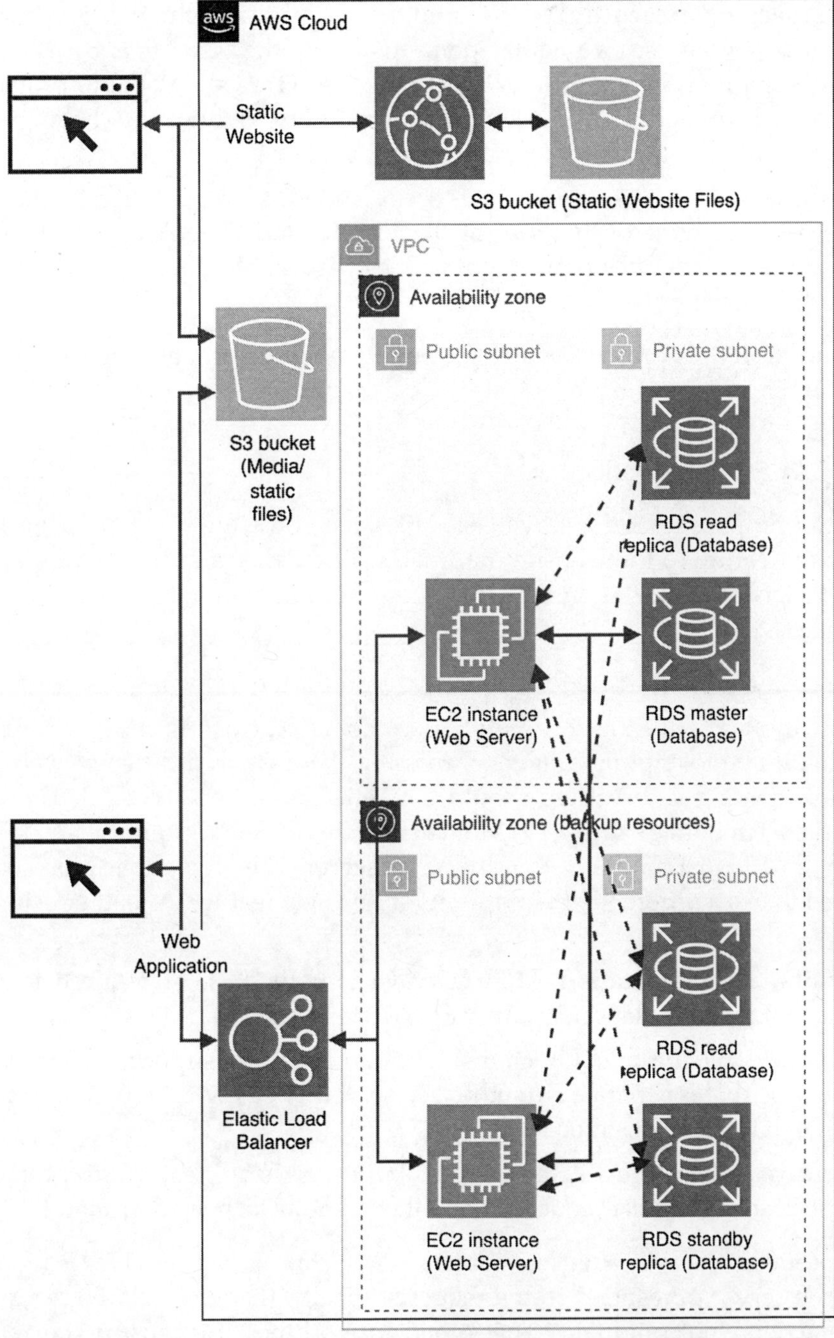

Figure 3.10: An example of an AWS architecture with a serverless website

Using this approach has the following benefits:

- **Reduced maintenance**: We no longer need to maintain our server by upgrading the operating system and web server software.
- **Improved cybersecurity**: We reduced the risk of a misconfigured web server that an attacker can use as an entry point to attack other servers and AWS resources. Furthermore, we can add a **Web Application Firewall (WAF)** to protect against attacks. Although a WAF was not shown in our architecture, having a WAF to protect Internet-facing servers is a highly recommended cybersecurity practice..
- **Lower costs**: We might reduce our costs. An EC2 server is billed by the hour, and the price depends on the size of the VM. S3 and CloudFront are billed by the usage. Static websites typically have files with small file sizes, and both services charge a small price per GB of data.

With the success of this project, we can propose the next step in adding serverless to our architecture.

Adding a serverless API

Next, we can propose to add a serverless API using API Gateway. For example, we are adding a new feature to the website that requires new modules in our web application code. The design team has determined these new modules will not affect other parts of the existing code.

This feature is a good candidate for a serverless API for the following reasons:

- **Low impact**: Since the new feature does not affect existing code, writing the code in a different scripting language, running the code in a different web server, or implementing it serverless should theoretically all be successful. The serverless approach requires using APIs. More than likely, the web application code is already using APIs that are hosted on the same server. The web application code would need to use a different API endpoint for this new feature instead of using the web server.
- **Flexible implementation**: API Gateway can redirect HTTP requests to a Lambda function, a load balancer, or another HTTP endpoint.
- **Reusable database connections**: Our architecture supports connecting to a database that is separate from the web server. The new code will need to connect to the database in a similar way.
- **Increased security**: API Gateway has built-in security features to protect against attacks and can reject requests that fail to meet the expected format.

As a compromise, we will suggest that the API Gateway redirect HTTP requests to a different web server to respond to the requests. Ideally, the team will be ready to adopt Lambda functions, but gradual changes tend to work best for most organizations. See *Figure 3.11* for an example of our updated AWS architecture with a serverless API:

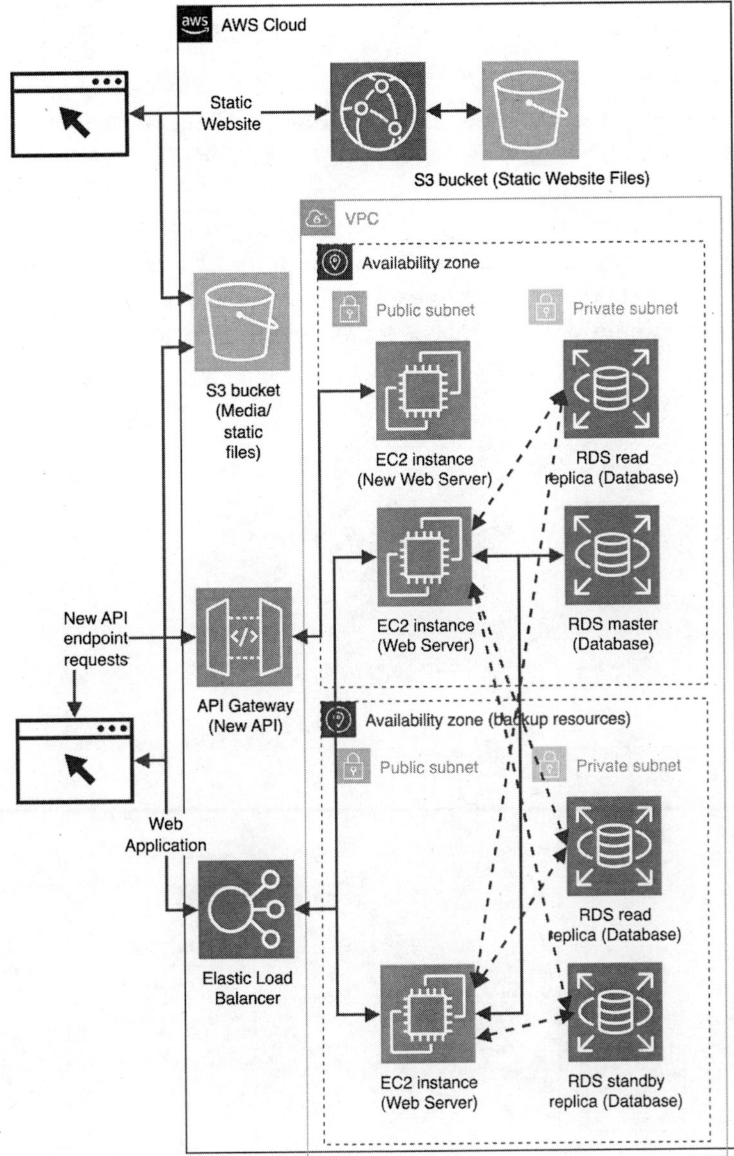

Figure 3.11: An example of an AWS architecture with a serverless API

With the success of this project, we can propose the next step in adding serverless to our architecture.

Adding serverless computing

Next, we can propose adding serverless computing using Lambda functions. For example, we can suggest completing the serverless API project by moving the new server to serverless functions. We can choose the API endpoint with the least complexity to introduce a serverless function. We will have API Gateway redirect the endpoint to a Lambda function rather than the web server.

This change might be exciting to some organizations, and a burden to others. For example, the web server uses PHP to run the web application code. Lambda does not natively support PHP. The Lambda function will need a custom runtime to add PHP. This increases complexity. The organization might need to write the function using Node.js, Python, or another natively supported runtime. If we can get past this hurdle, the organization can experience the benefits and drawbacks of serverless computing. Thereafter, the organization can evaluate when it makes sense to adopt serverless computing. We can suggest converting the newly added feature to use serverless functions for each endpoint. See *Figure 3.12* for an example of our updated AWS architecture with serverless compute:

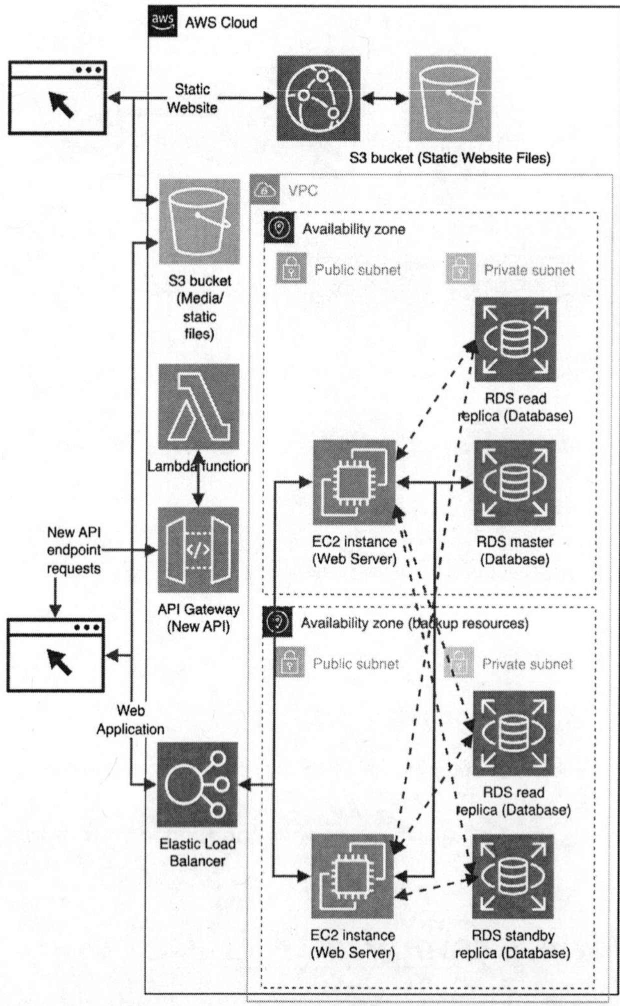

Figure 3.12: *An example of an AWS architecture with serverless compute*

With the success of this project, we can propose the next step in adding serverless to our architecture.

Adding or migrating to a serverless database

Next, we might want to suggest using a serverless database with either of two approaches:

- **Adding a serverless database**: Suppose the design needs a new database table. The table does not need to join with other tables to make it useful. This new table might be a good candidate for a serverless database (for example, a DynamoDB table).
- **Migrating to a serverless database**: Suppose the existing database needs to be restructured. The tables can be organized into groups and levels of importance. A group of tables with low importance could be migrated to a serverless database since they do not affect more important groups.

Adding a serverless database for a new database table is likely easier to start with. For example, we are adding yet another new feature. This new feature needs a new database table. The organization is ready to use API Gateway and Lambda functions to implement it. We suggest using a DynamoDB table as the serverless database.

Using a DynamoDB has the following benefits:

- **API-based**: Data is read and written to a DynamoDB table using the AWS APIs or SDK. This reduces the risk of SQL-based attacks.
- **Provisioning options**: The DynamoDB table can be configured to have provisioned or on-demand read-write capacity.
- **Built-in scaling**: The DynamoDB table will automatically increase its size, essentially providing unlimited storage.

See *Figure 3.13* for an example of our updated AWS architecture with a serverless database:

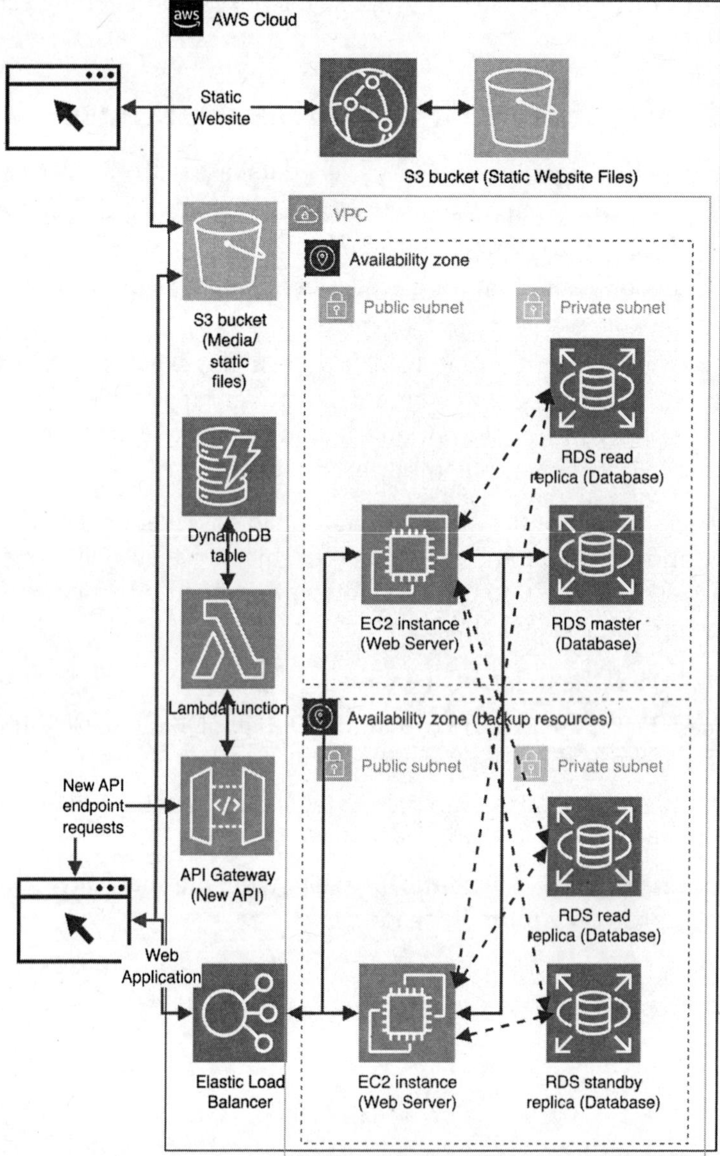

Figure 3.13: An example of an AWS architecture with a serverless database

With the success of this project, we can investigate the next steps in adding serverless to our architecture.

Additional serverless suggestions

At this point, we have explored the main serverless categories: storage, websites, APIs, computing and databases.

There are some other suggestions we can make:

- **Updating our serverless website to use serverless APIs**: The static website can use JavaScript to make it more dynamic. For example, the website can display recent company updates. JavaScript code can make a request to an API endpoint to get the content rather than having to modify the HTML code after every company update.
- **Converting scheduled jobs on the server to scheduled events**: The server might have schedule jobs. Depending on the complexity, we can create EventBridge scheduled events to trigger a Lambda function to do the same.
- **Migrate select APIs from the server to API Gateway and Lambda functions**: We can start moving some functionality from the web application code running on the web server and move them to an API on API Gateway. The organization now has experience implementing a new feature using serverless and can leverage that experience to start decoupling the web application code.

At this point, it might become more difficult to convince the organization to continue migrating to serverless. It will depend on the complexity of the web application and the willingness to embrace change. We should use our best judgment to determine when to leave good enough as is. We should look for opportunities to implement serverless in new projects.

Principles in serverless architectures

We have reviewed the traditional monolithic architecture, updated it to use services in the AWS cloud, and introduced serverless services to it. This journey was important in helping us design serverless architectures. By now, we have the foundational elements from the exercises in the previous architecture.

We can start designing an architecture that is meant to be serverless-first.

There are two common ways to create a serverless architecture:

- **Event-driven architecture:** This type of architecture relies on events for the application to work.
- **Microservices architecture:** This type of architecture organizes the components into logical groups of services.

We will explore both in this section.

Principles in event-driven architectures

An event-driven architecture is not specific to serverless. To some extent, a monolithic website architecture is event-driven. The client makes a request to the web server. This request is an HTTP request event that prompts the web server to send a response. For this architecture to be truly event-driven, the web server would do nothing else until it received another HTTP request.

Of course, this is not the case for the following reasons:

- The operating system runs processes.
- The web server runs its processes.
- The database runs its processes.
- There might be background processes or scheduled jobs (for example, an antivirus scan or cache cleaning).

Even when the server is idle, it is still active. The server will maintain itself and can run data processing even without an event.

Event-driven architectures are typically used when there are multiple components or systems that are decoupled, but they need to communicate with each other. For example, one server will not start a data processing activity until it gets an event from another server notifying it that all the data is ready for processing.

Event-driven architectures should also be asynchronous for the following reasons:

- The sender sends an event to a recipient that triggers an action.
- The sender does not need to wait for the response.
- The sender continues doing other activities.
- The recipient sends an event to the sender informing that the action was completed.
- The sender takes action on the next step if applicable.

An analogy might be helpful in this case. A restaurant follows the event-driven architecture concept and functions asynchronously.

The restaurant has the following components:

- **Patrons:** They enter the restaurant when they want to start eating. They exit the restaurant when they are done eating and have paid the bill.
- **Hosts:** They take the patrons to an available table.
- **Servers:** They take orders from patrons, deliver the food, provide the bill, and collect payment.
- **Cooks:** They receive an order, cook the food, and provide the cooked meal.

The components are dependent on each other, but they are not synchronous.

For example, suppose the restaurant was event-driven but synchronous:

- Patron Al arrives at the restaurant.
- The host takes nAl to a table.
- Al waits for the server. The server is serving patron Bob. The server cannot take Al's order because Bob has not finished eating.

- Bob eventually leaves the restaurant. The server can now take Al's order after having to wait.
- The server gives Al's order to the cook. The cook starts cooking the meal.
- Patron Cay arrives at the restaurant.
- The host takes Cay to a table.
- The server does not take Cay's order because the cook has not provided Al's cooked meal. Cay waits.
- The cook gives Al's meal to the server. The server delivers it to Al. Al starts to eat. The server kindly waits for Al to finish eating and paying the bill before taking Cay's order (assuming Cay was patient enough to wait all this time).

In this analogy, the events were the interactions (for example, a patron arriving). The host functioned asynchronously. The host did not wait for any patron to leave before taking a new patron to a table. The server functioned synchronously. The server served only one patron and did not serve another patron until finished with the prior one.

A real restaurant works asynchronously:

- The server will take a patron's order, give it to the cook, and move onto another task.
- The cook can receive multiple orders and start cooking them as they come.
- The host seats patrons as they come in.

Only the patrons work synchronously since they wait for each part of the process before they leave.

Let us explore an event-driven serverless architecture. Before defining an architecture, we must understand the purpose of the system. In this example, we will create a web application. The users will upload funny cat pictures. The backend will resize the pictures to a standard size. Once a week, the backend will send an email to the users with the week's most popular pictures.

We will have the following processes:

- **Process 1**: The website sends an API request to an API Gateway to get a list of the most recent pictures.
- **Process 2**: The website allows uploading image files. The image files are stored in an S3 bucket.
- **Process 3**: The website allows sending email notifications on a weekly basis. The status (that is, success or failure) is recorded to the database.
- **Process 4**: The website will attempt to resend the email if it fails to send.
- **Process 5**: The website will alert the administrator when the email fails to send three times.

See *Figure 3.14* for an illustration of the processes:

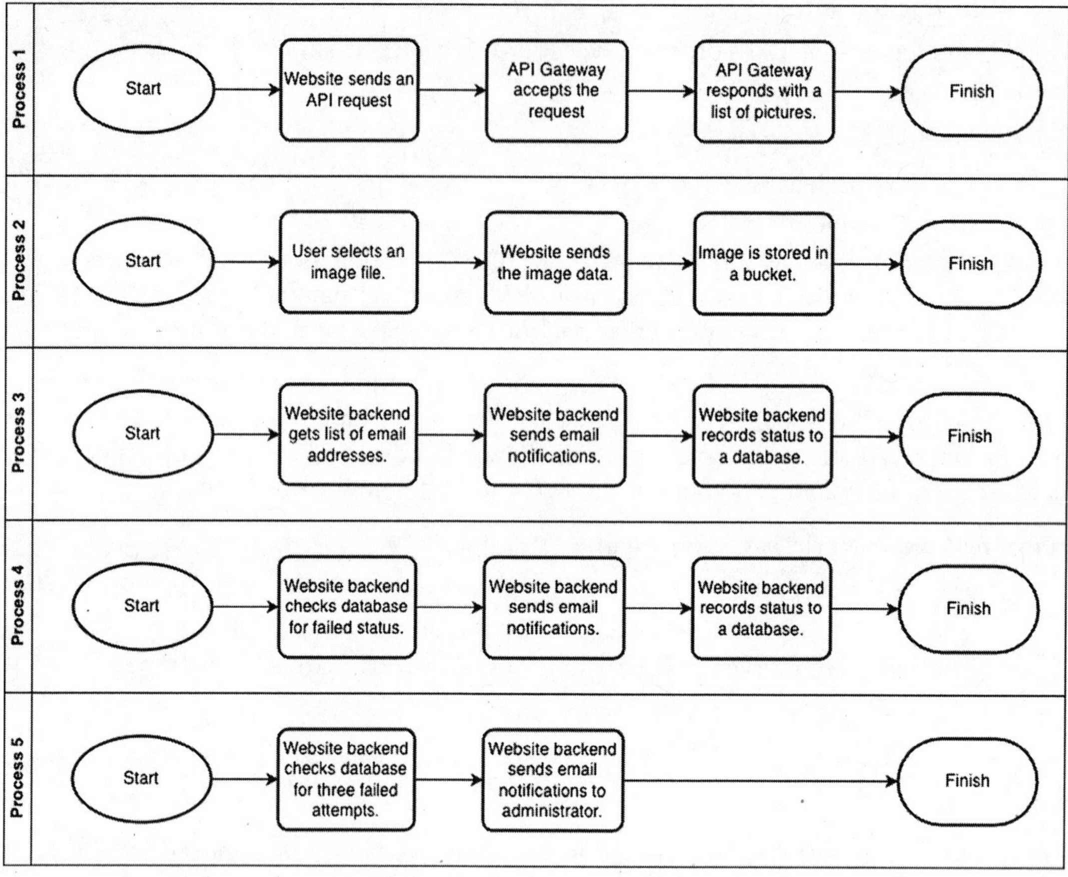

***Figure 3.14:** An illustration of an example event-driven architecture processes*

We omitted the login (that is, authentication) process from this example since it is a front end process and not part of the event-driven architecture.

We will have the following events:

- **HTTP events**: These events originate from the client when they make an HTTP request to the API Gateway.
- **Lambda triggers**: These triggers come from another AWS service (for example, API Gateway redirecting an HTTP event to a Lambda function).

- **Scheduled events**: These events originate from EventBridge to trigger a Lambda function.
- **SNS notifications**: These events originate when a message is sent to an SNS topic.
- **S3 event notifications**: These events originate when an object is created in an S3 bucket.
- **DynamoDB streams**: These events originate when the data in a DynamoDB table is updated.

Let us correlate the processes and the events:

- **Process 1**: An **HTTP event** will result when the website sends an API request to an API Gateway to get a list of the most recent pictures. The API Gateway will cause a **Lambda trigger** to the function assigned to that API request.
- **Process 2**: An **S3 event notification** will result when an image file is stored in an S3 bucket. The S3 event notification will cause a **Lambda trigger** to the function assigned to the event notification.
- **Process 3**: Some events need to be orchestrated for an email notification to be sent on a weekly basis. We will define subprocesses to achieve the desired outcome. After the email is sent, the Lambda function will write the status to a DynamoDB table.
    - **Process 3a**: EventBridge will send a scheduled event once per week to cause a Lambda trigger for a Lambda function.
    - **Process 3b**: The Lambda function will send an email using SES. Upon completion, the Lambda function will write the status to the DynamoDB table.
- **Process 4**: A **DynamoDB stream** event will be sent when the email delivery status is written to the table. It will cause a **Lambda trigger** to check the status and repeat **Process 3b** for a failure status.
- **Process 5**: On the fourth iteration of **Process 4**, the Lambda function will recognize the three failed attempts. It will send an **SNS notification** instead of trying to repeat **Process 3b**. The SNS notification will send the event to the administrator's email address and phone number as a text message.

See *Figure 3.15* for an illustration of an event-driven architecture:

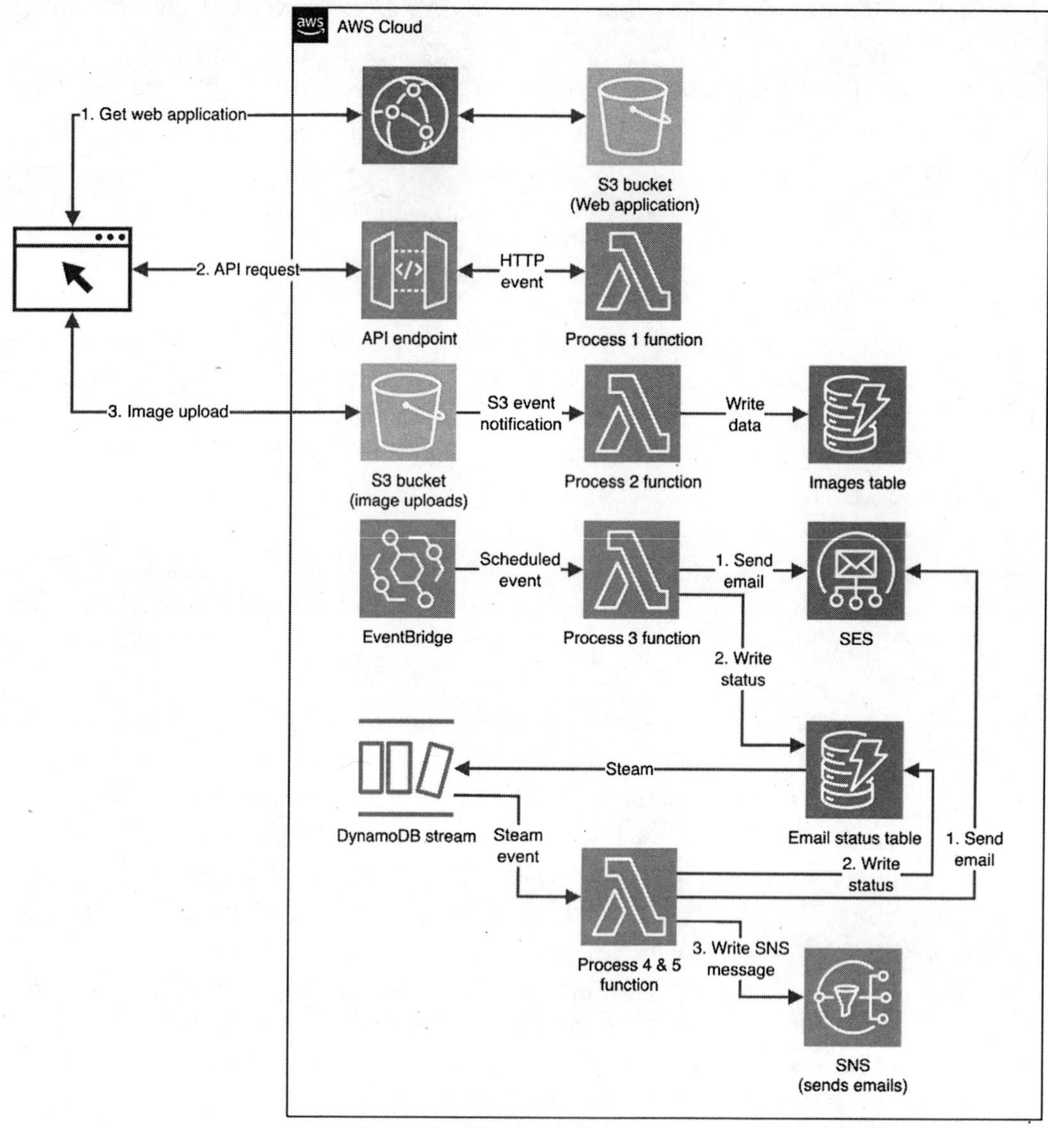

Figure 3.15: An illustration of an example event-driven architecture

As you can see, it relies on events. Next, we will explore a different type of architecture.

Principles in microservices architectures

Microservices architectures are not specific to serverless. It is possible that the monolithic architecture or our updated AWS server-based architecture have similarities to a microservices architecture. A microservice architecture assumes processes, resources, data, and other needed dependencies are organized into services.

Let us explore some of the concepts:

- **Modularity**: The architecture is organized into services. Each service provides different features (or a module) to the system. For example, there can be services for Authentication and Authorization, Catalog, Order, Analytics, and so on.
- **Independence**: Each service should be designed to be as independent as possible. Ideally, all the data and processes needed to make services useful will remain within that service. For example, the Authentication and Authorization service can be independent of the Catalog service.
- **Loose coupling**: Services sometimes need data from other services. Each service should have minimal dependence on any other service. If it does depend on another service, the service should remain mostly functional if its dependencies fail. For example, the Order service could make a request to the Catalog service for the quantity of a catalog item in stock before accepting the order. Instead, the Order service could accept the order and check the stock later. Another Order service process will check orders for valid items and refund the paid amount for items out of stock. The Order service can continue accepting orders regardless of the status of the Catalog service.
- **API-first**: Microservices rely on APIs as their external interfaces. A microservice that needs data from a database table in another microservice should not access that table directly. Instead, it should send an API request to the other microservice to get the data. For example, the Order service makes an API request to the Catalog service to check the quantity in stock for a catalog item instead of retrieving the data directly from the database table.

Using a microservices architecture provides some benefits:

- **Polyglot technology stack**: A microservice can use various technologies that provide the best solution. For example, the Catalog service might only use serverless technologies, but the Analytics service uses a server and external third-party services.
- **Autonomous development**: The development team responsible for a microservice can operate in autonomy. It can design and implement the microservice as they seem fit, but they must define the external interface and adhere to it. For example, the team publishes the Catalog service API that other microservices can use (for example, the Order service). The other teams can comment and influence the API, but they should not dictate how the inner workings are designed.
- **Scalability and flexibility**: Part of the architecture can scale and change to meet the current needs. Services with consistently high demand can provision greater resources and those with low demand or inconsistent demand can have lower resource or on-demand provisioning configurations. Services may be added and removed as the architecture evolves, which would be most difficult to achieve in a monolithic architecture.

- **Resilience**: As previously mentioned, services should be independent and loosely coupled. This provides built-in resilience and fault tolerance. When one microservice fails, the other microservices should not fail. The other microservices might be degraded but remain operational. For example, the failure of the Analytics service should not affect the Authentication and Authorization service. The failure of the Catalog service might degrade the Order service. The Order service may choose to accept orders but delay fulfilling them until the stock quantities are verified.

See *Figure 3.16* for an illustration of a microservices architecture:

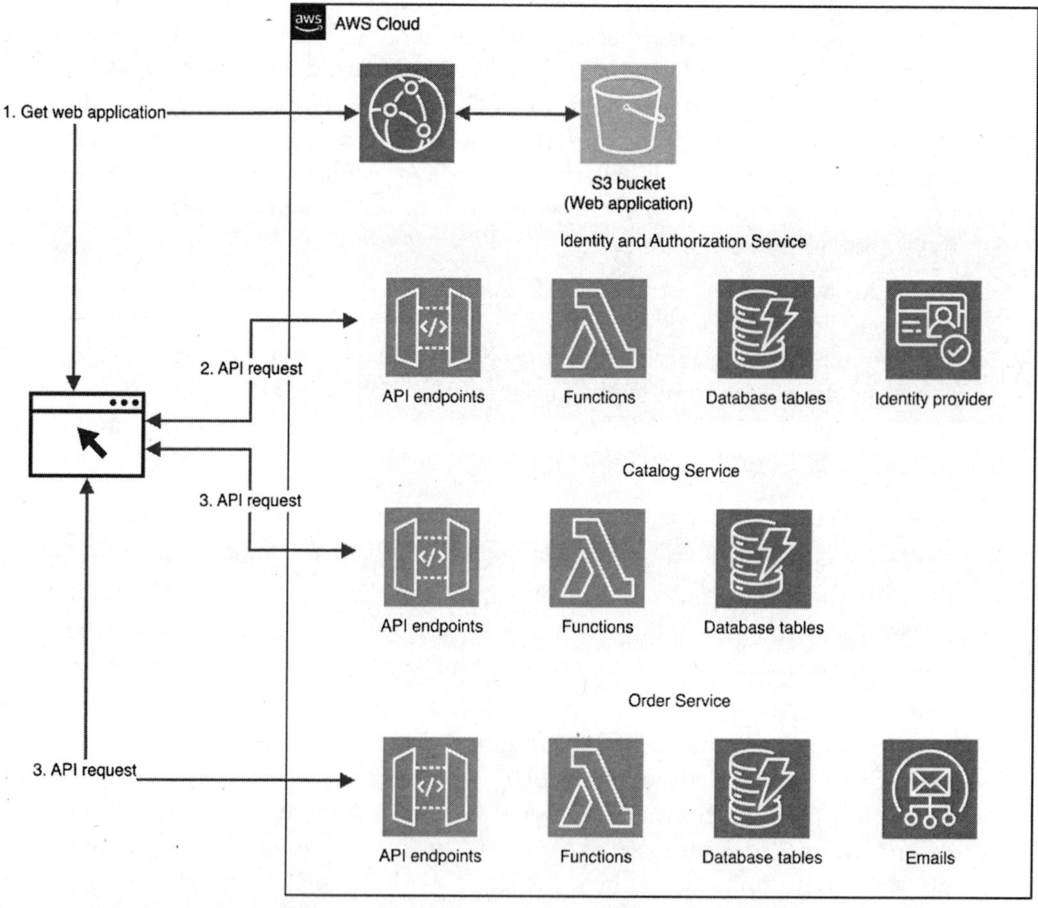

Figure 3.16: An illustration of an example microservices architecture

Although microservice architectures support polyglot technologies, we will limit ours to serverless technologies. Next, we will review some items to consider when creating our serverless application and choosing an architecture style.

Design considerations and potential drawbacks

Every architecture and design style has benefits and drawbacks. We will review some of these to consider for the types of architecture we have discussed.

Considerations for adding serverless to an existing architecture

Continuing to modify and grow an existing architecture might reach its limits. Adding serverless can help decouple parts to the system. Furthermore, keeping core functionality within the existing architecture and using serverless for non-core functionality might have some benefits as previously discussed.

There might be some drawbacks:

- The serverless code fails to follow the same coding language, patterns and styles as the existing architecture.
- The serverless components might be implemented differently and fail to follow reusable architecture patterns.
- New team members might have a longer learning curve since they need to learn the core design and the serverless additions.
- The documentation for the serverless components might be limited or inconsistent with the core documentation.
- Estimating costs might prove difficult or worrisome since many serverless services are billed based on usage.
- Existing code and features that were moved to serverless components might not have been deactivated. These result in *dead* code or *shadow* API endpoints in the core systems that could be exploited if not properly deactivated.

The drawbacks should be considered to avoid causing issues.

Considerations for event-driven architectures

As previously mentioned, event-driven architectures rely on events driving activity. There might be a temptation to assume that events are reliable.

Let us discuss some drawbacks:

- **Events might never be sent or could be lost during delivery**: As reliable and available the AWS cloud is, it does experience outages and failures. Our architecture and design need to account for an event not being sent as expected.

- **Events might be delivered late**: A process might expect an event to arrive within a certain time frame. If the event arrives after that time frame, it might result in unexpected behavior especially if the data is no longer relevant.
- **Events might arrive out of order**: When multiple events are being sent within a short time, it is possible some events might be received out of order. If this happens, the state of the data might be incorrect.
- **Duplicate events might be sent**: An event might be sent multiple times. If this happens, we might perform the operation multiple times and cause unexpected behavior.
- **Numerous events**: Sometimes, sending an event seems logical, but the volume of events might not have been considered. When the volume of events becomes too numerous, it is possible the system may stop responding as expected because it has exceeded its limits and thresholds.

These are some strategies to consider mitigating the drawbacks:

- **Scheduled events**: Our system might be designed to send events when states change. If an event is lost in transit, the receiving function will not be aware of a state change. We can use schedule events to trigger functions to check for unprocessed state changes.
- **Time windows**: When events have time stamps, we can check that the time stamp is within a certain time window. Data has a life expectancy and may lose its value when the life has been exceeded. Our functions can check whether an event arrived within the expected time window and discard any that are received beyond it.
- **Counters**: When sending data across networks and the Internet, routers attach a counter to the data packets. As the packets travel, they are sometimes split up as they are routed to the fastest and shortest path to the destination. As a result, some packets arrive out of order. The receiver uses the counter in each packet to assemble the message. We can consider adding a counter to our events to ensure they are processed in the correct order.
- **Idempotence**: This means that a function returns the same result and results in the same state when an input is received multiple times as if the input was only received once. Writing our Lambda functions to be idempotent reduces the risk that duplicate events result in unexpected behavior.
- **Throttling, batching, polling, or scheduled events**: We might be able to configure our system to throttle events to limit the number of events to a manageable amount per time period. We might also request that events be batched and sent as one event with multiple messages. We might be able to poll for messages on a regular interval. We may also consider scheduled events to have a function query the next set of data that needs processing.

Event-driven architectures should be designed to assume failures and issues.

Considerations for microservices architectures

As previously mentioned, microservice architectures organize the system into services. Well-designed microservice architectures have resilience and fault tolerance built in, but there are still some drawbacks to this style.

Let us discuss some drawbacks:

- **Proliferation**: Architects and designers might continually introduce a service for each additional feature. It is possible there might be more services than are actually needed.
- **Increased overhead**: In an attempt to minimize data and code dependencies across microservices, there might be duplicated data, functions, resources, and infrastructure. In a monolith, any part of the system can access a data source, for example. But in a microservice, that data source might be duplicated to avoid one service having to interact with another service.
- **Complexity and inconsistency**: Each service development team is encouraged to work autonomously, but this might result in each service being designed differently. The different services might fail to follow consistent coding standards and architecture patterns. The entire system can become complex as the number of services increases.
- **Broken contracts**: One service might have published an API schema that other services rely on. The service API schema might be updated in a way that causes a breaking change and is not backward compatible. When this change is published, the other dependent services are negatively affected.
- **Dead code and shadow APIs**: As services become obsolete or their API schemas change, the concerns of dead code and shadow APIs also apply.

These are some strategies to consider mitigating the drawbacks:

- **Keep it simple**: Existing services should be reviewed against the new features and changes. Adding new services should be considered when it would significantly alter the purpose and performance of existing services.
- **Shared resources**: Creating a service for shared resources (for example, database tables) could reduce overhead by centralizing them and avoiding duplicating in multiple services. Allow microservices to interact directly with shared resources rather than through a service API if the data is not sensitive to state changes. Common code libraries that functions can import minimizing the same code being copied into multiple functions.
- **Documentation and peer reviews**: Documenting coding standards, software patterns and architecture patterns can guide service teams how to develop their services. Implementing peer review across the different teams can help team members get constructive feedback from members from other teams.

- **Automated testing**: Implementing automated regression testing and end-to-end testing prior to releasing a change can help catch bugs and issues. These tests should be owned by an independent team to avoid the tests being evaluated against the update that might have a broken contract. Conducting peer reviews across different teams and performing "change management" process can also help.
- **Monitoring**: Checking logs and API usage metrics can help detect shadow APIs.

Microservice architectures should be designed to consider these drawbacks and mitigations.

Considerations when implementing ad hoc

When creating an application, it is tempting to design as we go. This approach might work for a small application but may become an issue for a large one. Some of the drawbacks previously discussed will likely surface by implementing ad hoc. We might experience *serverless spaghetti* or *serverless ping pong* which use the terms *spaghetti* and *ping pong* as an illustration of a complex, ad hoc design.

Spaghetti consists of multiple strands of noodles. By nature, these strands intertwine in a seemingly complex and random pattern. We might have heard of *spaghetti code* where code calls multiple functions in a way that it is difficult to trace the execution. Similarly, this can happen in a serverless design. Events can be routed to various destinations in a way that is difficult to trace. See *Figure 3.17* for an example of a serverless spaghetti:

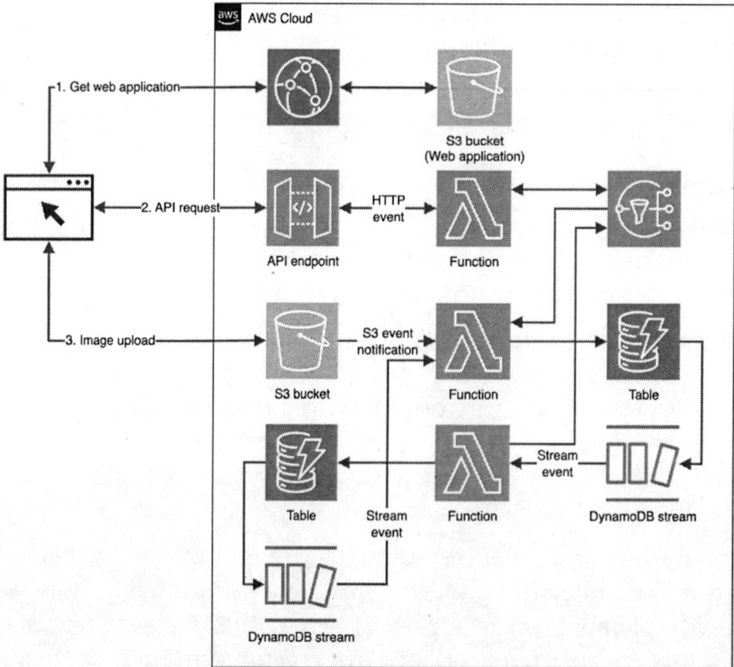

Figure 3.17: *An example of serverless spaghetti*

Ping pong is a game where two players use a wooden paddle to hit a plastic ball across a table and over a net. They keep hitting the ball back at each other. A similar situation can happen in a serverless design. An event can spark a reaction of events that are sent *back and forth*. See *Figure 3.18* for an example of serverless ping pong:

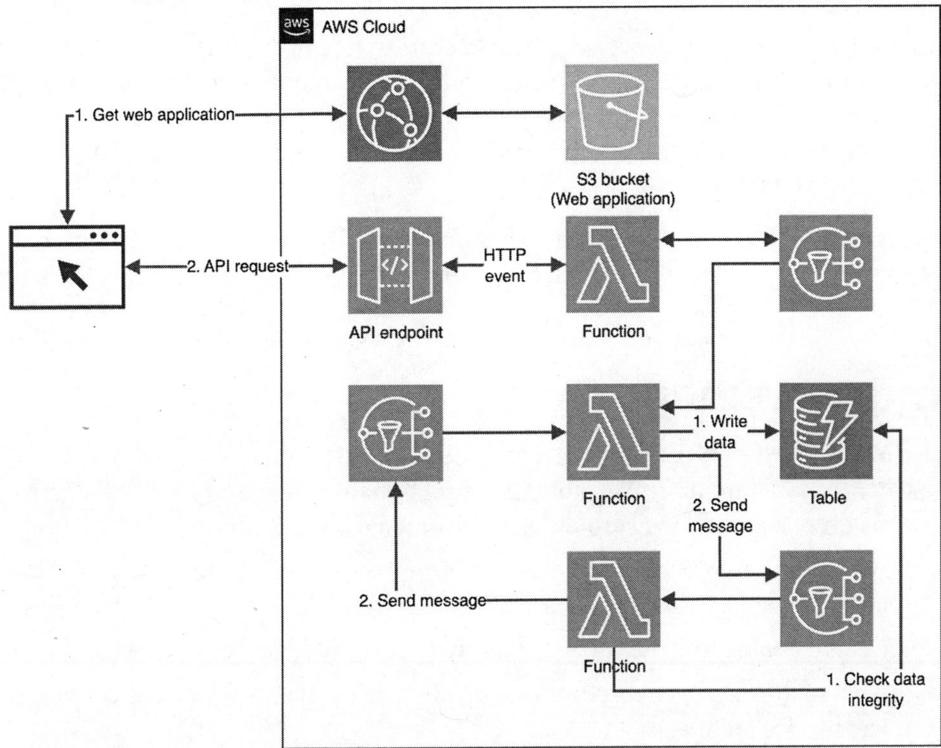

Figure 3.18: *An example of serverless ping pong*

Fortunately, serverless services provide so much flexibility that we can redesign and improve our architecture over time and as we learn more about user traffic patterns and cloud usage.

Conclusion

In this chapter, we discussed how to design serverless architectures. We reviewed a monolithic architecture where the web server, database and file storage are all on one server. We updated our architecture to a client-server architect that separated the web server and file storage into one server and the database in another server.

We moved our client-server architecture to the AWS cloud by using EC2. To make better use of the AWS cloud, we migrated some pieces of our architecture to AWS services. We moved the database EC2 server to use RDS. We moved our file storage to S3 or EFS. These changes introduced serverless services to our architecture.

We updated our architecture to have serverless services. We changed one of the web servers to a serverless website using S3 and CloudFront. We added a serverless API for a new feature using API Gateway. We introduced serverless computing by using Lambda. We added a serverless database by using DynamoDB. Modifying an existing architecture to use serverless helped us prepare for designing a serverless architecture.

We explored two types of serverless architectures. Event-driven architectures rely on events to run the system. Microservices architectures organize the system into services that are meant to be independent and loosely coupled. We discussed some drawbacks and mitigations of these approaches. We now have the foundation to create our serverless application.

In the next chapter, we will start putting these concepts into practice. We will discuss how to create a serverless website and work through hands-on exercises to create one using the AWS Management Console.

Points to remember

- Monolithic architectures run everything on one server.
- Client-server architectures split the functionality. Anything that is client-facing runs on one server. Everything else runs on a different server.
- Moving to the AWS cloud allows us to improve existing architectures by using a service instead of self-hosting a server.
- We can update our existing architecture to introduce serverless services.
- Fully serverless architectures typically use event-driven architectures or microservice architectures.
- Implementing a serverless application ad hoc might result in unwanted drawbacks.

Multiple choice questions

1. **Which of the following is not an architecture type we discussed?**
   a. Event-driven
   b. Microsystems
   c. Microservices
   d. Monolithic
   e. Client-server

   Answer: b

   Microsystems is not an architecture type we discussed.

2. **What was one of the first serverless service(s) we introduced for an existing architecture?**

   a. DynamoDB

   b. Lambda

   c. S3

   d. CloudFront

   e. FaaS

   Answer: c

   We introduced S3, but also mentioned EFS. Both are serverless services. S3 is a serverless object storage service. EFS is a serverless network file system service.

3. **Does S3 provide web hosting?**

   a. Yes

   b. No

   Answer: a

   Yes. Web hosting can be enabled for S3 buckets for static files.

4. **Does API Gateway only work with serverless service?**

   a. Yes

   b. No

   Answer: b

   Yes. API Gateway can redirect HTTP events to server-based destinations.

5. **Can Microservice architectures implement event-driven architectures?**

   a. Yes

   b. No

   Answer: a

   Yes. Microservice architectures use polyglot technologies. One service can be event-driven while another service is server-based.

6. **Which is not a possible outcome of an ad hoc architecture?**

   a. Spaghetti

   b. Idempotence

   c. Ping pong

   Answer: b

   Idempotence needs to be considered when using events to make sure the outcome is the same as if an event was only sent once when duplicate events are sent.

Join our book's Discord space

Join the book's Discord Workspace for Latest updates, Offers, Tech happenings around the world, New Release and Sessions with the Authors:

https://discord.bpbonline.com

Chapter 4
Launching a Website

Introduction

This chapter will provide hands-on exercises to create a serverless website.

Structure

We will cover the following topics in this chapter:

- Overview of serverless websites
- AWS account setup
- Register a new domain with Route 53
- Enabling S3 website hosting
- Creating a record in Route 53
- Disabling S3 website hosting
- Requesting a certificate from AWS Certificate Manager
- Creating a CloudFront distribution
- Creating aliases for the distribution in Route 53

Objectives

By the end of this chapter, you will understand how to use object storage with the Amazon **Simple Storage Service** (**S3**) to host web pages. You will also understand how to use a **content delivery network** (**CDN**) with Amazon CloudFront to speed up web page loading times.

Overview of serverless websites

In the previous chapter, we discussed creating serverless websites using Route 53, S3, ACM, and CloudFront. Let us review how these work in more detail.

We will use Route 53 to purchase a custom domain. When we purchase a domain with Route 53, it will automatically create a hosted zone, which is our DNS server. All the DNS records are created and managed in the hosted zone.

The S3 service provides static website hosting. S3 will provide us with an AWS-managed web address for our website. This website is long and complex. We can create a Route 53 record for the custom domain to point to the website.

By default, the S3 bucket that hosts our website files is not accessible via the Internet. AWS sets strict security settings when creating new buckets. We will need to update the bucket permissions to allow public access to all its objects. When we enable public access, we will be able to browse to our website.

The S3 hosting supports HTTP requests but not HTTPS requests. Many browsers give a warning or stop loading when a website uses HTTP instead of HTTPS. Using HTTP is considered a security risk because the data is transmitted over the Internet in plain text. Anyone can see the data. HTTPS sends the data encrypted between the browser and the web server. No one else should be able to see the data. We will want to make sure our website uses HTTPS, so users and search engines trust it.

To provide HTTPS, we need a **Secure Sockets Layer** (**SSL**) or **Transport Layer Security** (**TLS**) certificate. The certificate is installed on the browser, and it is registered with a certificate authority that verifies it is valid. When a browser connects to a website using HTTPS, it requests the certificate, the certificate is verified against the certificate authority, and the connection is established if the certificate is valid. We will create an SSL/TLS certificate for our website using the **AWS Certificate Manager** (**ACM**). We will let ACM manage the certificate.

We could work through adding the certificate to our S3 static website hosting, but we will use it for our CloudFront distribution. CloudFront is a CDN, and the distribution puts our static files on the CDN for faster delivery times and caching. The user will receive our website files from the closest CloudFront caching location in its global network. The user will experience lower latency since it is delivering a cached copy that has less distance to travel on the Internet. Furthermore, CloudFront provides built-in security protections, such as **Distributed Denial of Service** (**DDoS**) attack protection. For these reasons, we will configure our website to use a CloudFront distribution to our website. We will update the Route 53 records, so the custom domain points to the distribution.

The CloudFront distribution puts the website files into the CDN, but it needs to know where to get them. We will configure the distribution to get the requested files from the S3 bucket. Our S3 bucket will be configured to block public access at this point. We will update our bucket permissions to allow CloudFront to access the objects.

We will do hands-on exercises to implement what we discussed above.

We will do the following:

- Show screen captures of the AWS management console to provide visual aids in performing the steps.

  We will use **masteringawsserverlessbook.com** as the example domain and **masteringawsserverlessbook** as the name in the service settings through the book. You will substitute **masteringawsserverlessbook** with your custom domain name when performing these exercises.

Note: It is important that you select a unique name since the example domain and name for the service settings are already registered and you might run into conflicts when performing the exercises.

- Use the North Virginia (that is, us-east-1) region in the AWS web console. You will substitute the region you selected when performing these exercises.

Let us do some hands-on exercises to create our serverless website.

AWS account setup

We will assume we have already created an AWS account.

AWS recommends using multiple AWS accounts[1] for different purposes. It is a good practice to have one AWS account per project and per environment. For example, one web application in the development stage would be in one AWS account. The web application in the production stage would be in another AWS account. A different web application would be in yet another AWS account.

We will assume our serverless project will be in a new AWS account, but we will do our best to provide instructional steps for using an existing AWS account.

---

1 "Establishing your best practice AWS environment." AWS Organizations. Amazon Web Services. **https://aws.amazon.com/organizations/getting-started/best-practices/**

Security credentials

The security of our AWS account is important. Although this is not a book on cloud security, we must cover some basic cybersecurity.

We might use the root account to access the AWS web console. The root account is the account we created using our email address. This account has unlimited privileges. It is a super administrator account. As a result, it is important to protect it.

We can protect our root account by doing the following:

- Creating a strong, complex password.
- Not reusing an existing password.
- Adding **Multi-Factor Authentication** (MFA).

If an attacker guesses our password, MFA is the last line of defense. We will walk through the steps to set up MFA for our root account. We will assume our account already has a unique, strong, complex password.

Hands-on exercise 1: Setting up MFA

Let us set up MFA for our AWS root account:

1. Click the top right menu and click the **Security credentials** menu option or enter **https://us-east-1.console.aws.amazon.com/iam/home** in the browser address bar.
2. Go to the **Multi-factor authentication (MFA)** section. See *Figure 4.1* for reference:

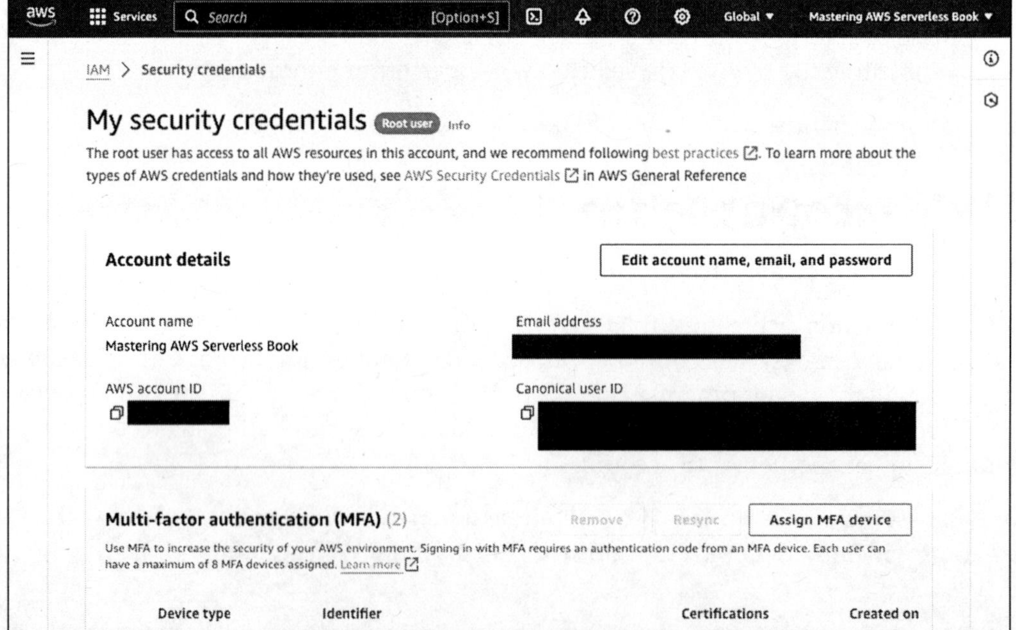

Figure 4.1: *The IAM security credentials page*

3. Click the **Assign MFA device** button.
4. Specify a name in the **Device name** field.
5. Select one of the following:
    a. Authenticator app
    b. Security key
    c. Hardware TOTP token
6. Click the **Next** button.
7. Follow the on-screen instructions to complete the process.
8. We should see the MFA device listed in the MFA section.
9. Open another web browser application (different than the one currently being used) and log in to your AWS root account to make sure all is working well.

IAM users and Identity Center

The IAM service allows us to create IAM users to log into our AWS account. Using IAM users is a better security practice because they do not have super administrator privileges. They will have the privileges we assign, which can be as low as read-only or as high as administrator. An IAM user with administrator privileges cannot have all the privileges as the root account.

Another approach is setting up the Identity Center. This service provides **Single Sign On** (**SSO**) into our AWS account. We will use AWS Organizations to create an organization for our AWS account(s). The account(s) part of that organization can enroll in the Identity Center and allow the creation of users with IAM privileges. These users will sign in with the Identity Center SSO website.

Reviewing both of these IAM concepts and providing hands-on exercises for them will be a distraction from mastering AWS serverless. We will assume you are securely logging into the AWS account and have sufficient privileges to work through the hands-on exercises.

Register a new domain with Route 53

In this section, we will register the **masteringawsserverlessbook.com** domain using Route 53.

Hands-on exercise 2: Registering a new domain with Route 53

Let us use Route 53 to register the **masteringawsserverlessbook.com** domain:

1. Search `route 53` in the top search bar and click the **Route 53** search result or enter **https://us-east-1.console.aws.amazon.com/route53/v2/home** in the browser address bar.
2. If the **Get started with Route 53** section is displayed, click on the **Get started** button. Check the **Register a domain** radio button and click the **Get started** button.
3. If the **Route 53 dashboard** page is displayed, click the **Register domain** button.
4. The **Register domains** page is displayed. See *Figure 4.2*:

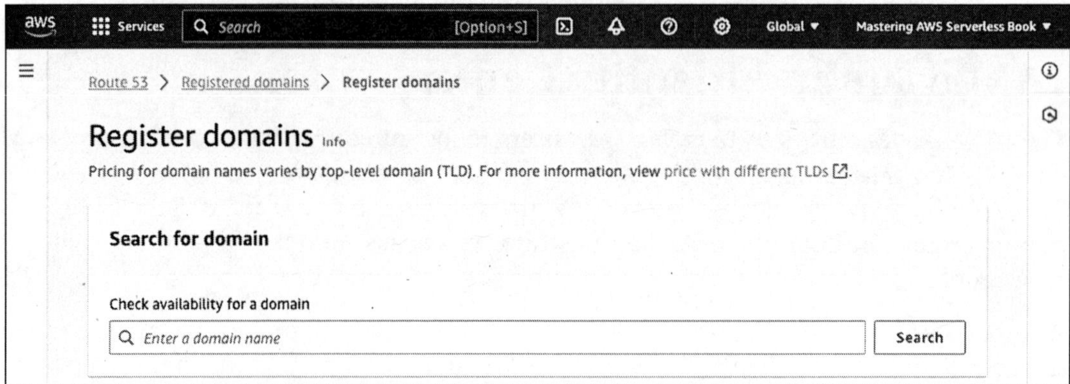

Figure 4.2: The Route 53 register domains page

5. Search for the desired domain.
6. Select the desired search result. See *Figure 4.3*:

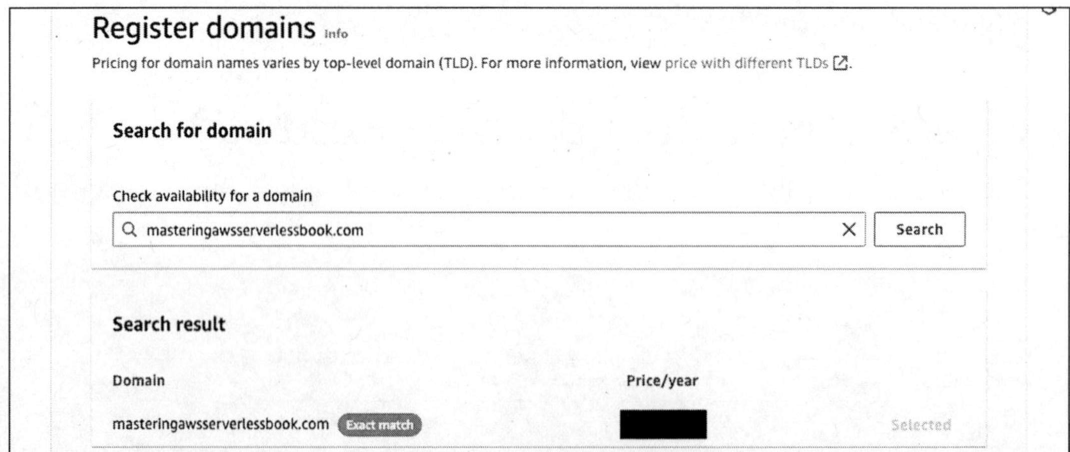

Figure 4.3: Searching for a domain

7. Click the **Proceed to checkout** button.
8. Check or uncheck the **Auto-renew On** checkbox as desired.
9. Follow the on-screen instructions to complete the process.
10. Observe **In progress** as the status. See *Figure 4.4* for your reference:

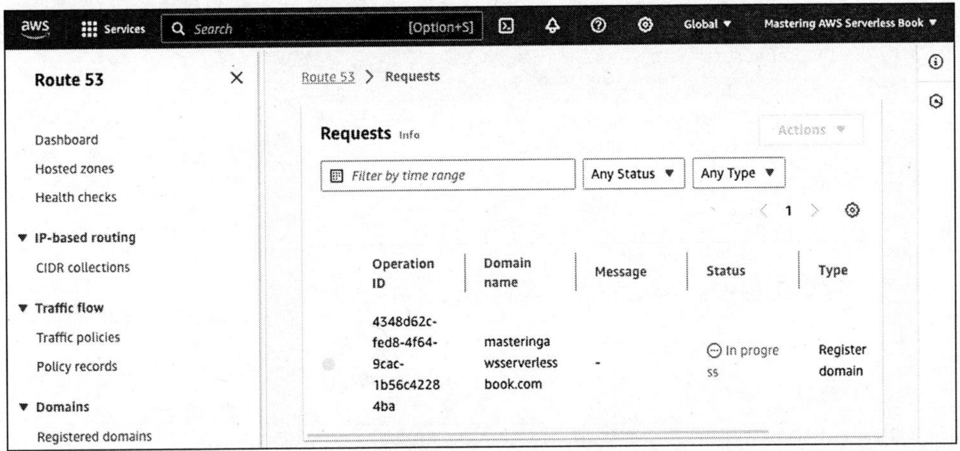

Figure 4.4: The in-progress domain registration

Note: We may need to refresh the page for the domain and status to be displayed.

11. We can check the status by refreshing the page. We should get an email when registration succeeds.

Note: It may take several minutes for the registration to complete.

12. Refresh the page and observe that the status is **Successful**. See *Figure 4.5*:

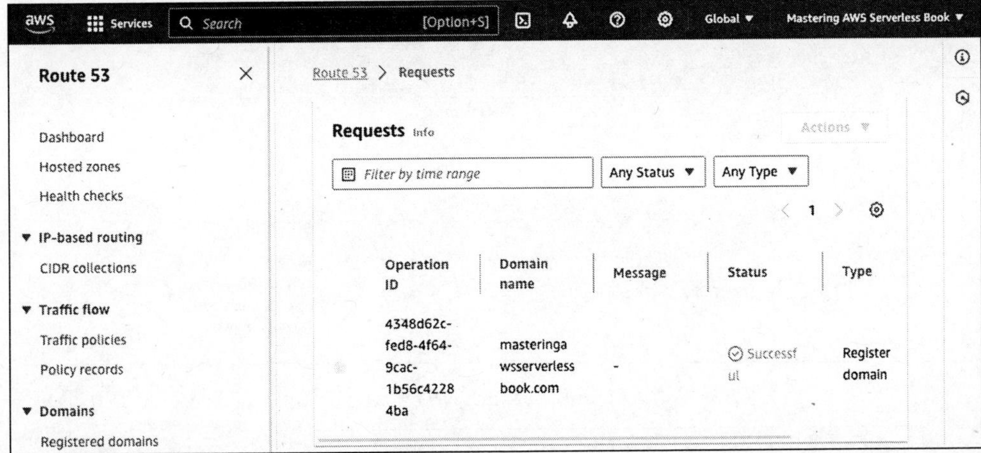

Figure 4.5: The successful domain registration

13. Go to the **Dashboard** menu option.
14. Click on the hosted zone link in the **Dashboard** page.
15. Observe that the hosted zone was automatically created. See *Figure 4.6*:

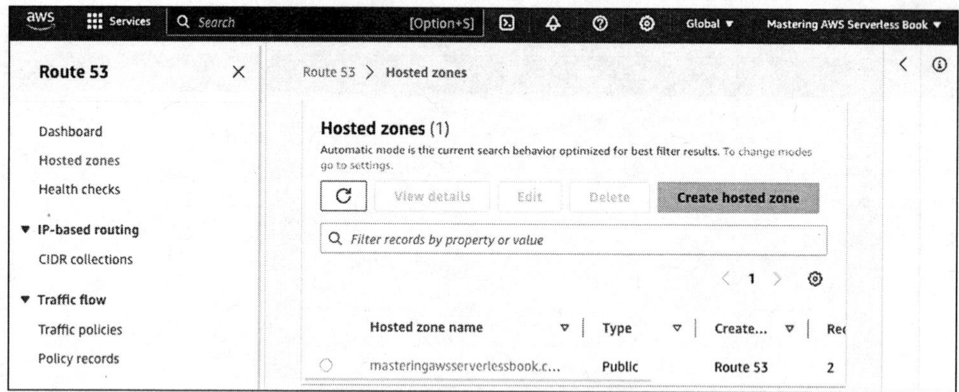

Figure 4.6: The hosted zone

16. Click on the hosted zone link in the **Hosted zones** page.
17. Observe DNS records were automatically created. See *Figure 4.7*:

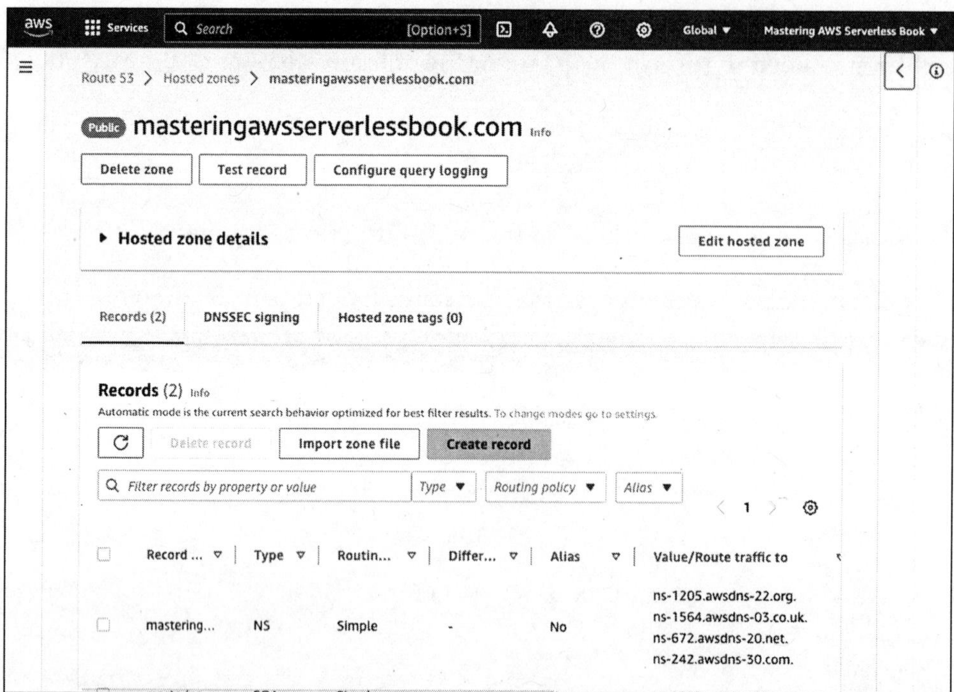

Figure 4.7: The DNS records

We have successfully registered our domain with Route 53 and have an active DNS.

Enabling S3 website hosting

In this section, we will:

- Create an HTML file.
- Upload the file to S3.
- Enable S3 website hosting.
- Configure S3 to allow public access.

Let us create our website.

Hands-on exercise 3: Enabling S3 website hosting

Let us create an HTML file, upload it to S3, and enable S3 website hosting:

1. Create a file named **`index.html`** on your computer.
2. Paste the following HTML code into the file.

Note: This file uses Bootstrap[2] that makes it easier to make website look nicer.

This will be nicer than a **`Hello world!`** web page:

```
<!doctype html>
<html lang="en" class="h-100" data-bs-theme="dark">
  <head>
    <title>Mastering AWS Book</title>
    <meta charset="utf-8">
    <meta name="viewport" content="width=device-width, initial-
    scale=1, shrink-to-fit=no">
    <link href="https://cdn.jsdelivr.net/npm/bootstrap@5.3.2/dist/
    css/bootstrap.min.css" rel="stylesheet" integrity="sha384-T3c6
    CoIi6uLrA9TneNEoa7RxnatzjcDSCmG1MXxSR1GAsXEV/Dwwykc2MPK8M2HN"
    crossorigin="anonymous">
  </head>
  <body class="d-flex h-100 text-center flex-column">
    <div class="d-flex w-100 h-100 mx-auto flex-column">
      <header class="mb-auto">
        <nav class="navbar">
          <div class="container-fluid">
            <span class="navbar-brand h1 mx-auto">
```

2 Bootstrap is released under the MIT license and is copyrighted by Twitter.

```
                Mastering AWS Serverless Book
              </span>
            </div>
          </nav>
        </header>
        <main role="main" class="my-auto">
          <div class="container">
            <h1>Coming soon</h1>
            <p class="lead">
              Check back soon.
            </p>
          </div>
        </main>
        <footer class="mt-auto">
          <div class="container text-center">
            <p>
              &copy; Miguel A. Calles. All rights reserved.
            </p>
          </div>
        </footer>
      </div>
    </body>
    <script src="https://cdn.jsdelivr.net/npm/bootstrap@5.3.2/
    dist/js/bootstrap.bundle.min.js" integrity="sha384-C6Rzsyn
    M9kWDrMNeT87bh95OGNyZPhcTNXj1NW7RuBCsyN/o0jlpcV8Qyq46cDfL"
    crossorigin="anonymous"></script>
  </html>
```

3. Save the file.
4. Search **s3** in the top search bar, click the **S3** search result, or enter **https://s3.console.aws.amazon.com/s3/get-started** in the browser address bar.
5. Click the **Create bucket** button.
6. Specify **masteringawsserverlessbook.com** in the **Bucket name** field.

Note: Bucket names must be globally unique. For example, we cannot create a bucket named masteringawsserverlessbook.com in a different AWS account or region.

7. Click the **Create bucket** button.
8. The new bucket is displayed. See *Figure 4.8*:

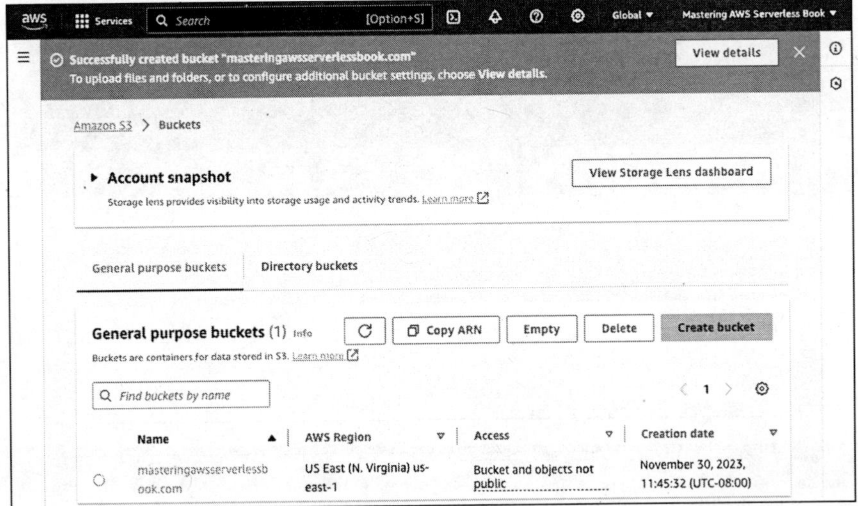

Figure 4.8: The bucket

9. Click the new bucket.
10. Click the **Upload** button.
11. Follow the on-screen instructions to upload the **`index.html`** file.
12. Click the **Upload** button.
13. Click the **Close** button when the upload finishes.
14. The **`index.html`** object is shown in the bucket objects list. See *Figure 4.9*:

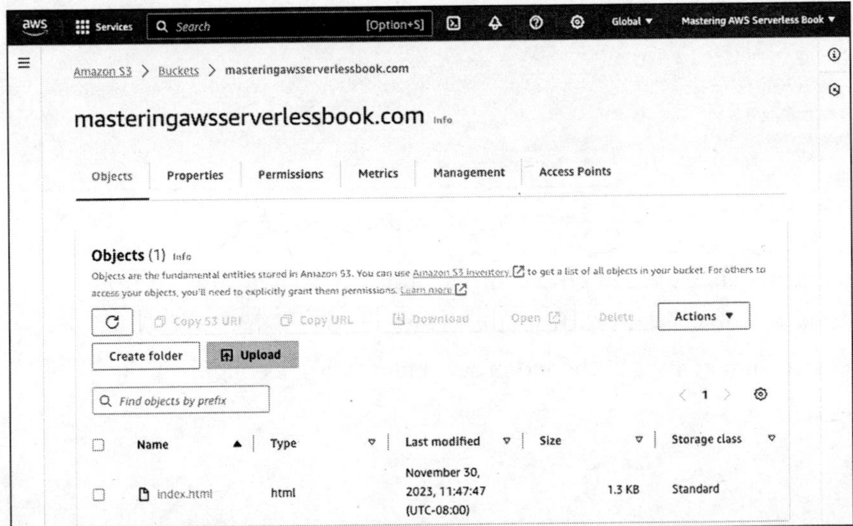

Figure 4.9: The object

15. Click the **`index.html`** object.
16. Click the link under the **Object URL** section.
17. An error is message is displayed. See *Figure 4.10*:

```
This XML file does not appear to have any style information associated with it. The document tree is shown below.

▾<Error>
   <Code>AccessDenied</Code>
   <Message>Access Denied</Message>
   <RequestId>YF64FMX2E6368RMB</RequestId>
   <HostId>97nc0e1GfS+GG2R0MIY9Wj2n/wZ1p2wn3mqd1g3jYbAYtAL3CLTNpT3lXB/5dVsRxe8zPdLpQ64=</HostId>
 </Error>
```

Figure 4.10: *The error message*

18. Click the browser back button.
19. Return to the bucket by clicking the bucket name link in the breadcrumbs at the top of the page.
20. Click on the **Properties** tab. See *Figure 4.11*:

Figure 4.11: *The bucket properties tab*

21. Go to the **Static website hosting** section and click the **Edit** button. See *Figure 4.12*:

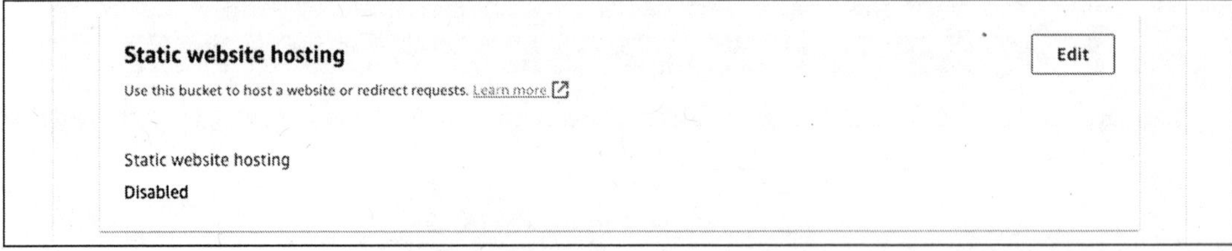

Figure 4.12: *The static website hosting section*

22. Check the **Enable** radio button in the **Static website hosting** section.
23. Check the **Host a static website** radio button.
24. Specify **`index.html`** in the **Index document** field. See *Figure 4.13*:

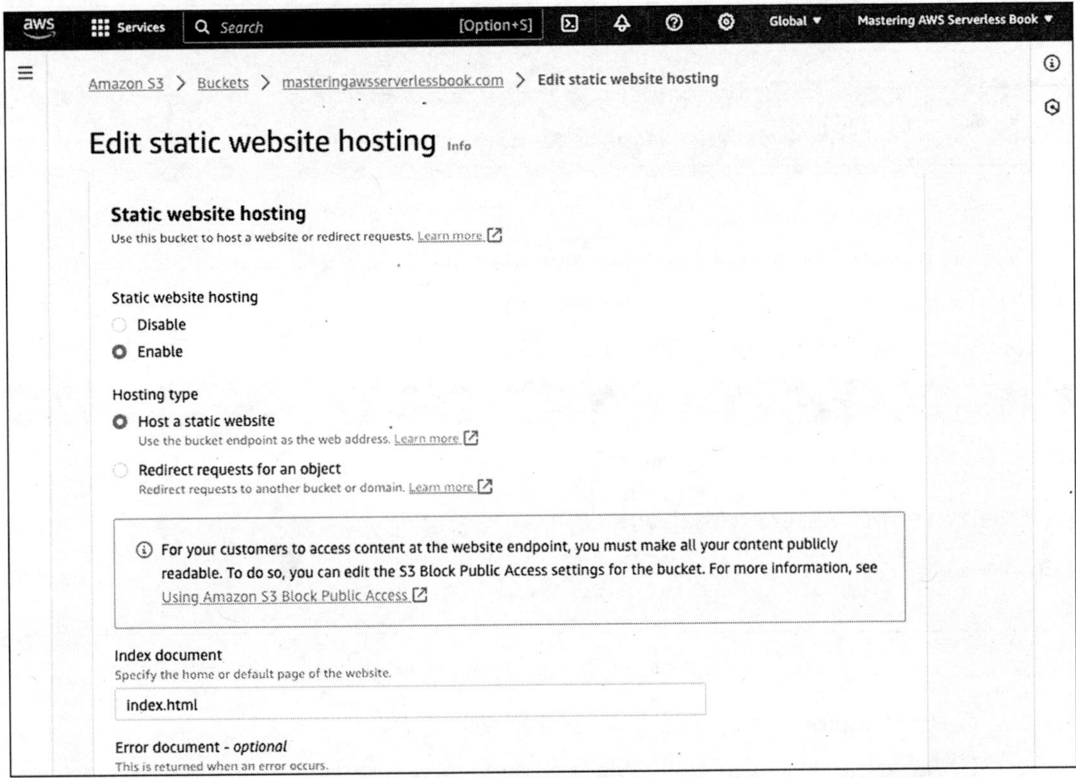

Figure 4.13: The static website hosting settings

25. Click the **Save changes** button.
26. Go to the **Static website hosting** section.
27. Observe the **Bucket website endpoint** link. See *Figure 4.14* for your reference:

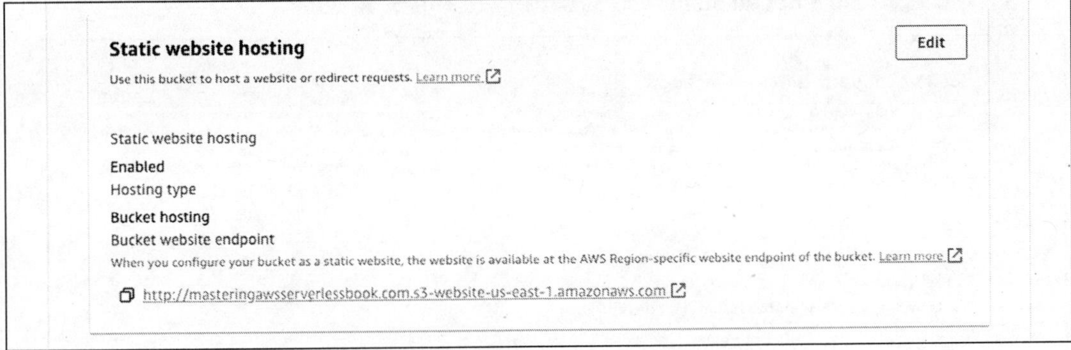

Figure 4.14: The bucket website endpoint

28. Click the website endpoint link.
29. An error is message is displayed. See *Figure 4.15*.

403 Forbidden

- Code: AccessDenied
- Message: Access Denied
- RequestId: DV6FTMRP51DW5442
- HostId: WZPB+yAHHX2Cz3XGSlgZ/eFzFKSy60xvLysJYN7c91f9NA++YKMkqhMAc7yU09HpKjWZvf61LrY=

Figure 4.15: The error message

30. We need to update the permission to allow public access.
31. Go back to the S3 bucket properties page.
32. Go to the **Permissions** tab. See *Figure 4.16*:

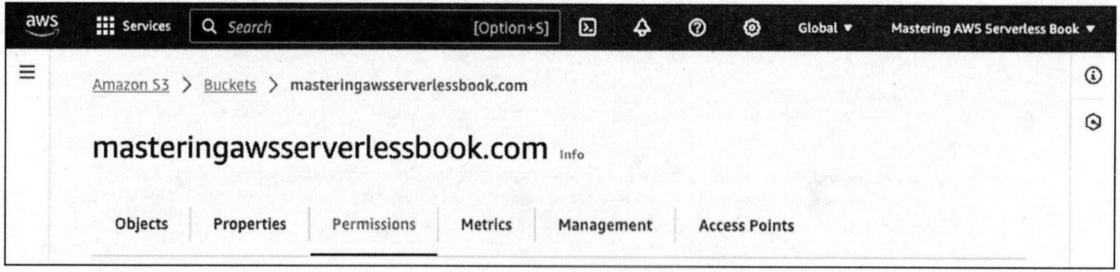

Figure 4.16: The bucket permissions tab

33. Go to the **Block public access (bucket settings)** section.
34. Observe the **On** setting in the **Block all public access** section.
35. Click the **Edit** button.
36. Uncheck the **Block all public access** checkbox.
37. Click the **Save changes** button.
38. Follow the on-screen instructions to confirm the change.
39. Observe the **Block all public access** setting to **Off**. See *Figure 4.17*:

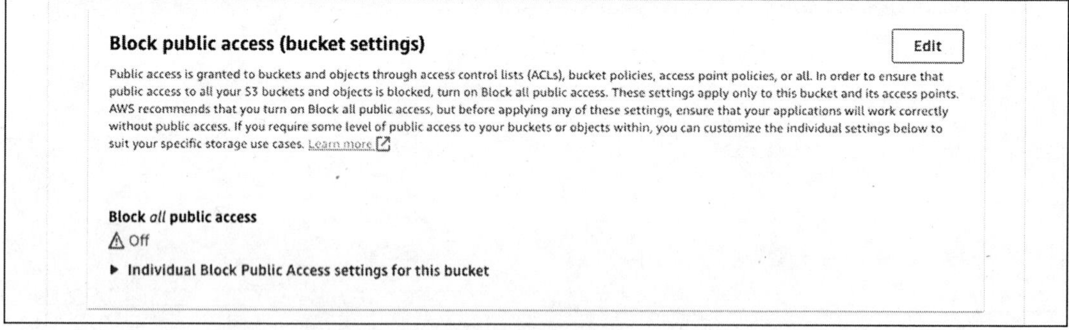

Figure 4.17: The block public access off status

40. Go to the **Bucket policy** section.
41. Observe the policy is empty. See *Figure 4.18*:

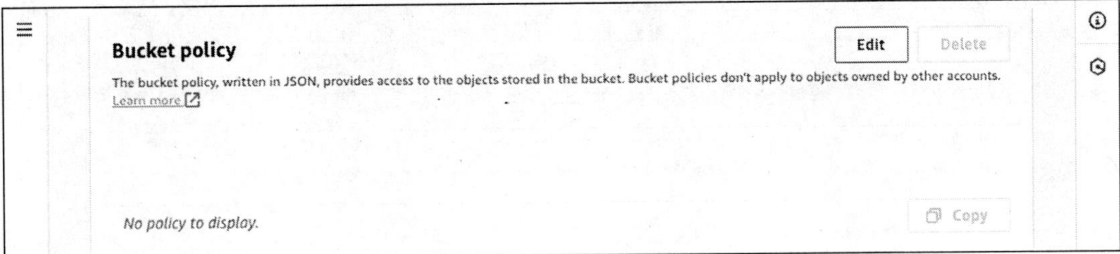

Figure 4.18: The empty bucket policy

42. Click the **Edit** button.
43. Enter the policy below.

Note: The text `masteringawsserverlessbook.com` in the policy refers to the bucket name.

```
{
  "Version": "2012-10-17",
  "Statement": [
  {
  "Sid": "PublicReadGetObject",
  "Effect": "Allow",
  "Principal": "*",
  "Action": [
  "s3:GetObject"
  ],
  "Resource": [
  "arn:aws:s3:::masteringawsserverlessbook.com/*"
  ]
  }
  ]
}
```

44. Click the **Save changes** button.
45. Go to the **Bucket policy** section.
46. Observe the policy exists. See *Figure 4.19*:

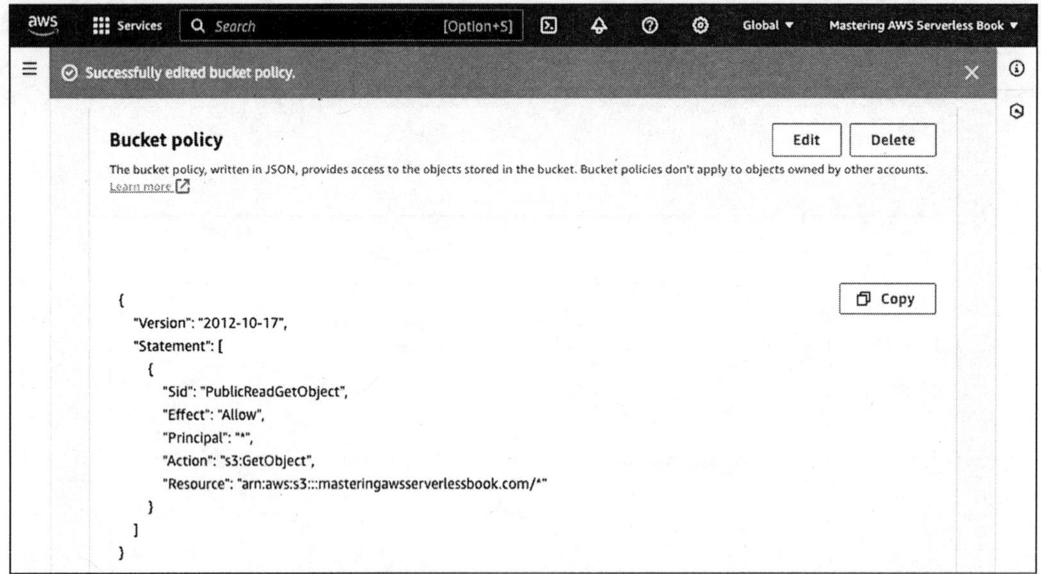

Figure 4.19: The bucket policy exists

47. Go to the other browser page, refresh the page, and observe that the web page loads properly.

Note: The browser may warn the website is not secure. This warning is presented because the protocol is HTTP and not HTTPS.

See *Figure 4.20*:

Figure 4.20: The website

We have successfully created our S3 website.

Creating a record in Route 53

The S3 website endpoint is long and difficult to remember. To improve UX, we want our website to display when we visit our custom domain. We will update our DNS to point the custom domain to the S3 website endpoint.

Hands-on exercise 4: Creating a record in Route 53

Let us create a DNS record in Route 53 to add a custom domain to our website using the given steps:

1. Go to the Route 53 service page and open the hosted zone for our domain.
2. Click the **Create record** button.
3. Change the **Record type** to the **A** dropdown option.
4. Check the **Alias** switch button.
5. In the **Route traffic to** section, select **Alias to S3 website endpoint** from the **Choose endpoint** dropdown.
6. Select **US East (N. Virginia)** in the **Choose Region** dropdown.
7. Search for the S3 endpoint for the bucket in the **Enter S3 endpoint** search field. See *Figure 4.21* for your reference:

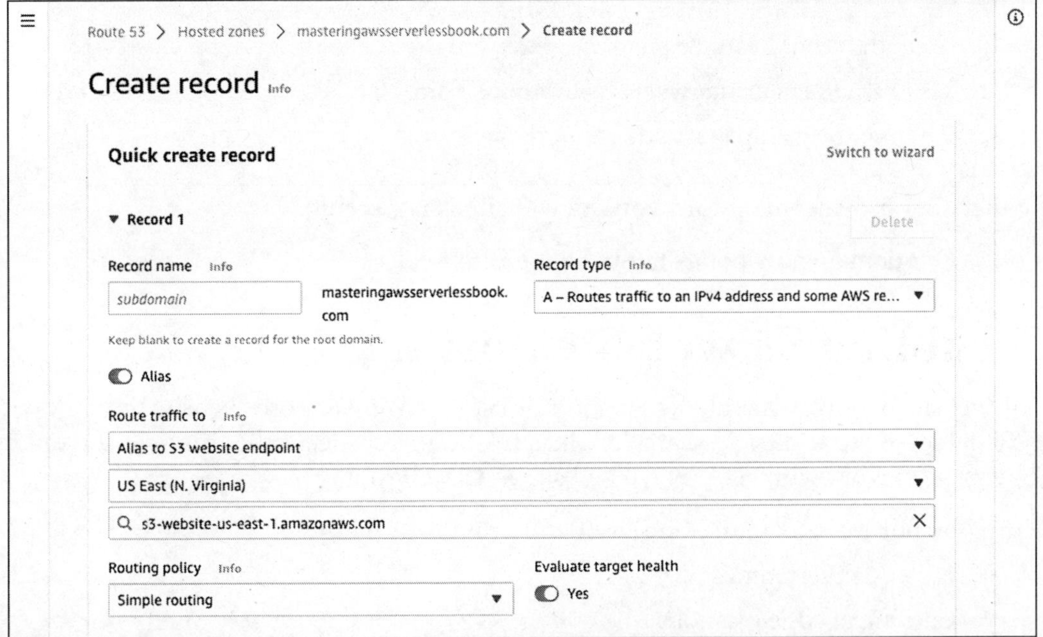

Figure 4.21: The record settings

8. Click the **Create records** button.
9. Observe the new A record in the hosted zone records list. See *Figure 4.22*:

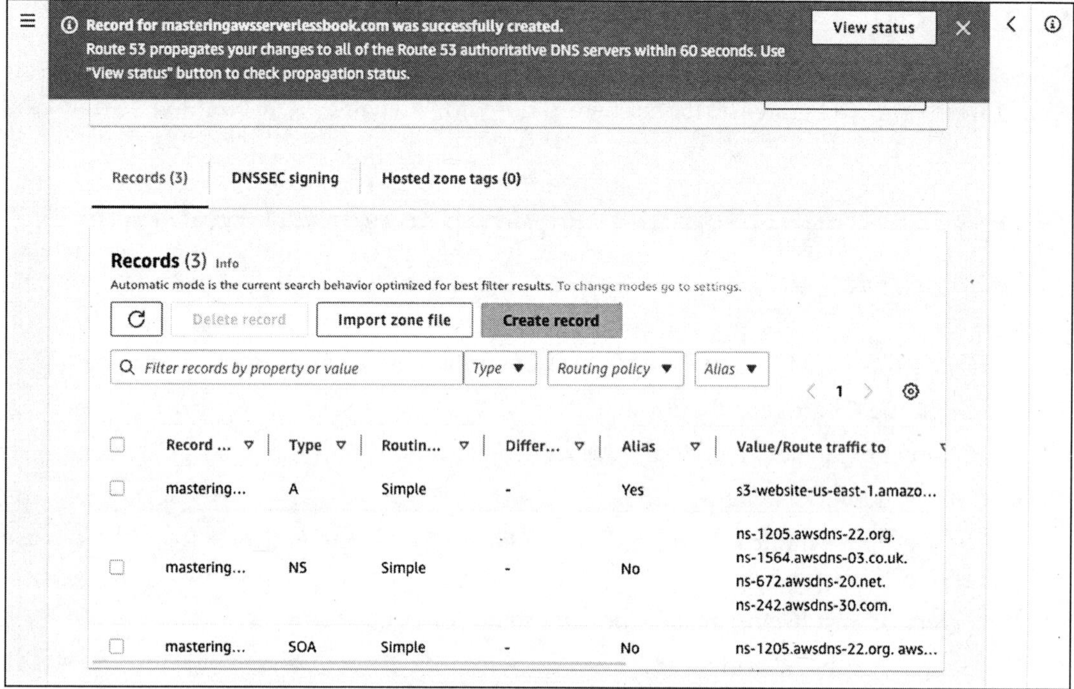

Figure 4.22: The DNS records

10. Go to the other browser page.
11. Visit **http://masteringawsserverlessbook.com.**
12. Observe the web page loads properly.

Note: Your browser may warn you the website is not secure.

13. Our domain now points to our S3 website.

Disabling S3 website hosting

Our website only works with HTTP and not HTTPS. We want our website to work with HTTPS too, so our users and search engines trust our website. Rather than setting up our S3 website to work with HTTPS, we will set up CloudFront.

Setting up our website with CloudFront will provide us with:

- Faster delivery times.
- Caching at edge locations.

- Keeping our bucket with private permissions.
- HTTPS support.

Let us remove the S3 website hosting.

Hands-on exercise 5: Disabling S3 website hosting

Let us disable the S3 website hosting since we will not use it going forward:

1. Go to the Route 53 service page and open the hosted zone for our domain.
2. Check the **A** record.
3. Click the **Delete record** button.
4. Follow the on-screen instructions to delete the **A** record.
5. Observe the record is no longer displayed in the hosted zone records list. See *Figure 4.23*:

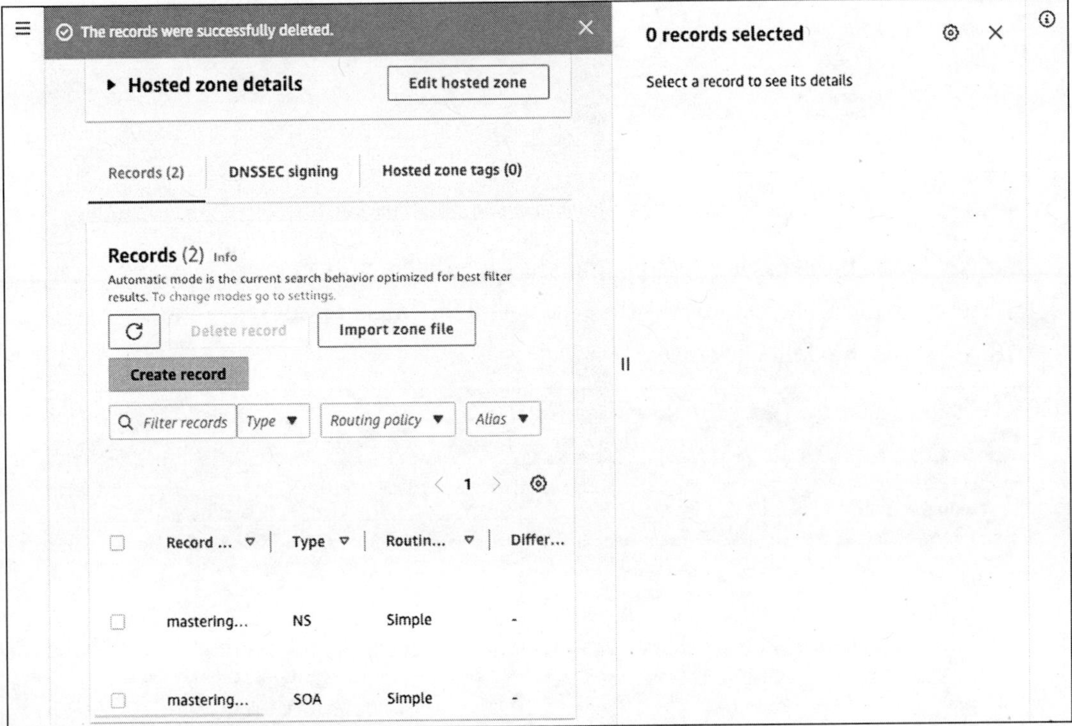

Figure 4.23: *The DNS records*

6. Go to the other browser page.
7. Visit **http://masteringawsserverlessbook.com**.
8. Observe the web page cannot be found or reached.

Note: It may take several minutes for the update to propagate.

9. Go to the S3 service page and open the bucket.
10. Go to the **Permissions** tab.
11. Go to the **Block public access (bucket settings)** and click the **Edit** button.
12. Check the **Block all public access** button.
13. Click the **Save changes** button.
14. Follow the on-screen instructions to confirm the changes.
15. Observe the **On** setting in the **Block all public access** section. See *Figure 4.24*:

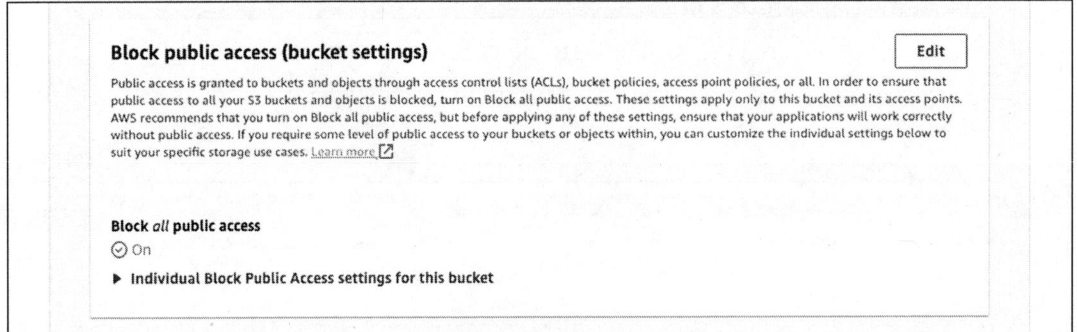

Figure 4.24: The block public access settings

16. Go to the **Bucket policy** section and click the **Delete** button.
17. Follow the on-screen instructions to delete the bucket policy.
18. Observe the policy is empty. See *Figure 4.25*:

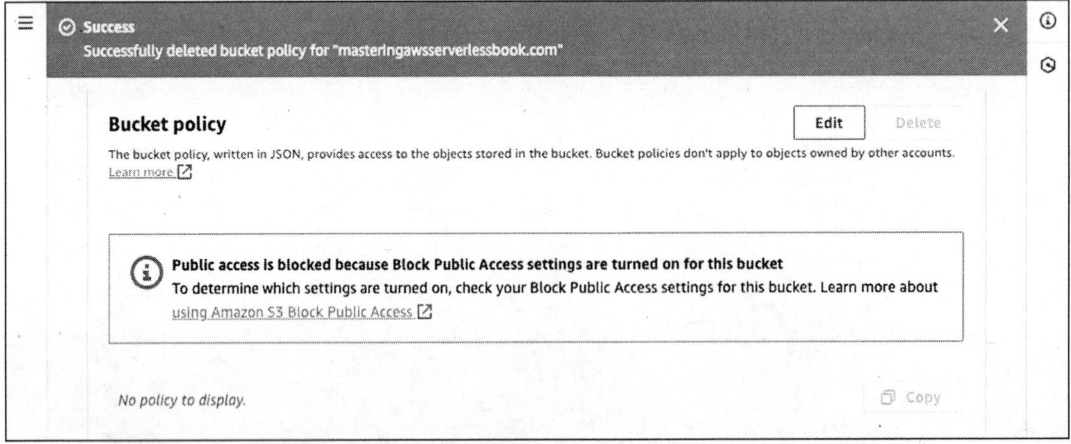

Figure 4.25: The empty bucket policy

19. Go to the **Properties** tab.
20. Go to the **Static website hosting** section and click the **Edit** button.
21. Check the **Disable** radio button in the **Static website hosting** section.
22. Click the **Save changes** button.
23. Observe the **Disabled** state and the **Bucket website endpoint** missing link in the **Static website hosting** section. See *Figure 4.26* for your reference:

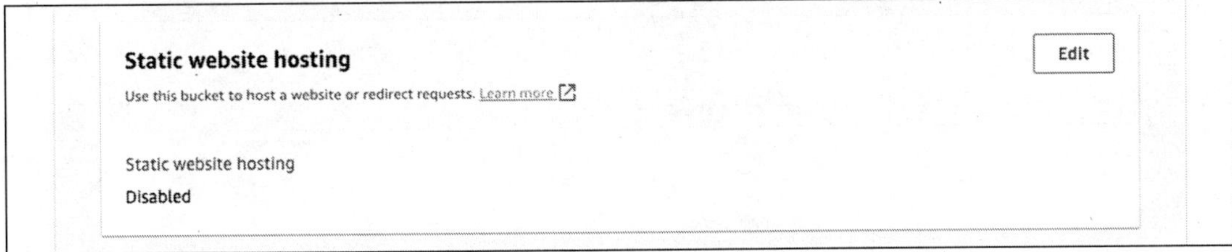

Figure 4.26: *The disabled static website hosting*

24. Go to the other browser page.
25. Visit **http://masteringawsserverlessbook.com.s3-website-us-east-1.amazonaws.com**.
26. Observe the web page cannot be found or reached.

Note: It may take several minutes for the update to propagate.

We have successfully disabled the S3 website hosting.

Requesting a certificate from AWS Certificate Manager

We need to request a certificate to support HTTPS. Let us request a certificate from the Certificate Manager.

Hands-on exercise 6: Requesting a certificate from ACM

Let us use Certificate Manager to request an SSL/TLS certificate we can use for the **masteringawsserverlessbook.com** domain and the website:

1. Search **acm** in the top search bar and click the **Certificate Manager** search result or enter **https://us-east-1.console.aws.amazon.com/acm/home** in the browser address bar.

2. If the **New ACM managed certificate** section is displayed, click the **Request a certificate** button.
3. If the **Certificates** page is displayed, click the **Request** button.
4. Check the **Request a public certificate** radio button in the **Certificate type** section. See *Figure 4.27* for your reference:

Figure 4.27: The certificate type

5. Click the **Next** button.
6. Specify `masteringawsserverlessbook.com` in the **Fully qualified domain name** field.
7. Click the **Add another name to this certificate** button.
8. Specify `"*.masteringawsserverlessbook.com` in the **Fully qualified domain name** field.

Note: This allows us to use www.masteringawsserverless.com and other subdomains.

9. Check the **DNS validation** radio button in the **Validation method** section. See *Figure 4.28*:

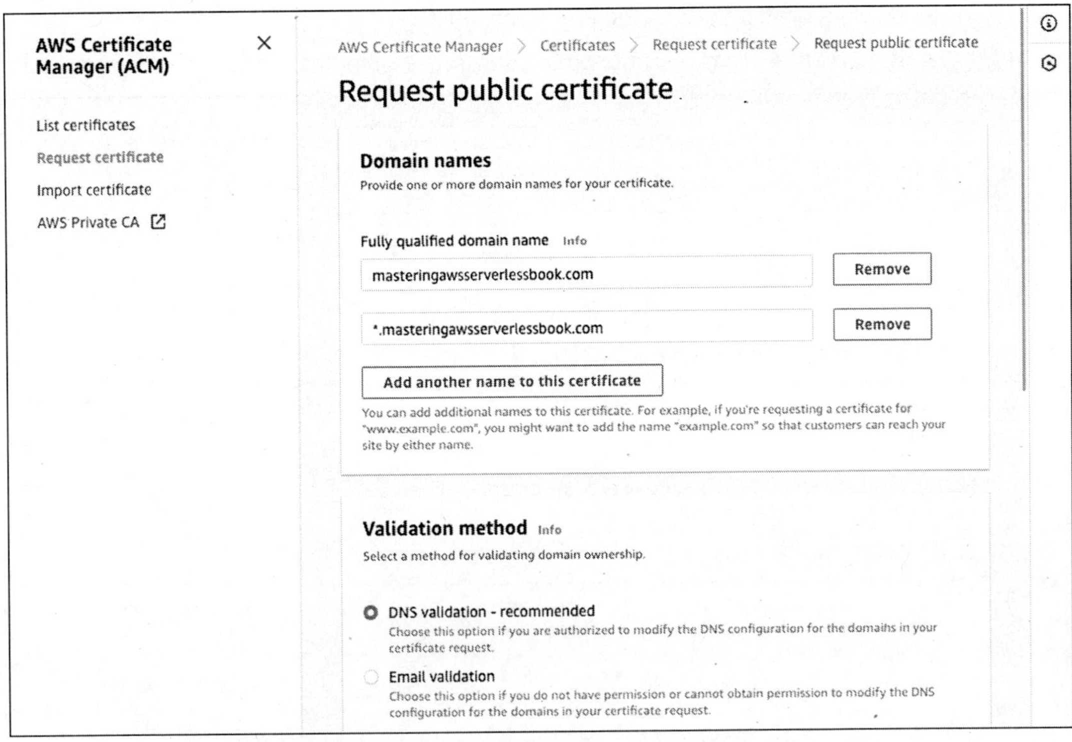

Figure 4.28: The domain names and validation method

10. Click the **Request** button.
11. Observe **Pending validation** as the status. See *Figure 4.29*:

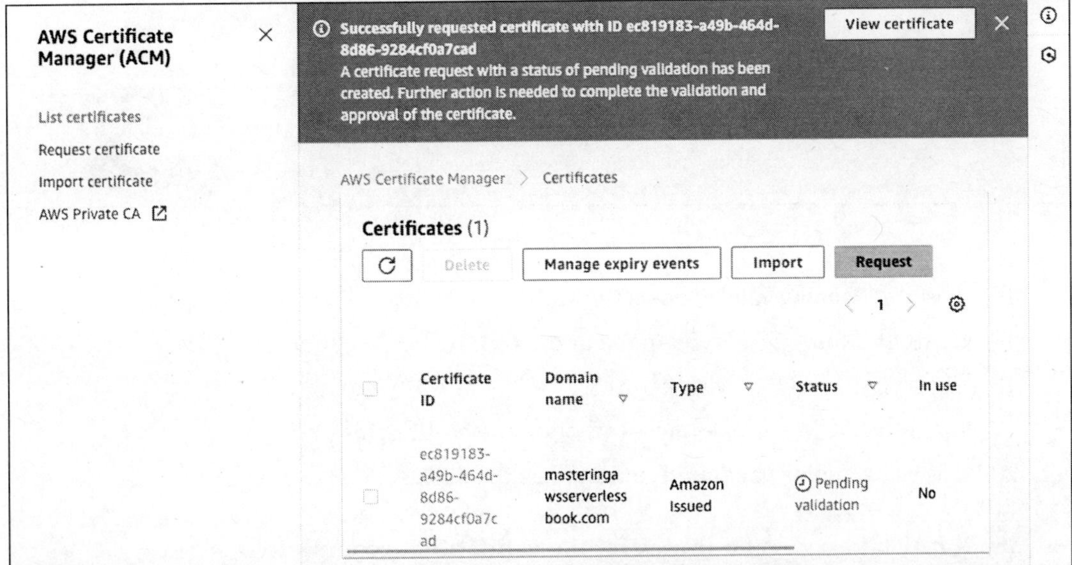

Figure 4.29: The certificate

12. Click on the **Certificate ID** in the certificates list.
13. Click the **Create records in Route 53** button in the **Domains** section. See *Figure 4.30*:

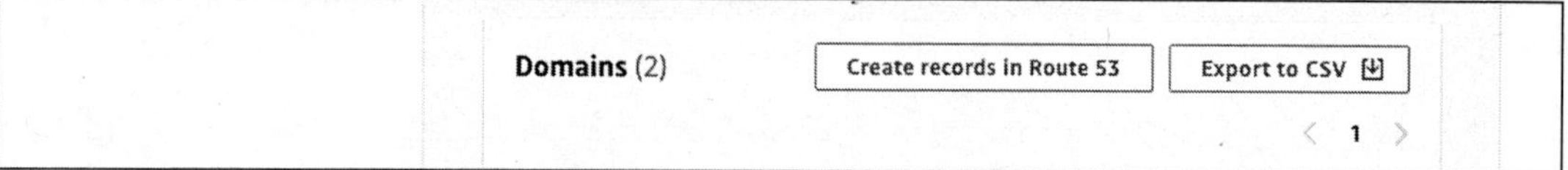

Figure 4.30: The button to create records in Route 53

14. Check all the listed domains.
15. Click the **Create records** button. See *Figure 4.31*:

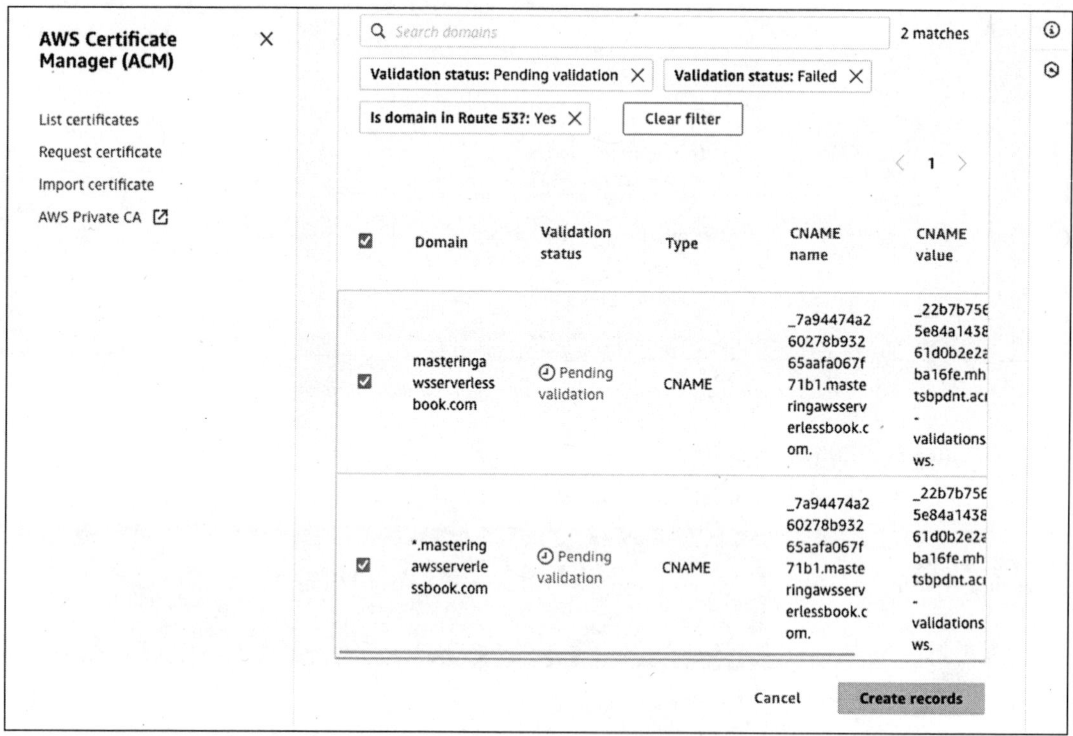

Figure 4.31: The records to create

16. Observe **Pending validation** as the status.
17. Go to the Route 53 service page and open the hosted zone.
18. Observe that a CNAME record was automatically created.
19. Go to the ACM service page and open the certificates page.
20. Observe **Pending validation** or **Issued** as the status.

Note: It may take several minutes for the validation to complete.

21. Refresh the page.
22. Observe **Issued** in the **Status** section. See *Figure 4.32*:

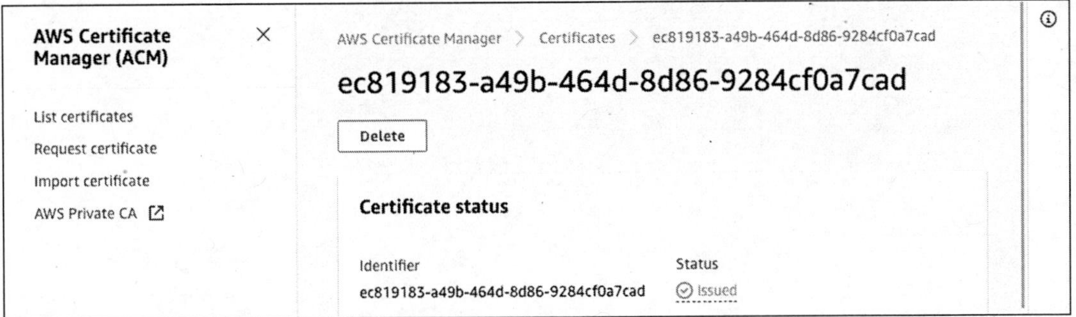

Figure 4.32: *The issued certificate*

We have successfully requested the certificate.

Creating a CloudFront distribution

We will set up our CloudFront distribution. We will need to do the following:

- Update the S3 bucket permission to give CloudFront distribution permissions to access the objects.
- Specify the domain names and certificate.

Let us create our distribution.

Hands-on exercise 7: Creating a CloudFront distribution

Let us create a CloudFront distribution to provide the website hosting and the CDN caching:

1. Search `cloudfront` in the top search bar and click the **CloudFront** search result or enter **https://us-east-1.console.aws.amazon.com/cloudfront/v4/home** in the browser address bar.
2. If the **Get started with CloudFront** section is displayed, click the **Create a CloudFront distribution** button.
3. If the **Distributions** page is displayed, click the **Create distribution** section.
4. Select the S3 endpoint for the bucket in the **Choose origin domain** search field under the **Origin domain** section. See *Figure 4.33* for your reference:

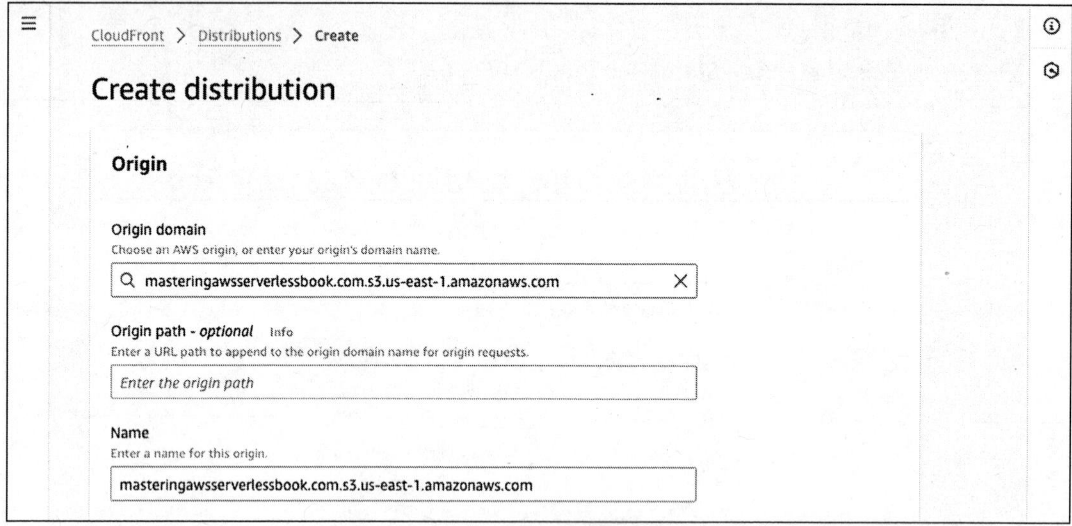

Figure 4.33: The origin domain setting

5. The name is automatically filled in.

Note: We could simplify the name to be the domain name if it is easier to read.

6. Check the **Origin access control settings (recommended)** in the **Origin access** section.
7. Click the **Create control setting** button. See *Figure 4.34*:

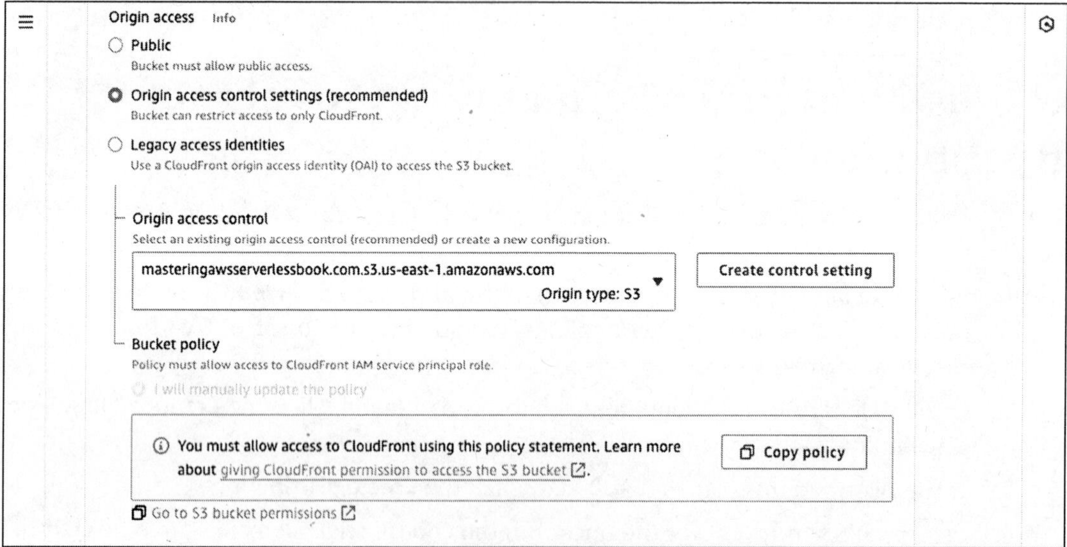

Figure 4.34: The origin access settings

8. Click the **Create** button in the **Create control setting** popup dialog.
9. Check the **Redirect HTTP to HTTPS** radio button in the **Viewer protocol policy** section.
10. Check the **Do not enable security protections** radio button in the **Web Application Firewall (WAF)** section.
11. Click the **Add item** button in the **Alternate domain name (CNAME)** section.
12. Specify `masteringawsserverlessbook.com` in the **Alternate domain name (CNAME)** field.
13. Click the **Add item** button in the **Alternate domain name (CNAME)** section.
14. Specify `www.masteringawsserverlessbook.com` in the **Alternate domain name (CNAME)** field. See *Figure 4.35*:

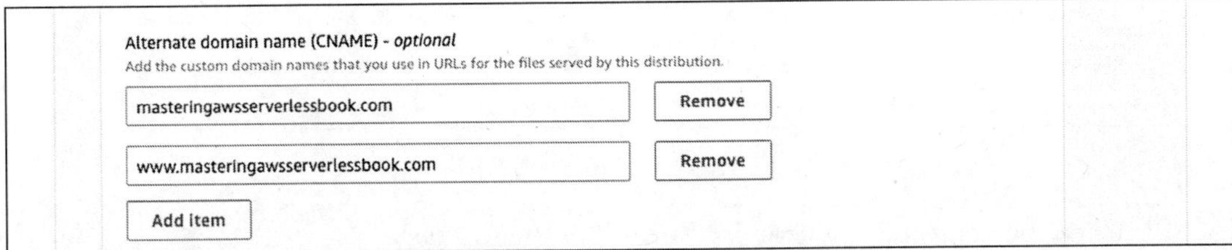

Figure 4.35: The alternate domain names

15. Select the certificate for our domain in the **Custom SSL certificate** search field. See *Figure 4.36*:

Figure 4.36: The SSL certificates

16. Specify `index.html` in the **Default root object** field.
17. Click the **Create distribution** button.
18. Observe **Deploying** as the **Last modified** value.

Note: It may take several minutes for the deployment to complete.

See *Figure 4.37:*

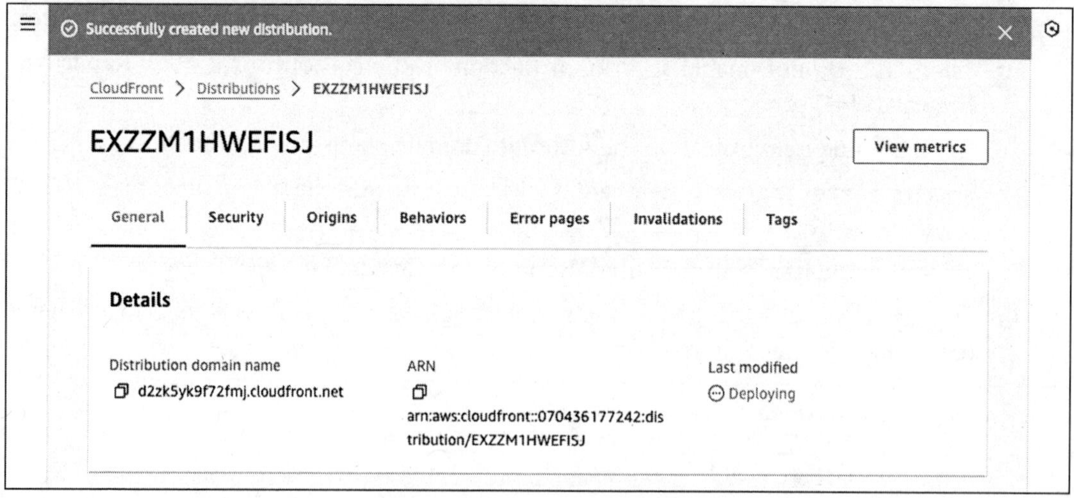

***Figure 4.37:** The distribution*

19. Click the **Copy policy** button in the alert at the top page.
20. Click the **Go to S3 bucket permissions to update policy** link in the alert at the top of the page.
21. In the S3 bucket page and **Permission** tab, click the **Edit** button in the **Bucket policy** section.
22. Paste the policy. See *Figure 4.38*:

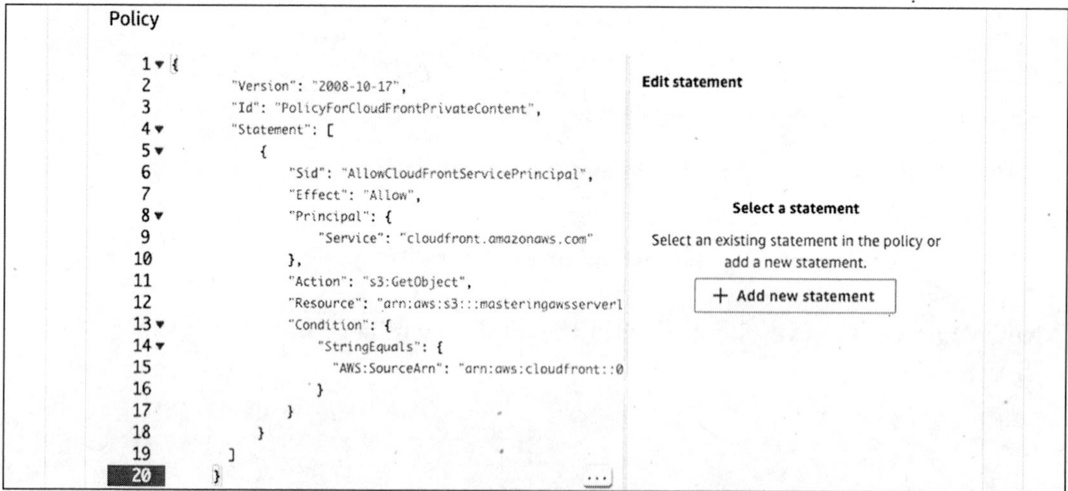

***Figure 4.38:** The bucket policy*

23. Click the **Save changes** button.
24. Go to the other browser page with the CloudFront distribution.
25. Refresh the page and observe a date in the **Last modified** value.
26. Copy the address in the **Distribution domain name** section.
27. Return to the distribution list by clicking the **Distributions** link in the breadcrumbs at the top of the page.
28. Observe **Enabled** as the **Status** for our distribution. See *Figure 4.39*:

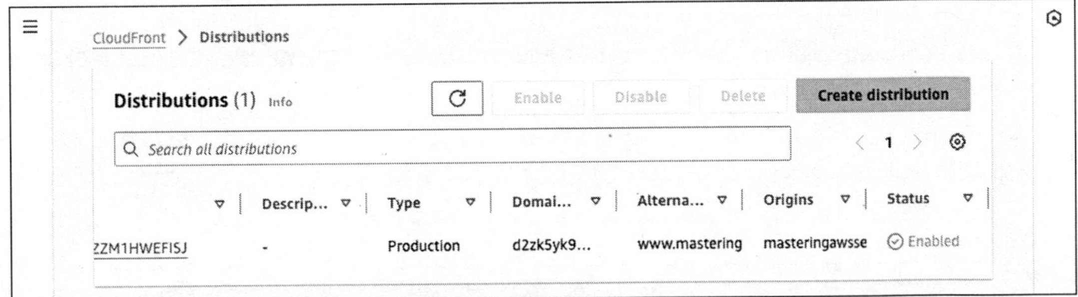

Figure 4.39: The distribution

29. Go to the other browser page.
30. Visit the distribution domain name (ending in `cloudfront.net`).
31. Observe the web page loads and the browser does not give a warning about the security.
32. Visit **https://masteringawsserverlessbook.com.**
33. Observe that the web page cannot be found or reached.

Note: We will need to update our DNS.

We have successfully created the CloudFront distribution.

Creating aliases for the distribution in Route 53

We want to update our DNS records to point our domain and the "www" subdomain to our distribution.

Let us create these aliases.

Hands-on exercise 8: Creating aliases for the distribution in Route 53

Let us create a DNS record in Route 53 to point to the CloudFront distribution, as shown:

1. Go to the Route 53 service page and open the hosted zone for our domain.
2. Click the **Create record** button.
3. Change the **Record type** to the **A** dropdown option.
4. Check the **Alias** switch button.
5. In the **Route traffic to** section, select **Alias to CloudFront distribution** from the **Choose endpoint** dropdown.
6. Search for the distribution in the **Choose distribution** search field. See *Figure 4.40*:

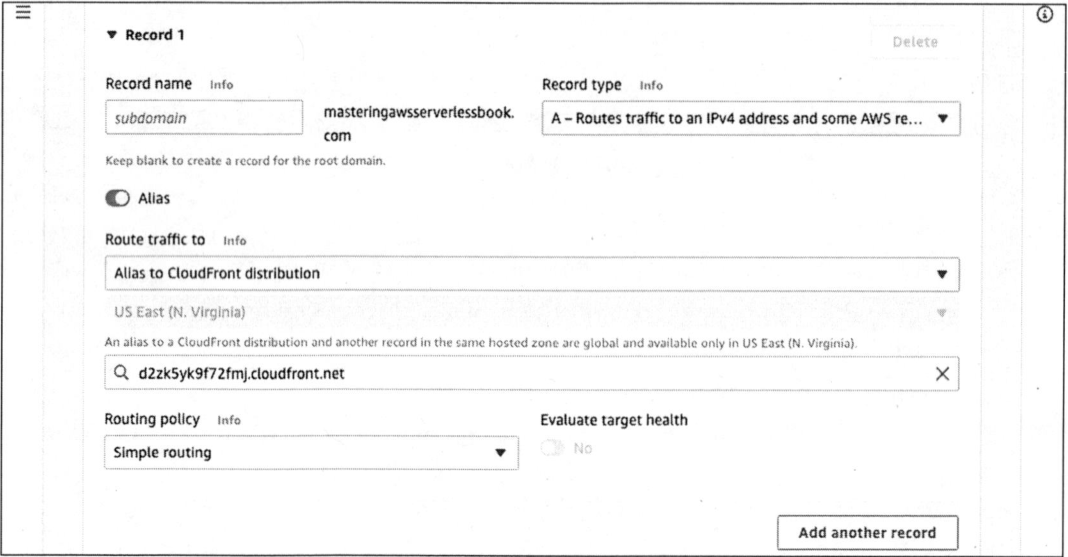

Figure 4.40: The record settings

7. Click the **Add another record** button.
8. Specify **www** in the **subdomain** field in the **Record name** section.
9. Change the **Record type** to the **A** dropdown option.
10. Check the **Alias** switch button.
11. In the **Route traffic to** section, select **Alias to CloudFront distribution** from the **Choose endpoint** dropdown.
12. Search for the distribution in the **Choose distribution** search field. See *Figure 4.41*:

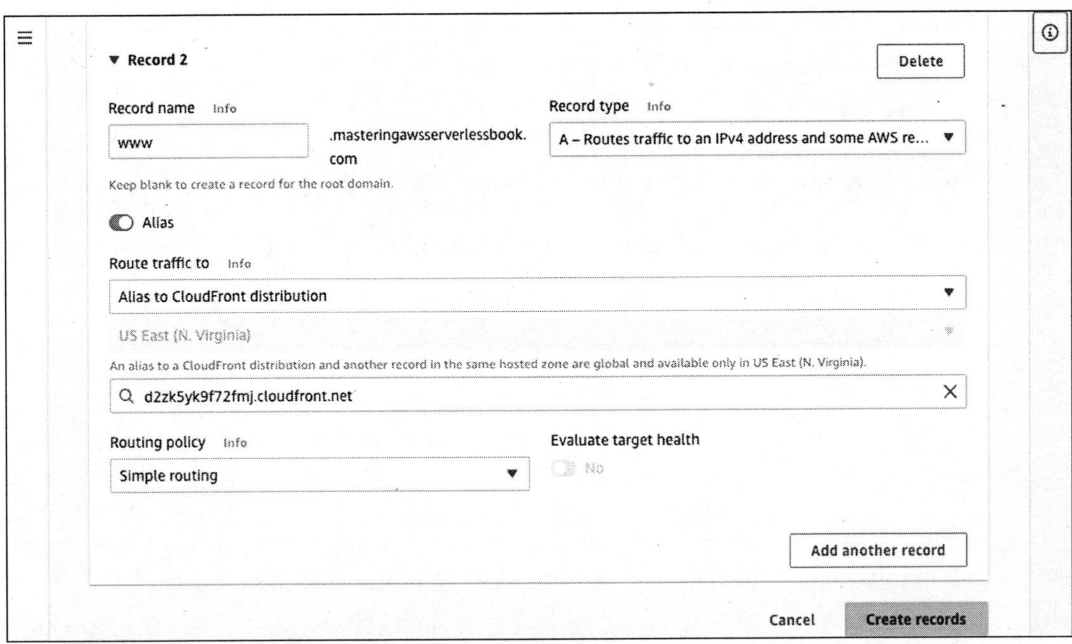

Figure 4.41: The record settings

13. Click the **Create records** button.
14. Observe the new **A** records in the hosted zone records list. See *Figure 4.42*:

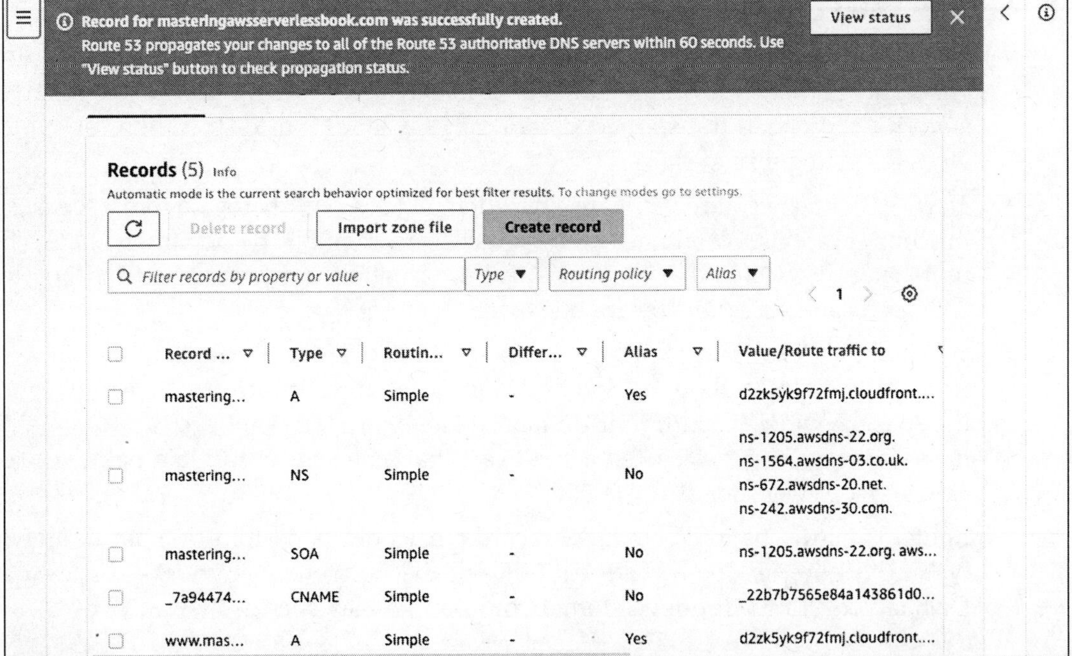

Figure 4.42: The DNS records

15. Go to the other browser page.
16. Visit **https://masteringawsserverlessbook.com.**
17. Observe the web page loads properly.

Note: It may take several minutes for the DNS update to propagate.

18. Visit **https://www.masteringawsserverlessbook.com.**
19. Observe that the web page loads properly.

Conclusion

In this chapter, we conducted hands-on exercises to create a serverless website. We started by registering a custom domain. We then created an HTML file and enabled S3 static website hosting for the web page. We updated our Route 53 DNS records to point our custom domain name to the S3 website hosting. After going through this exercise, we disabled it in favor of using a CloudFront distribution instead.

We created an SSL/TLS certificate using ACM to enable HTTPS for our custom domain. We created a CloudFront distribution and associated our S3 bucket, ACM certificate and custom domain. We updated our Route 53 DNS records to point our custom domain to the CloudFront distribution. Browsing to our custom domain showed our static website.

Points to remember

- S3 static website hosting only supports HTTP by default. HTTP provides no encryption, and all transmitted data is visible to anyone. It is better to use HTTPS since it encrypts all transmitted data. Using a CloudFront distribution for static website hosting provides HTTP.
- New S3 buckets are private by default, which helps avoid security misconfigurations. For many years, S3 buckets were public by default. Some AWS users later discovered that their sensitive information was being hosted in public S3 buckets and accessible by anyone on the Internet.
- We used the Certificate Manager to create an SSL/TLS certificate that we can use to enable HTTPS. Although CloudFront provides a certificate, it is only valid for the AWS-provided CloudFront domain name. Since we want a custom domain name for our website, we need a certificate that matches our domain name so we can serve our website using HTTPS.
- Route 53 allows us to create DNS records that point a custom domain to an S3 website hosting endpoint or a CloudFront distribution domain. We can create DNS records for the top-level domain or a subdomain, such as "www."

- The S3 bucket needed a bucket policy to allow the CloudFront distribution to access the bucket objects. Without this bucket policy, none of the S3 bucket objects are accessible since the bucket is private by default. The policy ensures only the CloudFront distribution can access the bucket objects. Any valid HTTP or HTTPS request to a valid bucket object path will return its content. We must be cautious not to upload sensitive data to the S3 bucket that was meant for the static website files.

Multiple choice questions

1. **Which of the following is needed to allow an S3 website to be accessible on the Internet?**
   a. Turn off the block public access settings.
   b. Specify a bucket policy.
   c. Both.

   Answer: c

   The S3 website needs both settings to allow public Internet access and a bucket policy.

2. **After creating the CloudFront distribution, we get an error when we browse to our custom domain. What might be the issue?**
   a. The certificate is missing.
   b. The bucket policy is missing.
   c. The alias record is missing.

   Answer: c

   The alias record is the first thing to check. Without it, a browser cannot resolve the custom domain to point to the distribution.

Join our book's Discord space

Join the book's Discord Workspace for Latest updates, Offers, Tech happenings around the world, New Release and Sessions with the Authors:

https://discord.bpbonline.com

CHAPTER 5
Creating an API

Introduction

In this chapter, we will create and manage an API, send requests to a serverless function, and learn about its OpenAPI specification.

Structure

We will cover the following topics in this chapter:

- Overview of serverless APIs
- Adding a new web page to use the API
- Invalidating the distribution to clear CDN cache
- Creating an API with API Gateway
- Integrating a Lambda function with the API
- OpenAPI specification

Objectives

By the end of this chapter, you will understand how to create an HTTP addressable API endpoint that responds to requests, sends the request to a function, and responds to the request.

Overview of serverless APIs

We will use the API Gateway service for our serverless API. There are multiple steps to create a functioning API:

1. Creating an API
2. Creating a resource
3. Creating a method
4. Defining the requests and responses for each method
5. Enabling CORS
6. Deploying the API
7. Creating an API stage
8. Creating a custom domain

We will create an API using the API Gateway service. This API provides us with a single web address to access all the API endpoints. When we create an API, AWS automatically creates an AWS-managed web address. We can use it, but we can improve our **Developer Experience** (**DX**) by using a custom domain name, for example, the **`api.masteringawsserverlessbook.com`** domain. We will need to create resources and methods for our API. The resource is appended to the web address, for example, the **`/chapters`** resources is appended to the web address, for example, the **`api.masteringawsserverlessbook.com/chapters`** address. The method, for example, **`GET`** is the HTTP method the API will respond to when addressed. The combination of a resource and a method is an API endpoint. API Gateway has built-in security features where it will respond with an error HTTP status code when an HTTP request fails to find the API endpoint by matching both the resource and the method.

We will quickly discuss some API endpoint strategies. One strategy is to define public and protected endpoints. For example, any resources that fail to start with **`/secure`** or **`/protected`** or another resource path will be a public resource that does not require a user to authenticate. Another strategy is to use plural words in the resource path name. For example, **`GET /chapters`** will return all the chapters, but **`GET /chapters/{id}`** will return a specific chapter. There are many other ways to define an API that will meet our needs. In this book, we will use both strategies. We will use the **`/account`** resource path prefix for our protected resources and use the **`/chapters`** resource path for our public resource that returns all chapters.

Next, we will define an integration for each resource method. We will start with a mock integration, which will return a static value. Mock integrations are useful when we want to return the same value every time. Using a mock integration helps us get the API working and respond to HTTP requests without introducing possible errors from dynamic integration, for example, a Lambda function. When we set up CORS, it will use a mock integration since the CORS values remain unchanged. Later in the chapter, we will change the mock integration to a Lambda integration that will send the HTTP request to a Lambda function.

Next, we will create a new page for a website that uses JavaScript to make an HTTP `GET` request to the **https://api.masteringawsserverlessbook.com/chapters** endpoint. When it gets the JSON data from the request, the JavaScript code will update the HTML to display the results as a list of cards of the book chapters. The browser, by default, will block the response from the API since it is using a different domain than the website. We will need to configure CORS in the API to inform the browser that the API is expecting traffic from the website. The browser will make a request with the `OPTIONS` method to get the CORS information. The CORS information will include the allowed origin (such as the website domain) and allowed methods (such as `GET` and `POST`). We will use a mock integration in the API to return the CORS information.

When we have proven we can get chapter data from the API, we will create a Lambda function to replace our mock integration. The Lambda function will return the same static response as our mock function. In a later chapter, we will update this function to get the data from a database table.

We will let the Lambda service automatically create the IAM permissions (that is, role and policy). The Lambda function needs an IAM role and the related policy to execute properly. The function will use the IAM role to know what permission the function has. The role contains the IAM policy or policies that define the permissions. The basic permissions allow the API Gateway to invoke the Lambda function execution and the Lambda function to write logs to a CloudWatch log group. Throughout this book, we will work with IAM to define specific roles and policies to allow the functions successfully execute, but with the least privileges.

When we execute the function, the Lambda service will automatically create a log group in CloudWatch. Any logs produced by executing the function code will appear in the log group. By default, CloudWatch sets an indefinite retention period. We will update it to one week to reduce keeping logs longer than needed and to reduce storage costs.

We will conclude by creating the API documentation. We will create it in the AWS management console and export using the OpenAPI specification in the YAML[1] format. (The YAML format is easier to read than JSON.) In a project following change management processes, we could use the export to track the changes. Projects that are API first, can programmatically create and update the API from the OpenAPI specification file. It is a good idea to keep copies of the OpenAPI specification file so we can see changes throughout the development and to have a backup where we can restore the API if needed.

As we progress through the book, we will provide less screen captures and shorter instructions. After having done an exercise, we should be familiar with the AWS service

1 YAML means "YAML Ain't Markup Language" and is defined under the **YAML.org** copyrighted website.

page and how to navigate the AWS management console. If we forget, we can revisit previous chapters for a refresher.

Adding a new web page to use the API

We will create a *Chapters* web page that will use our new API with the **api** subdomain. The **api.masteringawsserverlessbook.com** domain will be used when sending API requests. We will use JavaScript to make the API request using **XMLHttpRequest** which allows us to make an asynchronous HTTP request to the API. In a later chapter, we will use Fetch to make a request to the API.

The HTML code will show placeholders until the HTTP request is completed. When it is done, the JavaScript code will update the HTML code to show the chapters from the API response or an error message.

Hands-on exercise 1: Creating a new web page

Let us create a new web page for our website:

1. Create a new file named **chapters.html** on our computer.
2. Paste the following HTML code into the file.

```
<!doctype html>
<html lang="en" class="h-100" data-bs-theme="dark">
  <head>
    <title>Mastering AWS Book</title>
    <meta charset="utf-8">
    <meta name="viewport" content="width=device-width, initial-
    scale=1, shrink-to-fit=no">
    <link href="https://cdn.jsdelivr.net/npm/bootstrap@5.3.2/dist/
    css/bootstrap.min.css" rel="stylesheet" integrity="sha384-T3c6
    CoIi6uLrA9TneNEoa7RxnatzjcDSCmG1MXxSR1GAsXEV/DwwykC2MPK8M2HN"
    crossorigin="anonymous">
  </head>
  <body class="d-flex h-100 text-center flex-column">
    <div class="d-flex w-100 h-100 mx-auto flex-column">
      <header class="mb-auto">
        <nav class="navbar">
          <div class="container-fluid">
            <span class="navbar-brand h1 mx-auto">
              Mastering AWS Serverless Book
```

```
      </span>
    </div>
  </nav>
</header>
<main role="main" class="my-auto">
  <div class="container">
    <h1>Chapters</h1>
    <div id="chapters">
      <div class="card my-5" aria-hidden="true">
        <div class="card-body">
          <h2 class="card-title placeholder-glow">
            <span class="placeholder col-6"></span>
          </h2>
          <p class="card-text placeholder-glow">
            <span class="placeholder col-7"></span>
          </p>
        </div>
      </div>
      <div class="card my-5" aria-hidden="true">
        <div class="card-body">
          <h2 class="card-title placeholder-glow">
            <span class="placeholder col-6"></span>
          </h2>
          <p class="card-text placeholder-glow">
            <span class="placeholder col-7"></span>
          </p>
        </div>
      </div>
    </div>
  </div>
</main>
<footer class="mt-auto">
  <div class="container text-center">
    <p>
```

```
          &copy; Miguel A. Calles. All rights reserved.
        </p>
      </div>
    </footer>
  </div>
</body>
<script src="https://cdn.jsdelivr.net/npm/bootstrap@5.3.2/
dist/js/bootstrap.bundle.min.js" integrity="sha384-C6Rzsyn
M9kWDrMNeT87bh95OGNyZPhcTNXj1NW7RuBCsyN/o0jlpcV8Qyq46cDfL"
crossorigin="anonymous"></script>
<script>
  window.onload = function () {
    const url = 'https://api.masteringawsserverlessbook.com/
    chapters';
    const chaptersDiv = document.getElementById('chapters');
    const errorHtml = '<div class="alert alert-danger"
    role="alert">' +
      'Failed to get the chapters.</div>';
    const noneHtml = '<p>No chapters found.</p>';
    const chapterHtml = '<div class="card my-5" aria-
    hidden="true">' +
      '<div class="card-body">' +
      '<h2 class="card-title">{title}</h2>' +
      '<p class="card-text">{description}</p>' +
      '</div>' +
      '</div>';
    try {
      const xhr = new XMLHttpRequest();
      xhr.open('GET', url, true);
      xhr.setRequestHeader('Content-Type', 'application/json');
      xhr.onreadystatechange = function () {
        if (xhr.readyState == 4 && xhr.status == 200) {
```

```
            var responseData = JSON.parse(xhr.responseText);
            if (Array.isArray(responseData) && responseData.length >
            0) {
              chaptersDiv.innerHTML = '';
              for (let chapter of responseData) {
                chaptersDiv.innerHTML += chapterHtml.replace(
                  '{title}',
                  chapter.title
                ).replace('{description}', chapter.description);
              }
            } else {
              chaptersDiv.innerHTML = noneHtml;
            }
          } else {
            chaptersDiv.innerHTML = errorHtml;
            console.error('Request failed with status:', xhr.status);
          }
        };
        xhr.send();
      } catch (e) {
        chaptersDiv.innerHTML = errorHtml;
        console.error('Exception:', e);
      }
    }
  </script>
</html>
```

3. Take a moment to review the HTML and JavaScript.
4. Go to the S3 bucket page.
5. Upload the **`buckets.html`** file into the bucket.
6. Observe the file exists in the bucket. See *Figure 5.1*:

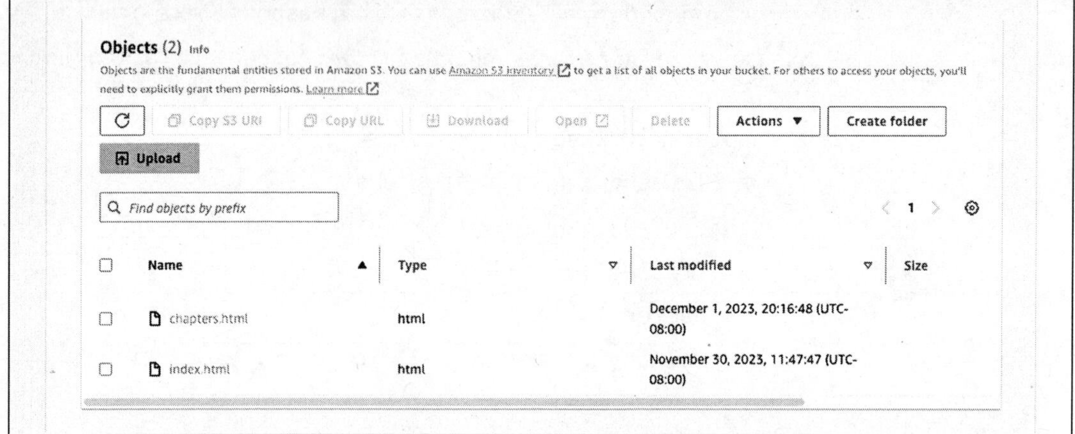

Figure 5.1: The S3 bucket objects

We successfully created our new file in the S3 bucket.

Invalidating the distribution to clear CDN cache

We need to clear the cache in the CDN whenever we update our static files. The CloudFront distribution is effective in caching the files, but they will stay there for a long time. We risk our website users getting an old copy of our files. To reduce this risk, we will send an invalidation request to the distribution to clear the cache.

Hands-on exercise 2: Invalidating the distribution

Let us clear the CDN cache by invalidating the distribution.

1. Go to the CloudFront distribution page.
2. Go to the **Invalidations** tab.
3. Click the **Create invalidation** button. See *Figure 5.2*:

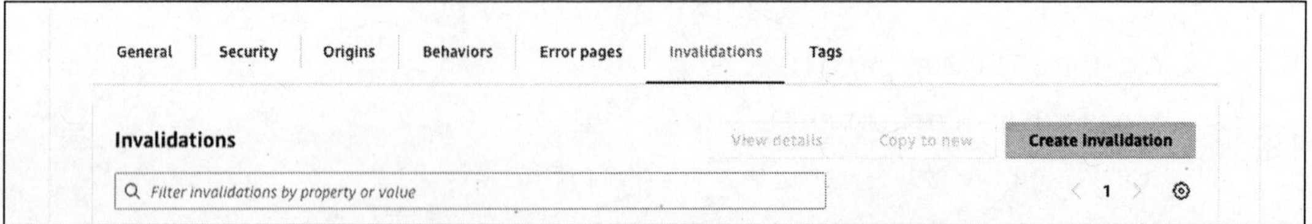

Figure 5.2: The CloudFront distribution invalidations tab

4. Specify **/*** in the **Add object pages** field to invalidate all files. See *Figure 5.3*:

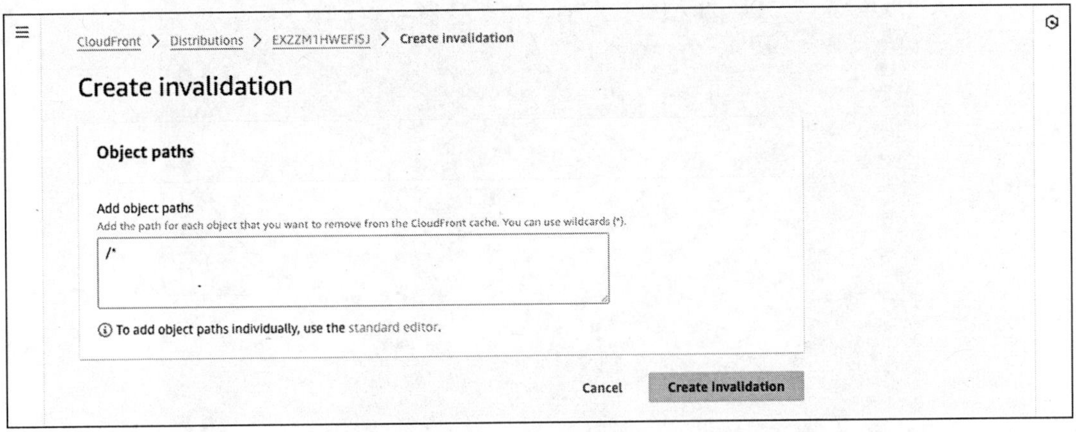

CloudFront > Distributions > EXZZM1HWEFISJ > Create invalidation

Create invalidation

Object paths

Add object paths

Add the path for each object that you want to remove from the CloudFront cache. You can use wildcards (*).

/*

To add object paths individually, use the standard editor.

Cancel Create invalidation

Figure 5.3: The create invalidation page

5. Click the **Create invalidation** button.
6. Observe **In progress** in the **Status** section.

Note: It may take several minutes for the invalidation to complete.

7. Observe **Completed** in the **Status** section. See *Figure 5.4*:

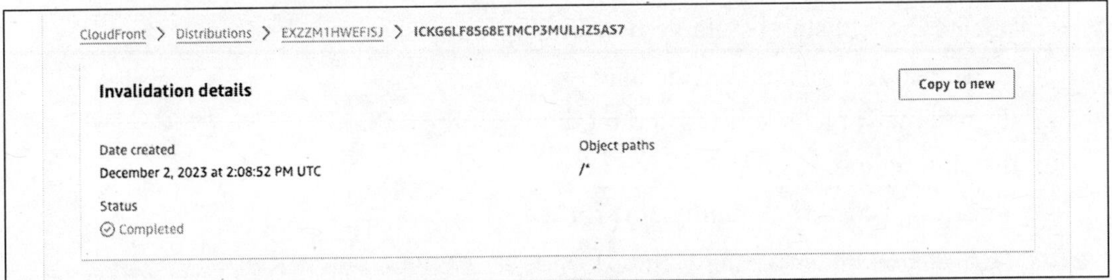

Figure 5.4: The invalidation details

8. We have successfully invalidated the distribution cache.
9. Visit **https://masteringawsserverlessbook.com/chapters.html.**
10. Observe the new web page loads and shows the error message. See *Figure 5.5*:

Figure 5.5: The chapters web page

Our new page is live.

Creating an API with API Gateway

We will create the API step-by-step. There are multiple steps involved:

1. Create an API using API Gateway.
2. Define the HTTP resources and methods for the API.
3. Deploying the API.
4. Creating a custom domain name for the API.
5. Creating an alias record for the API custom domain name.

We will work through hands-on exercises to set up a working API and update our website to use it.

Hands-on exercise 3: Creating the API

Let us create an API using the API Gateway service:

1. Search **api** in the top search bar and click the **API Gateway** service or enter **https://us-east-1.console.aws.amazon.com/apigateway/main/apis** in the browser address bar.
2. If the **Choose an API type** section is displayed, go to the **REST API** section and click the **Build** button.
3. If the **APIs** section is displayed, click the **Create API** button.

4. Click the **New API** radio button.
5. Specify **website** in the **API name** field.
6. Specify **API for the serverless website** in the **Description** field. See *Figure 5.6*:

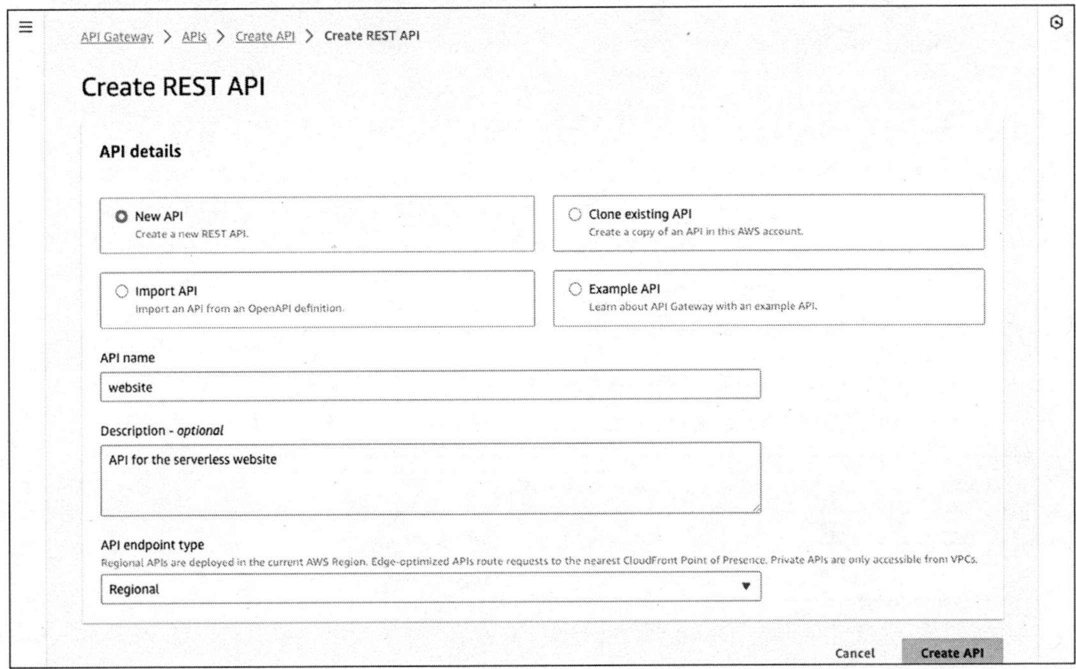

Figure 5.6: The API details

7. Click the **Create API** button.
8. Observe the API was created. See *Figure 5.7* for your reference:

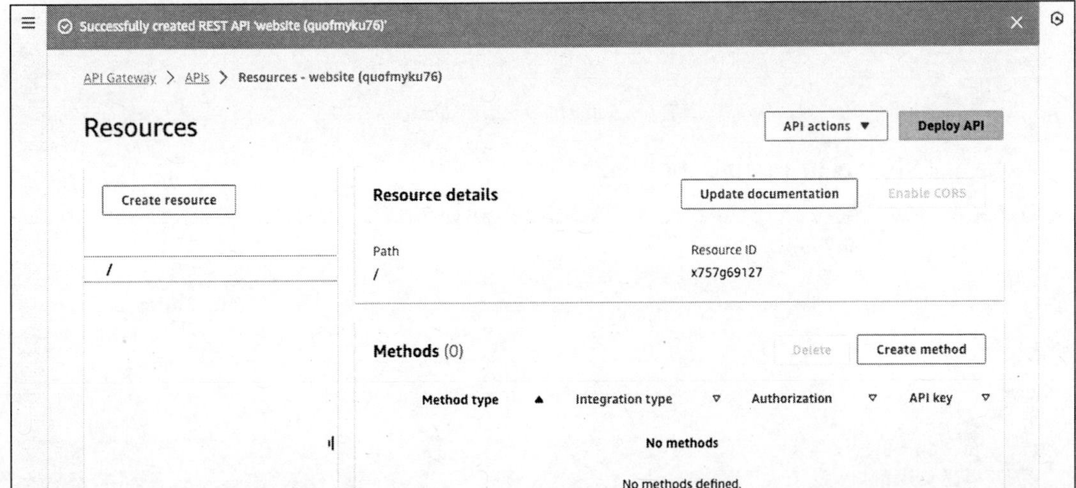

Figure 5.7: The API resources

9. Clear the alert at the top of the page.

Note: The alerts stack up on each other. We will clear them as we go but the exercise steps will not explicitly remind you to do it.

We successfully created our API.

Hands-on exercise 4: Defining resources and methods

Let us add resources and methods to the API:

1. Click the **Create resource** button.
2. Select **/** in the **Resource path** dropdown.
3. Specify **`chapters`** in the **Resource name** field.
4. Check the **CORS (Cross Origin Resource Sharing)** checkbox. See *Figure 5.8*:

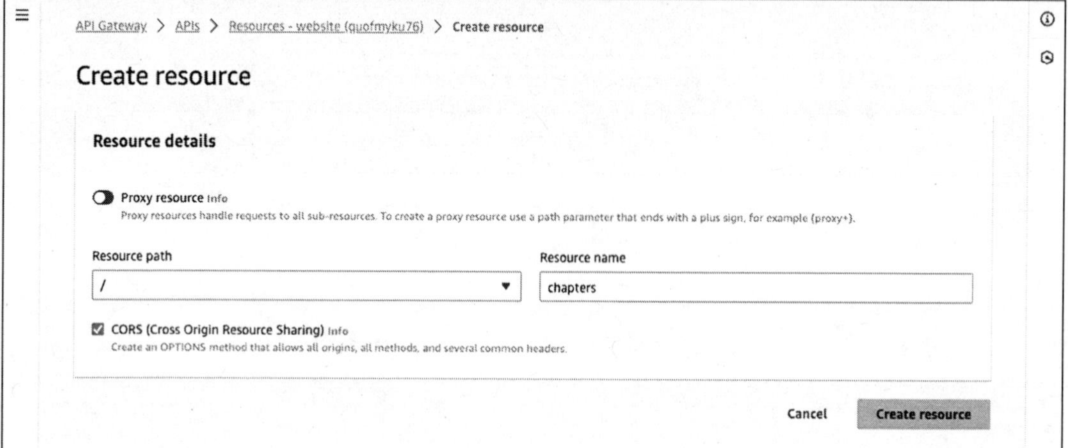

Figure 5.8: The resource details

5. Click the **Create resource** button.
6. Observe the **`/chapters`** resource and the **`OPTIONS`** method were automatically created. See *Figure 5.9*:

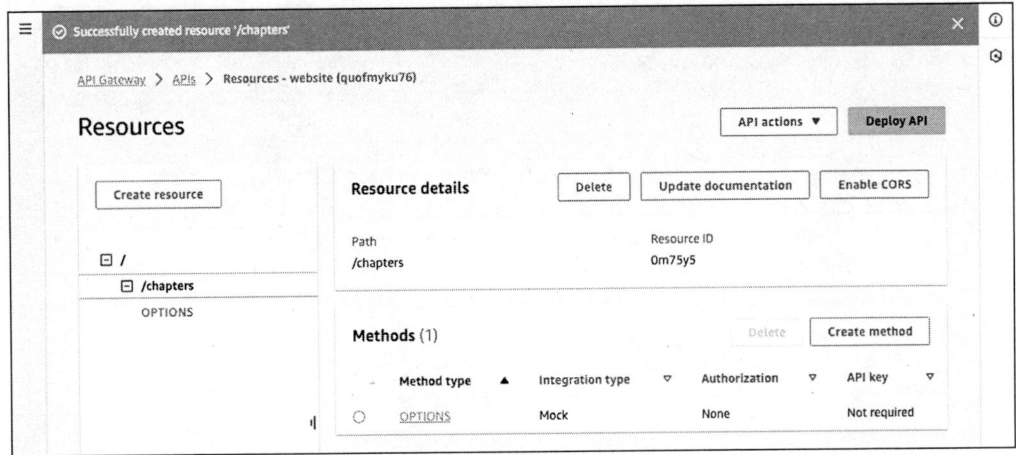

Figure 5.9: The API resources

7. Select the **`/chapters`** resource.
8. Click the **Create method** button.
9. Select **GET** in the **Method type** dropdown.
10. Click the **Mock** radio button in the **Integration type** section. See *Figure 5.10*:

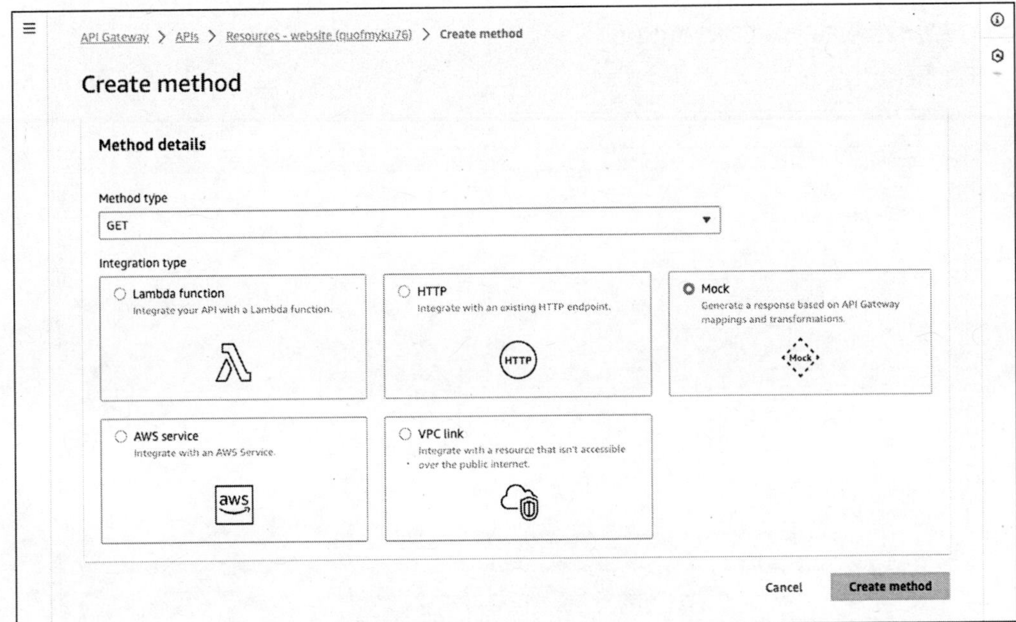

Figure 5.10: The method details

11. Click the **Create method** button.
12. Observe the **GET** method was created. See *Figure 5.11*:

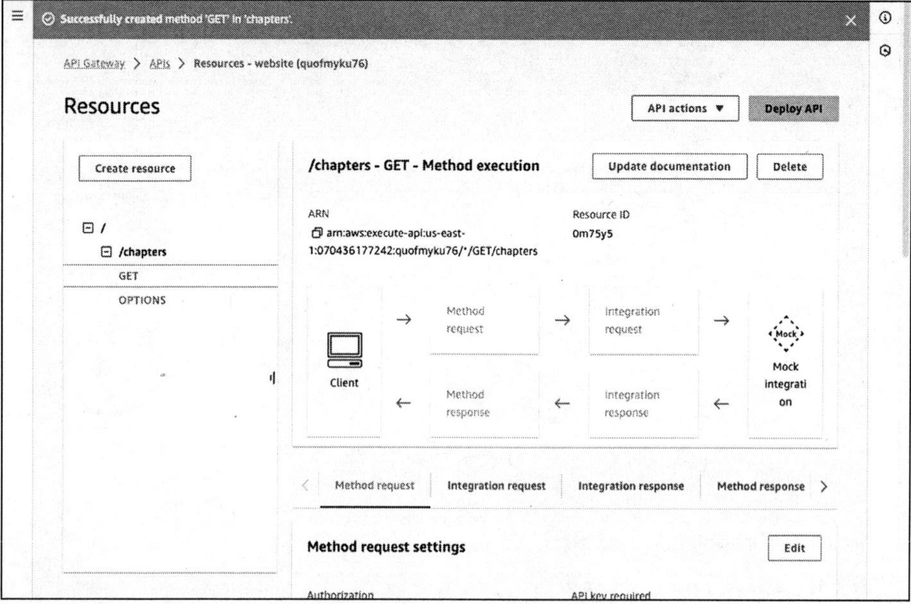

Figure 5.11: The API resources

13. Select the **`/chapters`** resource.
14. Click the **Enable CORS** button.
15. Check the **`GET`** and **`OPTIONS`** checkboxes in the **Access-Control-Allow-Methods** section. See *Figure 5.12*:

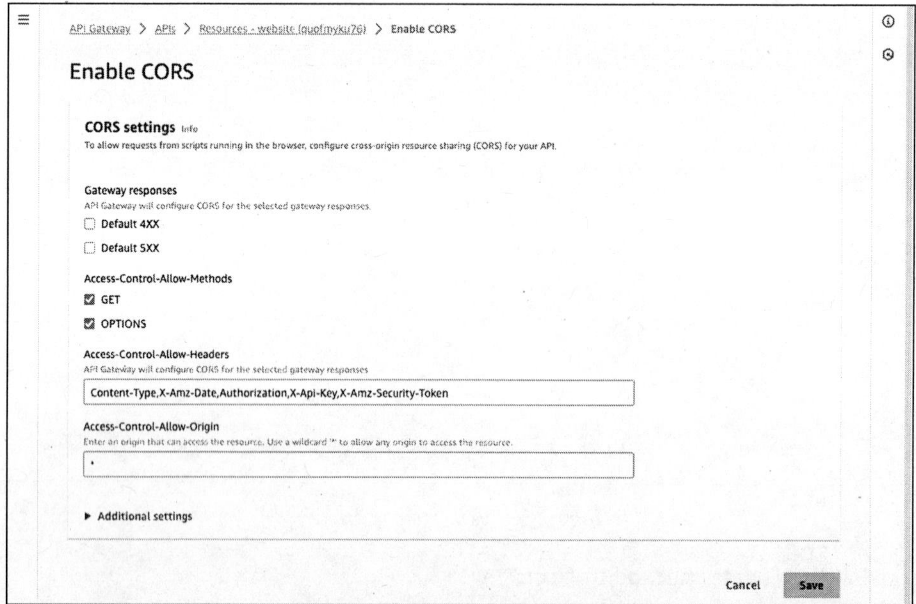

Figure 5.12: The CORS settings

16. Click the **Save** button.
17. Observe the success alert. See *Figure 5.13*:

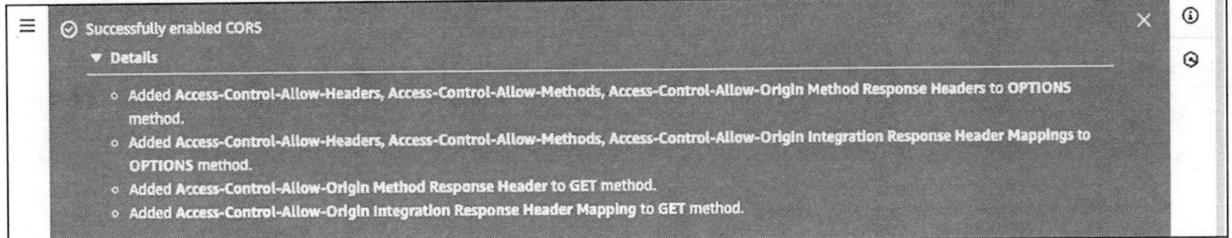

***Figure 5.13:** The CORS alert*

We successfully created the **`GET`** method with CORS enabled.

Hands-on exercise 5: Configuring the mock integration

Let us create a mock integration to return a static API response:

1. Click the **`GET`** method under the **`/chapters`** resource.
2. Select the **Integration response** tab.
3. Click the **Edit** button in the **`application/json`** section under the **Mapping templates** section. See *Figure 5.14*:

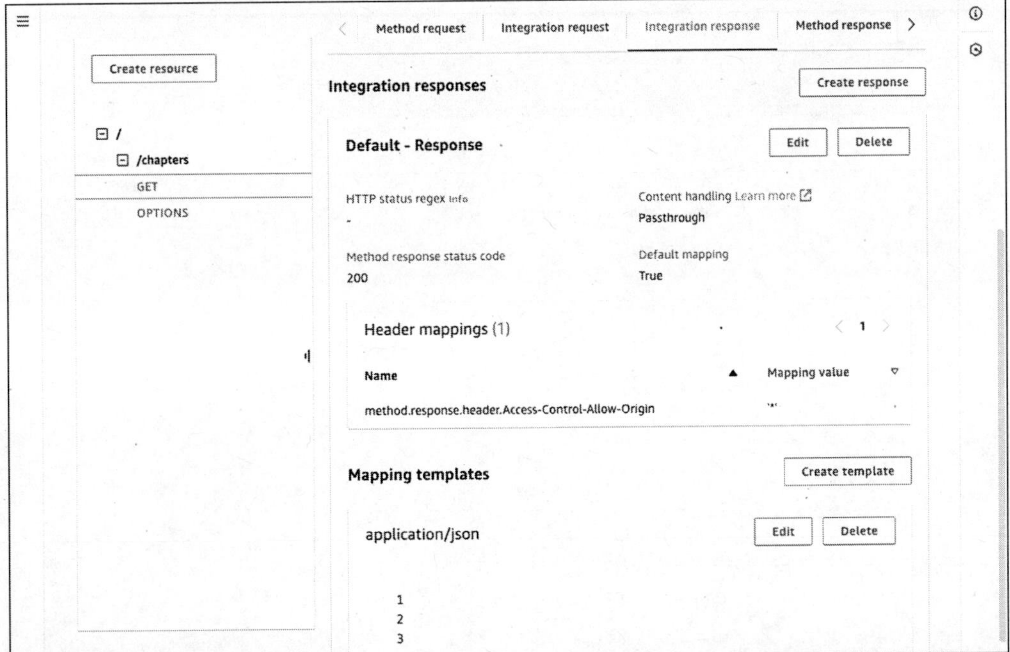

***Figure 5.14:** The integration responses section*

4. Select **application/json** in the **Content type** dropdown.
5. Enter the following text in the **Template body** field:

```
[
  {
    "id": 1,
    "title": "Chapter 1",
    "description": "The description for chapter 1."
  },
  {
    "id": 2,
    "title": "Chapter 2",
    "description": "The description for chapter 2."
  }
]
```

6. Click the **Save template** button. See *Figure 5.15*:

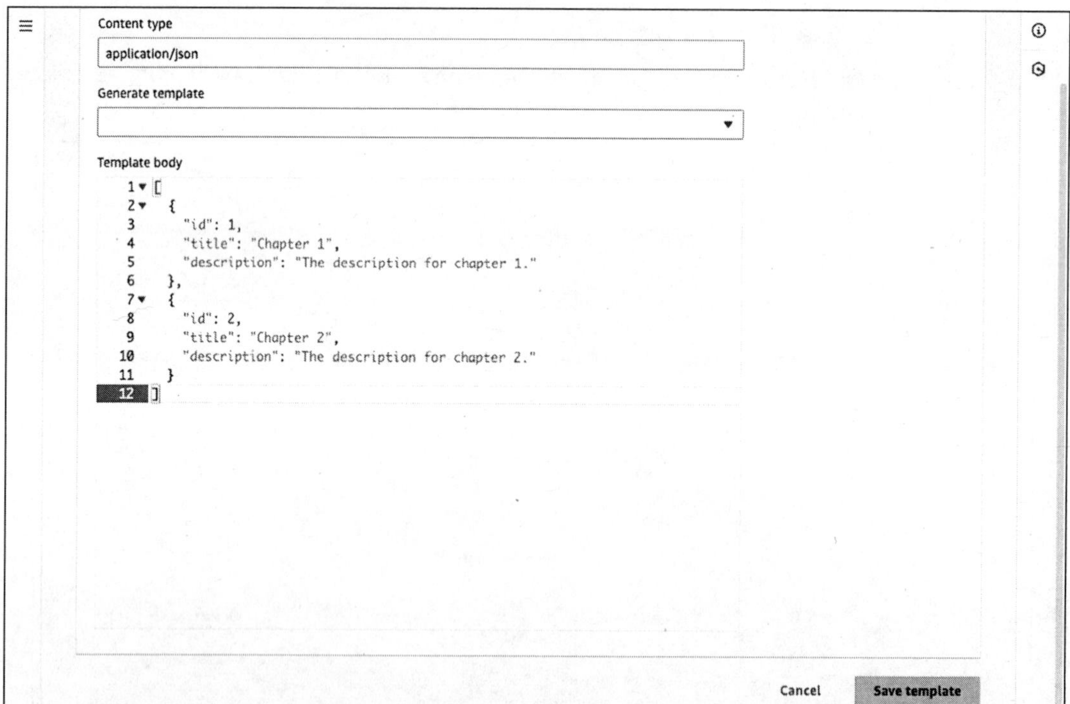

***Figure 5.15:** The mapping template settings*

7. Observe the updated mapping template in the **Integration response** section. See *Figure 5.16*:

Figure 5.16: *The mapping templates*

8. Select the **Test** tab.
9. Click the **Test** button. See *Figure 5.17*:

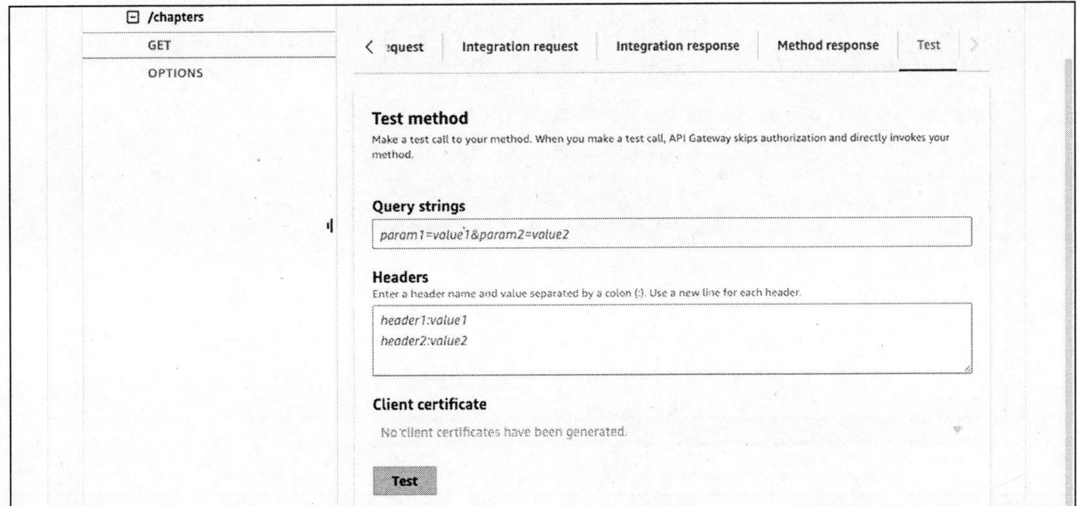

Figure 5.17: *The test tab*

10. Observe the test result returns the code above in the **Response body** section. See *Figure 5.18*:

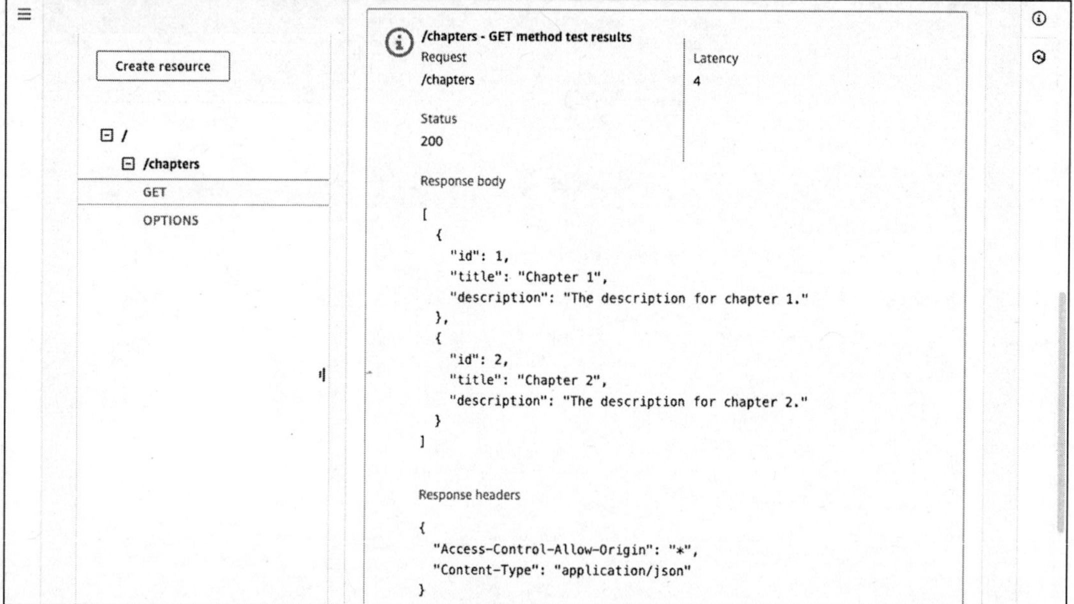

Figure 5.18: The test results

We successfully updated the mock integration.

Hands-on exercise 6: Deploying the API

Let us deploy the API using the given steps:

1. Click the **Deploy API** button at the top of the API resources page.
2. Select **New stage** in the **Stage** dropdown field.
3. Specify **v1** in the **Stage name** field. See *Figure 5.19*:

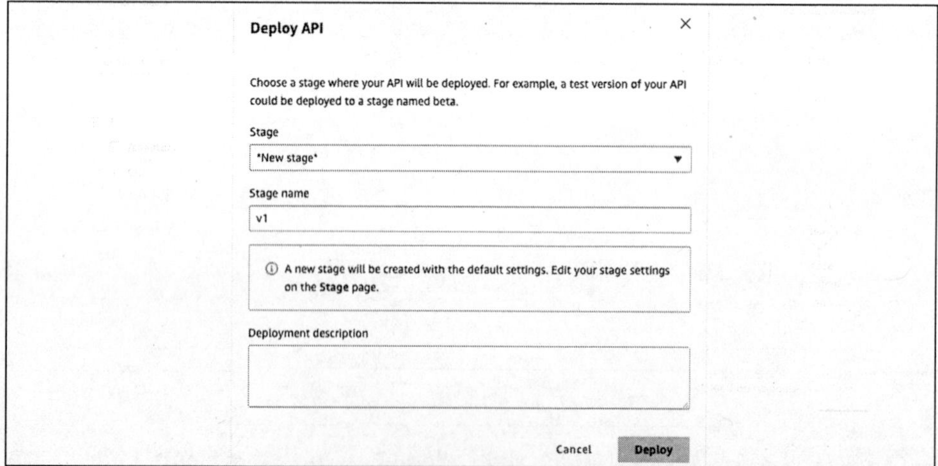

Figure 5.19: The deploy API settings

4. Click the **Deploy** button.
5. Observe the **v1** stage was created. See *Figure 5.20*:

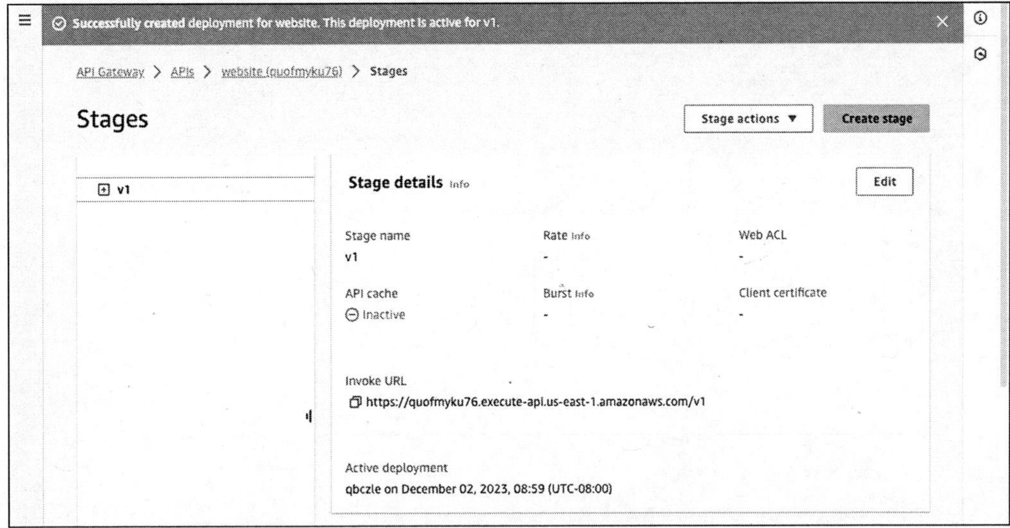

Figure 5.20: *The stage details*

We successfully deployed the API.

Hands-on exercise 7: Creating a custom domain

Let us add a custom domain for the API:

1. Click to the **Custom domain names** menu option in the **API Gateway** menu.
2. Click the **Create** button. See *Figure 5.21*:

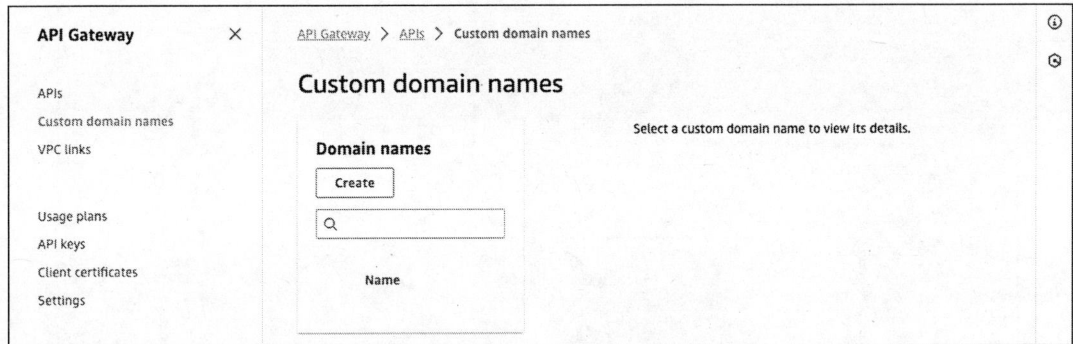

Figure 5.21: *The custom domain names page.*

3. Specify **`api.masteringawsserverlessbook.com`** in the **Domain name** field.
4. Select **`api.masteringawsserverlessbook.com`** from the **ACM certificate** dropdown. See *Figure 5.22*:

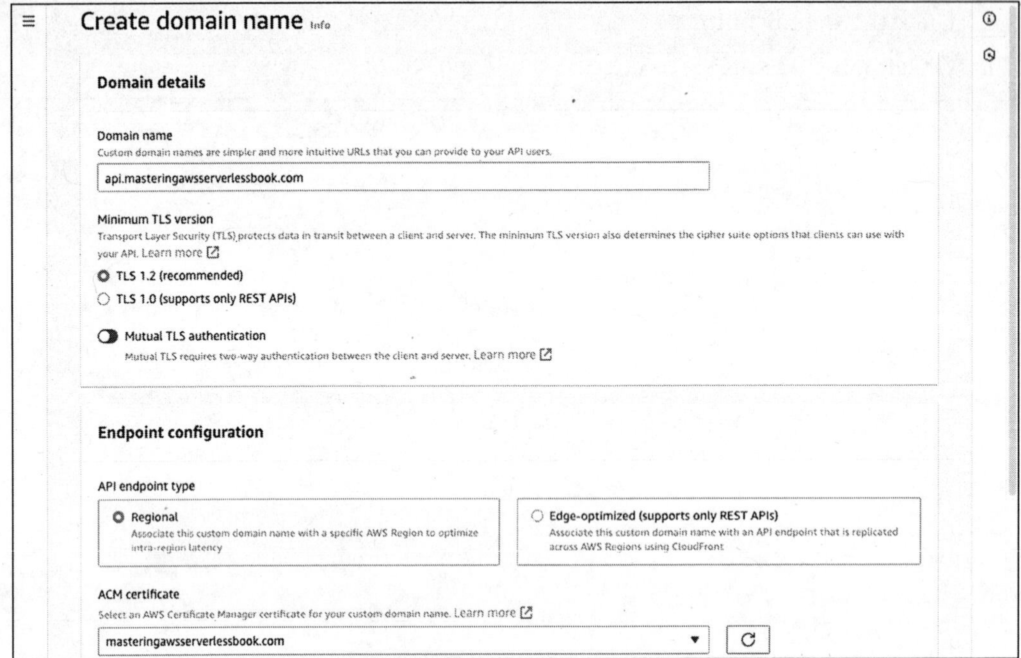

Figure 5.22: The stage details

5. Click the **Create domain name** button.
6. Observe the domain name was created. See *Figure 5.23*:

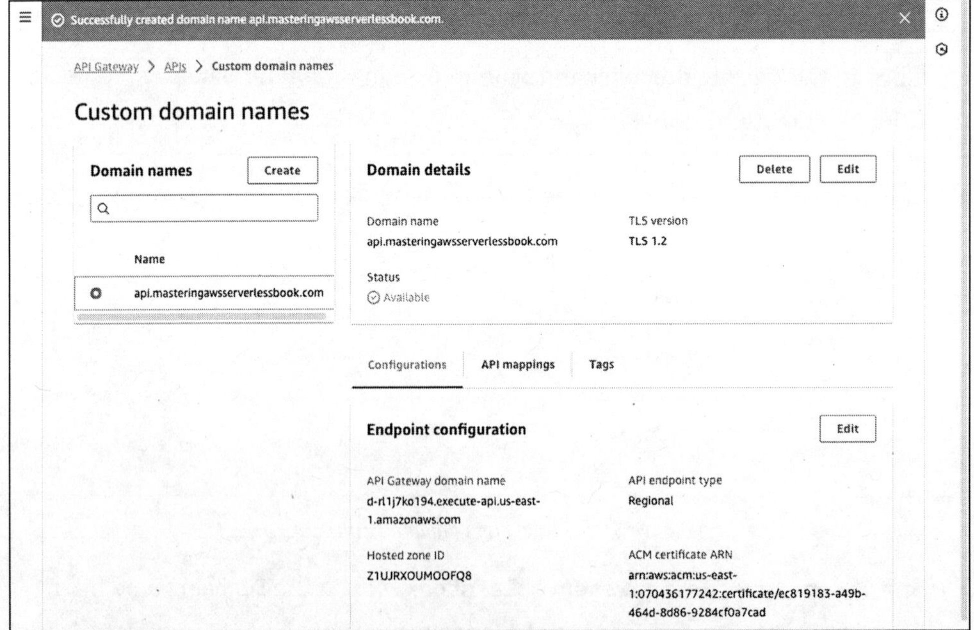

Figure 5.23: The custom domain name

7. Select the **API mappings** tab.
8. Click the **Configure API mappings** button. See *Figure 5.24*:

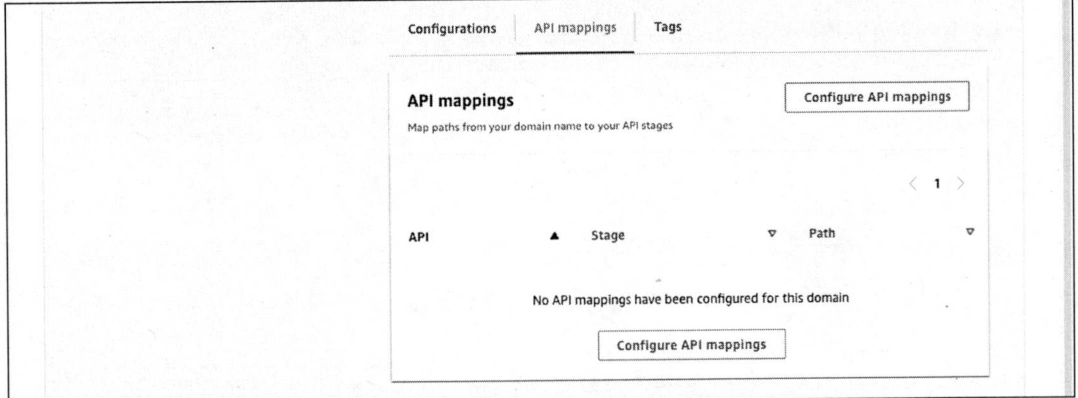

***Figure 5.24:** The API mappings*

9. Click the **Add new mapping** button.
10. Select **website** in the **API** dropdown.
11. Select **v1** in the **Stage** dropdown.

Note: If it is missing, try reloading the page.

See *Figure 5.25*:

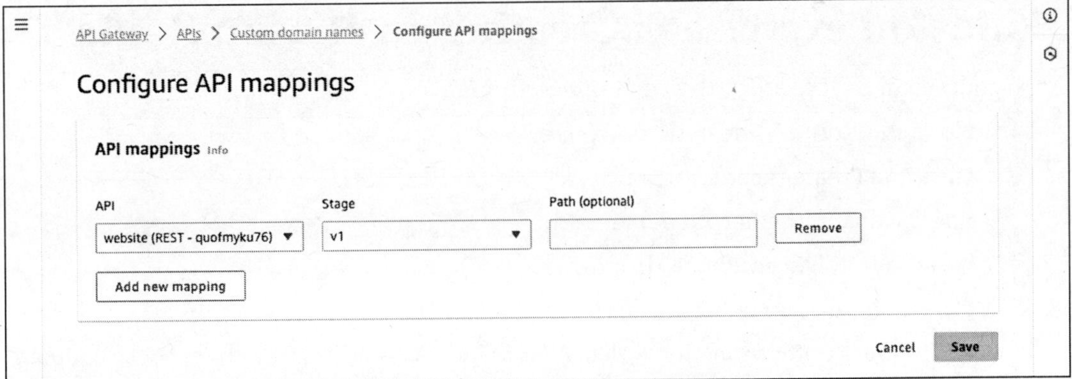

***Figure 5.25:** The API mappings settings*

12. Click the **Save** button.
13. Observe the API mapping was created. See *Figure 5.26*:

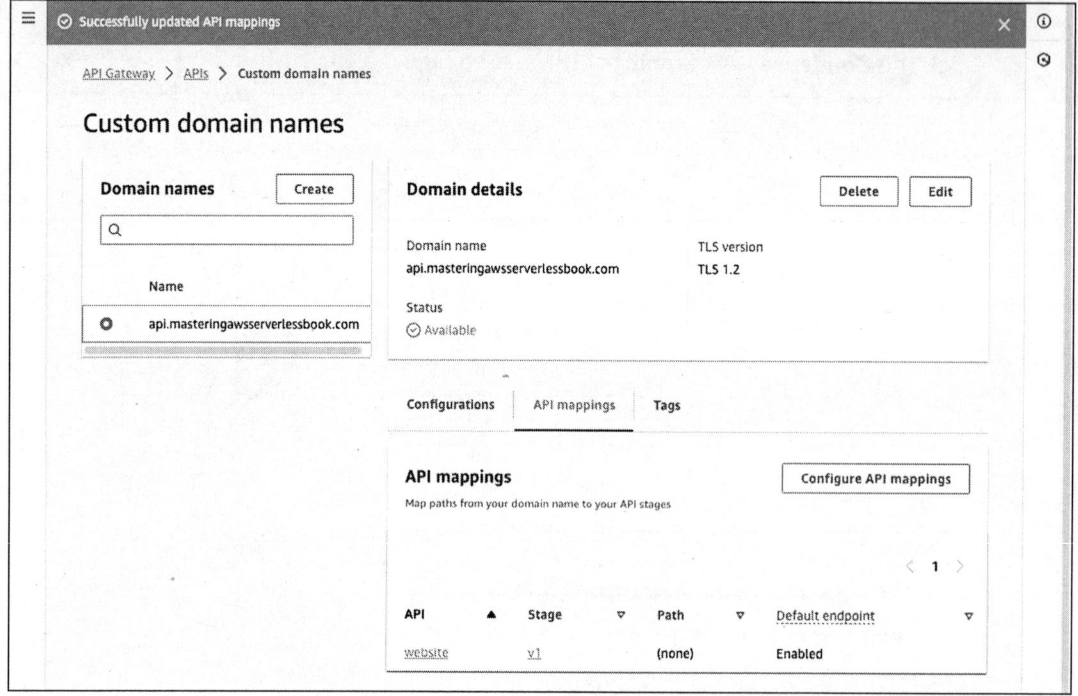

Figure 5.26: The API mappings

We successfully created our custom domain for the API.

Hands-on exercise 8: Creating an alias in Route 53

Let us add an alias record for the custom API domain:

1. Go to the Route 53 hosted zone page.
2. Click the **Create record** button.
3. Specify **api** in the **Record name** field.
4. Select **A** in the **Record type** dropdown.
5. Check the **Alias** switch button.
6. In the **Route traffic to** section, select **Alias to API Gateway API** from the **Choose endpoint** dropdown.
7. Select **US East (N. Virginia)** in the **Choose Region** dropdown.
8. Choose the available endpoint in the **Choose endpoint** field. See *Figure 5.27*:

Figure 5.27: The record settings

9. Click the **Create records** button.
10. Observe the new record was created. See *Figure 5.28*:

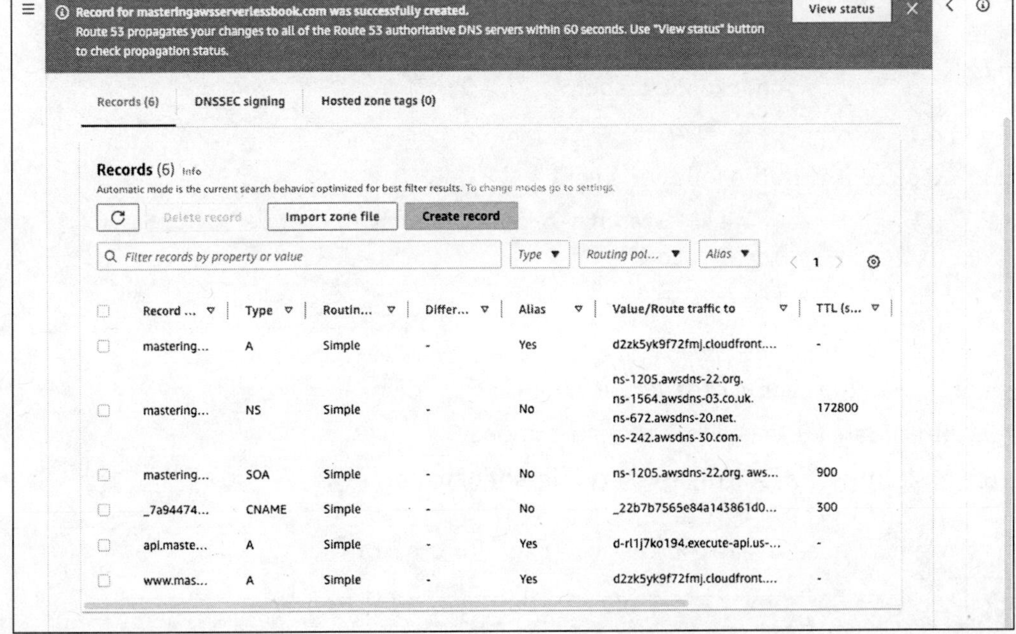

Figure 5.28: The hosted zone records

11. Visit **https://masteringawsserverlessbook.com/chapters.html.**
12. Observe the web page shows the chapters. See *Figure 5.29* for your reference:

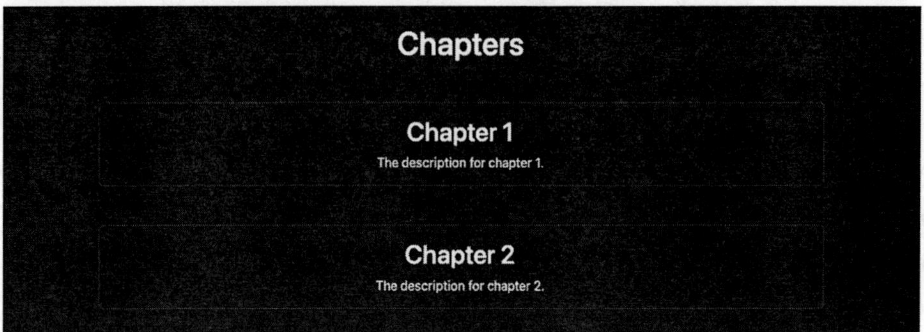

***Figure 5.29:** The chapters web page*

We have successfully created a working API that uses a custom domain.

Hands-on exercise 9: Updating the website home page

Let us update the `index.html` page to point to the `chapters.html` web page. Follow the given steps:

1. Open the `index.html` on our computer.
2. Select the following code:

```
<p class="lead">
  Check back soon.
</p>
```

3. Replace it with the following code:

```
<a class="btn btn-primary" href="/chapters.html"
role="button">
  Learn more
</a>
```

4. Upload the `index.html` to the S3 bucket.
5. Invalidate the cache for the distribution.
6. Visit **https://masteringawsserverlessbook.com.**

Note: We may need to refresh the web page for the browser to clear its local cache.

7. Observe the home page shows the button. See *Figure 5.30*:

Figure 5.30: The chapters web page

8. Click the button and observe the chapter web page loads.

We successfully updated the home page.

Integration a Lambda function with the API

We will create a Lambda function that will integrate with the API. We will have multiple hands-on exercises to work through the different aspects.

Hands-on exercise 10: Creating the function

Let us create a serverless function using the Lambda service, as shown:

1. Search `lambda` in the top search bar, click the **Lambda** service, or enter **https://us-east-1.console.aws.amazon.com/lambda/home** in the browser address bar.
2. Click the **Create function** button.
3. Select the **Author from scratch** radio button.
4. Specify `get-chapters` in the **Function name** field.
5. Select **Node.js** in the **Runtime** drop down.
6. Select the **arm64** radio button in the **Architecture** section. See *Figure 5.31*:

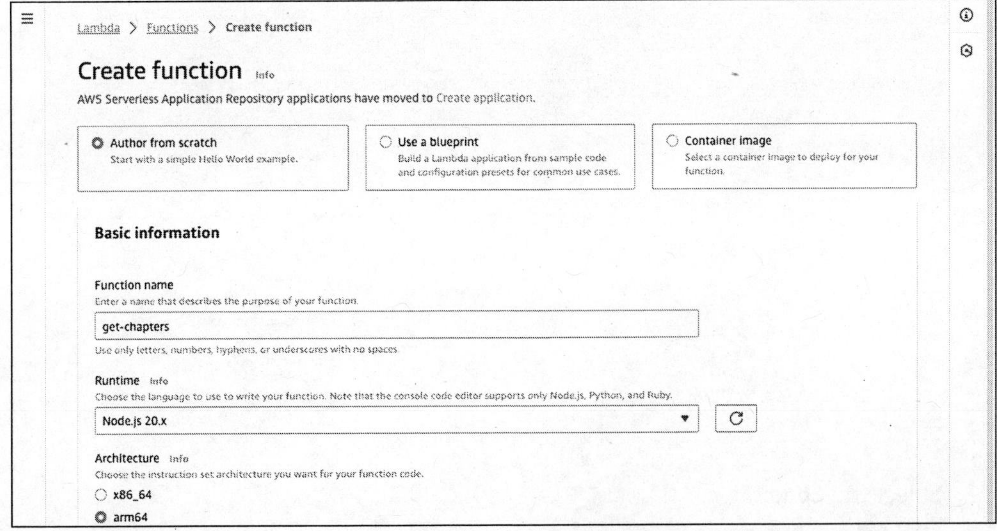

Figure 5.31: The function settings

7. Expand the **Change default execution role** section.
8. Select the **Create a new role with basic Lambda permission** radio button. See *Figure 5.32*:

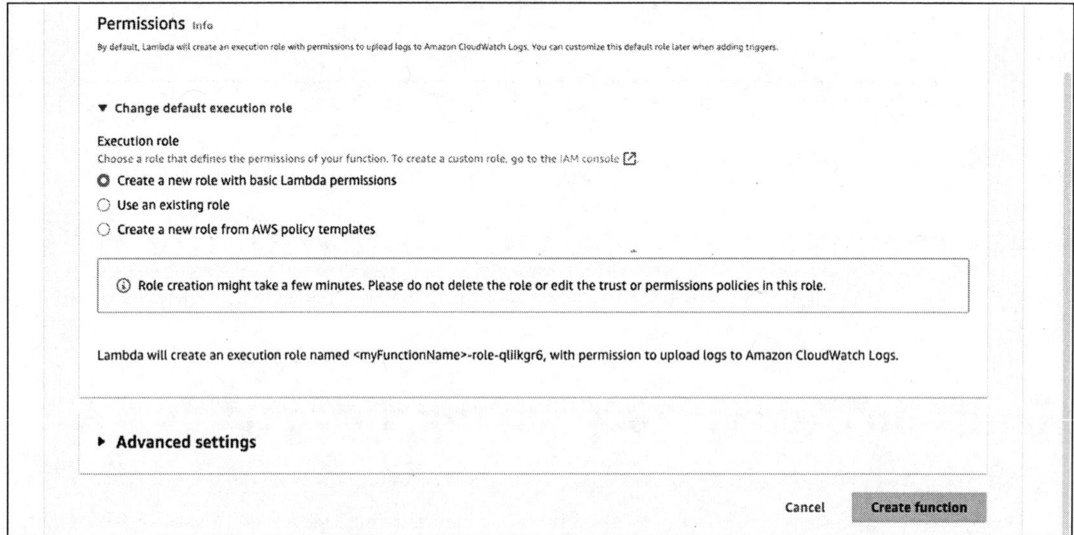

Figure 5.32: The function settings

9. Click the **Create function** button.
10. Observe the function was created. See *Figure 5.33*:

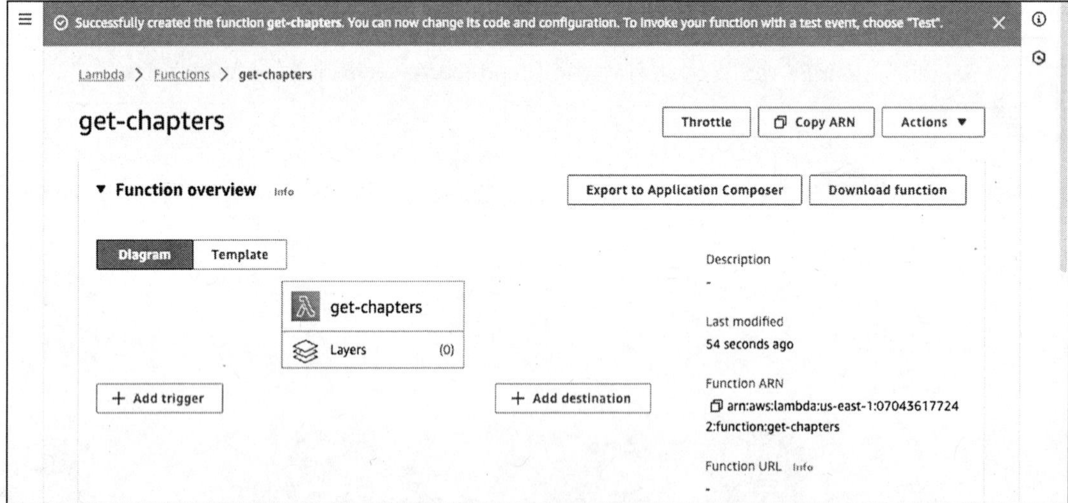

Figure 5.33: The function

11. Select the **Code** tab.
12. Go to the **Code source** section.

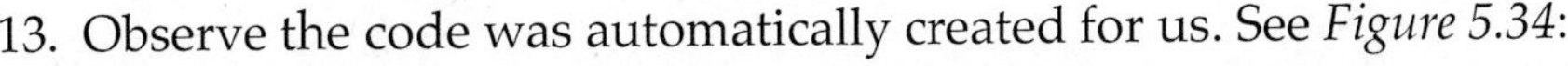

13. Observe the code was automatically created for us. See *Figure 5.34*:

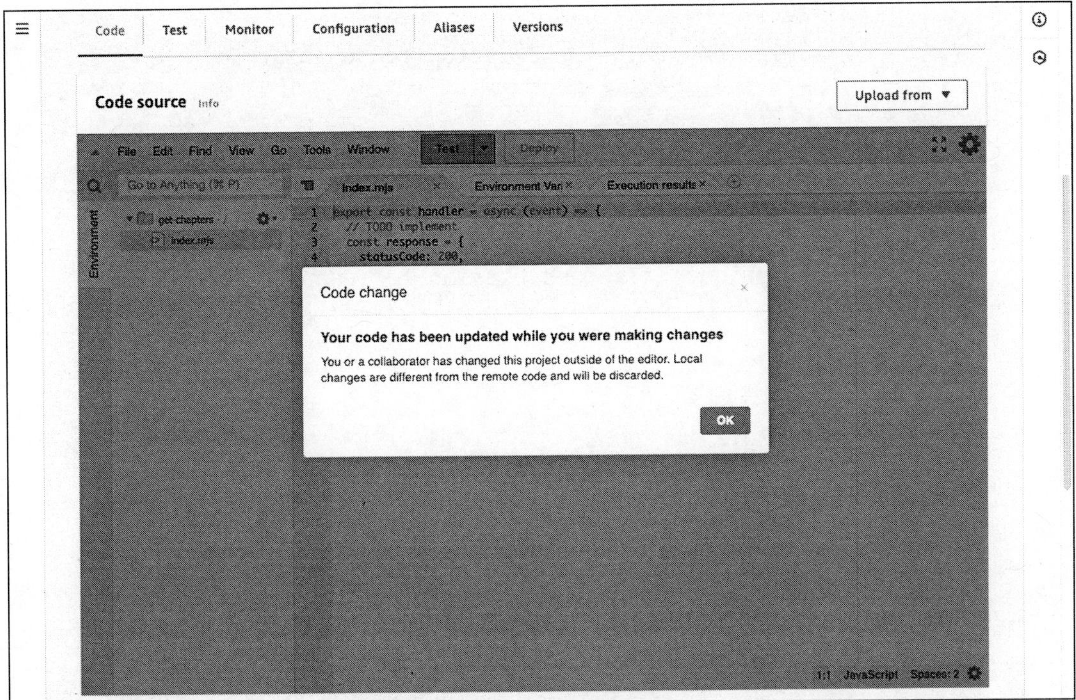

Figure 5.34: The function code

14. Replace the existing code with the code below:

```
export const handler = async (event) => {
  const response = {
    statusCode: 200,
    headers: {
      'Access-Control-Allow-Origin': '*',
      'Content-Type': 'application/json',
    },
    body: JSON.stringify([
      {
        'id': 1,
        'title': 'Chapter 1',
        'description': 'The description for chapter 1.'
      },
      {
```

```
            'id': 2,
            'title': 'Chapter 2',
            'description': 'The description for chapter 2.'
        },
        {
            'id': 3,
            'title': 'Chapter 3',
            'description': 'The description for chapter 3.'
        }
      ]),
    };
    return response;
};
```

15. Select the **File** menu and select the **Save** menu option.
16. Click the **Deploy** button.
17. Observe the code was deployed. See *Figure 5.35*:

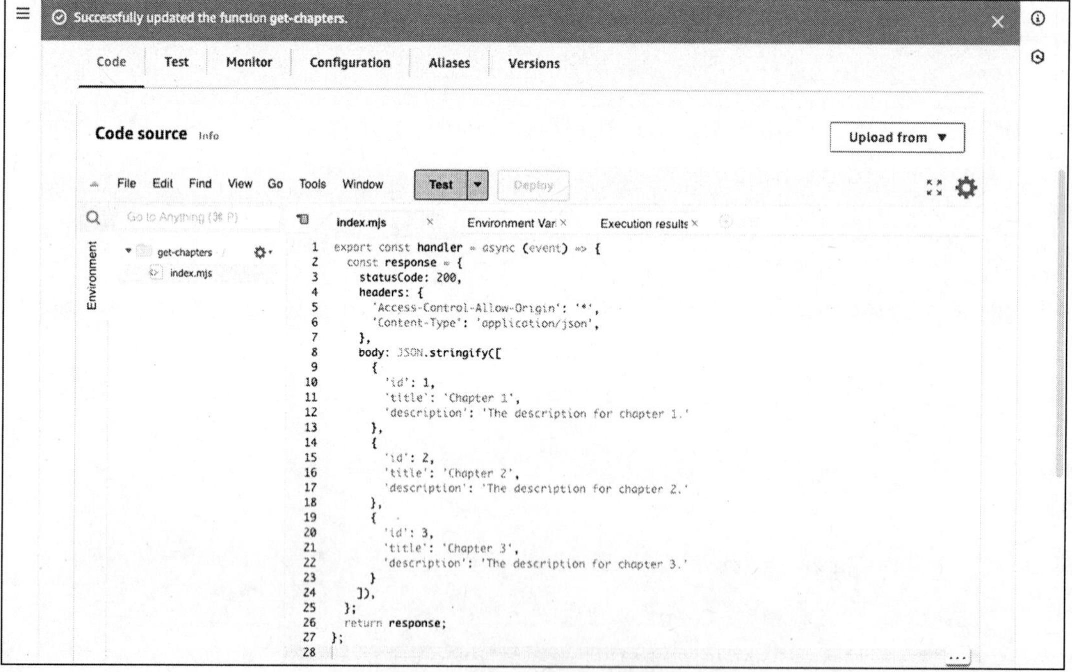

Figure 5.35: The function code

18. Click the **Test** button.
19. Select the **Create new event** radio button.
20. Specify **api** in the **Event name** field.
21. Select **API Gateway AWS Proxy** in the **Template** dropdown. See *Figure 5.36*:

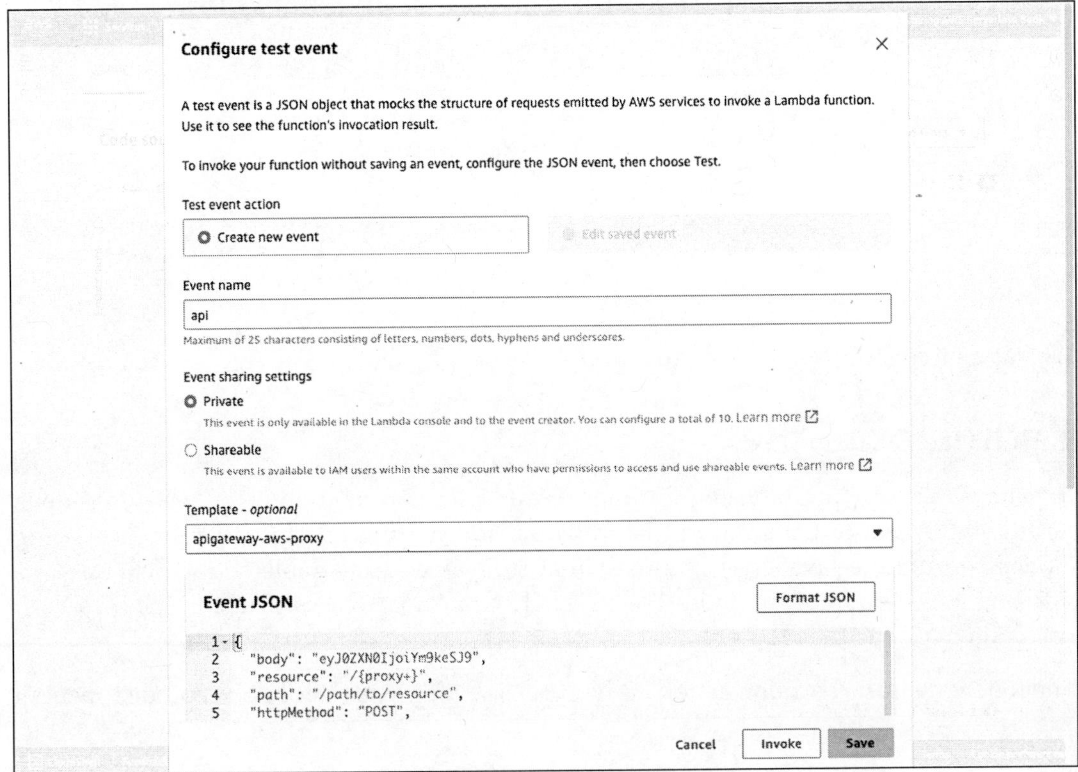

Figure 5.36: The test event settings

22. Click the **Save** button.
23. Click the **Test** button.
24. Observe the **Response** section show the response. See *Figure 5.37* for your reference:

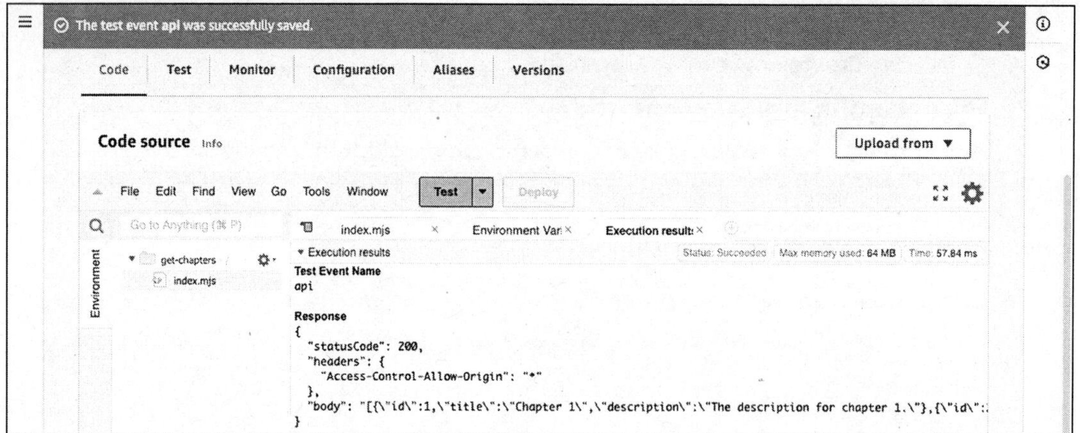

Figure 5.37: The test results

We have successfully created the function.

Python example

In general, we will not be using Python for our Lambda functions. The website code is written in JavaScript (running in the browser), and writing our Lambda function using Node.js (a runtime JavaScript language that runs as an executable script) will keep us thinking in JavaScript throughout the book. There are some cases where it will be best to use Python for our code though.

The following is the Python version of the Node.js code we used for our Lambda function:

```
import json

def lambda_handler(event, context):

  return {

    "statusCode": 200,

    "headers": {

      "Access-Control-Allow-Origin": "*",

      "Content-Type": "application/json",

    },

    "body": json.dumps([

      {

        "id": 1,
```

```
      "title": "Chapter 1",
      "description": "The description for chapter 1."
    },
    {
      "id": 2,
      "title": "Chapter 2",
      "description": "The description for chapter 2."
    },
    {
      "id": 3,
      "title": "Chapter 3",
      "description": "The description for chapter 3."
    }
  ])
}
```

If we feel adventurous, we can create a **`get-chapters1`** Lambda function and get it working with a **`/chapters1`** resource.

Hands-on exercise 11: Related resources

Let us create the typical resources that a Lambda function uses:

1. Search **`cloudwatch`** in the top search bar and click the **CloudWatch** service or enter **https://us-east-1.console.aws.amazon.com/cloudwatch/home** in the browser address bar.
2. Expand the **Logs** menu option in the CloudWatch menu.
3. Select the **Log groups** menu option.
4. Observe the **`/aws/lambda/get-chapters`** log group was automatically created. See *Figure 5.38*:

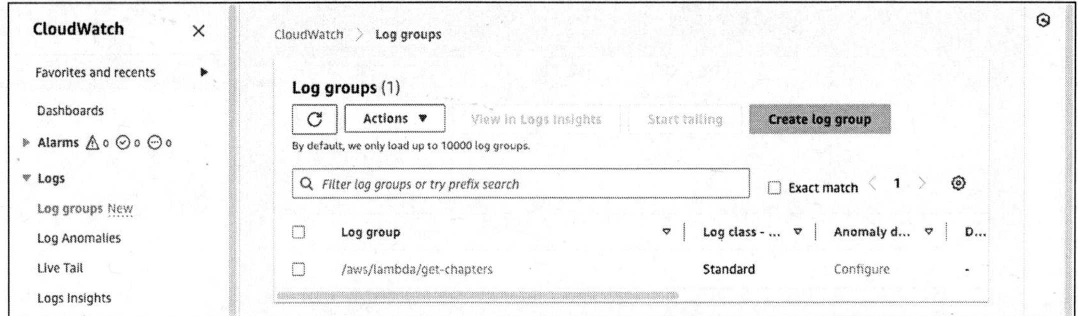

Figure 5.38: The log groups

5. Check the log group checkbox.
6. Select **Edit retention settings(s)** from the **Actions** dropdown.
7. Select **1 week (7 days)** from the **Expire events after** dropdown. See *Figure 5.39*:

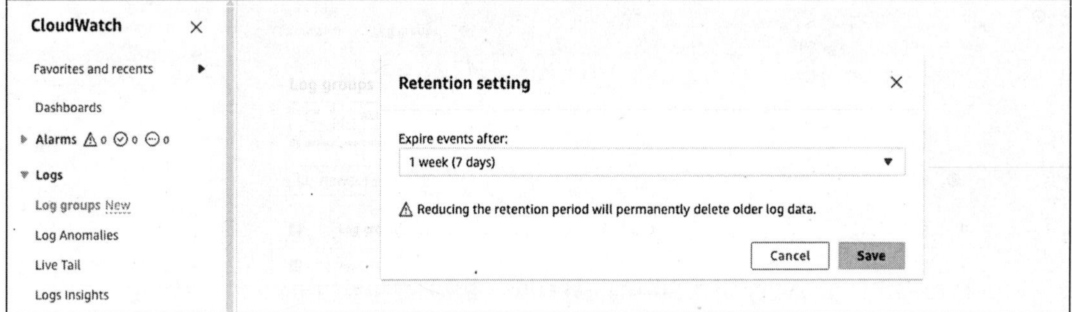

Figure 5.39: The retention settings

8. Click the **Save** button.
9. Observe the retention settings were updated. See *Figure 5.40*:

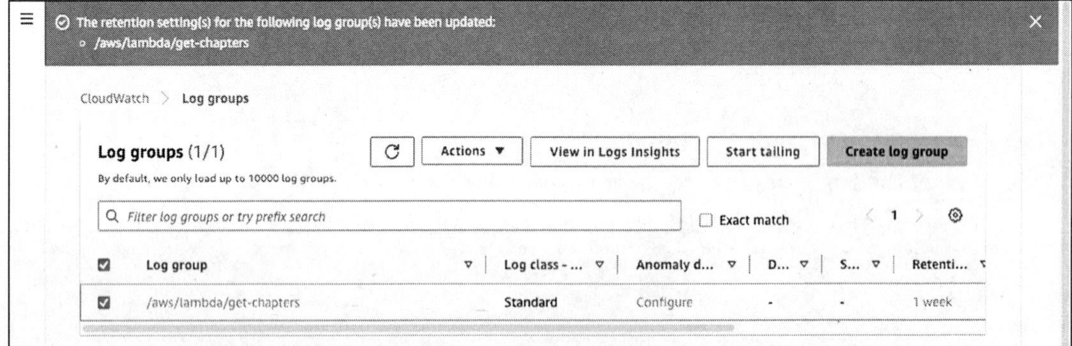

Figure 5.40: The log groups

10. Search **`iam`** in the top search bar and click the **IAM** service or enter **https://us-east-1.console.aws.amazon.com/iam/home** in the browser address bar.

11. Expand the **Access management** menu option in the IAM menu option.
12. Select the **Roles** menu option.
13. Observe the **`get-chapters-role`** role was automatically created. See *Figure 5.41* for your reference:

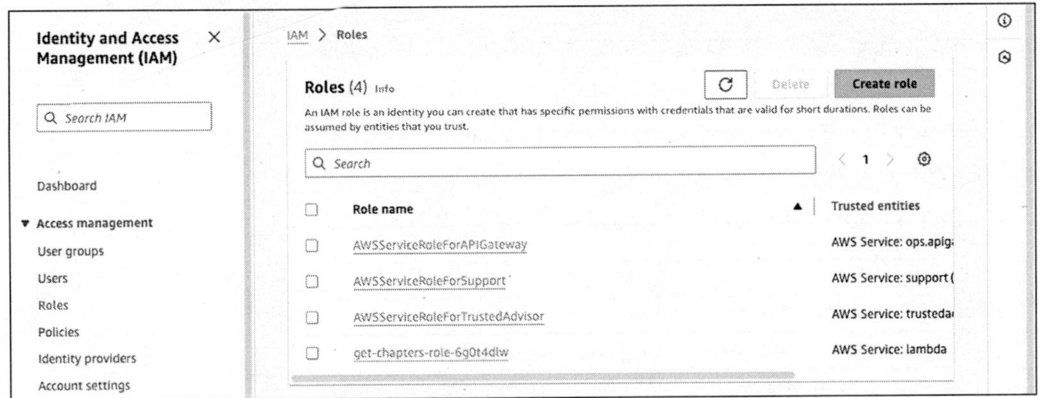

Figure 5.41: The IAM roles

14. Select the **Policies** menu option.
15. Select **Customer managed** from the **Filter by Type** dropdown.
16. Observe the **AWSLambdaBasicExecutionRole** policy was automatically created.
17. Expand the policy. See *Figure 5.42*:

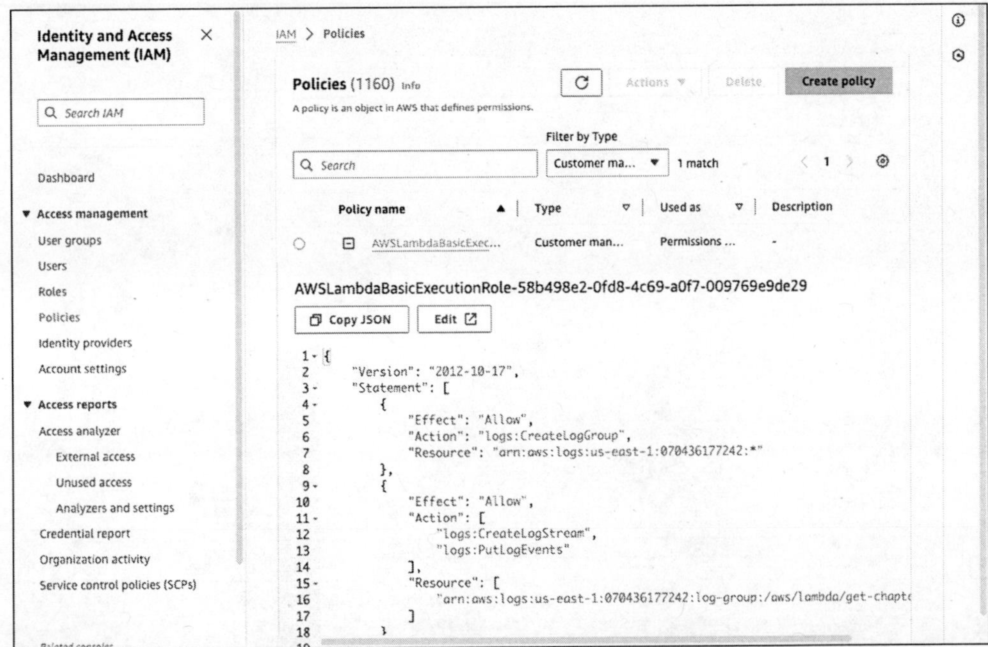

Figure 5.42: The IAM customer-managed policies

We observed that the resources were automatically created when we created our function.

Hands-on exercise 12: Updating the API integration

Let us update the API to use the Lambda function:

1. Go the website API settings page.
2. Select the **GET** method under the **/chapters** resource.
3. Click the **Delete** button.
4. Follow the on-screen instructions to delete it.
5. Select the **/chapters** resource.
6. Click the **Create method** button.
7. Select **GET** in the **Method type** dropdown.
8. Select the **Lambda function** radio button in the **Integration type** section.
9. Check the **Lambda proxy integration** switch button.
10. Select the **get-chapters** function in the **Choose a Lambda function or enter its ARN** search field. See *Figure 5.43*:

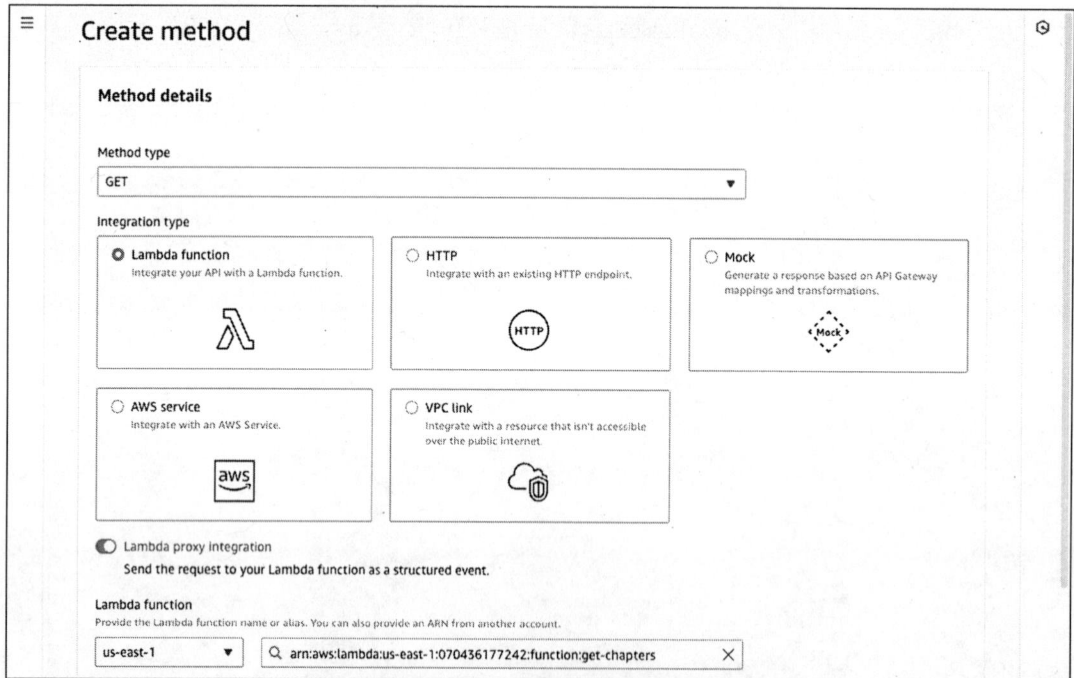

Figure 5.43: The method details

11. Uncheck the **Default timeout** switch button.

12. Specify **1000** in the **Custom timeout** field. See *Figure 5.44*:

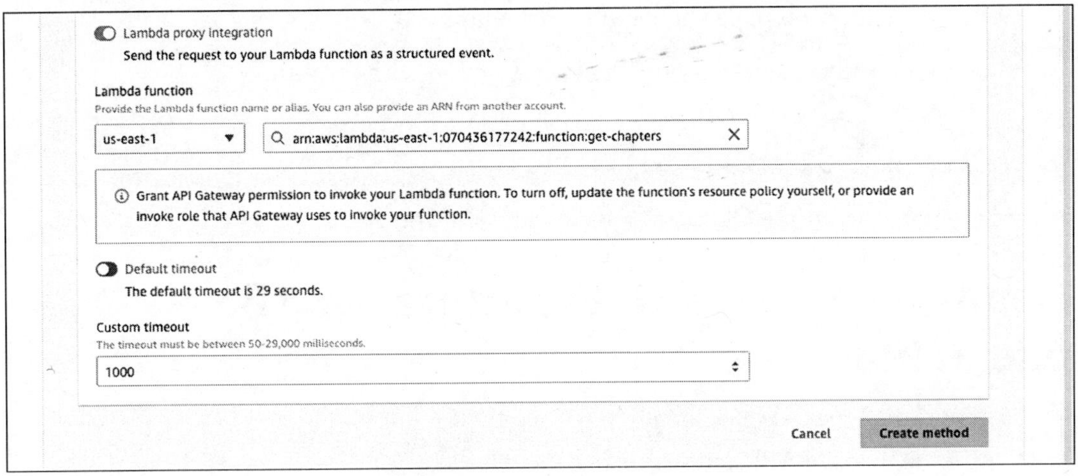

Lambda proxy integration
Send the request to your Lambda function as a structured event.
Lambda function
Provide the Lambda function name or alias. You can also provide an ARN from another account.
us-east-1
arn:aws:lambda:us-east-1:070436177242:function:get-chapters
Grant API Gateway permission to invoke your Lambda function. To turn off, update the function's resource policy yourself, or provide an invoke role that API Gateway uses to invoke your function.
Default timeout
The default timeout is 29 seconds.
Custom timeout
The timeout must be between 50-29,000 milliseconds.
1000
Cancel
Create method

Figure 5.44: The method details

13. Click the **Create method** button.
14. Observe the **GET** method was successfully created with the Lambda integration. See *Figure 5.45*:

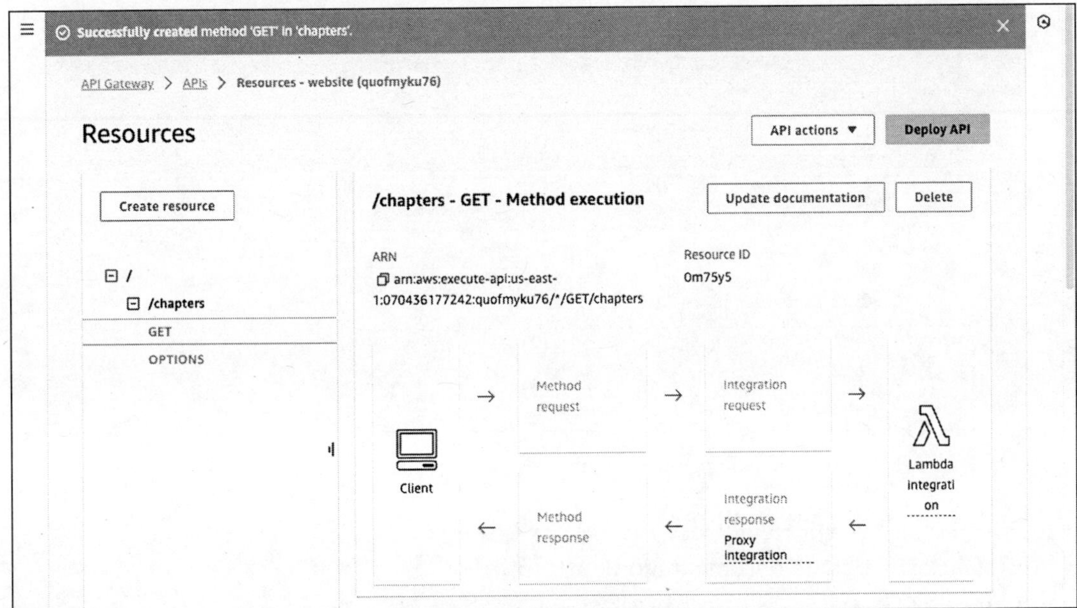

Figure 5.45: The API resources

15. Click the **Deploy API** button.
16. Select the **v1** stage in the **Stage** dropdown.
17. Click the **Deploy** button.

18. Visit **https://masteringawsserverlessbook.com/chapters.html.**
19. Observe the web page shows the three chapters.

We have successfully integrated our Lambda function with the API.

OpenAPI specification

We are going to export the OpenAPI specification for our API.

Hands-on exercise 13: Exporting the API integration

Let us export the OpenAPI specification for the API:

1. Go the website API settings page.
2. Select the **/** resource.
3. Click the **Update documentation** button.
4. Specify **The API for the website** in the JSON **description** property. See *Figure 5.46*:

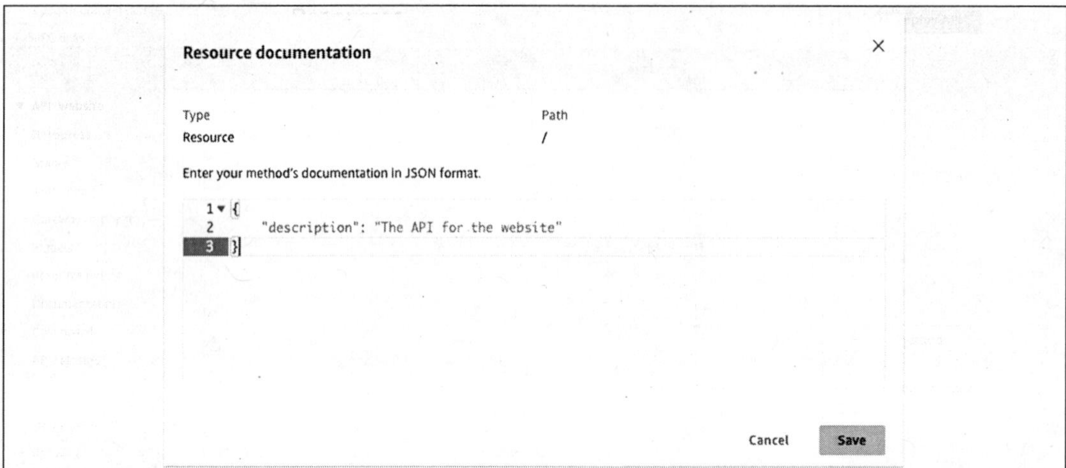

Figure 5.46: The resource documentation

5. Select the **/chapters** resource.
6. Click the **Update documentation** button.
7. Specify **Book chapters** in the JSON **description** property.
8. Click the **Save** button.
9. Select the **GET** method under the **/chapters** resource.
10. Click the **Update documentation** button.
11. Specify **Get book chapters** in the JSON **description** property.

12. Click the **Save** button.
13. Select the `OPTIONS` method under the `/chapters` resource.
14. Click the **Update documentation** button.
15. Specify **CORS** in the JSON **description** property.
16. Click the **Save** button.
17. Select the **Documentation** menu option in the **API: website** menu in the left pane.
18. Select the **website** resource.
19. Click the **Create documentation part** button. See *Figure 5.47* for your reference:

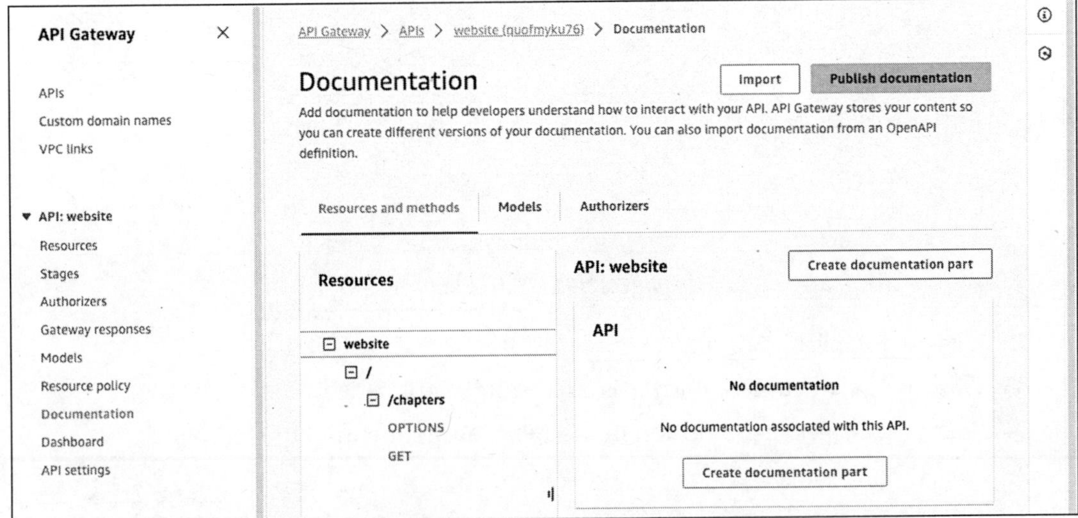

Figure 5.47: The documentation

20. Select **API** in the **Documentation type** dropdown.
21. Specify **The API for the website** in the JSON **description** property.
22. Click the **Create documentation part** button.
23. Observe that the documentation exists.
24. Select the **/** resource.
25. Observe that the documentation exists.
26. Select the `/chapters` resource.
27. Observe that the documentation exists.
28. Click the **Publish documentation** button.
29. Select **v1** in the **Stage** dropdown.
30. Specify `0.1` in the **Version** field.

Note: This value must be unique every time the API documentation is published.

31. Specify **Initial revision** in the **Description** field. See *Figure 5.48*:

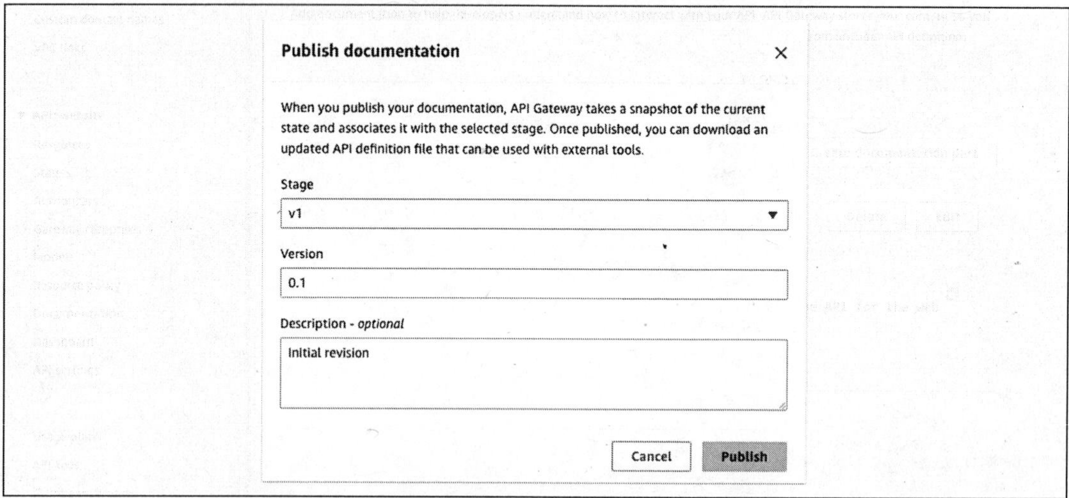

Figure 5.48: The documentation

32. Click the **Publish** button.
33. Observe the documentation was successfully published.
34. Select the **Stages** menu option in the **API: website** menu in the left pane.
35. Select the **v1** stage.
36. Select **Export** in the **Stage actions** dropdown. See *Figure 5.49*:

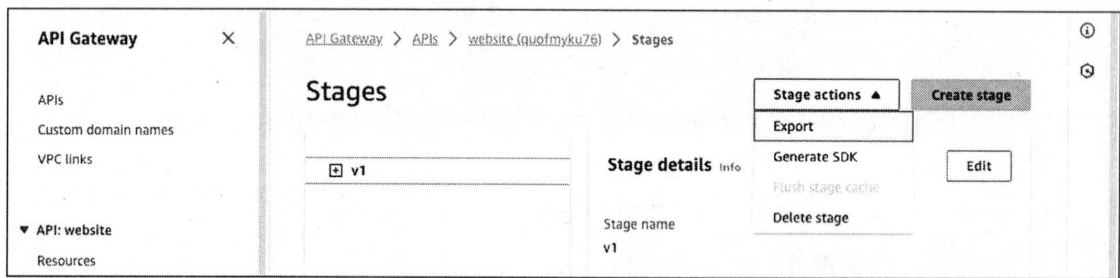

Figure 5.49: The stage

37. Select the **Open API 3** radio button in the **API specification type** section.
38. Select the **YAML** radio button in the **Format** section.
39. Select the **Export the API Gateway extension** in the **Extension** section. See *Figure 5.50*:

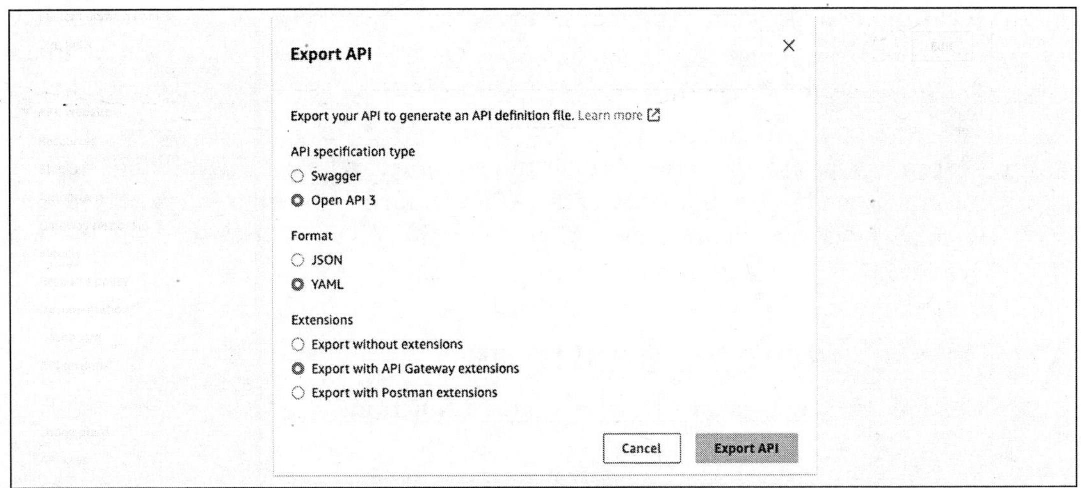

***Figure 5.50:** The export API settings*

40. Click the **Export API** button.
41. We will save the file to our computer.

We have successfully created the OpenAPI specification file.

Conclusion

In this chapter, we created an API with a custom domain. We defined the "/chapters" endpoint for the HTTP GET method and enabled CORS. The endpoint was first integrated with a mock integration to make sure we could get our web page to make a successful HTTP request. We changed the endpoint to a Lambda integration with a function that returned the data. We created our API documentation and exported the OpenAPI specification.

Points to remember

- The CORS settings are needed whenever a browser makes a request to a domain that is different from the website's domain. Our API domain uses a subdomain and our website uses the top-level domain. Since those addresses are different, we need set the CORS settings in the API resources and methods to allow HTTP requests from the webpage via JavaScript.
- The function response needs to include the CORS headers to allow HTTP requests from the webpage via JavaScript. Having the headers provides protection from unwanted website traffic. The website will not accept the HTTP response if the header's response fails to include the website's domain name in the allowed origin and the HTTP method in the allowed methods.

- A custom domain name is defined in the API Gateway settings. An alias record is needed in the Route 53 hosted zone also. Without it, a request to the API subdomain will fail since there is no DNS record to direct the request to the API hosted in the API Gateway.
- We can export and import the API documentation as a JSON or YAML file. Having this file provides us with a copy of the API. We can compare the API export files to track changes. We can import the API documentation file to recreate the API if it is ever lost or if we want to create a new development environment.

Multiple choice questions

1. **Can mock integrations work with Lambda functions?**
   a. True
   b. False

   Answer: b

   False. The mock integrations do not integrate with any other AWS service.

2. **The web page gives errors when trying to connect to the API endpoint. What might be the issue?**
   a. Incorrect address.
   b. Incorrect HTTP method.
   c. The API CORS was not enabled in the API Gateway.
   d. There is an issue with integration.
   e. The Lambda function is not returning the CORS headers.
   f. All of the above.

   Answer: f

   All of the above.

Join our book's Discord space

Join the book's Discord Workspace for Latest updates, Offers, Tech happenings around the world, New Release and Sessions with the Authors:

https://discord.bpbonline.com

Chapter 6
Saving and Using Data

Introduction

This chapter focuses on different ways to save and use data using serverless services.

Structure

We will cover the following topics in this chapter:

- Overview of saving and using data
- Creating a new S3 bucket
- Getting the object contents from a Lambda function
- Creating a DynamoDB table
- Getting the table data from a Lambda function
- Clean up

Objectives

By the end of this chapter, you will understand how to use object storage and serverless databases with Amazon S3 and Amazon DynamoDB to store and query data.

Overview of saving and using data

We previously have discussed using object storage and databases. We have been using object storage for our website. We can also use it for our data. Reading and writing to S3 is typically slower than writing to a database. As a result, we can use S3 when the speed is not a factor. Furthermore, S3 data storage is typically less expensive than database storage. Using object storage works well for storing large amounts of data that need to be processed in the backend. We will typically use databases for the data the website needs to load.

We will focus on DynamoDB for our database. DynamoDB is a non-relational database and works well with JSON data. We can specify on-demand or provisioned capacity. The on-demand capacity is more expensive per read-and-write transaction but is best suited for unpredictable traffic. Predictable traffic would be reading the same amount of data every minute. With on-demand capacity, the monthly cost would be $0 if there are no transactions. With provisioned capacity, the lowest monthly cost would be $0.59 if there were no transactions (based on the pricing at the time of writing).

We will also work with **Identity and Access Management** (**IAM**). We previously let the AWS management console automatically create the IAM role and policy for the Lambda function. We will now create our own policy and role and update them throughout the chapter. When we create the IAM policy, we will use the principle of least privilege to assign only the necessary permissions that the Lambda function needs to execute. The policy will thus specify the permissions to create a log group, create a log stream and write log events.

We will update our Lambda function first to read that from an S3 object and later update it to read data from a DynamoDB table, so we get practice working with both data sources. First, we will update the `get-chapters` function in the Lambda service to read the data from an S3 object. We will need to specify the permission to get an object from the desired S3 bucket in the IAM policy. We will put a JSON file in an S3 bucket. When the function executes, the function will retrieve the JSON file and return its data in the function response.

Then, we will update the function to get the data from a DynamoDB table. We will create a table and add data to it. We will update the IAM policy to remove the permission to access the S3 object since it is no longer needed and add the permission to get all the data from the table. When the function executes, it will scan the DynamoDB table and return its data in the function response.

Let us update our serverless application.

Creating a new S3 bucket

We will create a new bucket to store data and upload a JSON file representing the chapter data. Our Lambda function reads the JSON file and returns its data in the response. This bucket will be private by default and cannot be accessed on the Internet. We will not need to update the other bucket settings as we did in *Chapter 4: Launching a Website,* since we are not trying to make the bucket data publicly accessible on the Internet.

Hands-on exercise 1: Creating a new S3 bucket

We will create a new S3 bucket for data using the given steps:

1. Go to the S3 service page.
2. Click the **Create bucket** button.
3. Specify `masteringawsserverlessbook-data` in the **Bucket name** field.
4. Click the **Create bucket** button.
5. Observe that the bucket was created.
6. Click the `masteringawsserverlessbook-data` bucket.
7. Create a `chapters.json` file on our computer.
8. Paste the following text into the file:

```
[
  {
    "id": 1,
    "title": "Chapter 1",
    "description": "The description for chapter 1."
  },
  {
    "id": 2,
    "title": "Chapter 2",
    "description": "The description for chapter 2."
  },
  {
    "id": 3,
    "title": "Chapter 3",
    "description": "The description for chapter 3."
```

```
    },
    {
      "id": 4,
      "title": "Chapter 4",
      "description": "The description for chapter 4."
    }
  ]
```

9. Upload the file into the bucket.
10. Observe that the **chapters.json** object was created.

We have successfully created a new bucket.

Getting the object contents from a Lambda function

We will update our Lambda function to get the contents of the **chapters.json** object. There will be multiple aspects to updating our function. We will do a few hands-on exercises to make the changes.

Creating an IAM policy

We will create a new IAM policy. We could update the automatically created IAM policy, but it may become difficult to know its purpose from its name. We will create a new IAM policy that allows creating a CloudWatch log group and log stream and getting an object from the new S3 bucket.

Hands-on exercise 2: Creating an IAM policy

Let us create the IAM policy:

1. Go to the IAM service page.
2. Expand the **Access management** menu option in the IAM menu option.
3. Select the **Policies** menu option.
4. Click the **Create policy** button.
5. Click the **Visual** button in the **Policy editor** section.
6. Select **CloudWatch Logs** in the **Choose a service** dropdown.
7. Search **create** in the **Filter Actions** search field.
8. Check the **CreateLogGroup** and **CreateLogStream** checkboxes in the **Write** section. See *Figure 6.1*:

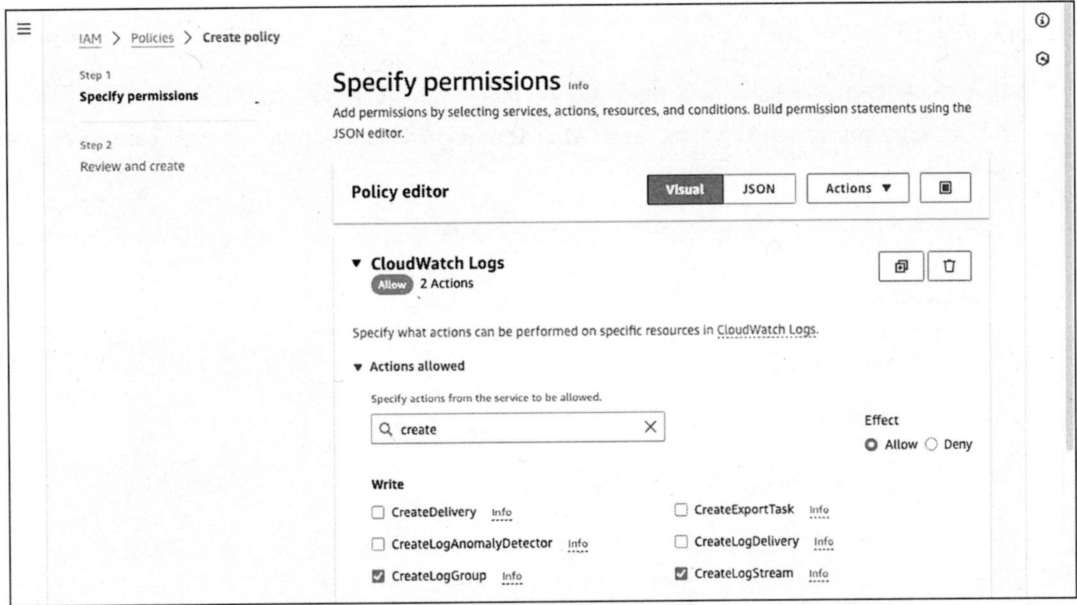

Figure 6.1: Specifying permissions

9. Search **put** in the **Filter Actions** search field.
10. Check the **PutLogEvents** checkbox in the **Write** section. See *Figure 6.2*:

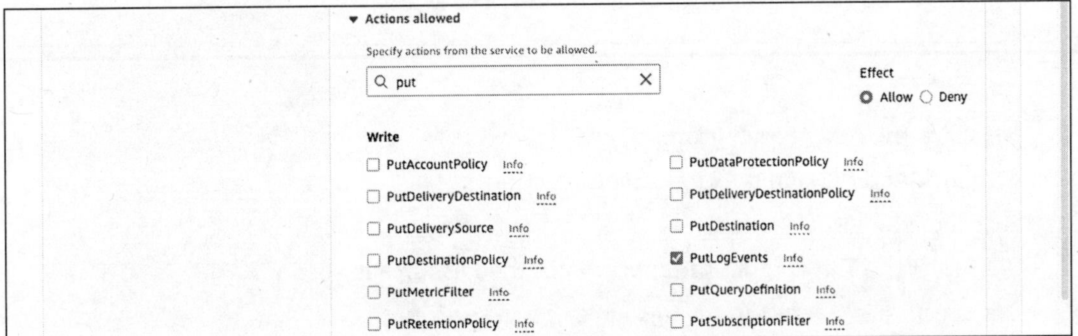

Figure 6.2: Specifying permissions

11. Select the **Specific** radio button in the **Resources** section.
12. Click **Add ARNs** in the **log-group** section.
13. Click the **Visual** button.
14. Select the **This account** radio button in the **Resource in** section.
15. Specify **us-east-1** in the **Resource region** section.
16. Specify **/aws/lambda/get-chapters** in the **Resource log group name** section.

Note: CloudWatch log groups names follow the `/aws/lambda/{functionName}` naming convention.

17. Observe **`arn:aws:logs:us-east-1:{accountId}:log-group:/aws/lambda/get-chapters`** is in the **Resource ARN** field.

Note: The account ID will be different for your AWS account.

See *Figure 6.3*:

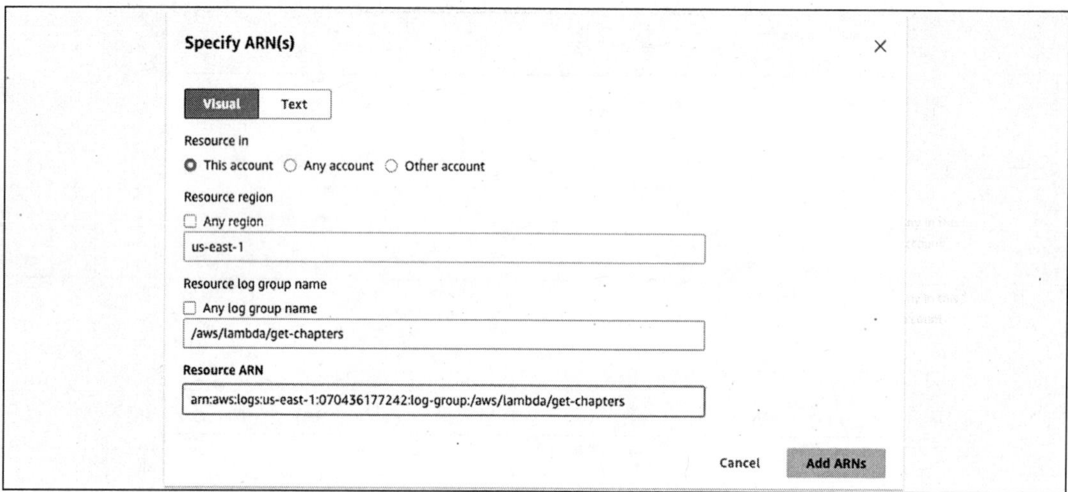

***Figure 6.3:** Specifying ARNs*

18. Click the **Add ARNs** button.
19. Click **Add ARNs** in the **`log-stream`** section.
20. Click the **Visual** button.
21. Select the **This account** radio button in the **Resource in** section.
22. Specify **`us-east-1`** in the **Resource region** section.
23. Specify **`/aws/lambda/get-chapters`** in the **Resource log group name** section.
24. Check the **Any log stream name** in the **Resource log stream name** section.
25. Observe that **`arn:aws:logs:us-east-1:{accountId}:log-group:/aws/lambda/get-chapters:log-stream:*`** is in the **Resource ARN** field. See *Figure 6.4* for your reference:

Note: The account ID will be different for your AWS account.

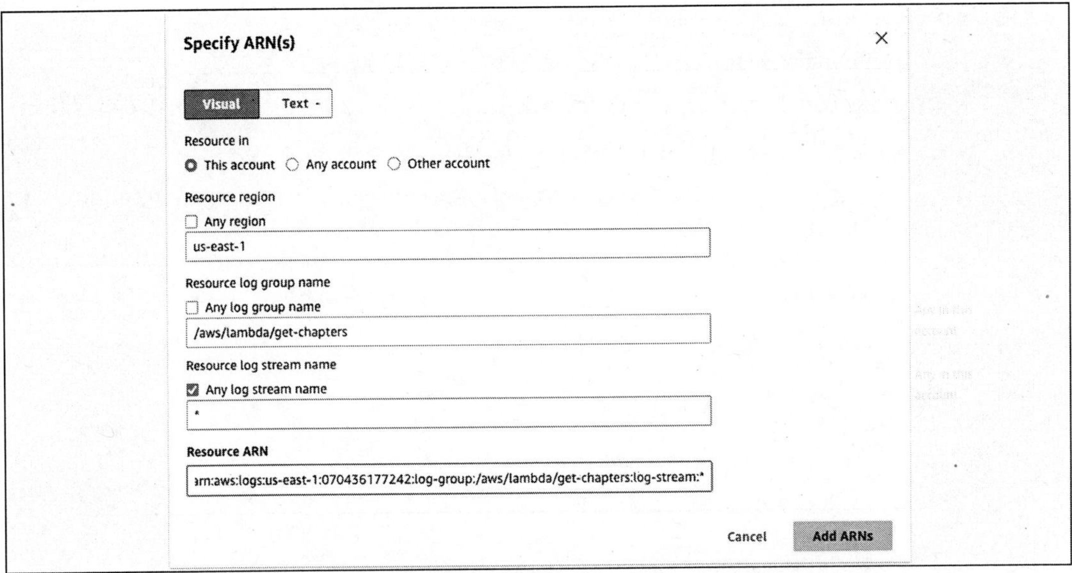

Figure 6.4: Specifying ARNs

26. Click the **Add ARNs** button.
27. Click the **Add more permissions** button. See *Figure 6.5*:

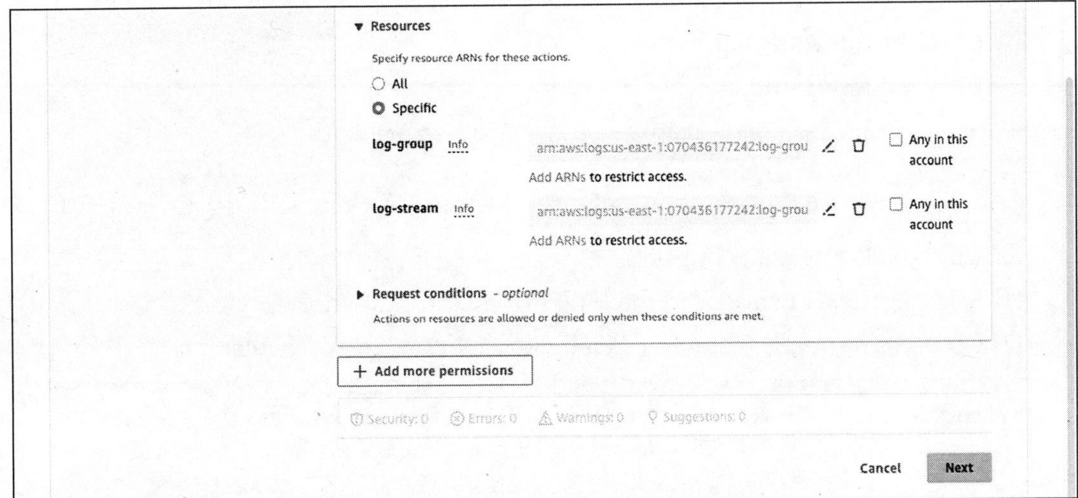

Figure 6.5: Specifying permissions

28. Select **S3** in the **Choose a service** dropdown.
29. Search **`object`** in the **Filter Actions** search field.
30. Check the **GetObject** checkbox in the **Read** section.
31. Select the **Specific** radio button in the **Resources** section.

32. Click **Add ARNs** in the `object` section.
33. Click the **Visual** button.
34. Specify `masteringawsserverlessbook-data` in the **Resource bucket name** section.
35. Specify `chapters.json` in the **Resource object name** section.
36. Observe that `arn:aws:s3:::masteringawsserverlessbook-data/chapters.json` is in the **Resource ARN** field. See *Figure 6.6*:

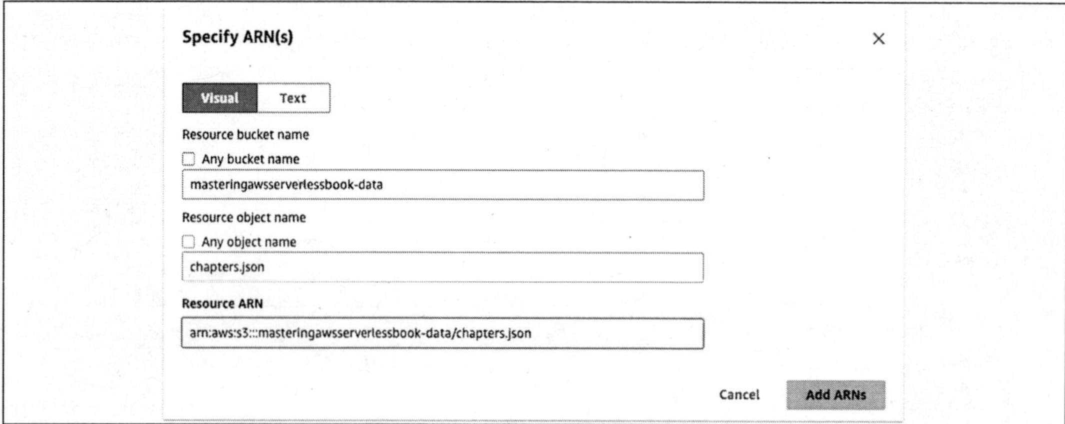

Figure 6.6: *Specifying permissions*

37. Click the **Add ARNs** button.
38. Click the **Next** button.
39. Specify `function-get-chapters` in the **Policy name** field.

Note: The name was chosen to help identify the resource that will use the policy.

40. Click the **Create policy** button.
41. Select **Customer managed** in the **Filter by Type** dropdown.
42. Observe the policy that was created. See *Figure 6.7* for your reference:

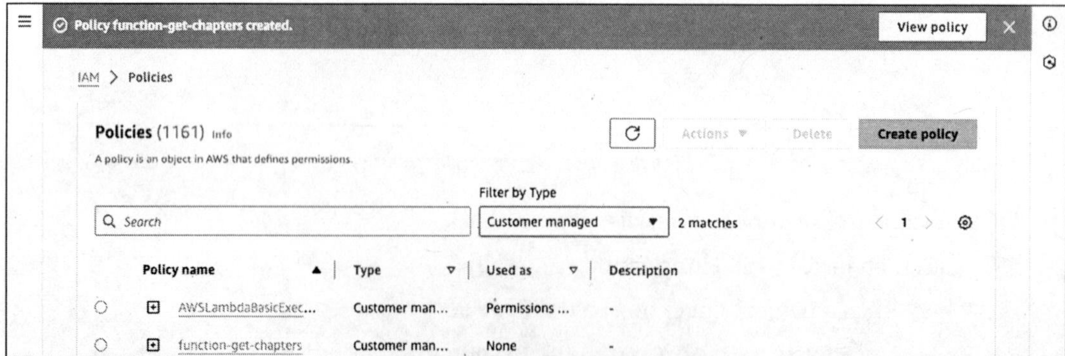

Figure 6.7: *The customer-managed IAM policies*

We have successfully created an IAM policy. Later in the book, we will use the **AWSLambdaBasicExecutionRole** AWS-managed policy to assign the CloudWatch permissions we assigned. We went through this exercise to bring awareness of the necessary permissions to help you master AWS serverless.

Creating an IAM role

We will now create a new IAM role. We could update the automatically created IAM role, but knowing how to create a role is a good exercise. We will create a new IAM role that uses our new IAM policy.

Hands-on exercise 3: Creating an IAM role

Let us create an IAM role:

1. Go to the IAM service page.
2. Expand the **Access management** menu option in the IAM menu option.
3. Select the **Roles** menu option.
4. Click the **Create role** button.
5. Select the **AWS service** radio button in the **Trusted entity type** section.
6. Select **Lambda** in the **Service or use case** dropdown.
7. Select the **Lambda** radio button. See *Figure 6.8*:

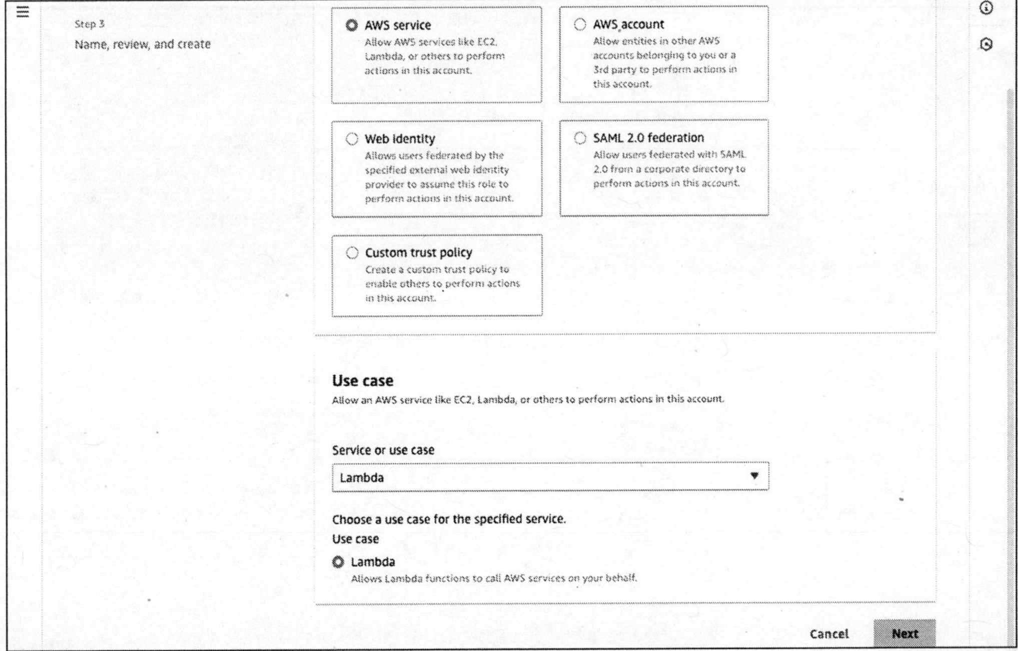

***Figure 6.8:** Selecting the trusted entity*

8. Click the **Next** button.
9. Search **`get-chapters`** in the search field.
10. Check the **`function-get-chapters`** policy. See *Figure 6.9*:

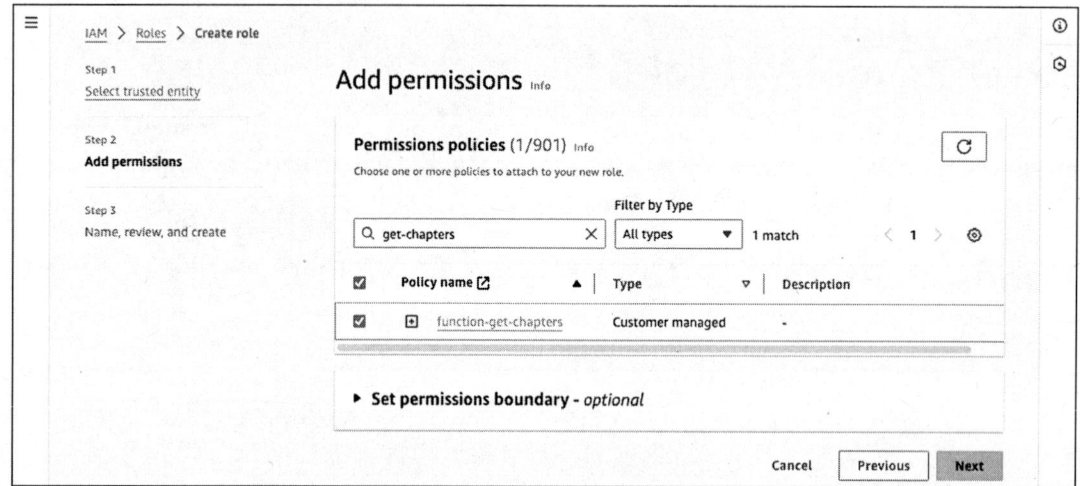

Figure 6.9: *Selecting permissions policies*

11. Click the **Next** button.
12. Specify **`function-get-chapters`** in the **Role name** field.

Note: The name was chosen to help identify the resource that will use the role.

13. Click the **Create role** button.
14. Observe the role was created. See *Figure 6.10*:

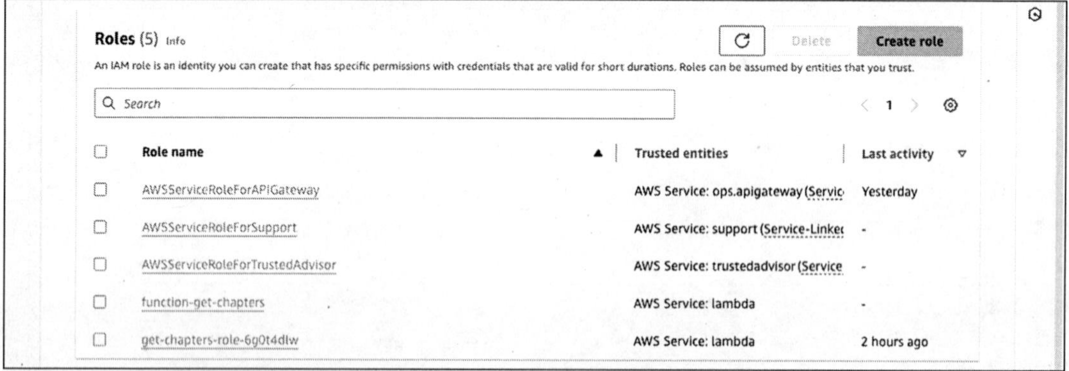

Figure 6.10: *The IAM roles*

We have successfully created a new role.

Updating the Lambda function settings

We are going to change the IAM role to get the data from the S3 bucket object. We will update the configuration to increase the memory since it will need to run more code. We will also update the timeout since it takes longer to get the data from the bucket.

Hands-on exercise 4: Updating the Lambda function settings

Let us update the Lambda function settings:

1. Go to the Lambda service page.
2. Go to the **`get-chapters`** function.
3. Select the **Configuration** tab.
4. Select the **Permission** tab.
5. Click the **Edit** button. See *Figure 6.11*:

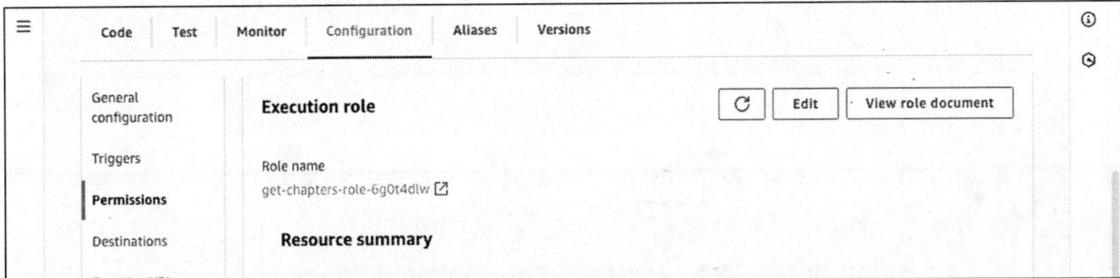

Figure 6.11: *The execution role*

6. Specify **`1024`** in the **Memory** field.
7. Specify **`0`** in the **min** field under the **Timeout** section.
8. Specify **5** in the **sec** field under the **Timeout** section.
9. Select **`function-get-chapters`** in the **Existing role** dropdown. See *Figure 6.12*:

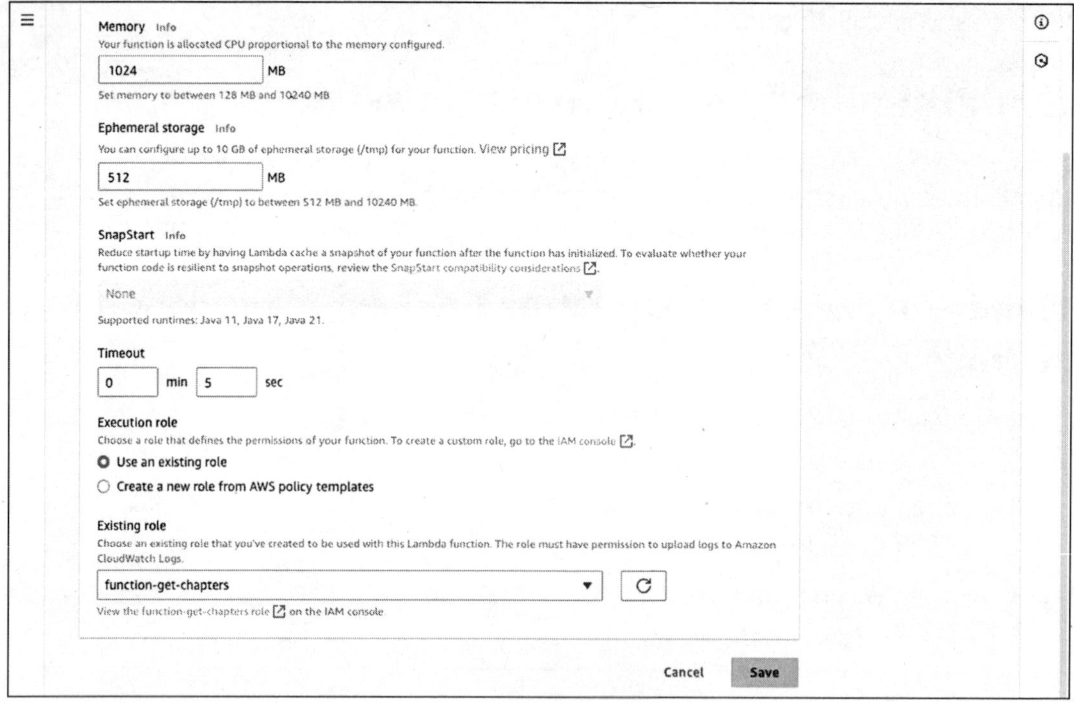

Figure 6.12: The function settings

10. Click the **Save** button.
11. Observe the **General configuration** tab has the updated settings.
12. Observe the **Permissions** tab has the updated settings.
13. Visit **https://masteringawsserverlessbook.com/chapters.html.**
14. Observe three chapters loaded on the page.

We have successfully updated the function settings.

Updating the Lambda function code

We are going to update the function code. We will use the AWS JavaScript SDK version 3[1] to get the object data from the bucket. We will return the contents of the file in the response. If something goes wrong, we will return an HTTP error status code.

Hands-on exercise 5: Updating the Lambda function code

Let us update the Lambda function code to get data from an S3 bucket:

1. Go to the Lambda service page.

1 "GetObjectCommand." AWS SDK for JavaScript v3. Amazon Web Services. **https://docs.aws.amazon.com/AWSJavaScriptSDK/v3/latest/client/s3/command/GetObjectCommand/**

2. Go to the **get-chapters** function.
3. Select the **Code** tab.
4. Paste the following code.

```
import { S3Client, GetObjectCommand } from "@aws-sdk/client-s3";
export const handler = async (event) => {
  const response = {
    statusCode: 500,
    headers: {
      'Access-Control-Allow-Origin': '*',
      'Content-Type': 'application/json',
    },
    body: JSON.stringify([]),
  };
  try {
    const s3Client = new S3Client({ region: 'us-east-1' });
    const s3Command = new GetObjectCommand({
      Bucket: 'masteringawsserverlessbook-data',
      Key: 'chapters.json',
    });
    const s3Response = await s3Client.send(s3Command);
    const objectData = await s3Response.Body.transformToString();
    response.statusCode = 200;
    response.body = objectData;
  } catch (e) {
    console.error(e);
  }
  return response;
};
```

5. Click the **Deploy** button.
6. Visit **https://masteringawsserverlessbook.com/chapters.html.**
7. Observe four chapters loaded on the page.

We have successfully updated the function code to get the data from the bucket object.

Creating a DynamoDB table

We are going to create a DynamoDB table for our chapter data. We will choose on-demand capacity instead of provisioned capacity. Our website traffic will most likely be idle the majority of the time. We will start with on-demand capacity to start.

Hands-on exercise 6: Creating a DynamoDB table

Let us create a DynamoDB table.

1. Search for **dynamodb** in the top search bar and select the **DynamoDB** service or enter **https://us-east-1.console.aws.amazon.com/dynamodbv2/home** in the browser address bar.
2. Go to the **Tables** menu option in the left pane.
3. Click the **Create table** button.
4. Specify **`chapters`** in the **Table name** field.
5. Specify **`id`** in the **Partition key** field.
6. Select **Number** in the dropdown for the **Partition key** section.
7. Specify **`title`** in the **Sort key** field.
8. Select **String** in the dropdown for the **Sort key** section. See *Figure 6.13* for your reference:

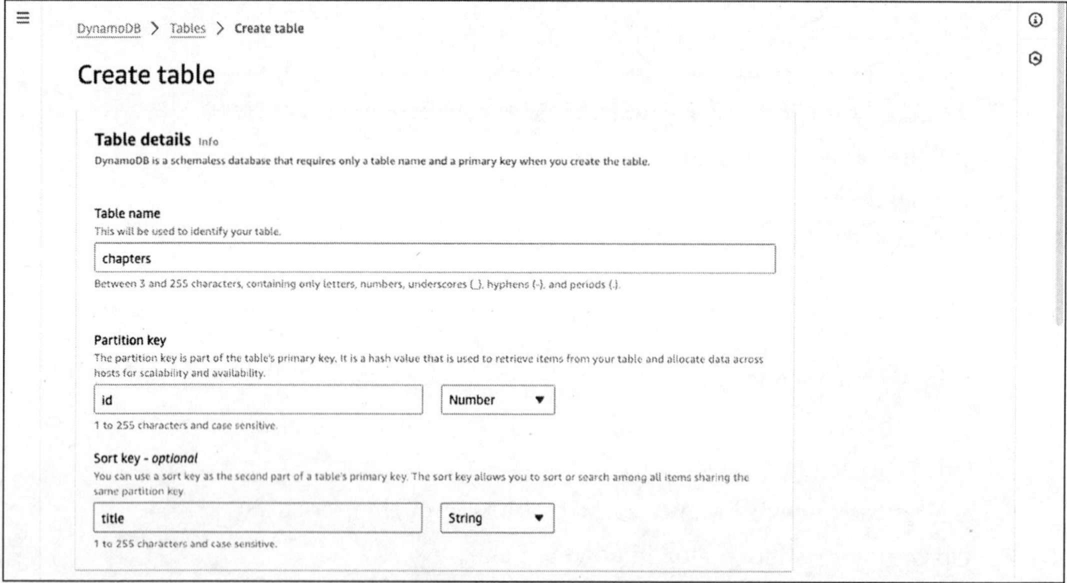

Figure 6.13: The table details

9. Select the **Customize settings** radio button in the **Table settings** section.

10. Select the **DynamoDB Standard** radio button in the **Table class** section.
11. Select the **On-demand** radio button in the **Capacity mode** section. See *Figure 6.14*:

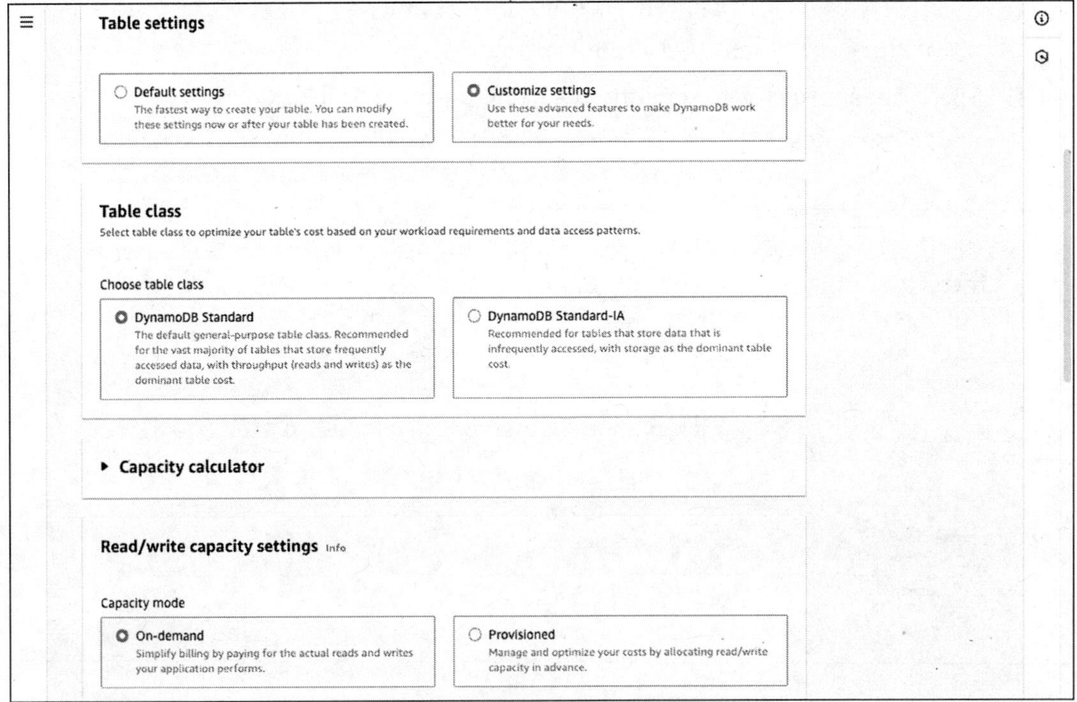

Figure 6.14: The table settings

12. Click the **Create table** button.
13. Observe that the table was created.

Note: It may take several minutes for the table to be created.

See *Figure 6.15*:

Figure 6.15: The tables

14. Click the table.

15. Select **Create item** in the **Actions** dropdown.
16. Specify `1` in the **Value** column for the **id** row.
17. Specify `Chapter 1` in the **Value** column for the **title** row.
18. Select **String** in the **Add new attribute** dropdown.
19. Specify `description` in the **Attribute name** column for the new row.
20. Specify `The description for chapter 1` in **Value** column for the new row. See *Figure 6.16*:

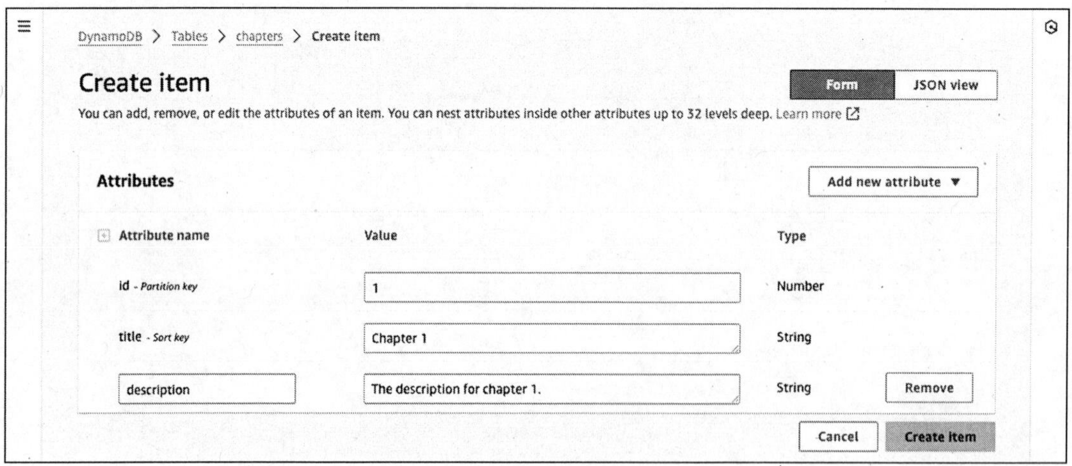

***Figure 6.16:** Creating a new item*

21. Click the **Create item** button.
22. Observe that the item was created.

We have successfully created the DynamoDB table.

Getting the table data from a Lambda function

We will update our Lambda function to get the table data. There will be multiple aspects to updating our function.

Updating the IAM policy

We need to update our IAM policy to remove the permission to get bucket objects from and add the permission to scan the table. Querying a table is typically better than scanning the entire table, but the number of entries is extremely small in this case.

Hands-on exercise 7: Updating the IAM policy

Let us update the IAM policy:

1. Go to the IAM service page.
2. Go to the **Policies** page.
3. Select the `function-get-chapters` policy.
4. Click the **Edit** button.
5. Click the **Visual** button.
6. Delete the **S3** action.
7. Click the **Add more permissions** button.
8. Select **DynamoDB** in the **Choose a service** dropdown.
9. Search `scan` in the **Filter Actions** search field.
10. Check the **Scan** checkbox in the **Read** section.
11. Select the **Specific** radio button in the **Resources** section.
12. Click **Add ARNs** in the **index** section.
13. Click the **Visual** button.
14. Select the **This account** radio button in the **Resource in** section.
15. Specify `us-east-1` in the **Resource region** section.
16. Specify `chapters` in the **Resource table name** section.
17. Check the **Any index name** checkbox in the **Resource index name** section.
18. Observe that `arn:aws:dynamodb:us-east-1:{accountId}:table/chapters/index/*` is in the **Resource ARN** field.

Note: The account ID will be different for your AWS account.

19. Click the **Add ARNs** button.
20. Click **Add ARNs** in the **table** section.
21. Click the **Visual** button.
22. Select the **This account** radio button in the **Resource in** section.
23. Specify `us-east-1` in the **Resource region** section.
24. Specify `chapters` in the **Resource table name** section.
25. Observe `arn:aws:dynamodb:us-east-1:{accountId}:table/chapters` in the **Resource ARN** field.

Note: The account ID will be different for your AWS account.

26. Click the **Add ARNs** button.

27. Click the **Next** button.
28. Click the **Save changes** button.

We have successfully updated the IAM policy.

Updating the Lambda function code

We are going to update the function code. We will use the AWS JavaScript SDK version 3[2] to get the data from the table. We will return the contents of the file in the response. If something goes wrong, we will return an HTTP error status code.

We will use the document client with the DynamoDB client. This library converts the DynamoDB items into the JSON format we are using in our application.

Hands-on exercise 8: Updating the Lambda function code

Let us update the Lambda function code to get data from a DynamoDB table, as follows:

1. Go to the Lambda service page.
2. Go to the **get-chapters** function.
3. Select the **Code** tab.
4. Paste the following code:

```
import { DynamoDBClient } from "@aws-sdk/client-dynamodb";
import { DynamoDBDocument, ScanCommand } from "@aws-sdk/lib-dynamodb";
export const handler = async (event) => {
  const response = {
    statusCode: 500,
    headers: {
      'Access-Control-Allow-Origin': '*',
      'Content-Type': 'application/json',
    },
    body: JSON.stringify([]),
  };
  try {
    const ddbClient = new DynamoDBClient({ region: 'us-east-1' });
    const ddbDocClient = DynamoDBDocument.from(ddbClient);
```

2 "ScanCommand." AWS SDK for JavaScript v3. Amazon Web Services. **https://docs.aws.amazon.com/AWSJavaScriptSDK/v3/latest/Package/-aws-sdk-lib-dynamodb/Class/ScanCommand/**

```
      const ddbCommand = new ScanCommand({
        TableName: 'chapters',
      });
      const ddbResponse = await ddbDocClient.send(ddbCommand);
      response.statusCode = 200;
      response.body = JSON.stringify(ddbResponse.Items);
    } catch (e) {
      console.error(e);
    }
    return response;
  };
```

5. Click the **Deploy** button.
6. Visit **https://masteringawsserverlessbook.com/chapters.html.**
7. Observe one chapter loads on the page.

We have successfully updated the function code to get the data from the bucket object.

Clean up

There are some items we need to clean up. We will add a robots.txt file to tell search engines not to crawl our website. We also want to delete the automatically created IAM role for our function. It is a good practice to remove unused resources whenever we make changes.

Adding a robots.txt file

We will include a robots.txt file on our website to tell search engines not to crawl. This will reduce the risk of getting an expensive bill. Later, we will need to update the robots.txt file if we want our website to be found by search engines.

Hands-on exercise 9: Adding a robots.txt file

Let us add a robots file to our S3 bucket using the given steps:

1. Go to the S3 service page.
2. Click the `masteringawsserverlessbook.com` bucket.
3. Create a `robots.txt` file on our computer.
4. Paste the following text into the file:

```
User-agent: *
Disallow: /
```

5. Upload the file into the bucket.
6. Observe the **robots.txt** object was created.
7. Visit **https://masteringawsserverlessbook.com/robots.txt**.
8. Observe that the text above is displayed.

We have successfully created the **robots.txt** object.

Cleaning up IAM

We will delete the automatically created role and policy for the **get-chapters** function since we no longer need them.

Hands-on exercise 10: Deleting the old IAM policy and role

Let us delete the unused IAM role and policy:

1. Go to the IAM service page.
2. Select the **Roles** menu option in the left pane.
3. Check the **get-chapters-role** role.
4. Click the **Delete** button.
5. Follow the on-screen instructions to delete the role.
6. Observe the role was deleted.
7. Select the **Policies** menu option in the left pane.
8. Select **Customer managed** in the **Filter by Type** field.
9. Select the **AWSLambdaBasicExecutionRole** policy.

Note: There is also an AWS-managed policy with the same name which we cannot delete.

10. Click the **Delete** button.
11. Follow the on-screen instructions to delete the policy.
12. Observe that the policy was deleted.

We have successfully deleted the unused role.

Conclusion

In this chapter, we created a new S3 bucket and DynamoDB table for our website data. Both contain the chapter data we coded into the initial version of our Lambda function. We created a new IAM policy and role for the function. We first updated the policy to give permission to get the S3 bucket object and updated the function code to get the data from the object. We then updated the policy, gave permission to scan the DynamoDB table, removed the S3 bucket permissions, and updated the function code to get the data from the database. We concluded with some clean up.

Points to remember

- Storing data in an S3 bucket is best when data is processed offline. Speed is not a factor, and lower costs are preferred. We typically would avoid retrieving data from an S3 bucket for a Lambda function triggered by an API.
- Storing data in a DynamoDB table is best when speed is a factor, such as the website requesting data using an API. DynamoDB table storage costs are typically higher than S3 bucket storage costs and we would typically avoid storing large objects, such as images, in a table.
- The IAM policy and role should limit the permissions based on what the function needs to do. We created an IAM policy that limited the Lambda function permissions to creating a log group, creating a log stream, writing to a log stream, and accessing the data from a specific S3 bucket or DynamoDB table.
- If we find our Lambda function cannot write logs to CloudWatch, we might have a misconfiguration in our Lambda policy.
- If we find our Lambda function cannot read the data from the S3 bucket object or a DynamoDB table, we might have a misconfiguration in our Lambda policy.

Multiple choice questions

1. **Should the Dynamo on-demand capacity be avoided since the read-and-write transaction costs are more expensive?**

    a. Yes

    b. No

    Answer: b

    No. On-demand might be more cost-effective when the read/write operations are not consistent and unpredictable.

2. **It is better to let the AWS management console create the IAM role and policy:**

    a. True

    b. False

    Answer: b

    False. The automatically generated names might become confusing if they are named with unique IDs instead of logical names. Furthermore, the policy will need to be updated to give the function permissions to the AWS services it needs to use.

Join our book's Discord space

Join the book's Discord Workspace for Latest updates, Offers, Tech happenings around the world, New Release and Sessions with the Authors:

https://discord.bpbonline.com

CHAPTER 7

Adding Authentication and Authorization

Introduction

This chapter will demonstrate how a website could add authentication and authorization to restrict certain pages to logged-in users. We will conduct hands-on exercises to add authentication and authorization using Amazon Cognito.

Structure

We will cover the following topics in this chapter:

- Overview of authentication and authorization
- Creating a new Cognito user pool
- Updating the website
- Testing the authentication
- Adding an authorized API endpoint

Objectives

By the end of this chapter, you will understand how to use an identity provider with Amazon Cognito to allow users to sign up and log in. The reader will also be able to restrict access to some web pages if a user is not logged in.

Overview of authentication and authorization

Authentication and authorization are two parts used in websites to allow users to sign in and access allowed data. Authentication consists of signing in and signing out of the website. Users typically experience authentication by using a login form where they enter a username and their password. Authorization consists of verifying that a user can perform certain actions. Users typically experience authorization by the menu options they see on the website. They would not see unauthorized menu options such as administrator functions. If they tried to access an administrator function, they would get an error message.

Let us review these concepts with an analogy. Suppose you want to enter a secure building protected by security guards. When we want to enter the building, the security guard will check our identification card. If the identification card is valid, the security guard will let us inside the building. This is authentication since we have verified who we claimed. We now have access to the front lobby. There are various doors for different purposes. Some doors are protected by a security guard. Let us assume that we are trying to enter the door of the administration office. The security guard checks our identification card. The identification is valid, but the security guard says, *You do not have the privilege to enter*. Our authentication passed, but the authorization failed. We did not have the proper authority to enter the administration office. Suppose we were an employee of that office. The security guard will have let us in because we have the authorization to enter. Suppose we tried to enter the door that goes to the cafeteria. There was no security guard at the door. This door does not require authorization. Hopefully, this analogy helps explain both concepts.

In our serverless website, we will implement authentication and authorization differently than a server-based website. We will use an identity provider to handle our authentication since we cannot protect the user account information on the website itself.

In a server-based website, we could implement local authentication. This would work since the server can be configured to hide any secret information by preventing it from being displayed in the HTML code. But out serverless website is all HTML code and all the S3 bucket objects are accessible on the Internet. We should not put any secret information on our website since it will be accessible by anyone on the Internet. Therefore, we will use an identity provider, such as Cognito, to keep our authentication safe.

We will use the Cognito service that will manage the user accounts and provide us with a way for users to authenticate. We will create a Cognito user pool with a hosted **User Interface** (**UI**) that our users will use to authenticate. This hosted UI is a website where our users can sign up and sign in. The hosted UI is configured to allow our website to use it. When a user logs in, the hosted UI will provide our website with authentication information. Our website will use authentication information to show or hide certain information. It will also store the authentication information in the browser's local storage.

We will use our API Gateway to authorize certain API calls. The API Gateway allows us to authorize request to API endpoints. We will use an authorization function that will validate that the authorization information is valid before the API will allow the API request to start. If the authorization information is invalid or expired, the API will return an error code.

We will create an authorizer that will use the authentication information and verify it with the user pool. AWS performs this inside their services and the user will not get any of the sensitive or secret information returned to them. The API Gateway authorizer function executes inside of AWS and makes a direct request to the Cognito user pool to verify the authorization information. Furthermore, the authentication information is transmitted securely using HTTPS and it has an expiration date built in. Since our serverless website is public, our serverless design must put greater importance on security. Therefore, we can use the authentication information securely since we are using HTTPS, API Gateway authorizers and using the Cognito user pool to validate the authorization information.

Furthermore, the Cognito user pool will provide us with two types of authentication information. One is an access token that is more focused on the access privileges that an authenticated user has. Another is an identity token that is more focused on the identity information of an authenticated user. Both tokens are formatted using the **JSON Web Token (JWT)** standard[1]. The Cognito user pool will sign the authorization information in the JWT so it can be used securely and only it can check whether the token is valid.

We will perform multiple hands-on exercises to step through the different authentication and authorization concepts we discussed.

Creating a new Cognito user pool

We will create a user pool. The user pool will take care of authentication. We will configure it to allow users to create a new account with their email address after they have verified it. For now, we will use the AWS-provided Cognito email address to send the email address. We will cover custom email messaging in a later chapter. We will enforce MFA with an authenticator to protect the account. We will not choose SMS for MFA since it will increase costs, and we will cover messaging in a later chapter. We will set up a custom subdomain and hosted UI that our website will use to redirect authentication requests. Our hosted UI will use authentication code grants and OpenID since the website is a static website, and we cannot safely protect any secrets.

Creating a new Cognito user pool

We will create our user pool.

1 The JWT standard is defined in RFC 7519. RFC 7519 is available at **https://datatracker.ietf.org/doc/html/rfc7519**

Hands-on exercise 1: Creating a new Cognito user pool

Let us create a Cognito user pool to be our identity provider.

1. Search for `cognito` in the top search bar and select the **Cognito** service or enter **https://us-east-1.console.aws.amazon.com/cognito/v2/idp/user-pools** in the browser address bar.
2. Click the **Create user pool** button.
3. Check the **Email** checkbox in the **Cognito user pool sign-in options** section.
4. Click the "**Next**" button. See *Figure 7.1*:

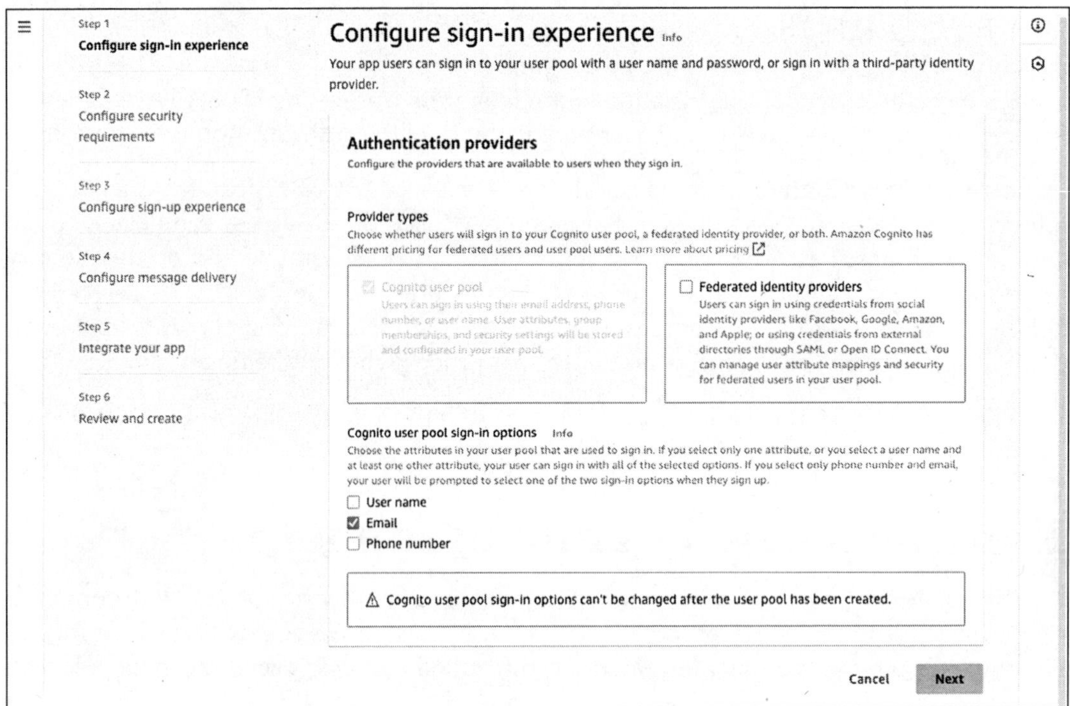

Figure 7.1: The Cognito user pool sign-in options

5. Select the **Cognito default** radio button in the **Password policy** section. See *Figure 7.2*:

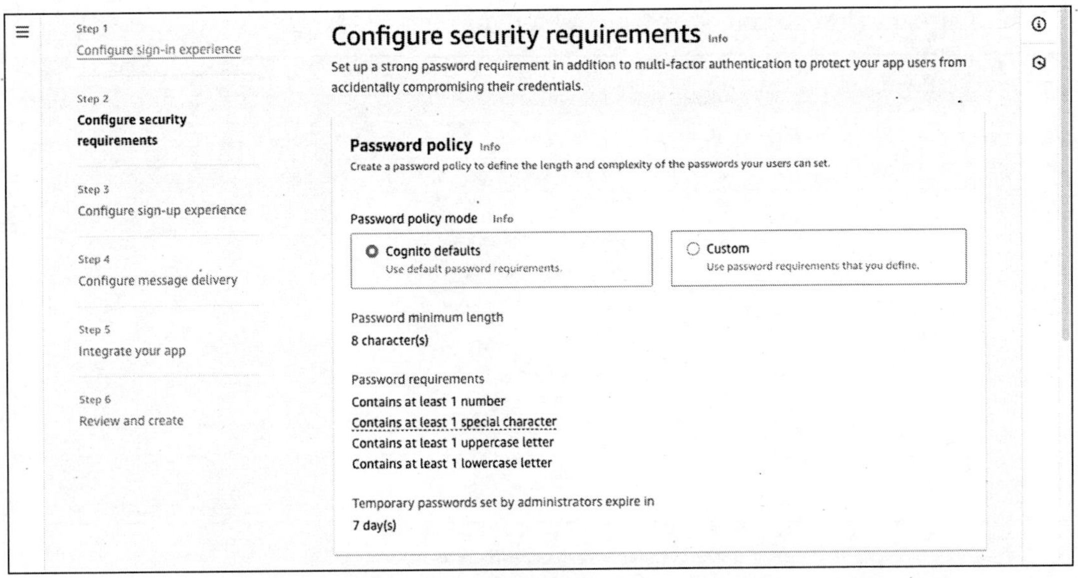

Figure 7.2: The password policy settings

6. Select the **Require MFA** radio button in the **MFA enforcement** section.
7. Check the **Authenticator apps** checkbox in the **MFA methods** section. See *Figure 7.3*:

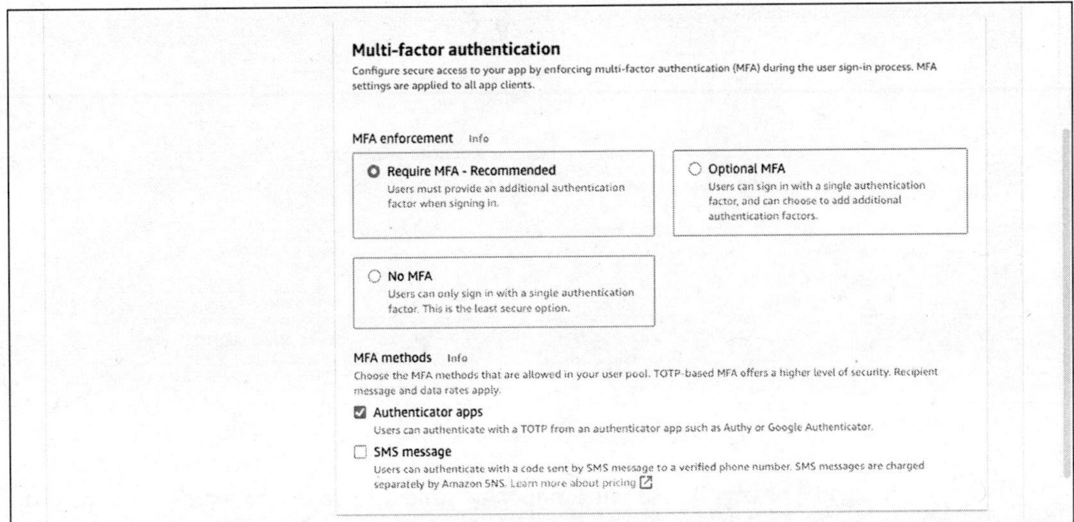

Figure 7.3: The multi-factor authentication settings

8. Check the **Enable self-service account recovery** checkbox in the **Self-service account recovery** section.
9. Select the **Email only** radio button in the **Delivery method for user account recovery messages** section.

10. Click the **Next** button. See *Figure 7.4* for your reference:

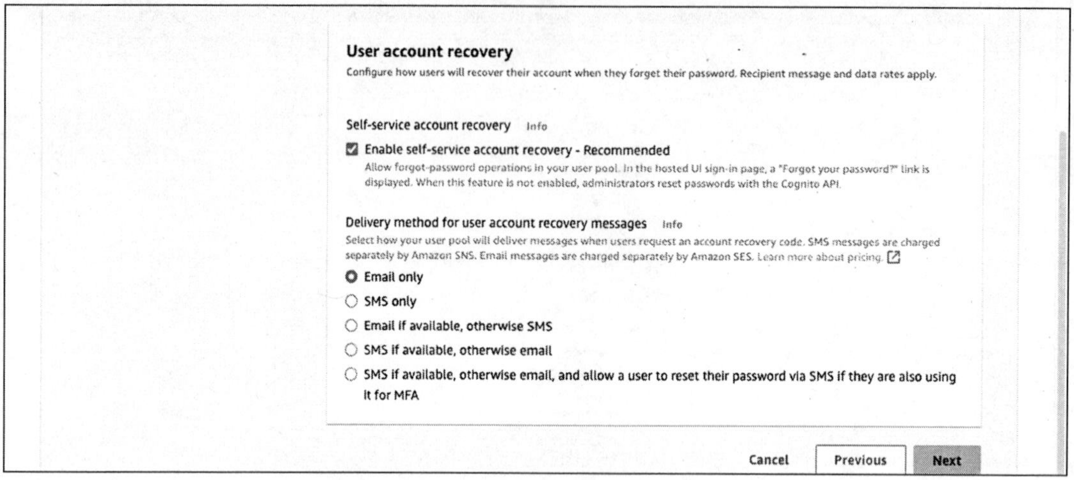

Figure 7.4: The user account recovery settings

11. Check the **Enable self-registration** checkbox in the **Self-registration** section. See *Figure 7.5*:

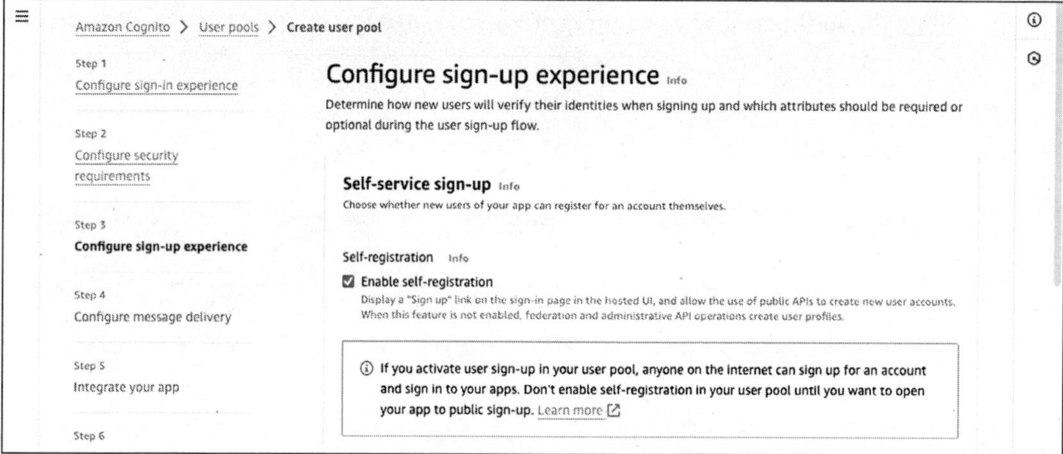

Figure 7.5: The self-service sign-up settings

12. Check the **Allow Cognito to automatically send messages to verify and confirm** checkbox in the **Cognito-assisted verification and confirmation** section.
13. Select the **Send email message, verify email address** radio button in the **Attributes to verify** section.
14. Check the **Keep original attribute value active when an update is pending** checkbox in the **Verify attribute changes** section.
15. Select the **Email address** radio button in the **Active attribute values when an update is pending** section. See *Figure 7.6*:

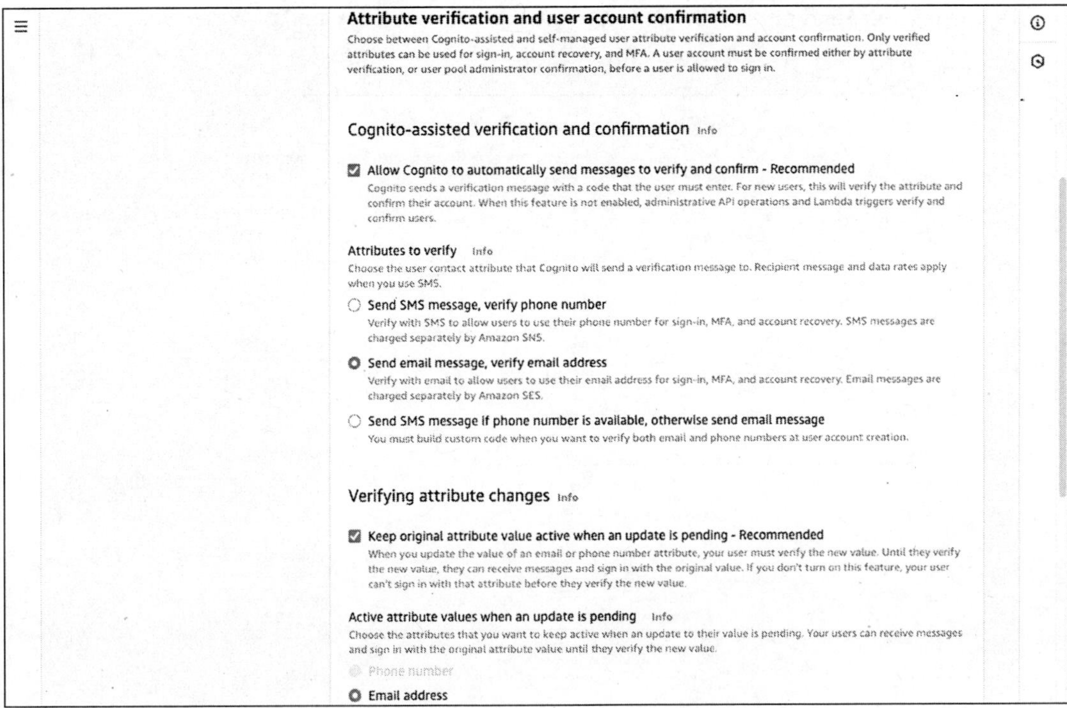

Figure 7.6: The attribute verification and user account confirmation settings

16. Select **`given_name`** in the **Additional required attributes** dropdown.
17. Skip the **Custom attributes** section.
18. Click the "**Next**" button. See *Figure 7.7*:

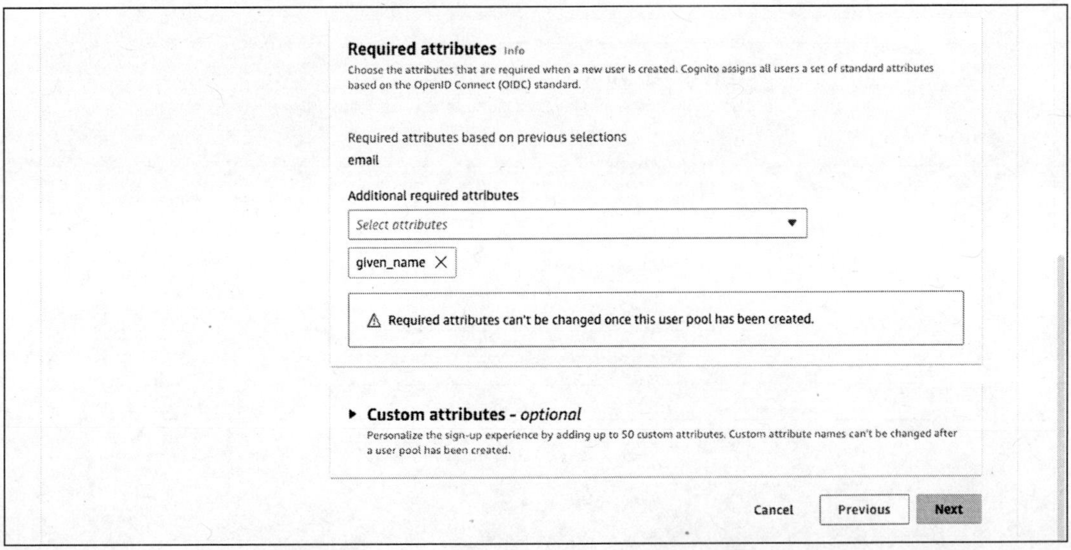

Required attributes Info

Choose the attributes that are required when a new user is created. Cognito assigns all users a set of standard attributes based on the OpenID Connect (OIDC) standard.

Required attributes based on previous selections

email

Additional required attributes

Select attributes

given_name ✕

⚠ Required attributes can't be changed once this user pool has been created.

▸ **Custom attributes** - *optional*

Personalize the sign-up experience by adding up to 50 custom attributes. Custom attribute names can't be changed after a user pool has been created.

Cancel | Previous | **Next**

Figure 7.7: The required attributes and custom attributes settings

19. Select the **Send email with Cognito** radio button in the **Email provider** section.
20. Click the **Next** button. See *Figure 7.8*:

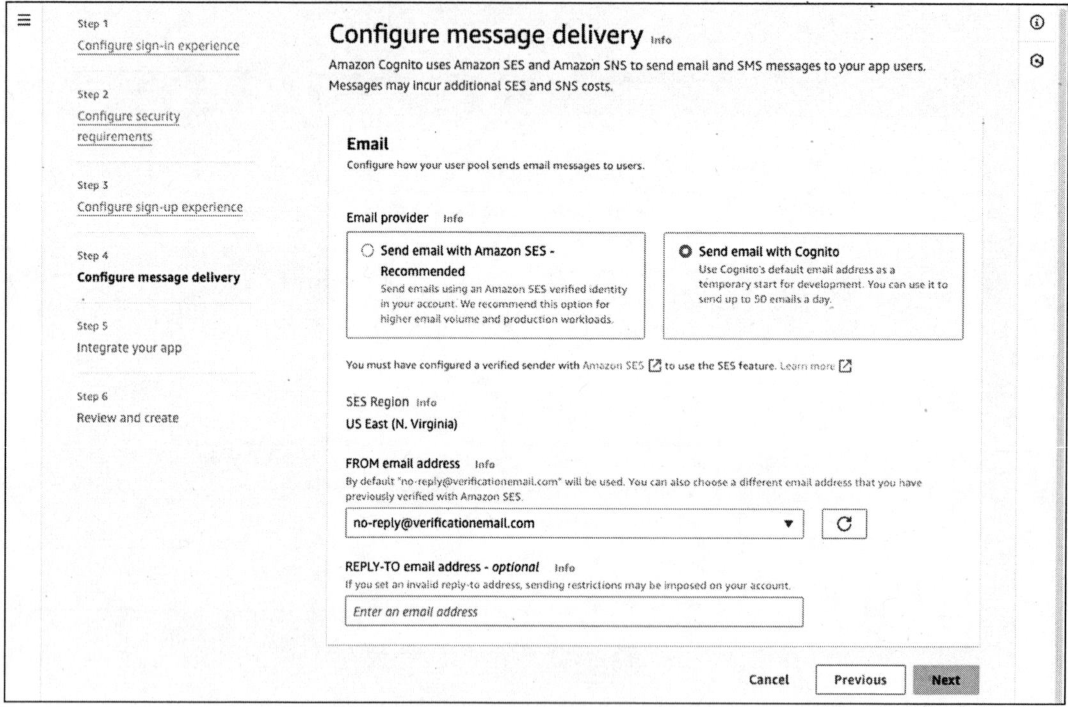

Figure 7.8: The email settings

21. Specify **`masteringawsserverlessbook.com`** in the **User pool name** field. See *Figure 7.9*:

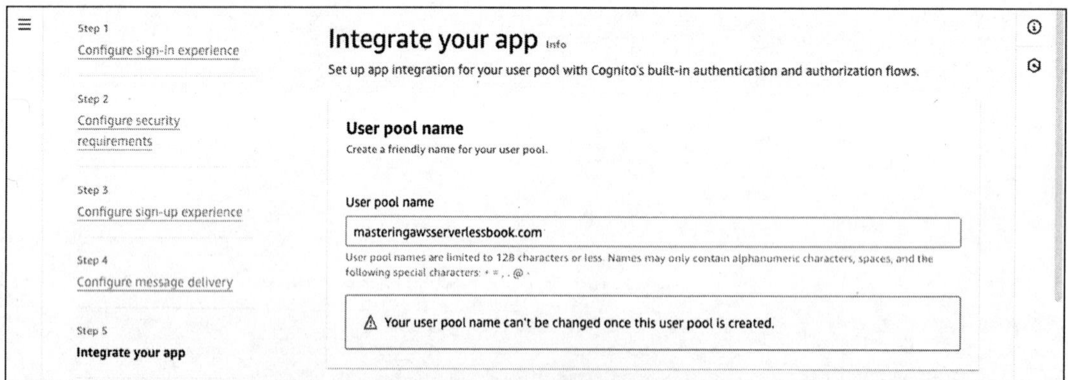

Figure 7.9: The user pool name

22. Check the **Use the Cognito Hosted UI** checkbox in the **Hosted authentication pages** section.
23. Select the **Use a custom domain** radio button in the **Domain type** section.
24. Specify `https://auth.masteringawsserverlessbook.com` in the **Custom domain** field.
25. Select the `masteringawsserverlessbook.com` certificate in the **ACM certificate** dropdown. See *Figure 7.10*:

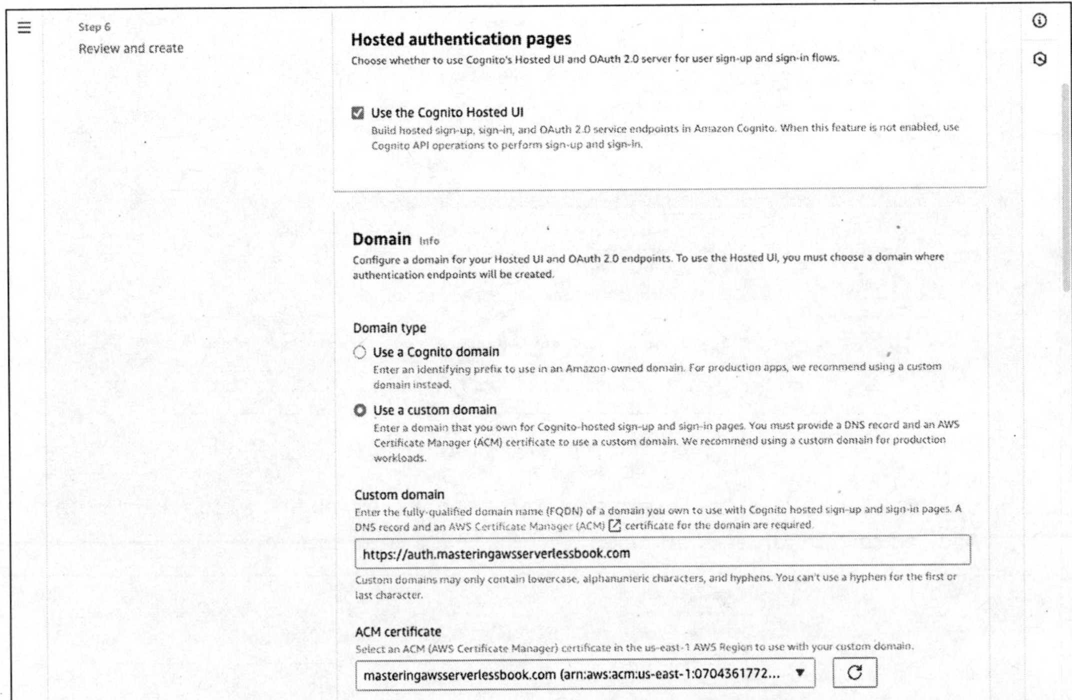

Figure 7.10: *The hosted authentication pages and domain settings*

26. Select the **Public type** radio button in the **App type** section.
27. Specify `masteringawsserverlessbook.com` in the **App client name** field.
28. Select the **Don't generate a client secret** radio button in the **Client secret** section. See *Figure 7.11*:

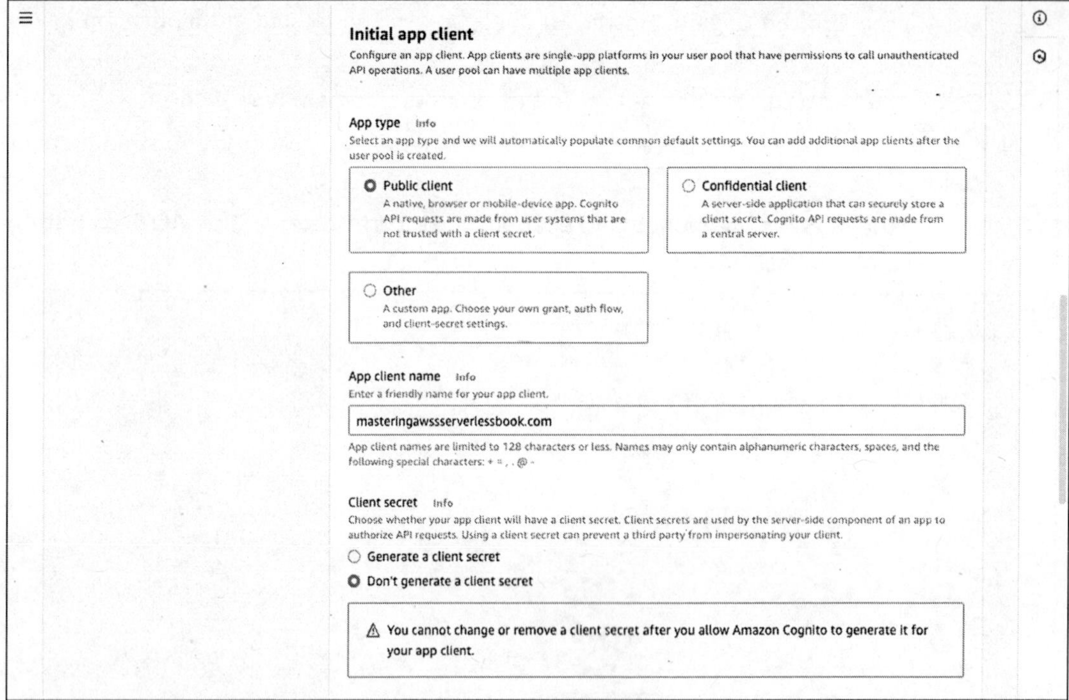

Figure 7.11: The initial app client settings

29. Specify **`https://masteringawsserverlessbook.com/auth-callback.html`** in the **Allowed callback URLs** section. See *Figure 7.12* for your reference:

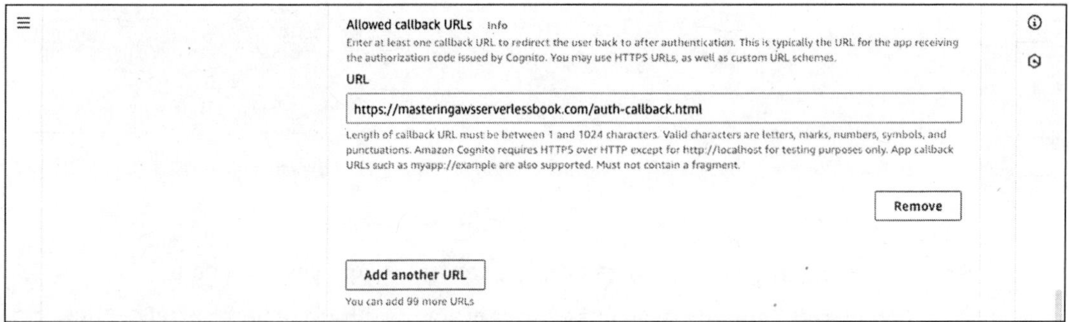

Figure 7.12: The allowed callback URLs

30. Expand the **Advanced app client settings** section.
31. Confirm that **`ALLOW_REFRESH_TOKEN_AUTH`** and **`ALLOW_USER_SRP_AUTH`** are the only selections in the **Authentication flows** sections. See *Figure 7.13*:

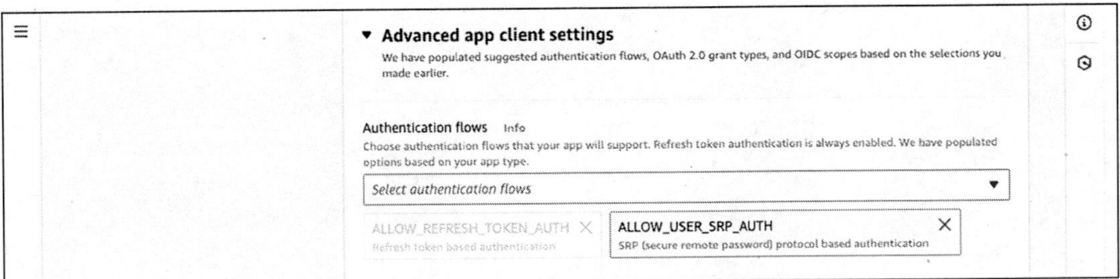

Figure 7.13: The authentication flow settings

32. Confirm that only **Cognito user pool** is selected in the **Identity providers** section.
33. Confirm that only **Authorization code grant** is selected in the **OAuth 2.0 grant types** section.
34. Select **OpenID**, **`aws.cognito.signin.user.admin`**, **Email** and **Profile** in the **OpenID Connect scopes** section. See *Figure 7.14*:

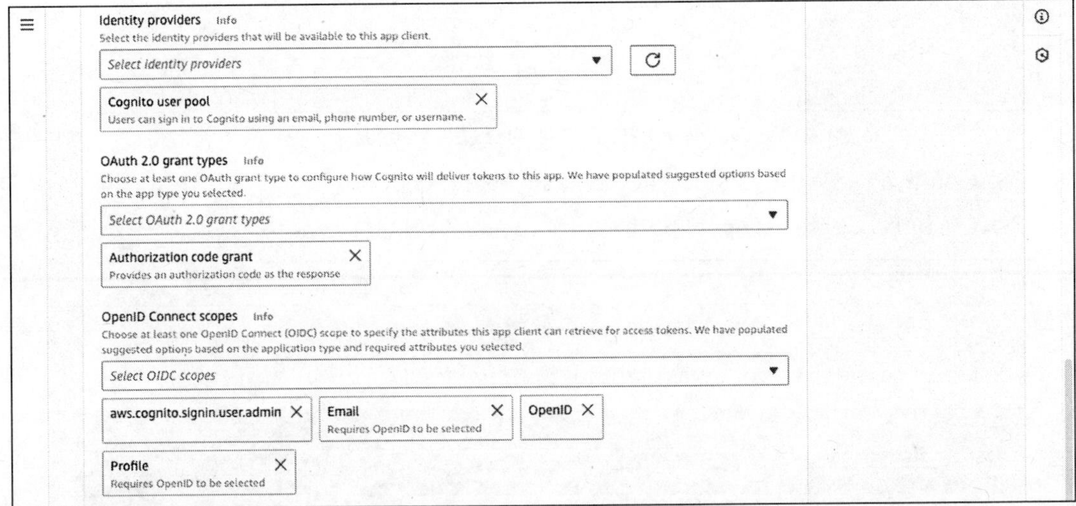

Figure 7.14: The identity providers, OAuth 2.0 grant types and OpenID Connect scopes settings

35. Specify **`https://masteringawsserverlessbook.com/logout.html`** in the **Allow sign-out URLs** section.
36. Skip the **Attribute read and write permissions** section.
37. Click the **Next** button. See *Figure 7.15*:

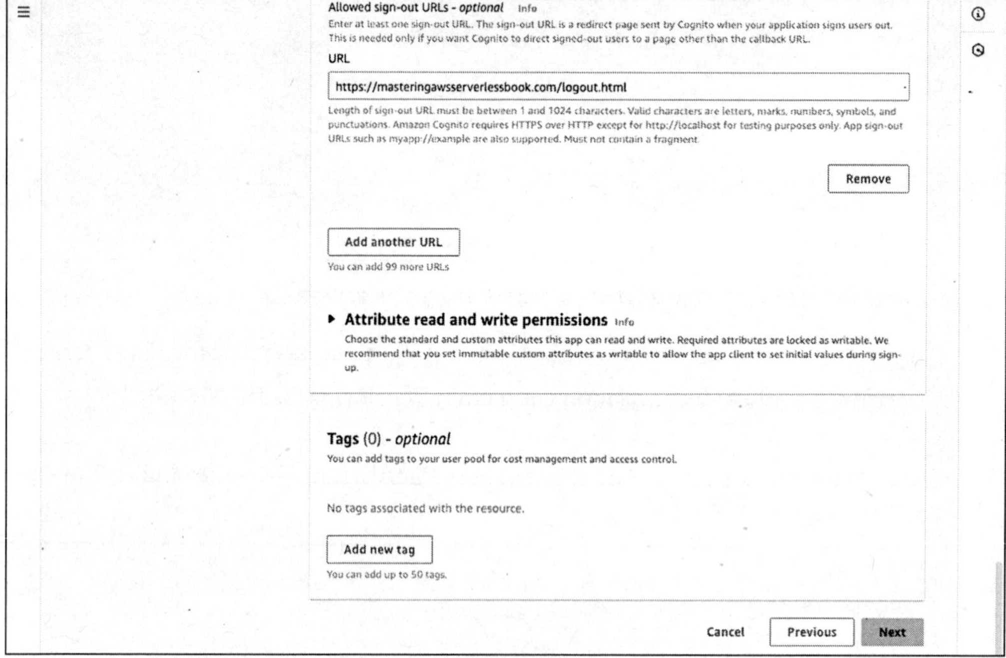

Figure 7.15: The sign-out URL settings

38. Confirm the settings in the **Review and create** section.
39. Click the **Create user pool** button. See *Figure 7.16*:

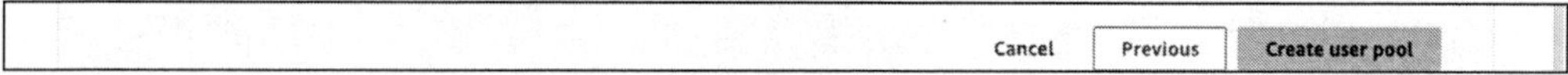

Figure 7.16: Creating the user pool

40. Observe the user pool was created. See *Figure 7.17*:

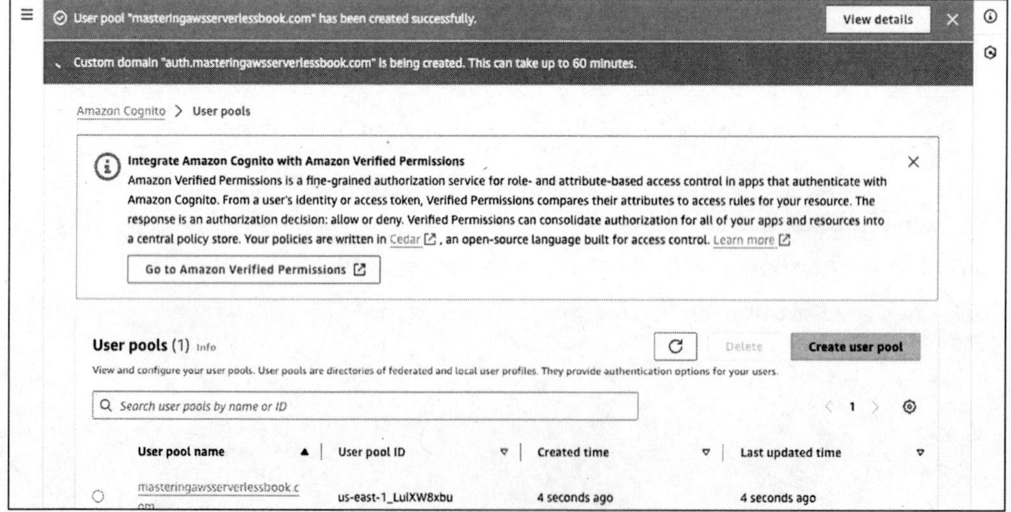

Figure 7.17: The user pools

We have successfully created the user pool.

Adding an alias in Route 53

We will create an alias record in our DNS to point to the custom user pool subdomain we created.

Hands-on exercise 2: Adding an alias in Route 53

Let us add an alias for the Cognito user pool:

1. Go to the **masteringawsserverlessbook.com** user pool.
2. Go to the **App integration** tab.
3. Copy the **cloudfront.net** domain name in the **Alias target** section. See *Figure 7.18*:

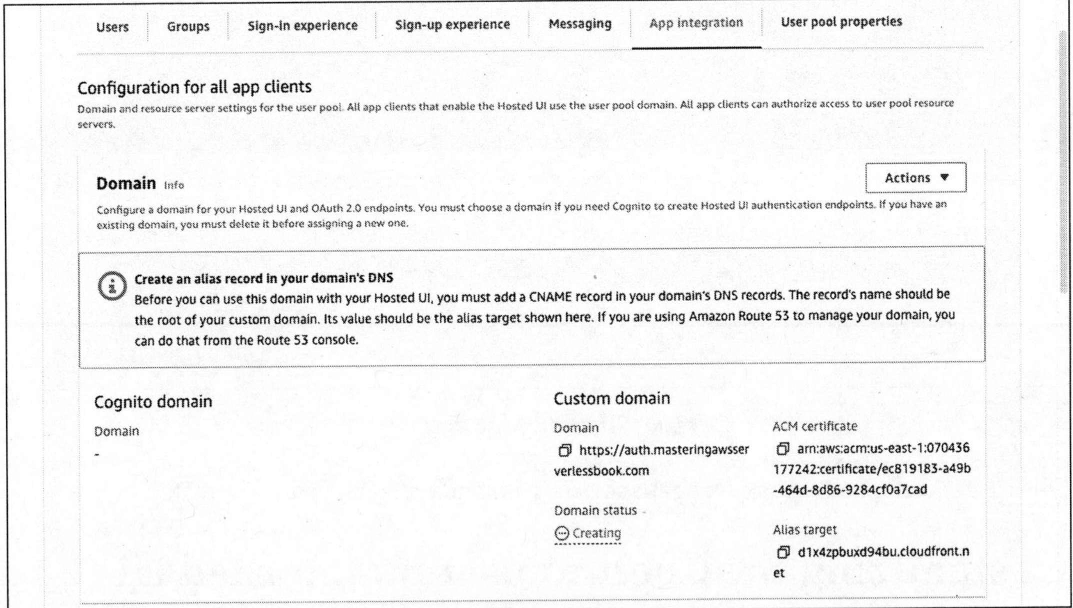

Figure 7.18: An example of the custom domain

4. Go to the Route 53 service page.
5. Go to the **masteringawsserverlessbook.com** hosted zone page.
6. Click the **Create record** button.
7. Specify **auth** in the **Record name** field.
8. Select **A** in the **Record type** dropdown.

9. Check the **Alias** switch button.
10. Select **Alias to Cloudfront distribution** in the **Choose endpoint** dropdown.
11. Specify the **`cloudfront.net`** domain name in the **Choose distribution** field.
12. Click the **Create records** button. See *Figure 7.19* for your reference:

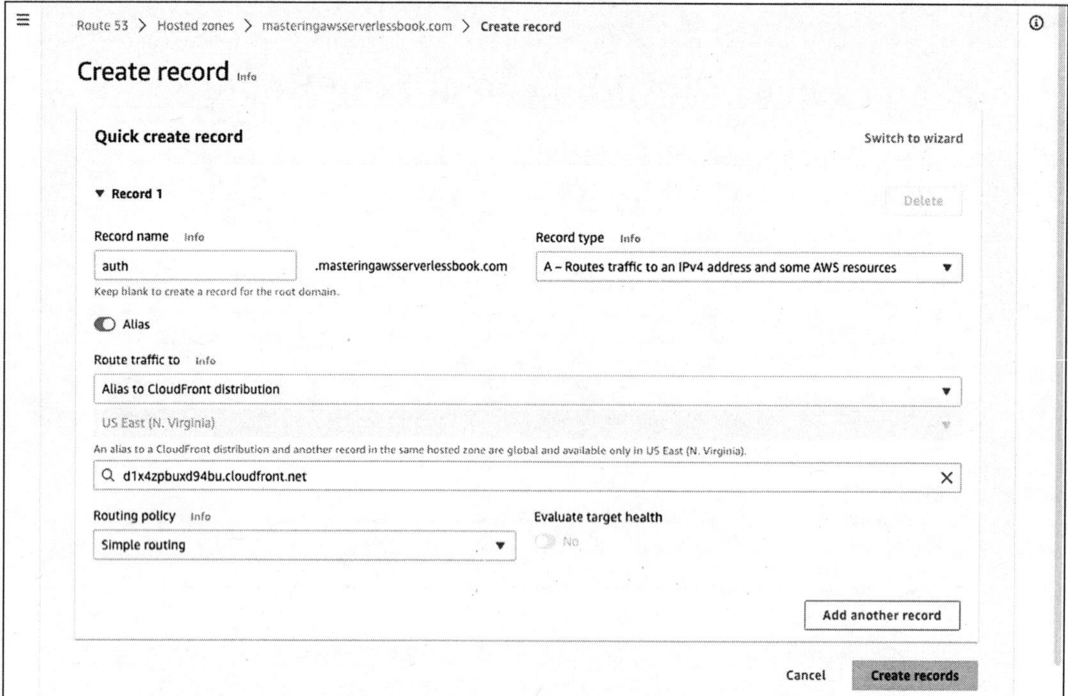

Figure 7.19: The Route 53 record

Observe that the **`auth.masteringawsserverlessbook.com`** record was created.

Customizing the Cognito user pool hosted UI

We will configure our user tool to use a hosted UI. We will upload a custom logo and a CSS file that updates the colors. We will obtain the CSS file from Cognito and modify the allowed CSS properties. We will also change the sign-up experience to send an email to verify the user's email address.

Hands-on exercise 3: Customizing the user pool hosted UI

Let us customize the user pool UI to match our website colors and logo:

1. Go to the **`masteringawsserverlessbook.com`** user pool.
2. Go to the **App integration** tab.
3. Go to the **Hosted UI customization** section.
4. Click the **Edit** button. See *Figure 7.20*:

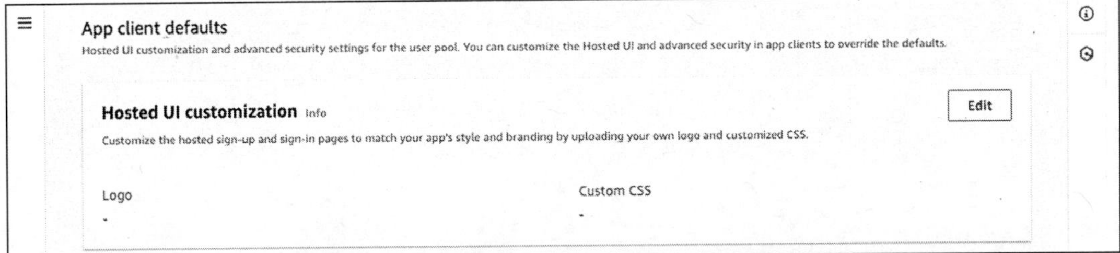

Figure 7.20: The hosted UI customization section

5. Take a screen capture of the title of the **`masteringawsserverlessbook.com`** website.

Note: Try to capture the image as close to the title text so the logo image looks as big as possible in the hosted UI.

6. Click the **Choose file** button in the **Upload a logo** button and select the image file.
7. Click the **`CSS template.css`** link in the **Upload CSS customization** section to download the CSS template file.
8. Open the file and change the CSS code for the **`banner-customizable`** class. See the following code:

```
.banner-customizable {
  padding: 25px 0px 25px 0px;
  background-color: #212529;
}
```

9. Click the **Choose file** button in the **Upload CSS customization** section and select the CSS file.
10. Click the **Save changes** button. See *Figure 7.21*:

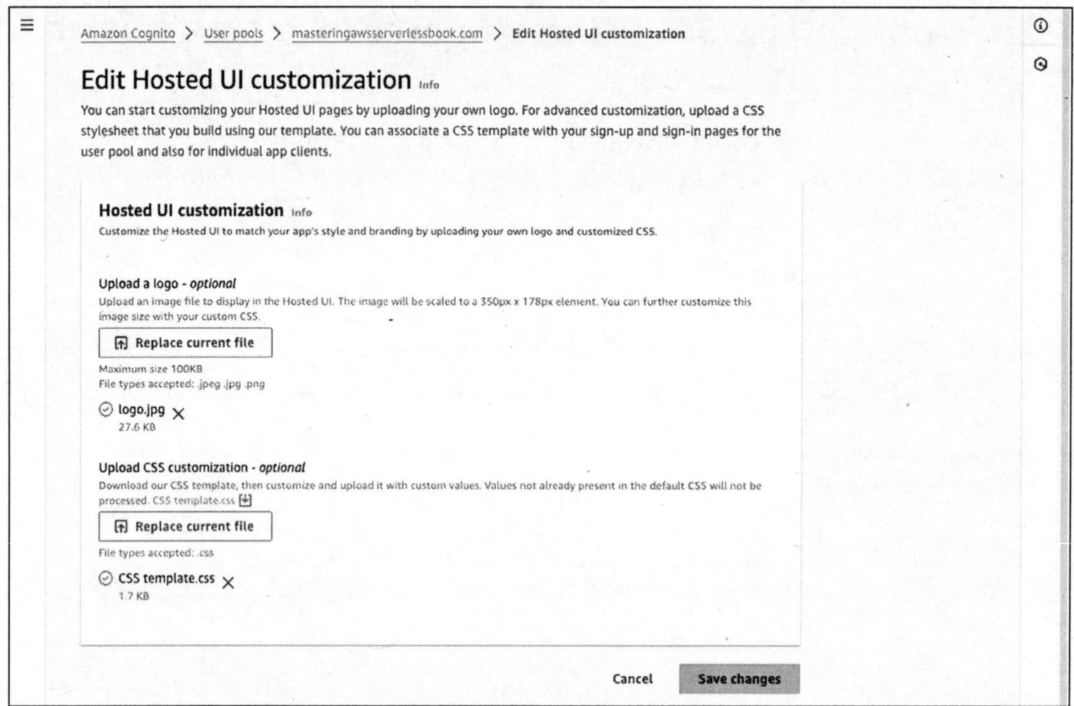

Figure 7.21: Editing the hosted UI customization

11. Go to the **Messaging** tab.
12. Select the **Verification message** radio button in the **Message templates** section.
13. Click the **Edit** button. See *Figure 7.22*:

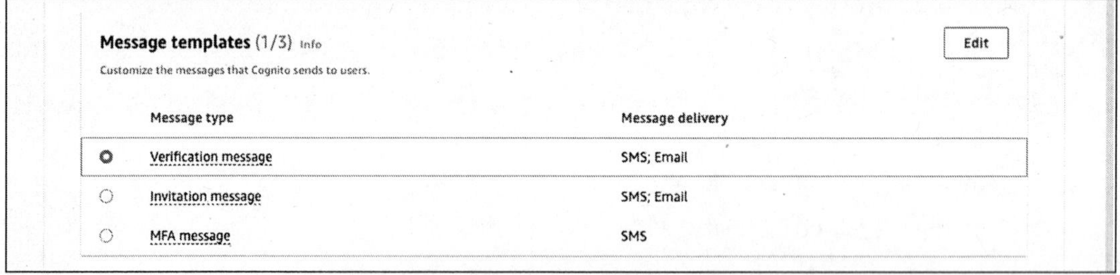

Figure 7.22: The message templates

14. Select the **Link** radio button in the **Verification type** section.
15. Specify `Your verification link for masteringawsserverlessbook.com` in the **Email subject** field.
16. Click the **Save changes** button. See *Figure 7.23* for your reference:

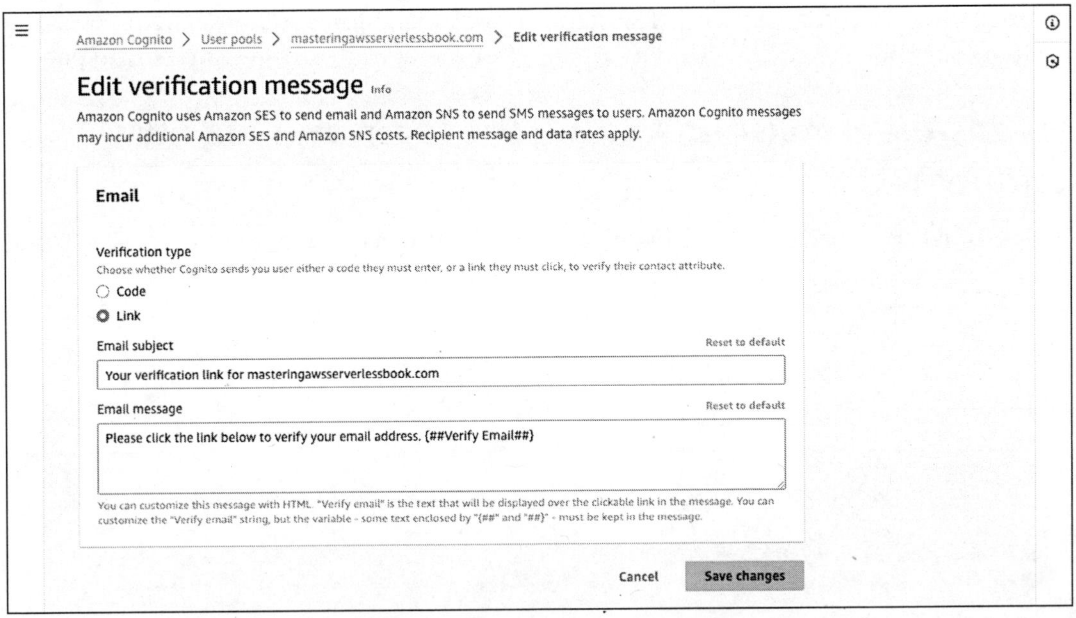

Figure 7.23: Editing the verification message

We have successfully customized the user pool.

Updating the website

We will update the website to add authentication and authorization. We will use the custom user pool hosted UI to take care of signing up, signing in, and signing out. The website will redirect to the hosted UI. The hosted UI will take care of the authorization process. When the process is complete, it will redirect to the authentication callback or log out web page. The authentication callback web page will verify that the authentication was successful and store the authentication tokens in local storage. It will use the tokens to verify the user is logged in. The logout web page will invalidate and delete the tokens from local storage.

The website will not perform the authentication, but delegate that process to the hosted UI. The website will use authentication information to send authorization information to protected API endpoints that have an authorizer.

Adding the login and log out buttons

We will update the home page and chapters page to add the signup, login, log-out, and account buttons. The web pages will use JavaScript to check for the authentication tokens. If they exist, it will show the log out and account buttons. If not, it will show the signup and log in button.

All the buttons redirect to a URL. The sign up, log in, and log out buttons redirect to the custom user pool hosted UI URL. The account button redirects to the account web page.

Hands-on exercise 4: Adding the login and log out buttons

Let us update our website to add login and logout buttons that work with the user pool:

1. Go to the user pool.
2. Go to the **App integration** tab.
3. Go to the **App client and analytics** section.
4. Copy the **Client ID** value. See *Figure 7.24*:

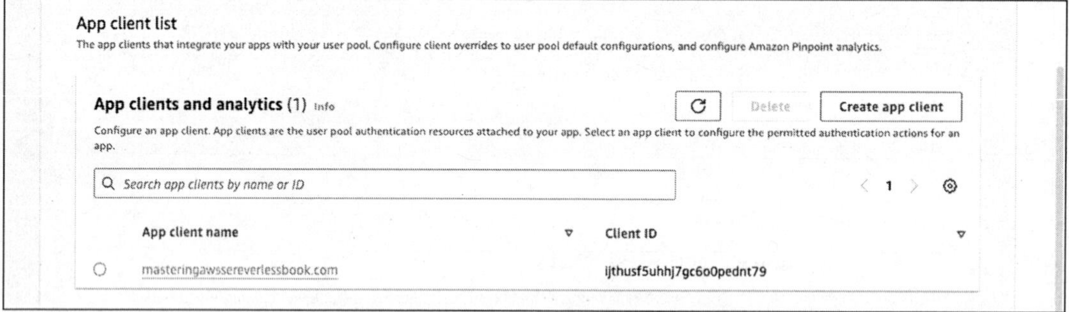

Figure 7.24: *An example of the Client ID*

5. Open the **index.html** file.
6. Select the following code:

```
<nav class="navbar">
  <div class="container-fluid">
    <span class="navbar-brand h1 mx-auto">
      Mastering AWS Serverless Book
    </span>
  </div>
</nav>
```

7. Replace it with the following code:

```
<nav class="navbar">
  <div class="container-fluid">
    <div class="col"></div>
    <div class="col navbar-brand h1 pt-3">
      Mastering AWS Serverless Book
```

```
        </div>
        <div class="col text-md-end">
          <div id="is-logged-out-btn" class="visually-hidden">
            <a class="btn btn-primary" href="https://
            auth.masteringawsserverlessbook.com/
            signup?client_id={clientId}&response_
            type=code&scope=openid+profile+aws.cognito.
            signin.user.admin&redirect_uri=https://
            masteringawsserverlessbook.com/auth-callback.html">
              Sign Up
            </a>
            <a class="btn btn-secondary" href="https://
            auth.masteringawsserverlessbook.com/
            login?client_id={clientId}&response_
            type=code&scope=openid+profile+aws.cognito.
            signin.user.admin&redirect_uri=https://
            masteringawsserverlessbook.com/auth-callback.html">
              Log In
            </a>
          </div>
          <div id="is-logged-in-btn" class="visually-hidden">
            <a class="btn btn-primary" href="https://
            auth.masteringawsserverlessbook.com/
            logout?client_id={clientId}&logout_uri=https://
            masteringawsserverlessbook.com/logout.html">
              Log Out
            </a>
          <a class="btn btn-secondary" href="/account/index.html">
              My Account
            </a>
          </div>
        </div>
      </div>
    </nav>
```

8. Replace the **`{clientId}`** placeholder with the Client ID from the user pool app integration settings.
9. Make the same changes in the **`chapters.html`** file.

10. The **chapters.html** file was successfully updated.
11. Open the **index.html** file.
12. Add the following code right above the closing HTML tag at the bottom of the file:

```
<script>
  window.onload = function () {
    const jwt = localStorage.getItem('jwt');
    if (jwt) {
      document.getElementById('is-logged-out-btn')
        .classList.add('visually-hidden');
      document.getElementById('is-logged-in-btn')
        .classList.remove('visually-hidden');
    } else {
      document.getElementById('is-logged-out-btn')
        .classList.remove('visually-hidden');
      document.getElementById('is-logged-in-btn')
        .classList.add('visually-hidden');
    }
  }
</script>
```

13. The **index.html** file was successfully updated.
14. Open the **chapters.html** file.
15. Update the last script tag to include the code changes identified with comments:

```
<script>
  window.onload = function () {
    console.error('onload');
    const url = 'https://api.masteringawsserverlessbook.com/
    chapters';
    const chaptersDiv = document.getElementById('chapters');
    const errorHtml = '<div class="alert alert-danger"
    role="alert">' +
      'Failed to get the chapters.</div>';
    const noneHtml = '<p>No chapters found.</p>';
    const chapterHtml = '<div class="card my-5" aria-
    hidden="true">' +
      '<div class="card-body">' +
```

```
    '<h2 class="card-title">{title}</h2>' +
    '<p class="card-text">{description}</p>' +
    '</div>' +
    '</div>';
  try {
    const xhr = new XMLHttpRequest();
    xhr.open('GET', url, true);
    xhr.setRequestHeader('Content-Type', 'application/json');
    xhr.onreadystatechange = function () {
      if (xhr.readyState == 4 && xhr.status == 200) {
        var responseData = JSON.parse(xhr.responseText);
        if (Array.isArray(responseData) && responseData.length >
        0) {
          chaptersDiv.innerHTML = '';
          for (let chapter of responseData) {
            chaptersDiv.innerHTML += chapterHtml.replace(
              '{title}',
              chapter.title
            ).replace('{description}', chapter.description);
          }
        } else {
          chaptersDiv.innerHTML = noneHtml;
        }
      } else {
        chaptersDiv.innerHTML = errorHtml;
        console.error('Request failed with status:', xhr.status);
      }
    };
    xhr.send();
  } catch (e) {
    chaptersDiv.innerHTML = errorHtml;
    console.error('Exception:', e);
  }
  /* !!!! START OF CHANGES !!!! */
```

```
    /* check jwt */
    const jwt = localStorage.getItem('jwt');
    if (jwt) {
      document.getElementById('is-logged-out-btn')
        .classList.add('visually-hidden');
      document.getElementById('is-logged-in-btn')
        .classList.remove('visually-hidden');
    } else {
      document.getElementById('is-logged-out-btn')
        .classList.remove('visually-hidden');
      document.getElementById('is-logged-in-btn')
        .classList.add('visually-hidden');
    }
    /* !!!! END OF CHANGES !!!! */
  }
```

The **chapters.html** file was successfully updated.

Adding the auth callback page

We will create a new web page to finish the sign-in process. When the user signs up, or signs in, the user pool will redirect to the provided redirect URL. We specified the redirect URL to be the authentication (auth) callback web page. The web page will use JavaScript to verify the authentication code provided by the user pool, save the authentication tokens to local storage, and redirect to the account web page. If it fails to verify the code, it will redirect to the home page.

Hands-on exercise 5: Adding the auth callback page

Let us add an authentication callback page to verify the authentication request is valid using the given steps:

1. Create a new **auth-callback.html** file on a computer.
2. Insert the following code into the file.

```
<!doctype html>
  <head>
  </head>
  <body>
    <script type="module" src="auth-callback.js"></script>
```

```
  </body>
</html>
```

3. The **auth-callback.html** file was successfully created.
4. Create a new **auth-callback.js** file.
5. Insert the following code into the file:

```
const url = new URL(location.href);
const code = url.searchParams.get('code');
const clientId = '{clientId}';
const redirectUri = `${url.origin}${url.pathname}`;
const cognitoDomain = 'auth.masteringawsserverlessbook.com';
const tokenEndpoint = `https://${cognitoDomain}/oauth2/token`;
const grantType = 'authorization_code';
if (code) {
  try {
    const resp = await fetch(tokenEndpoint, {
      method: 'POST',
      headers: {
        'Content-Type': 'application/x-www-form-urlencoded',
      },
      body: `grant_type=${grantType}&client_id=${clientId}&` +
        `code=${code}&redirect_uri=${redirectUri}`,
    });
    const data = await resp.json();
    if (typeof data == 'object' && data.access_token) {
      localStorage.setItem('jwt', JSON.stringify(data));
    }
  } catch (e) {
    console.error(e);
    history.replaceState(null, '', url.origin);
    location.href = `${url.origin}/`;


  }
}
```

```
history.replaceState(null, '', url.origin);
location.href = `${url.origin}/account/index.html`;
```

6. Replace the **{clientId}** placeholder with the Client ID from the user pool app integration settings.

Note: The ${clientId} variable is not a placeholder. Do not replace it with the Client ID.

The **auth-callback.js** file was successfully created.

Creating the logout page

We will create a new web page to log out the user. The web page will use JavaScript to invalidate the tokens provided from the user pool. It will also delete them from local storage.

Hands-on exercise 6: Creating the logout page

Let us create a log out page to logout the user:

1. Create a **logout.html** file on a computer.
2. Insert the following code into the file:

```
<!doctype html>
  <head>
  </head>
  <body>
    <script type="module" src="logout.js"></script>
  </body>
</html>
```

3. The **logout.html** file was successfully created.
4. Create a **logout.js** file on a computer.
5. Insert the following code into the file:

```
const url = new URL(location.href);
const clientId = '{clientId}';
const cognitoDomain = 'auth.masteringawsserverlessbook.com';
const tokenEndpoint = `https://${cognitoDomain}/oauth2/revoke`;
try {
  const jwt = localStorage.getItem('jwt');
```

```
    if (jwt) {
      const jwtObj = JSON.parse(jwt);
      if (jwtObj.refresh_token) {
        await fetch(tokenEndpoint, {
          method: 'POST',
          headers: {
              'Content-Type': 'application/x-www-form-urlencoded',
          },
          body: `token=${jwtObj.refresh_token}&client_id=${clientId}`,
        });
      }
    }
  } catch (e) {
    console.error(e);
  }
  localStorage.removeItem('jwt');
  history.replaceState(null, '', url.origin);
  location.href = url.origin;
```

6. Replace the **`{clientId}`** placeholder with the Client ID from the user pool app integration settings.

> **Note: The `${clientId}` variable is not a placeholder. Do not replace it with the Client ID.**

The **`logout.js`** file was successfully created.

Creating the account page

We will create a new web page for signed-in accounts. The accounts page will use JavaScript to check whether the access token was saved to local storage and whether it is valid. If it is valid, it will show the web page content. It will redirect to the log out web page if it is not.

Hands-on exercise 7: Creating the account page

Let us create an account page that is restricted to logged-in users, as shown:

1. Create an **`account`** folder on a computer.
2. Create an **`index.html`** file inside the **`account`** folder.
3. Insert the following code into the file:

```
<!doctype html>
<html lang="en" class="h-100" data-bs-theme="dark">
  <head>
    <title>Mastering AWS Book</title>
    <meta charset="utf-8">
    <meta name="viewport" content="width=device-width, initial-
    scale=1, shrink-to-fit=no">
    <link href="https://cdn.jsdelivr.net/npm/bootstrap@5.3.2/dist/
    css/bootstrap.min.css" rel="stylesheet" integrity="sha384-T3c6
    CoIi6uLrA9TneNEoa7RxnatzjcDSCmG1MXxSR1GAsXEV/Dwwykc2MPK8M2HN"
    crossorigin="anonymous">
  </head>
  <body class="d-flex h-100 text-center flex-column">
    <div class="d-flex w-100 h-100 mx-auto flex-column">
      <header class="mb-auto">
        <nav class="navbar">
          <div class="container-fluid">
            <div class="col"></div>
            <div class="col navbar-brand h1 pt-3">
              Mastering AWS Serverless Book
            </div>
            <div class="col text-md-end">
              <a class="btn btn-primary" href="https://
              auth.masteringawsserverlessbook.com/
              logout?client_id={clientId}&logout_uri=https://
              masteringawsserverlessbook.com/logout.html">
                  Log Out
              </a>
            </div>
          </div>
        </nav>
      </header>
      <main role="main" class="my-auto visually-hidden">
        <div id="is-logged-in" class="container visually-hidden">
          <h1>My Account</h1>
```

```
        <p id="greeting">Hello {firstName}!</p>
        <p>
          <a href="/account/info.html" class="btn btn-
          primary">Update info</a>
        </p>
      </div>
      <div id="is-logged-out" class="container placeholder-glow">
        <h1><span class="placeholder col-4"></span></h1>
        <p><span class="placeholder col-3"></span></p>
      </div>
    </main>
    <footer class="mt-auto">
      <div class="container text-center">
        <p>
          &copy; Miguel A. Calles. All rights reserved.
        </p>
      </div>
    </footer>
  </div>
</body>
<script src="https://cdn.jsdelivr.net/npm/bootstrap@5.3.2/
dist/js/bootstrap.bundle.min.js" integrity="sha384-C6Rzsyn
M9kWDrMNeT87bh95OGNyZPhcTNXj1NW7RuBCsyN/o0jlpcV8Qyq46cDfL"
crossorigin="anonymous"></script>
<script type="module" src="auth-check.js"></script>
<script>
  window.onload = function () {
    const firstName = localStorage.getItem('userFirstName');
    const greetingEl = document.getElementById('greeting');
    const updatedGreeting = greetingEl.innerHTML.replace(
      '{firstName}',
      firstName
    );
    greetingEl.innerHTML = updatedGreeting;
```

```
  }
  </script>
</html>
```

4. The **account/index.html** file was successfully created.
5. Create an **auth-check.js** file in the **account** folder.
6. Insert the following code into the file:

```
const jwt = localStorage.getItem('jwt');
const url = new URL(location.href);
const cognitoDomain = 'auth.masteringawsserverlessbook.com';
const tokenEndpoint = `https://${cognitoDomain}/oauth2/userInfo`;
let validLogin = false;
document.getElementsByTagName('main')[0].classList
  .add('visually-hidden');;
document.getElementById('is-logged-in').classList
  .add('visually-hidden');
document.getElementById('is-logged-out').classList
  .remove('visually-hidden');
if (jwt) {
  document.getElementsByTagName('main')[0].classList
    .remove('visually-hidden');;
  try {
    const jwtObj = JSON.parse(jwt);
    if (jwtObj.access_token) {
      const resp = await fetch(tokenEndpoint, {
        method: 'GET',
        headers: {
            'Content-Type': 'application/x-amz-json-1.1',
            Authorization: `Bearer ${jwtObj.access_token}`,
        },
      });
      if (resp.ok) {
        validLogin = true;
        const data = await resp.json();
        localStorage.setItem('userFirstName', data.given_name);
```

```
          document.getElementById('is-logged-in').classList
            .remove('visually-hidden');
          document.getElementById('is-logged-out').classList
            .add('visually-hidden');
        }
      }
    } catch (e) {
      console.error(e);
    }
  }
  if (!validLogin) {
    history.replaceState(null, '', url.origin);
    location.href = `${url.origin}/logout.html`;
  }
```

The **account/auth-check.js** file was successfully created.

Uploading the files to S3 bucket

We will upload all the website files into the S3 bucket to ensure it has the latest versions of our files.

Hands-on exercise 8: Uploading the files to S3 bucket

Let us upload the most recent website files to the bucket:

1. Go to the S3 service page.
2. Click the **masteringawsserverlessbook.com** bucket.
3. Click the **Upload** button.
4. Select all the website files from the computer.
5. Drag and drop all the files onto the bucket page.
6. Click the **Upload** button.
7. Wait for the files to finish uploading.

Invalidating the CloudFront distribution cache

We will invalidate all the cache to make sure all our website updates load properly in the browser.

Hands-on exercise 9: Invalidating the CloudFront distribution cache

Let us invalidate the distribution to clear the CDN cache:

1. Go to the CloudFront service page.
2. Click the CloudFront distribution.
3. Go to the **Invalidations** tab.
4. Click the **Create invalidation** button.
5. Specify **/*** in the **Add object pages** field to invalidate all files.
6. Click the **Create invalidation** button.
7. Observe **In progress** in the **Status** section.

Note: It may take several minutes for the invalidation to complete.

8. Observe **Completed** in the **Status** section.
9. Visit **https://masteringawsserverlessbook.com**.
10. Observe the web page shows the **Sign up** and **Log in** buttons. See *Figure 7.25*:

Figure 7.25: *The sign up and log in buttons*

We have successfully updated the website.

Testing the authentication

We set up our Cognito user pool. We will test signing up, signing in, and signing out with a new user account we will create.

Sign up using the Cognito user pool

We will test signing up for our new user account.

Hands-on exercise 10: Signing up using the Cognito user pool

Let us sign up on the website as a new user:

1. Click the **Sign Up** button on the website.
2. Observe the sign up page. See *Figure 7.26*:

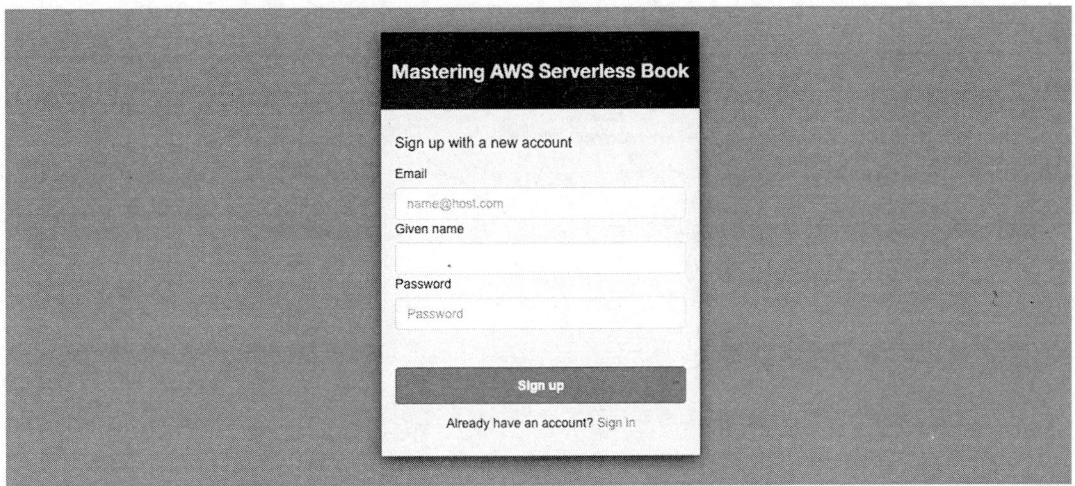

Figure 7.26: The sign up page

3. Specify an email address in the **Email** field.
4. Specify a name in the **Given name** field.
5. Specify a password in the **Password** field.
6. Click the **Sign up** button.
7. The page updates to indicate that a confirmation link was sent. See *Figure 7.27* for your reference:

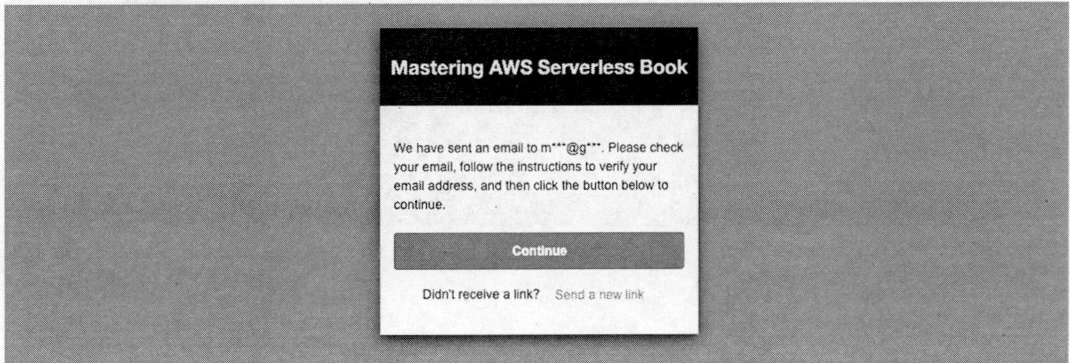

Figure 7.27: The confirmation pages

8. Click the link in the verification email.
9. Close the page.
10. Return to the confirmation page.
11. Click the **Continue** button.
12. Observe the authentication dialog on the page. See *Figure 7.28*:

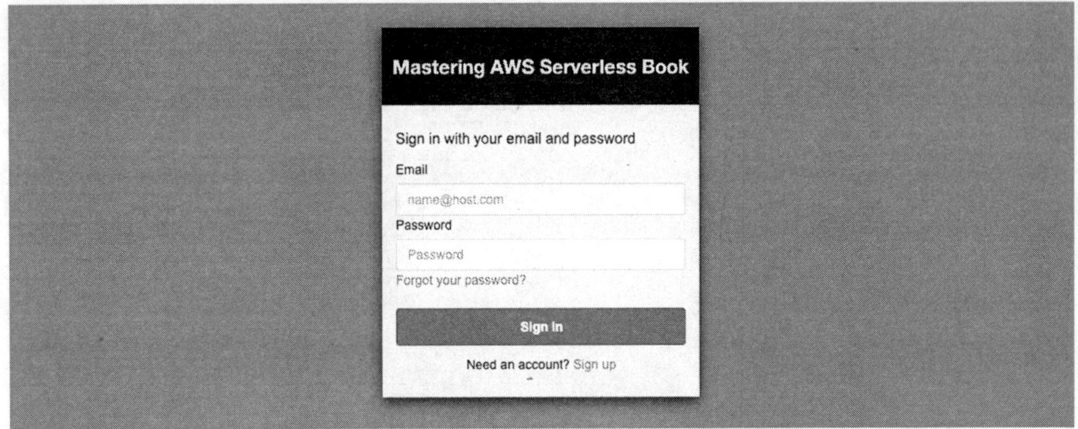

Figure 7.28: The sign in page

13. Enter the email address and password.
14. Click the **Sign in** button.
15. Follow the on-screen instructions to set up the authenticator app MFA.
16. The page redirects to the **My Account** page. See *Figure 7.29*:

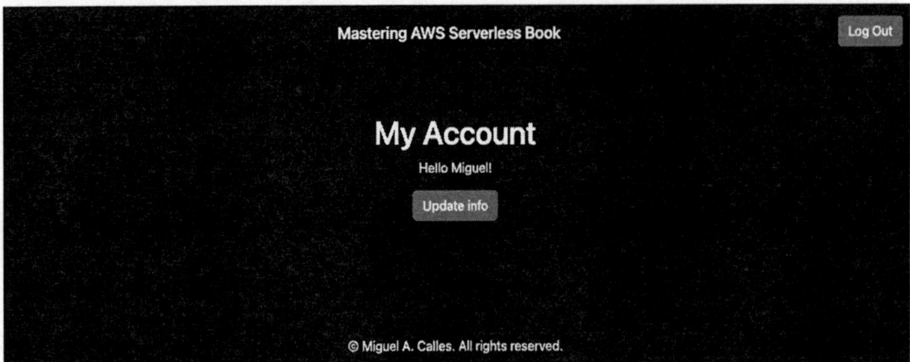

Figure 7.29: The my account page

We have successfully signed up.

Sign out from the Cognito user pool

We will test signing out from our new user account.

Hands-on exercise 11: Signing out from the Cognito user pool

Let us sign out from the website:

1. Click the **Log Out** button.
2. The page redirects to the home page.

3. Visit **https://masteringawsserverlessbook.com/account/index.html.**
4. The page redirects to the home page.

Sign in using the Cognito user pool

We will test signing into our new user account.

Hands-on exercise 12: Signing in using the Cognito user pool

Let us sign in to the website with the new user account, as shown:

1. Click the **Sign in** button.
2. Enter the email address and password.
3. Click the **Sign in** button.
4. The page redirects to the **My Account** page.

We have successfully authenticated.

Adding an authorized API endpoint

We will create a new page on our website to allow users to update their names. We will create an API endpoint dedicated to updating the first name. We want to protect this endpoint since it is specific to a user and contains user information. We will protect it with an authorizer.

The API Gateway will send the authorized HTTP request to a Lambda function. This Lambda function will use the authorization and the HTTP body information to make an AWS SDK request to the Cognito user pool to update the user information.

Creating an authorizer

We will create a Cognito authorizer. We have the option to create a custom Lambda function authorizer. This would be a good choice if we want to authorize with a different identity provider or a different authorization strategy.

We have the option to authorize with an identity token or access token. Either will work for the API Gateway authorization, but we will set up the access token authorization because the Lambda function will need the access token.

Hands-on exercise 13: Creating an authorizer

Let us create an authorizer to protect some API endpoints, using the given steps:

1. Go to the API Gateway service page.

2. Click the **website** API.
3. Click the **Authorizers** menu option.
4. Click the **Create authorizer** button. See *Figure 7.30*:

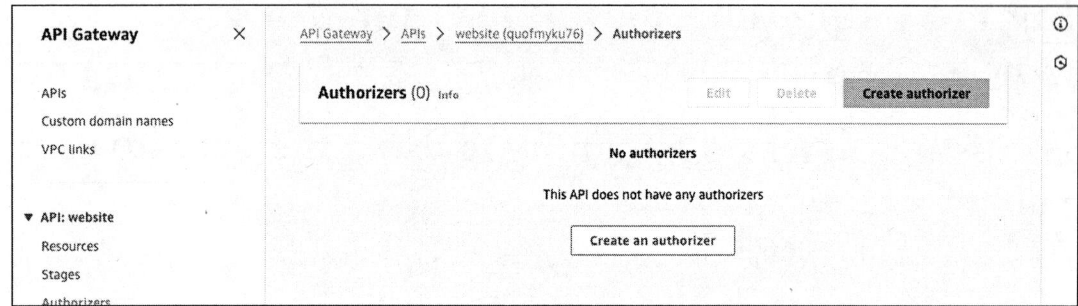

***Figure 7.30:** The API Gateway authorizers*

5. Click on the **Authorizers** menu option.
6. Specify **`cognitoAuthorizer`** in the **Authorizer name** field.
7. Select the **Cognito** radio button in the **Authorizer type** section.
8. Specify the **`us-east-1`** region in the **Cognito user pool** section.
9. Select the **`masteringawsserverlessbook.com`** user pool in the **Cognito user pool** section.
10. Specify **Authorization** in the **Token source** field.
11. Click the **Create authorizer** button. See *Figure 7.31*:

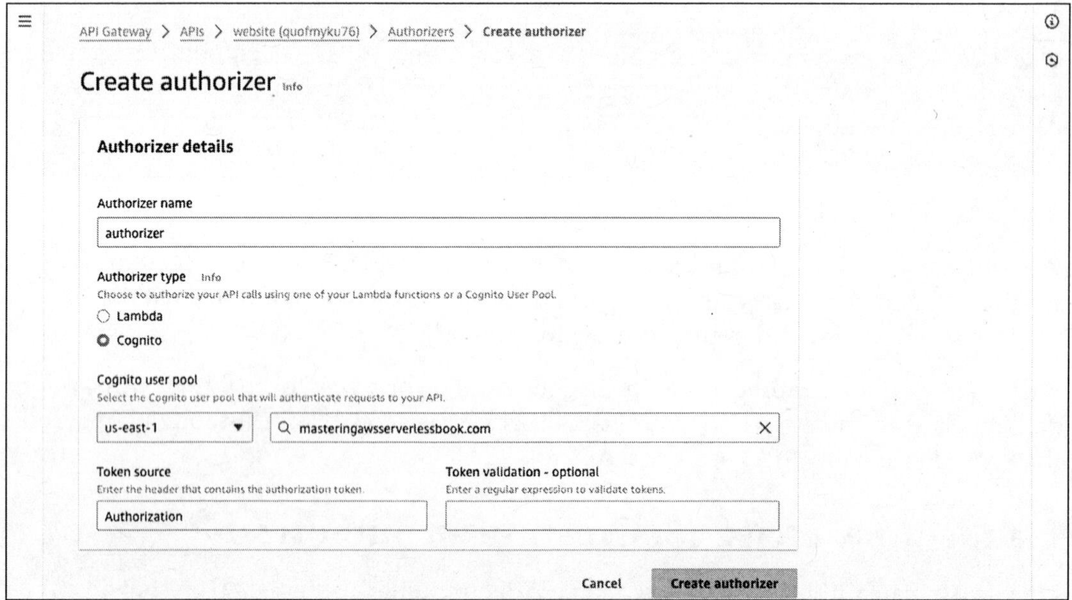

***Figure 7.31:** The authorizer settings*

12. Observe that the authorizer was created. See *Figure 7.32*:

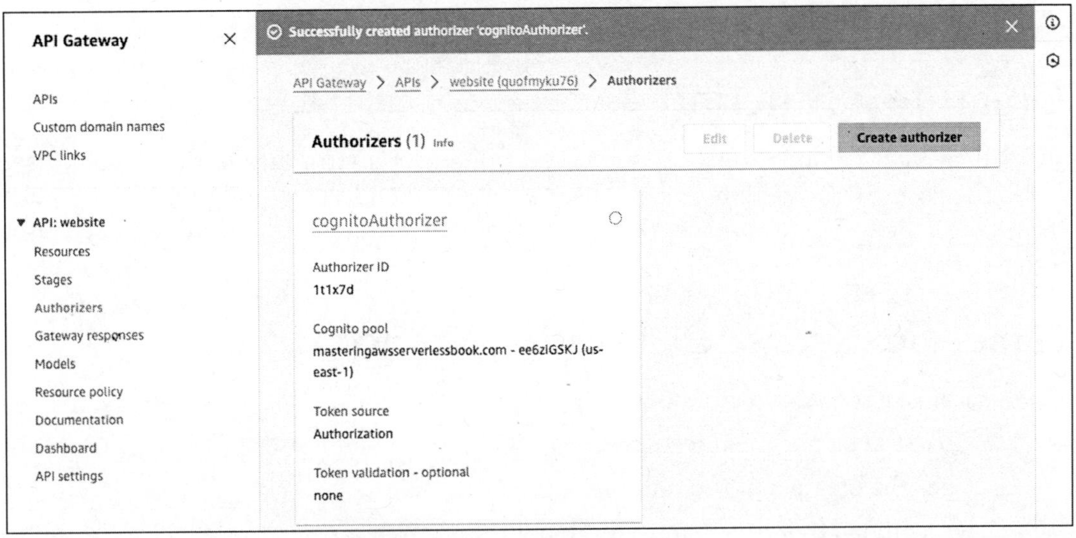

Figure 7.32: *The authorizer settings*

The Cognito authorizer has been successfully created.

Creating an IAM role

We will create an IAM role for our new function. We would typically create an IAM policy, too, but the function will use the user's access token for authorization instead of the Lambda's role. The role will use the AWS-provided policy to create logs in a log group.

Hands-on exercise 14: Creating an IAM role

Let us create an IAM role for a new Lambda function:

1. Go to the IAM service page.
2. Go to the **Roles** menu option.
3. Click the **Create role** button.
4. Select the **AWS service** radio button in the **Trusted entity type** section.
5. Select **Lambda** in the **Service or use case** drop down.
6. Click the **Next** button.
7. Search for **AWSLambdaBasicExecutionRole** in the **Permissions policies** section.
8. Check the **AWSLambdaBasicExecutionRole** checkbox.
9. Click the **Next** button.
10. Specify `function-put-account-info` in the **Role name** field.

11. Click the **Create role** button.

We have successfully created an IAM role.

Creating a function

We will create a Lambda function that updates the user's attributes in the Cognito user pool. The AWS SDK function uses the user's access token to gain authorization to make the changes. It will also use the body from the HTTP request to get the updated user information.

Hands-on exercise 15: Creating a function

Let us create a new Lambda function:

1. Go to the Lambda service page.
2. Click the **Create function** button.
3. Select the **Author from scratch** radio button.
4. Specify **`put-account-info`** in the **Function name** field.
5. Select **Node.js** in the **Runtime** dropdown.
6. Select the **arm64** radio button in the **Architecture** section.
7. Expand the **Change default execution role** section.
8. Select the **Use an existing role** radio button in the **Execution role** section.
9. Select **`function-put-account-info`** in the **Existing role** dropdown.
10. Click the **Create function** button.
11. Enter the following code into the **Code source** section:

```
import {
  CognitoIdentityProviderClient,
  UpdateUserAttributesCommand,
} from "@aws-sdk/client-cognito-identity-provider";
export const handler = async (event) => {
 const response = {
    statusCode: 500,
    headers: {
      'Access-Control-Allow-Origin': '*',
      'Content-Type': 'application/json',
    },
    body: JSON.stringify({}),
```

```
    };
    try {
      if (!event.body) {
        throw new Error('Empty body');
      }
      const bodyObj = JSON.parse(event.body);
      if (!bodyObj.given_name) {
        throw new Error('No given_name');
      }
      const cognitoClient = new CognitoIdentityProviderClient({
        region: process.env.AWS_REGION,
      });
      const cognitoCommand = new UpdateUserAttributesCommand({
        AccessToken: event.headers.Authorization,
        UserAttributes: [
          {
            Name: 'given_name',
            Value: bodyObj.given_name,
          },
        ],
      });
      await cognitoClient.send(cognitoCommand);
      response.statusCode = 200;
    } catch (e) {
      console.error(e);
    }
    return response;
  };
```

12. Go to **File** | **Save** to save the code.
13. Click the **Deploy** button.
14. Click the **Test** button.
15. Click the **Create new event** radio button.
16. Specify **TestEvent** in the **Event name** field.
17. Select **API Gateway AWS Proxy** in the **Template** dropdown.

18. Click the **Save** button.
19. Click the **Test** button.

We have successfully created the Lambda function.

Updating the log group settings

We will update the log group retention settings to one week.

Hands-on exercise 16: Updating the log group settings

Let us update the log group retention settings, as shown:

1. Go to the CloudWatch service page.
2. Go to the **Logs | Log groups** menu option.
3. Check the **`/aws/lambda/put-account-info`** log group.
4. Click the **Actions** dropdown.
5. Select the **Edit retention setting(s)** dropdown option.
6. Select **1 week (7 days)** in the **Expire events after** dropdown.
7. Click the **Save** button.

We have successfully updated the log group retention settings.

Creating an API endpoint

We will create an **`/account/info`** API endpoint with a **PUT** method. We will protect it with the authorizer we created earlier.

Hands-on exercise 17: Creating an API endpoint

Let us create a new API endpoint for the new Lambda function:

1. Go to the API Gateway service page.
2. Click the **website** API.
3. Go to the **Resources** menu option.
4. Select the **/** resource.
5. Click the **Create resource** button.
6. Select **/** in the **Resource path** dropdown.
7. Specify **`account`** in the **Resource name** field.
8. Click the **Create resource** button.

   We have successfully created the **`/account`** resource.

9. Select the **`/account`** resource.
10. Click the **Create resource** button.
11. Select **`/account/`** in the **Resource name** field.
12. Specify **`info`** in the **Resource name** field.
13. Check the **CORS (Cross Origin Resource Sharing)** checkbox.
14. Click the **Create resource** button.

    We have successfully created the **`/account/info`** resource.
15. Select the **`/info`** resource under the **`/account`** resource.
16. Click the **Create method** button.
17. Select **PUT** in the **Method type** dropdown.
18. Select the **Lambda function** radio button in the **Integration type** section.
19. Check the **Lambda proxy integration** switch button.
20. Select **`us-east-1`** in the dropdown in the Lambda function section.
21. Select **`arn:aws:lambda:us-east-1:{accountId}:function:put-account-info`** in the **Choose a Lambda function or enter its ARN** field in the Lambda function section.

Note: The `{accountId}` is the AWS account ID.

22. Uncheck the **Default timeout** switch button.
23. Specify **`5000`** in the **Custom timeout** field.
24. Click the **Create method** button.

    We have successfully created the **PUT** method.
25. Select the **PUT** method under the **`/info`** resource.
26. Go to the **Method request** tab.
27. Click the **Edit** button in the **Method request settings** section.
28. Select **`cognitoAuthorizer`** in the **Authorizer** dropdown.
29. Specify **`openid`** in the **Add a scope** field.
30. Click **Add** in the **Authorization Scopes** section.
31. Select **None** in the **Request validator** dropdown.
32. Click the **Save** button.

    We have successfully added an authorizer to the **PUT** method.
33. Click the **Deploy API** button.
34. Select **`v1`** in the **Stage** dropdown.
35. Click the **Deploy** button.

We have successfully created a new API endpoint.

Creating an account information page

We will create a restricted web page that allows the user to update the account information using the new API endpoint.

Hands-on exercise 18: Creating an account information page

Let us create the web page:

1. Go to the **account** folder on a computer.
2. Create an **info.html** file inside the **account** folder.
3. Insert the following code into the file:

```
<!doctype html>
<html lang="en" class="h-100" data-bs-theme="dark">
  <head>
    <title>Mastering AWS Book</title>
    <meta charset="utf-8">
    <meta name="viewport" content="width=device-width, initial-
    scale=1, shrink-to-fit=no">
    <link href="https://cdn.jsdelivr.net/npm/bootstrap@5.3.2/dist/
    css/bootstrap.min.css" rel="stylesheet" integrity="sha384-T3c6
    CoIi6uLrA9TneNEoa7RxnatzjcDSCmG1MXxSR1GAsXEV/Dwwykc2MPK8M2HN"
    crossorigin="anonymous">
  </head>
  <body class="d-flex h-100 text-center flex-column">
    <div class="d-flex w-100 h-100 mx-auto flex-column">
      <header class="mb-auto">
        <nav class="navbar">
          <div class="container-fluid">
            <div class="col"></div>
            <div class="col navbar-brand h1 pt-3">
              Mastering AWS Serverless Book
            </div>
            <div class="col text-md-end">
              <a class="btn btn-primary" href="https://
              auth.masteringawsserverlessbook.com/
              logout?client_id={clientId}&logout_uri=https://
```

```
            masteringawsserverlessbook.com/logout.html">
              Log Out
            </a>
          </div>
        </div>
      </nav>
    </header>
    <main role="main" class="my-auto visually-hidden">
      <div id="is-logged-in" class="container visually-hidden">
        <h1>Account Information</h1>
        <div id="put-user-info-alert" class="alert w-50 mx-auto
        visually-hidden"></div>
        <form id="put-user-info-form" class="row g-3 mx-auto"
        style="max-width:600px">
          <div class="col-3 col-md-2">
            <label for="name-field" class="form-label pt-2">Name:</
            label>
          </div>
          <div class="col-9 col-md-6">
            <input id="given-name" type="text" class="form-
            control" id="name-field" placeholder="">
          </div>
          <div class="col-12 col-md-4">
            <button type="submit" class="btn btn-primary">Update</
            button>
            <a href="/account/index.html" class="btn btn-
            secondary">Cancel</a>
          </div>
        </form>
      </div>
      <div id="is-logged-out" class="container placeholder-glow">
        <h1><span class="placeholder col-4"></span></h1>
        <p><span class="placeholder col-3"></span></p>
      </div>
    </main>
    <footer class="mt-auto">
```

```
      <div class="container text-center">
        <p>
          &copy; Miguel A. Calles. All rights reserved.
        </p>
      </div>
    </footer>
  </div>
</body>
<script src="https://cdn.jsdelivr.net/npm/bootstrap@5.3.2/
dist/js/bootstrap.bundle.min.js" integrity="sha384-C6Rzsyn
M9kWDrMNeT87bh95OGNyZPhcTNXj1NW7RuBCsyN/o0jlpcV8Qyq46cDfL"
crossorigin="anonymous"></script>
<script type="module" src="auth-check.js"></script>
<script>
  const alert = document.getElementById('put-user-info-alert');
  const formEl = document.getElementById('put-user-info-form');
  const givenNameEl = document.getElementById('given-name');
  const url = 'https://api.masteringawsserverlessbook.com/account/
  info';
  const jwt = localStorage.getItem('jwt');
  function clearAlertStatus() {
    alert.classList.add('visually-hidden');
    alert.classList.forEach(function (x) {
      if (x.startsWith('alert-')) {
        alert.classList.remove(x);
      }
    });
  }
  function updateAlertStatus(status, text) {
    clearAlertStatus();
    alert.classList.add(`alert-${status}`);
    alert.classList.remove('visually-hidden');
    alert.innerText = text;
  }
  formEl.addEventListener('submit', async function (event) {
```

```
            event.preventDefault();
            event.stopPropagation();
            updateAlertStatus('info', 'Updating...');
            try {
              const jwtObj = JSON.parse(jwt);
              const resp = await fetch(url, {
                method: 'PUT',
                mode: 'cors',
                headers: {
                  'Authorization': jwtObj.access_token ?? '',
                  'Content-Type': 'application/json',
                },
                body: JSON.stringify({
                  given_name: givenNameEl.value ?? '',
                }),
              });
              if (resp.ok) {
                updateAlertStatus('success', 'Successfully updated.');
                localStorage.setItem('userFirstName', givenNameEl.value);
              } else {
                throw new Error(`HTTP status: ${resp.status}`);
              }
            } catch (e) {
              console.error(e);
              updateAlertStatus('danger', 'Something went wrong.');
            }
          });
        </script>
      </html>
```

The **account/info.html** file was successfully created.

Uploading the files to S3 bucket

We will upload all the website files into the S3 bucket to ensure it has the latest versions of our files.

Hands-on exercise 19: Uploading files to the S3 bucket

Let us update the most recent files to the bucket:

1. Go to the S3 service page.
2. Click the `masteringawsserverlessbook.com` bucket.
3. Click the **Upload** button.
4. Select all the website files from the computer.
5. Drag and drop all the files onto the bucket page.
6. Click the **Upload** button.
7. Wait for the files to finish uploading.

Invalidating the CloudFront distribution cache

We will invalidate all the cache to make sure all our website updates load properly in the browser.

Hands-on exercise 20: Invalidating the CloudFront distribution cache

Let us invalidate the distribution to clear the CDN cache:

1. Go to the CloudFront service page.
2. Click the **CloudFront** distribution.
3. Go to the **Invalidations** tab.
4. Click the **Create invalidation** button.
5. Specify **/*** in the **Add object pages** field to invalidate all files.
6. Click the **Create invalidation** button.
7. Observe **In progress** in the **Status** section.

Note: It may take several minutes for the invalidation to complete.

8. Observe **Completed** in the **Status** section.

Testing the new function

We have all the parts put together. We will use the website to update the user's first name.

Hands-on exercise 21: Testing the new function

Let us test the API endpoint and function works by using the website:

1. Visit **https://masteringawsserverlessbook.com/account/index.html** or reload the page if already there.

2. Log in if prompted.
3. We have successfully updated the website.
4. Click the **Update info** button.
5. Specify a different name in the **Name** field.
6. Click the **Update** button.
7. Observe the success dialog.
8. Click the **Cancel** button.
9. Observe the account page shows the updated name.

Conclusion

In this chapter, we added authentication and authorization to our website. We updated our website to add sign up, login, log out and account buttons that will show or hide depending on the authentication. The website relies on JavaScript to modify the web page and check the authentication information. We also used JavaScript to send API requests that contain the authorization information based on the authentication information.

We used a Cognito user pool with a hosted UI to handle all the sign up, log in and log out requests. The hosted UI provides the website with authentication information. The website stores that information in the browser's local storage.

We used an API Gateway authorizer that integrates with the user pool to verify authorization for a new API endpoint. The new API endpoint allows the user to update the name if the authorization passes.

Points to remember

- Serverless websites use plain HTML, JavaScript, and CSS files and cannot securely store secret information.
- Using an identity provider, such as Cognito, provides a secure authentication process and allows a website to delegate authentication to the identity provider. Cognito will provide the website with an access token or identity token using the JWT standard when a user successfully authenticates.
- An API Gateway API can host public and authorized API endpoints. The public endpoints do not require authorization information, such as a JWT. An authorized endpoint will first validate the JWT with the Cognito user pool before returning any data. An invalid or expired JWT will result in the endpoint returning an error code.
- The web pages use JavaScript to provide dynamic functionality (for example, updating the web page contents, verifying the authentication information, and sending API requests).

Multiple choice questions

1. **A hosted UI is required to authenticate with a Cognito user pool?**

   a. True

   b. False

   Answer: b

   False. Some websites use the AWS SDK or AWS Amplify libraries to perform the authentication process. The hosted UI is an additional feature that we used to delegate authentication from the website.

2. **A request to an API endpoint protected by an authorizer is failing. What might be the issue?**

   a. CORS is misconfigured.

   b. Sending the incorrect token.

   c. The token has expired.

   d. The authorizer is configured for the incorrect token type.

   e. The incorrect HTTP method is being used.

   f. All of the above.

   Answer: f

   All of the above can be true. Check the browser console logs and the CloudWatch logs to get an idea of what might be the issue.

Chapter 8

Processing Data Using Automation and Machine Learning

Introduction

This chapter will focus on how to use serverless computing to process data.

Structure

We will cover the following topics in this chapter:

- Overview of data processing
- Tracking authentication callbacks
- Transforming data
- Analyzing data using machine learning

Objectives

By the end of this chapter, you will learn how to use an event-driven architecture to extract and transform data. You will also be introduced to machine learning using a serverless approach.

Overview of data processing

We want to avoid data processing that involves user interaction. We want our users to use the web application to get the data they need and request any data inputs when we need from the users. The data the user needs could be their own information or data our application has already processed. Any data they provide could be their own information or data we can process later. Since the user interacts with the web application in a sporadic and asynchronous manner, it is best to leave the user out of data processing and perform it in the backend.

As previously discussed, we can use event-driven architectures in our serverless application. We can schedule events and create event triggers that will process data and automate tasks. For example, we can create a schedule to invoke a Lambda function every 10 minutes. The Lambda function will extract data, transform it, and load it into a different data location. This type of approach allows us to process data independently of user activity.

In this chapter, we will update our authentication process to write analytics data. Whenever a user logs in and the identity provider redirects to the authentication callback web page, the JavaScript code will send an HTTP **`POST`** request to an API endpoint that will write information to a DynamoDB table that stores analytics data. We can keep track of user sign-ins.

We will create an EventBridge schedule rule to process the analytics table data. The rule will trigger every 10 minutes. The rule will send a trigger to a Lambda function that will count the successful authentication callbacks within a 30-minute time window. It will append the count to an object in an S3 bucket. This S3 object will provide us with analytics on the number of successful logins every 30 minute period.

We will discuss how we can use the analytics data to run machine learning. Machine learning is a method of artificial intelligence that looks for patterns. We will use an AWS-provided machine learning algorithm to analyze the analytics data. The algorithm is designed to detect unusual patterns or anomalies in the data. For example, the website might typically average 100 logins within a 30-minute period during daylight hours in the United States Eastern time zone but less than 10 logins outside of those hours. Suppose one day the average logins increase to 200 one night. The machine learning algorithm will identify that nighttime 30-minute periods as anomalies.

We will have two parts when performing machine learning. The first part is training where the machine learning algorithm will process the data and determine the typical patterns. The second part is inference where the algorithm will look for anomalies. This two-part process allows us to create an event-driven design where we first trigger the training on a periodic basis and trigger the inference when training is done.

Tracking authentication callbacks

We will create a new table for our analytics data. We will also create a new API endpoint that will write a successful login to the analytics table. We do not need a Lambda function in this case because the API Gateway can write directly to DynamoDB.

Create a DynamoDB table

We will create the analytics table that has `dataType` as the primary key and the `timestamp` as the secondary key. This key schema allows us to save other types of analytics without having to create a new table.

Hands-on exercise 1: Creating a DynamoDB table

Let us create a DynamoDB table using the given steps:

1. Go to the DynamoDB service page.
2. Click the **Create table** button.
3. Specify `analytics` in the **Table name** field.
4. Specify `dataType` in the **Partition key** field.
5. Select **String** in the dropdown in the **Partition key** section.
6. Specify `timestamp` in the **Sort key** field.
7. Select **Number** in the dropdown in the **Sort key** section.
8. Select the **Customize settings** radio button in the **Table settings** section.
9. Select the **DynamoDB Standard** radio button in the **Table class** section.
10. Select the **On-demand** radio button in the **Capacity mode** section.
11. Select **Owned by Amazon DynamoDB** radio button in the **Encryption key management** section.
12. Click the **Create table** button.

We have successfully created the table.

Creating an IAM policy

We will create a policy that will allow the API Gateway API endpoint to write to DynamoDB.

Hands-on exercise 2: Creating an IAM policy

Let us create an IAM policy:

1. Go to the IAM service page.
2. Go to the **Access Management | Policies** menu option.

3. Click the **Create policy** button.
4. Select **DynamoDB** in the **Service** dropdown.
5. Search for **PutItem** in the **Filter Actions** search field.
6. Check the **PutItem** checkbox.
7. Select the **Specific** radio button in the **Resources** section.
8. Click the **Add ARNs** link in the **table** section.
9. Click the **Visual** button.
10. Select the **This account** radio button in the **Resource in** section.
11. Specify **us-east-1** in the **Resource region** field.
12. Specify **analytics** in the **Resource table name** field.
13. Click the **Add ARNs** button.
14. Click the **Next** button.
15. Specify **apigateway-post-analytics-auth-callback** in the **Policy name** field.
16. Click the **Create policy** button.

We have successfully created the IAM policy.

Creating an IAM role

We will be creating a role that uses the new policy.

Hands-on exercise 3: Creating an IAM role

Let us create an IAM role:

1. Go to the IAM service page.
2. Go to the **Access Management | Roles** menu option.
3. Click the **Create role** button.
4. Select the **Custom trust policy** radio button in the **Trusted entity type** section.
5. Specify the following code in the **Custom trust policy** section:

```
{
  "Version": "2012-10-17",
  "Statement": [
    {
      "Sid": "Statement1",
      "Effect": "Allow",
      "Principal": {
        "Service": "apigateway.amazonaws.com"
```

```
            },
            "Action": "sts:AssumeRole"
        }
    ]
}
```

6. Click the **Next** button.
7. Specify **AmazonAPIGatewayPushToCloudWatchLogs** in the **Search** field.
8. Check the **AmazonAPIGatewayPushToCloudWatchLogs** checkbox.
9. Specify **`apigateway-post-analytics-auth-callback`** in the **Search** field.
10. Check the **`apigateway-post-analytics-auth-callback`** checkbox.
11. Click the **Next** button.
12. Specify **`apigateway-post-analytics-auth-callback`** in the **Role name** field.
13. Click the **Create role** button.

We have successfully created the role.

14. Click the **`apigateway-post-analytics-auth-callback`** role.
15. Copy the value in the **ARN** section.

We will use the copied ARN value in the next section.

Creating an API endpoint

We will create an API endpoint that will make a direct request to DynamoDB to write the data. The endpoint will be protected by a Cognito authorizer. The authorization information will provide us with the information we want to write to the database table.

Hands-on exercise 4: Creating an API endpoint

Let us create an API endpoint:

1. Go to the API Gateway service page.
2. Click on the **website** API.
3. Select the **/** resource.
4. Click the **Create resource** button.
5. Select **/** in the **Resource path** dropdown.
6. Specify **`analytics`** in the **Resource name** field.
7. Click the **Create resource** button.
8. We successfully created the **`/analytics`** resource.
9. Select the **`/analytics`** resource.

10. Click the **Create resource** button.
11. Select **`/analytics/`** in the **Resource path** dropdown.
12. Specify **`auth-callback`** in the **Resource name** field.
13. Check the **CORS (Cross Origin Resource Sharing)** checkbox.
14. Click the **Create resource** button.
15. We successfully created the **`/analytics/auth-callback`** resource.
16. Select the **`/auth-callback`** resource under the **`/analytics`** resource.
17. Click the **Create method** button.
18. Select **POST** in the **Method type** dropdown.
19. Select the **AWS service** radio button in the **Integration type** section.
20. Select **`us-east-1`** in the **AWS Region** dropdown.
21. Select **DynamoDB** in the **AWS service** dropdown. See *Figure 8.1*:

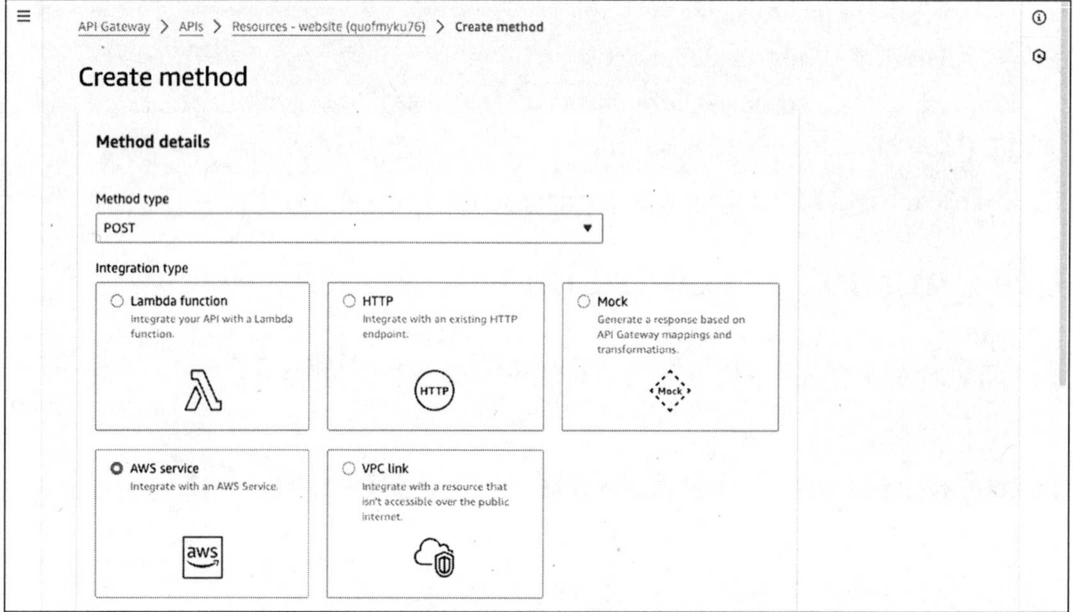

Figure 8.1: The method details

22. Select **POST** in the **HTTP method** dropdown.
23. Select the **Use action name** radio button in the **Action type** section.
24. Specify **`PutItem`** in the **Action name** field.
25. Paste the **`arn:aws:iam::{accountId}:role/apigateway-post-analytics-auth-callback`** ARN value copied earlier in the **Execution role** field.

Note: The `{accountId}` is the AWS account ID.

26. Uncheck the **Default timeout** switch button.
27. Specify **5000** in the **Custom timeout** field.
28. Click the **Create method** button. See *Figure 8.2*:

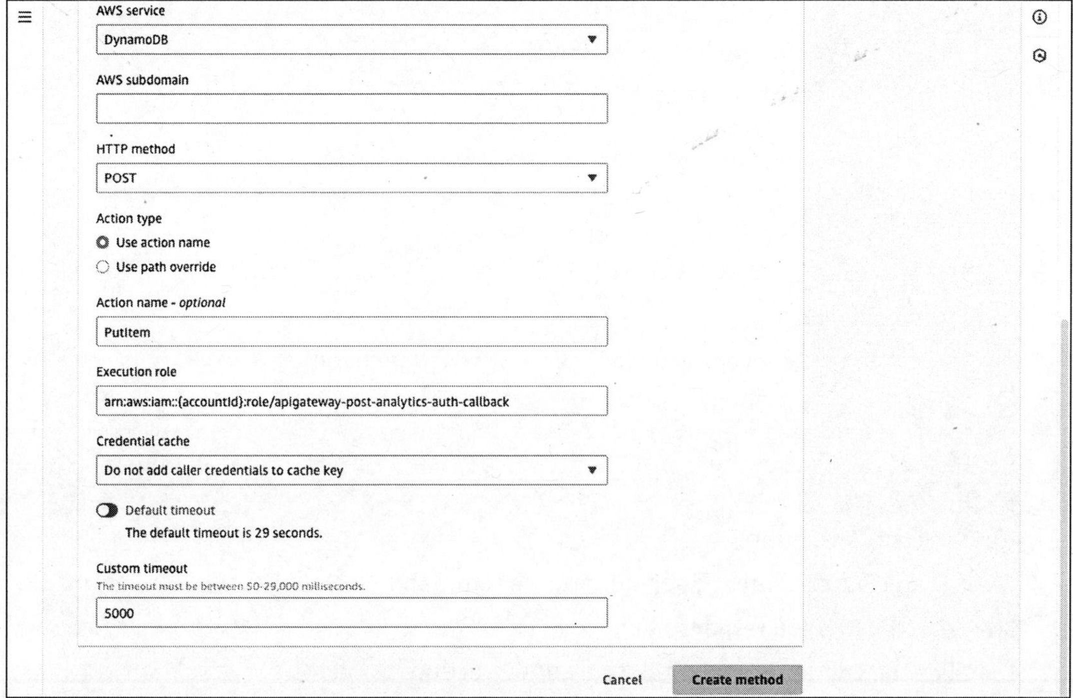

Figure 8.2: The method details

We have successfully created the method.

29. Go to the **Method request** tab.
30. Click the **Edit** button in the **Method request settings** section.
31. Select **cognitoAuthorizer** in the **Authorization** dropdown.
32. Specify **openid** in the **Authorization Scopes** field.
33. Click the **Add** button in the **Authorization Scopes** section.
34. Click the **Save** button.

    We have successfully added an authorizer to the method request settings.

35. Go to the **Integration request** tab.
36. Click the **Edit** button in the **Integration request settings** tab.
37. Expand the **Mapping templates** section.
38. Specify **application/json** in the **Content type** field.

39. Enter the following code in the **Template body** section:

```
{
  "TableName": "analytics",
  "Item": {
    "dataType": {
      "S": "auth-callback"
    },
    "timestamp": {
      "N": "$context.requestTimeEpoch"
    },
    "username": {
      "S": "$context.authorizer.claims.username"
    }
  }
}
```

40. Click the **Save** button.

    We have successfully added a mapping template.

41. Go to the **Method response** tab.
42. Click the **Edit** button in the **Response 200** section.
43. Click the **Add header** button.
44. Specify **Access-Control-Allow-Origin** in the **Header name** field.
45. Click the **Save** button.

    We have successfully edited the method response.

46. Go to the **Integration response** tab.
47. Click the **Edit** button in the **Default - Response** section.
48. Specify '*' in the **Access-Control-Allow-Origin** field.

Note: Make sure the value is *single quote asterisk single quote* with no spaces. The single quote should be straight like ' and not curly like '.

49. Expand the **Mapping templates** section.
50. Specify **`application/json`** in the **Content type** field.
51. Specify the following code in the **Template body** section:

```
{
  "errorMessage": "$context.error.message"
}
```

52. Click the **Save** button.

    We have successfully edited the integration response.

53. Click the **Deploy API** button.
54. Select **v1** in the **Stage** dropdown.
55. Click the **Deploy** button.

    We have successfully created the API endpoint.

Updating the auth callback web page

We will update the JavaScript code to make an HTTP POST request to the new API endpoint after the authorization code has been verified.

Hands-on exercise 5: Updating the auth callback web page

Let us update the authentication callback web page.

1. Open the **account/auth-callback.js** file on a computer.
2. Update the file to add the code noted as changes:

```
const url = new URL(location.href);
const code = url.searchParams.get('code');
const clientId = '{clientId}';
const redirectUri = `${url.origin}${url.pathname}`;
const cognitoDomain = 'auth.masteringawsserverlessbook.com';
const tokenEndpoint = `https://${cognitoDomain}/oauth2/token`;
const grantType = 'authorization_code';
const analyticsEndpoint = 'https://api.masteringawsserverlessbook.
com/analytics/auth-callback';
if (code) {
  try {
    const resp = await fetch(tokenEndpoint, {
      method: 'POST',
      headers: {
        'Content-Type': 'application/x-www-form-urlencoded',
      },
      body: `grant_type=${grantType}&client_
      id=${clientId}&code=${code}&redirect_uri=${redirectUri}`,
```

```
    });
    const data = await resp.json();
    if (typeof data == 'object' && data.access_token) {
      localStorage.setItem('jwt', JSON.stringify(data));
      /* !!!! START OF CHANGES !!!! */
      /* post analytics */
      await fetch(analyticsEndpoint, {
        method: 'POST',
        mode: 'cors',
        headers: {
          Authorization: data.access_token ?? '',
          'Content-Type': 'application/json',
        },
        body: JSON.stringify({}),
      }).catch(function(e) {
        console.warn(e);
      });
      /* !!!! END OF CHANGES !!!! */
    }
  } catch (e) {
    console.error(e);
    history.replaceState(null, '', url.origin);
    location.href = `${url.origin}/`;
  }
}
history.replaceState(null, '', url.origin);
location.href = `${url.origin}/account/index.html`;
```

3. Replace the `{clientId}` placeholder with the Client ID from the user pool app integration settings.

> **Note: The `${clientId}` variable is not a placeholder. Do not replace it with the Client ID.**

We have successfully updated the **`auth-callback.js`** file.

Uploading the files to S3 bucket

We will upload all the website files into the S3 bucket to ensure it has the latest versions of our files.

Hands-on exercise 6: Uploading the files to S3 bucket

Let us upload all the website files to the S3 bucket:

1. Go to the S3 service page.
2. Click the `masteringawsserverlessbook.com` bucket.
3. Click the **Upload** button.
4. Select all the website files from the computer.
5. Drag and drop all the files onto the bucket page.
6. Click the **Upload** button.
7. Wait for the files to finish uploading.

Invalidating the CloudFront distribution cache

We will invalidate all the cache to make sure all our website updates load properly in the browser.

Hands-on exercise 7: Invalidating the CloudFront distribution cache

Let us invalidate the distribution:

1. Go to the CloudFront service page.
2. Click the CloudFront distribution.
3. Go to the **Invalidations** tab.
4. Click the **Create invalidation** button.
5. Specify **/*** in the **Add object pages** field to invalidate all files.
6. Click the **Create invalidation** button.
7. Observe **In progress** in the **Status** section.

Note: It may take several minutes for the invalidation to complete.

8. Observe **Completed** in the **Status** section.

Testing the new API endpoint

We have all the parts put together. We will use the website to log in to see the auth callback analytics data written to the database.

Hands-on exercise 8: Testing the new API endpoint

Let us test the new API endpoint:

1. Visit **https://masteringawsserverlessbook.com.**
2. Log out if already logged in.
3. Click the **Log in** button.
4. Follow the on-screen instructions to log in.
5. Observe the account page.
6. Open the DynamoDB service page.
7. Go to the **Tables | Explore Items** menu option.
8. Click the **`analytics`** table.
9. Observe a table entry exists.
10. Copy the username.
11. Go to the Cognito service page.
12. Click on the **`masteringawsserverlessbook.com`** user pool.
13. Go to the **Users** tab.
14. Search for the username.
15. The search returns the user account as the result.

We have successfully verified the new analytics API endpoint.

Transforming data

We will extract, transform, and load the analytics data from the DynamoDB table to an S3 bucket. We will query the DynamoDB table to get the count of records within a 30-minute period. This count is written to an object in S3 that is formatted for machine learning.

Creating SSM parameters

We will use an SSM parameter to keep track of the next period we want to process. Also, we will specify the period is 30 minutes in milliseconds.

Hands-on exercise 9: Creating SSM parameters

Let us create SSM parameters.

1. Search **ssm** in the top search bar and click the **Systems Manager** search result or enter **https://us-east-1.console.aws.amazon.com/systems-manager/home** in the browser address bar.
2. Go to **Application Management | Parameter Store** menu option.
3. Click the **Create parameter** button.
4. Specify **/function-rule-analytics-auth-callback/next-start-iso-timestamp** in the **Name** field.
5. Select the **Standard** radio button in the **Tier** section. See *Figure 8.3* for your reference:

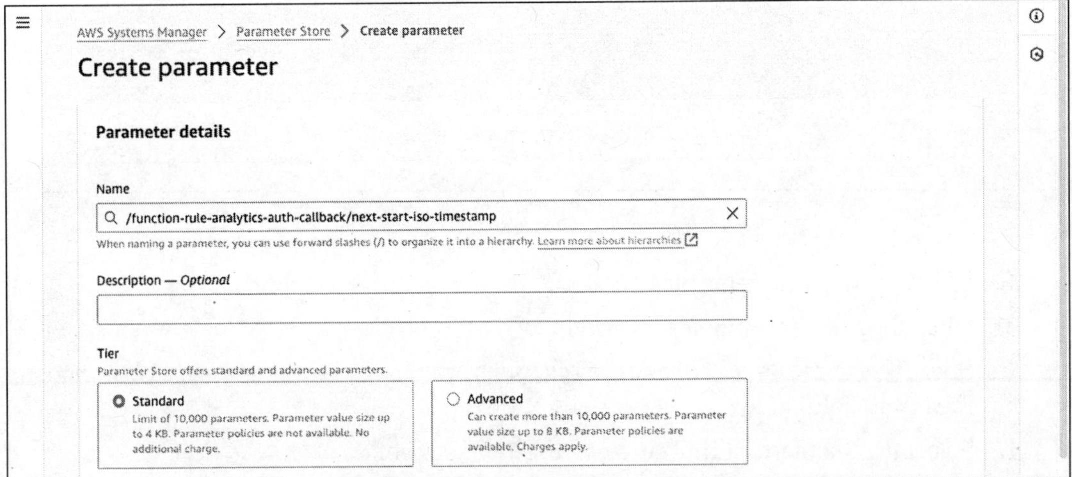

Figure 8.3: The parameter details

6. Select the **String** radio button in the **Type** section.
7. Select **text** in the **Data type** dropdown.
8. Specify an ISO timestamp in the **Value** field.

Note: Use the start time for today's date (for example, 2024-01-01T00:00:00.000Z as the value). Consider searching *utc time now* in a search engine to get the current ISO date and time.

9. Click the **Create parameter** button. See *Figure 8.4*:

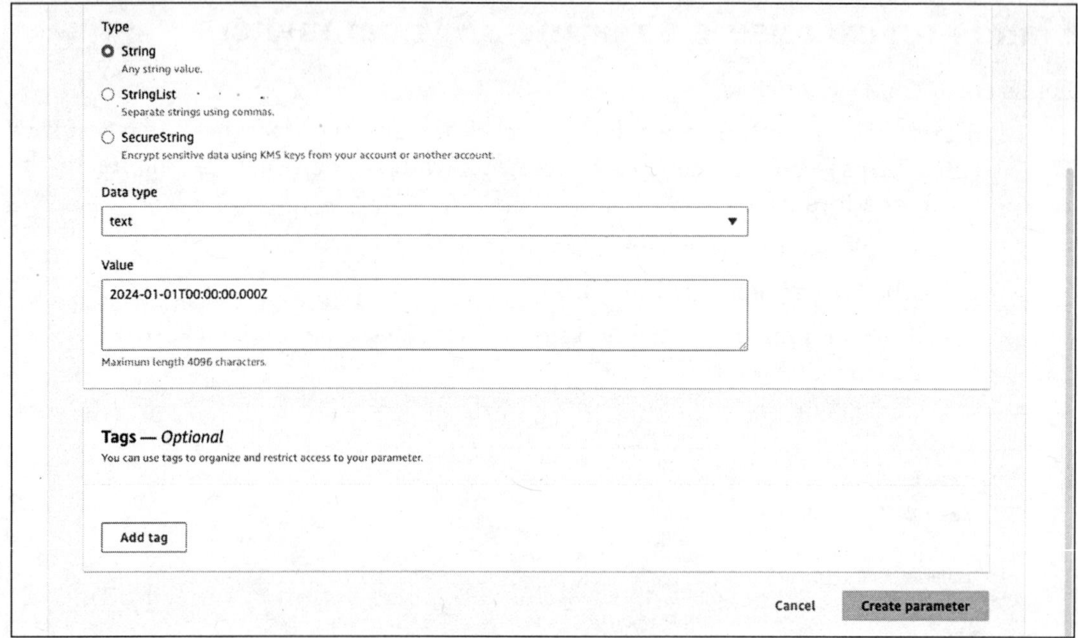

Figure 8.4: The parameter details

10. Observe the parameter was created.
11. Click the **Create parameter** button.
12. Specify **`/function-rule-analytics-auth-callback/interval-milliseconds`** in the **Name** field.
13. Select the **Standard** radio button in the **Tier** section.
14. Select the **String** radio button in the **Type** section.
15. Select **text** in the **Data type** dropdown.
16. Specify **`1800000`** in the **Value** field.

Note: This is 30 minutes in milliseconds.

17. Click the **Create parameter** button.
18. Observe the parameter was created.
19. Observe the parameter was created.

We have successfully created the parameters.

Creating an IAM policy

We will create an IAM policy for a new Lambda function so it can read the SSM parameters, get the current analytics data from DynamoDB table and S3 bucket, write the updated data to the S3 bucket, and update the SSM parameters.

Hands-on exercise 10: Creating an IAM policy

Let us create an IAM policy using the given steps:

1. Go to the IAM service page.
2. Go to the **Access Management | Policies** menu option.
3. Click the **Create policy** button.
4. Select **DynamoDB** in the **Service** dropdown.
5. Search **Query** in the **Filter Actions** search field.
6. Check the **Query** checkbox.
7. Check the **Specific** radio button in the **Resources** section.
8. Click the **Add ARNs** in the **table** section.
9. Click the **Visual** button.
10. Check the **This account** radio button in the **Resource in** section.
11. Specify `us-east-1` in the **Resource region** field.
12. Specify `analytics` in the **Resource table name** field.
13. Click the **Add ARNs** button.
14. Click the **Add more permissions** button.
15. Select **S3** in the **Service** dropdown.
16. Search `PutObject` in the **Filter Actions** search field.
17. Check the `PutObject` checkbox.
18. Check the **Specific** radio button in the **Resources** section.
19. Click the **Add ARNs** in the **object** section.
20. Click the **Visual** button.
21. Specify `masteringawsserverlessbook-data/analytics` in the **Resource bucket name** field.
22. Specify `auth-callback.csv` in the **Resource object name** section.

Note: The object key is `analytics/auth-callback.csv` but the AWS console UI automatically moves the `analytics/` key prefix to the bucket name.

23. Click the **Add ARNs** button.
24. Click the **Add more permissions** button.
25. Select **Systems Manager** in the **Service** dropdown.
26. Specify `GetParametersByPath` in the search field.
27. Check the `GetParametersByPath` checkbox.
28. Specify `PutParameter` in the search field.

29. Check the `PutParameter` checkbox.
30. Check the **Specific** radio button in the **Resources** section.
31. Click the **Add ARNs** link in the **parameter** section.
32. Click the **Visual** button.
33. Select the **This account** radio button in the **Resource in** section.
34. Specify `us-east-1` in the **Resource region** field.
35. Specify `function-rule-analytics-auth-callback/*` in the **Resource parameter name without leading slash** section.
36. Click the **Add ARNs** button.
37. Click the **Next** button.
38. Specify `function-rule-analytics-auth-callback` in the **Policy name** field.
39. Click the **Create policy** button.

We have successfully created the IAM policy.

Creating an IAM role

We will create an IAM role that uses the new policy.

Hands-on exercise 11: Creating an IAM role

Let us create an IAM role:

1. Go to the IAM service page.
2. Go to the **Access Management | Roles** menu option.
3. Click the **Create role** button.
4. Select the **AWS service** radio button in the **Trusted entity type** section.
5. Select **Lambda** in the **Service or use case** dropdown.
6. Click the **Next** button.
7. Specify `function-rule-analytics-auth-callback` in the search field.
8. Check the `function-rule-analytics-auth-callback` checkbox.
9. Specify **AWSLambdaBasicExecutionRole** in the search field.
10. Check the **AWSLambdaBasicExecutionRole** checkbox.
11. Click the **Next** button.
12. Specify `function-rule-analytics-auth-callback` in the **Role name** field.
13. Click the **Create role** button.

We have successfully created the IAM role.

Creating a Lambda function

We will create a Lambda function that will read the SSM parameters, get the current analytics data from DynamoDB table and S3 bucket, write the updated data to the S3 bucket, and update the SSM parameters.

Hands-on exercise 12: Creating a Lambda function

Let us create a Lambda function.

1. Go to the Lambda service page.
2. Click the **Create function** button.
3. Specify **`rule-analytics-auth-callback`** in the **Function name** field.
4. Specify **Node.js** in the **Runtime** dropdown.
5. Select the **arm64** radio button in the **Architecture** section.
6. Expand the **Change default execution role** section.
7. Check the **Use an existing role** radio button in the **Execution role** section.
8. Select **`function-rule-analytics-auth-callback`** in the **Execution role** dropdown.
9. Click the "**Create function**" button.
10. Enter the following code in the "**Code source**" section:

```
import {
  SSMClient,
  GetParametersByPathCommand,
  PutParameterCommand,
} from '@aws-sdk/client-ssm';
import {
  DynamoDBClient,
  QueryCommand,
} from '@aws-sdk/client-dynamodb';
import {
  S3Client,
  GetObjectCommand,
  PutObjectCommand,
} from '@aws-sdk/client-s3';
export const handler = async (event) => {
  /* get ssm parameters */
  const ssmClient = new SSMClient({
```

```
  region: process.env.AWS_REGION,
});
const ssmGetCmd = new GetParametersByPathCommand({
  Path: '/function-rule-analytics-auth-callback/',
  Recursive: true,
  WithDecryption: false,
});
const ssmGetResp = await ssmClient.send(ssmGetCmd);
if (!ssmGetResp.Parameters) {
  throw new Error('No ssm parameters found');
}
const startIsoTimestampParam = ssmGetResp.Parameters.find(
  (x) => x.Name ===
    '/function-rule-analytics-auth-callback/next-start-iso-
    timestamp'
);
if (!startIsoTimestampParam) {
  throw new Error('Empty startIsoTimestampParam');
}
const startIsoTimestamp = startIsoTimestampParam.Value;
const intervalParam = ssmGetResp.Parameters.find(
  (x) => x.Name ===
    '/function-rule-analytics-auth-callback/interval-milliseconds'
);
if (!intervalParam) {
  throw new Error('Empty intervalParam');
}
const intervalMilliseconds = Number(intervalParam.Value);
/* time check */
const now = new Date().valueOf();
const start = new Date(startIsoTimestamp).valueOf();
const end = new Date(start + intervalMilliseconds - 1).valueOf();
if (now < end) {
  console.warn('Too early');
```

```
  return;
}
/* query dynamodb table */
const ddbClient = new DynamoDBClient({
  region: process.env.AWS_REGION,
});
let count = 0;
const queryInput = {
  TableName: 'analytics',
  ExpressionAttributeNames: {
    '#PK': 'dataType',
    '#SK': 'timestamp',
  },
  ExpressionAttributeValues: {
    ':pk': {
      S: 'auth-callback',
    },
    ':sk1': {
      N: `${start}`,
    },
    ':sk2': {
      N: `${end}`,
    },
  },
  KeyConditionExpression: '#PK = :pk AND #SK BETWEEN :sk1 and :sk2',
  Select: 'COUNT',
  ExclusiveStartKey: undefined,
};
const queryCmd = new QueryCommand(queryInput);
do {
  const queryResp = await ddbClient.send(queryCmd);
  queryInput.ExclusiveStartKey = queryResp.LastEvaluatedKey;
  count += queryResp.Count;
} while (queryInput.ExclusiveStartKey);
```

```
/* get s3 object data */
const s3Client = new S3Client({
  region: process.env.AWS_REGION,
});
let objectBody = 'timestamp,value';
try {
  const getObjCmd = new GetObjectCommand({
    Bucket: 'masteringawsserverlessbook-data',
    Key: 'analytics/auth-callback.csv',
  });
  const getObjectResp = await s3Client.send(getObjCmd);
  if (getObjectResp.Body) {
    objectBody = await getObjectResp.Body.transformToString();
  }
} catch (e) {
  console.warn('Object does not exist');
}
/* write s3 object data */
const objectStartTimestamp = startIsoTimestamp
  .replace('T', ' ').replace('.000Z', '');
if (objectBody.search(objectStartTimestamp) === -1) {
  console.info('Data already exists in the S3 object.');
  objectBody += `\n${objectStartTimestamp},${count}`;
}
const putObjCmd = new PutObjectCommand({
    Bucket: 'masteringawsserverlessbook-data',
    Key: 'analytics/auth-callback.csv',
    Body: objectBody,
  });
await s3Client.send(putObjCmd);
/* update ssm parameter */
const putParamCmd = new PutParameterCommand({
  Name:
    '/function-rule-analytics-auth-callback/next-start-iso-
    timestamp',
```

```
        Value: new Date(end + 1).toISOString(),
        Overwrite: true,
      });
      await ssmClient.send(putParamCmd);
    };
```

11. Go to **File** | **Save**.
12. Click the **Deploy** button.
13. Click the **Test** button.
14. Click the **Create new event** radio button in the **Test event action** section.
15. Specify **TestEvent** in the **Event name** field.
16. Specify `{}` in the **Event JSON** field.
17. Click the **Save** button.
18. Click the **Test** button.
19. Go to the **Configuration** tab.
20. Go to the **General configuration** menu option.
21. Click the **Edit** button in the **General configuration** section. See *Figure 8.5*:

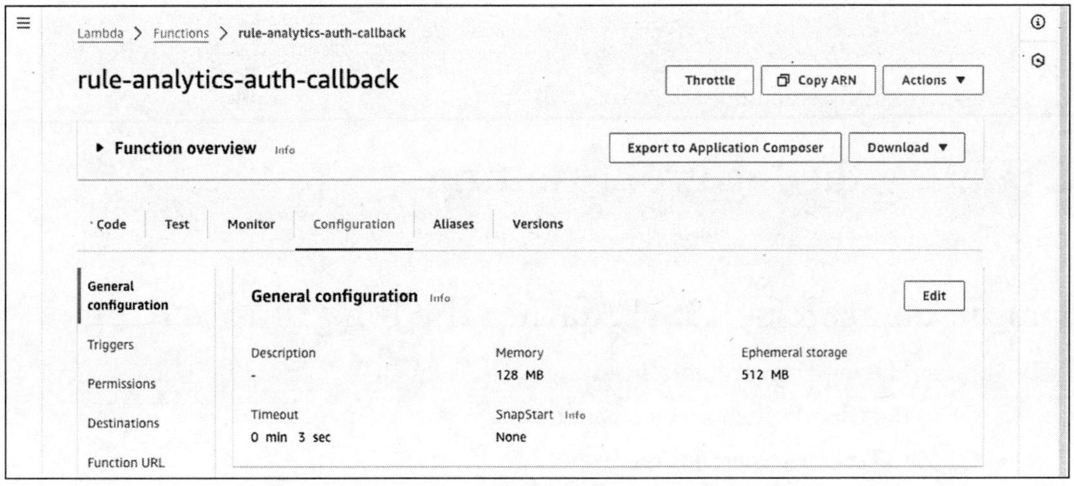

Figure 8.5: *The general configuration sections*

22. Specify `1024` MB in the **Memory** field.
23. Specify `0` min and `10` sec in the **Timeout** section.

Note: When the website gets super popular, the timeout will likely need to be longer since there will be more data in the DynamoDB table.

24. Click the **Save** button. See *Figure 8.6*:

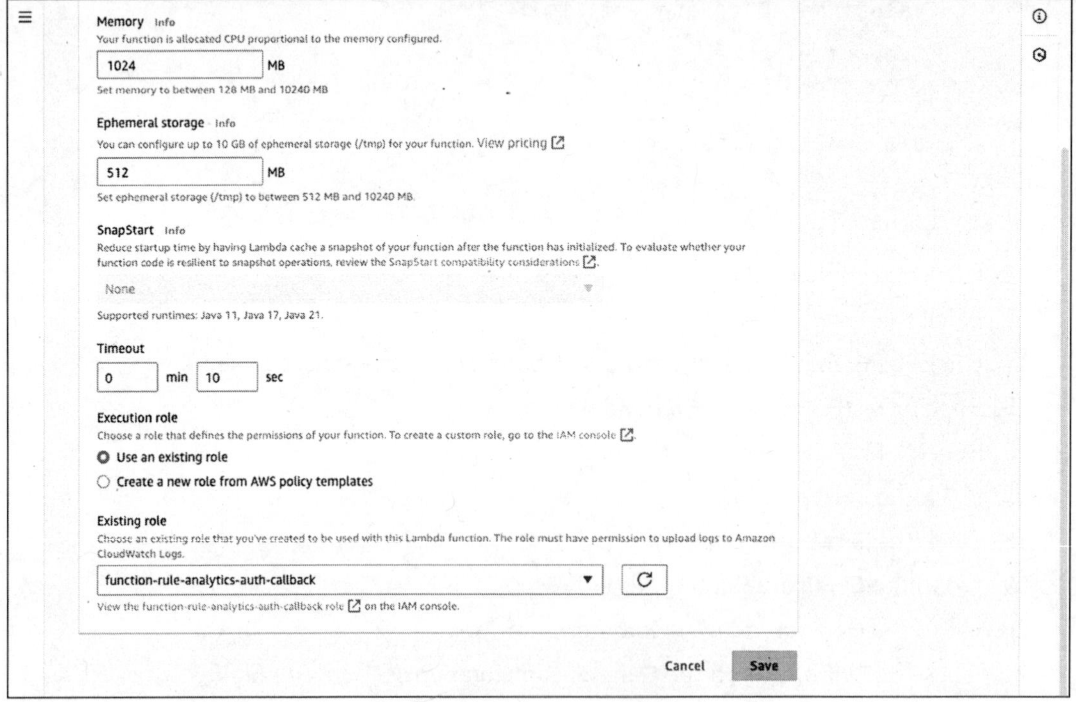

Figure 8.6: The basic settings

We have successfully created the Lambda function.

Updating the log group settings

We will update the log group retention settings to be one week.

Hands-on exercise 13: Updating the log group settings

Let us update the log group retention settings.

1. Go to the CloudWatch service page.
2. Go to the **Logs** | **Log groups** menu option.
3. Check the **`/aws/lambda/rule-analytics-auth-callback`** log group.
4. Click the **Actions** dropdown.
5. Select the **Edit retention setting(s)** dropdown option.
6. Select **1 week (7 days)** in the **Expire events after** dropdown.
7. Click the **Save** button.

We have successfully updated the log group retention settings.

Creating an EventBridge schedule rule

We will create a schedule rule that runs every 10 minutes. We want the rule to run more periodically than the data time window, so the data processing does not fall behind in the event there is a service outage.

Hands-on exercise 14: Creating an EventBridge schedule rule

Let us create an EventBridge schedule rule.

1. Search **eventbridge** in the top search bar and click the **Amazon EventBridge** search result or enter **https://us-east-1.console.aws.amazon.com/events/home** in the browser address bar.
2. Go to the **Scheduler | Schedules** menu option.
3. Click the **Create schedule** button.
4. Specify **function-rule-analytics-auth-callback** in the **Schedule name** field. See *Figure 8.7*:

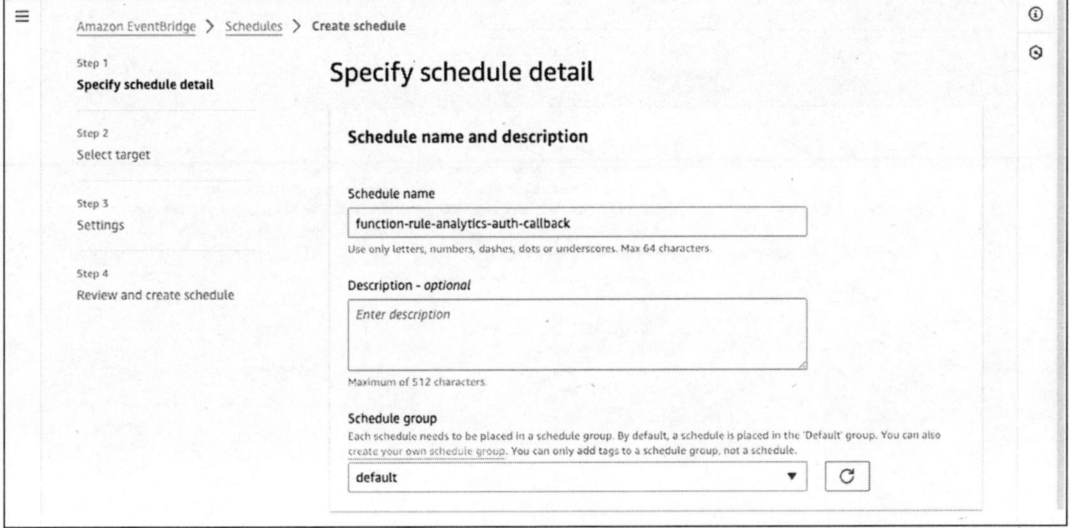

Figure 8.7: The schedule details

5. Select the **Recurring schedule** radio button in the **Occurrence** section.
6. Select the **Rate-based schedule** radio button in the **Schedule type** section.
7. Specify **10** in the **Value** field in the **Rate expression** section.
8. Select **minutes** in the **Unit** dropdown in the **Rate expression** section.
9. Select **Off** in the **Flexible time window** dropdown. See *Figure 8.8* for your reference:

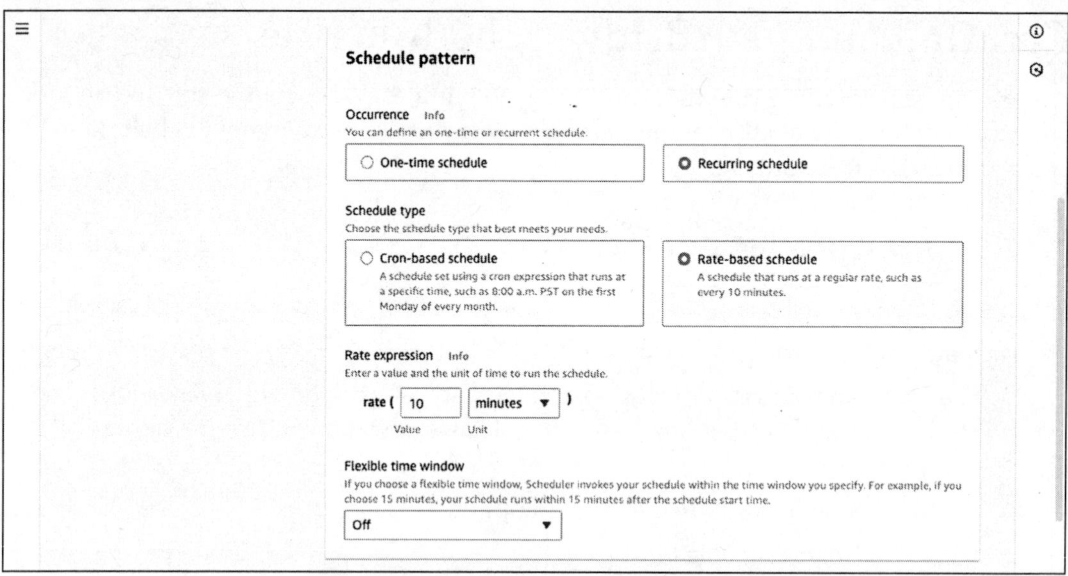

Figure 8.8: The schedule details

10. Click the **Next** button. See *Figure 8.9*:

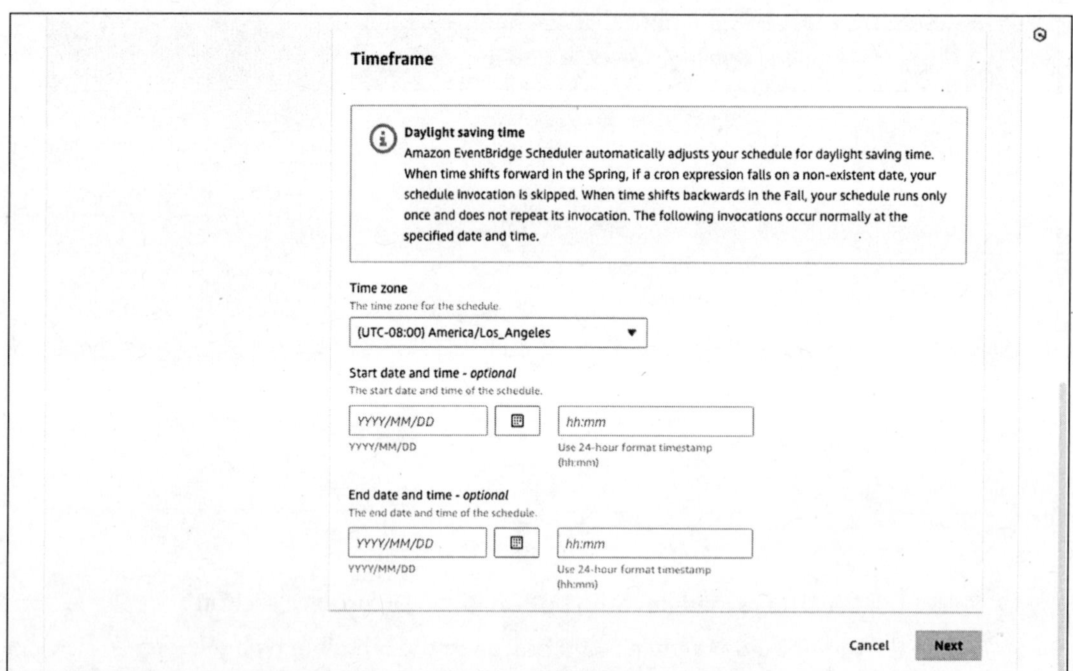

Figure 8.9: The schedule details

11. Select the **Templated targets** radio button in the **Target API** section.

12. Select the **AWS Lambda Invoke** radio button in the **Target API** section. See *Figure 8.10*:

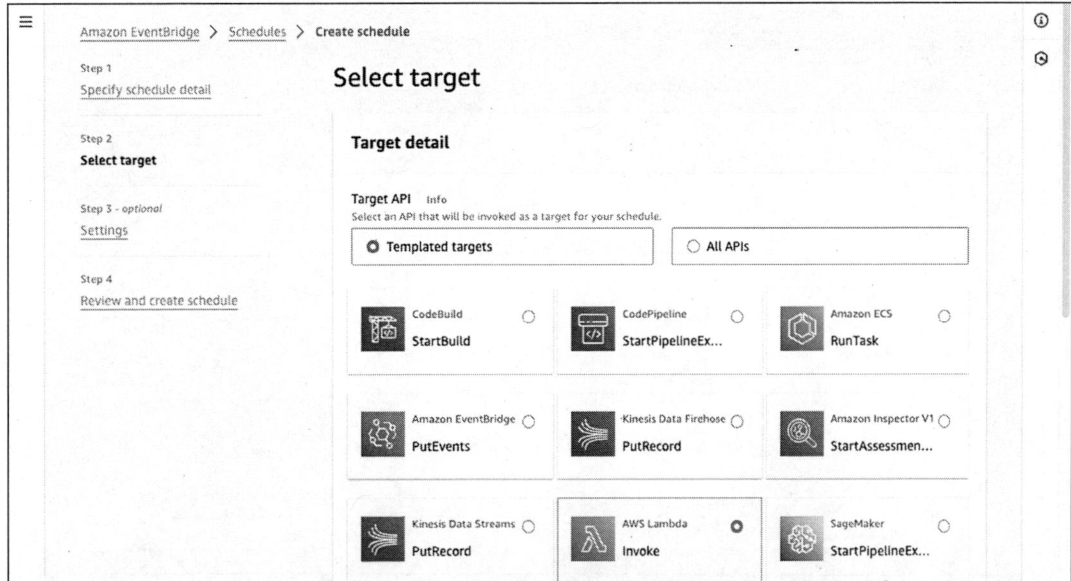

Figure 8.10: The target details

13. Select `rule-analytics-auth-callback` in the **Lambda function** dropdown.
14. Leave the **Payload** section empty. See *Figure 8.11*:

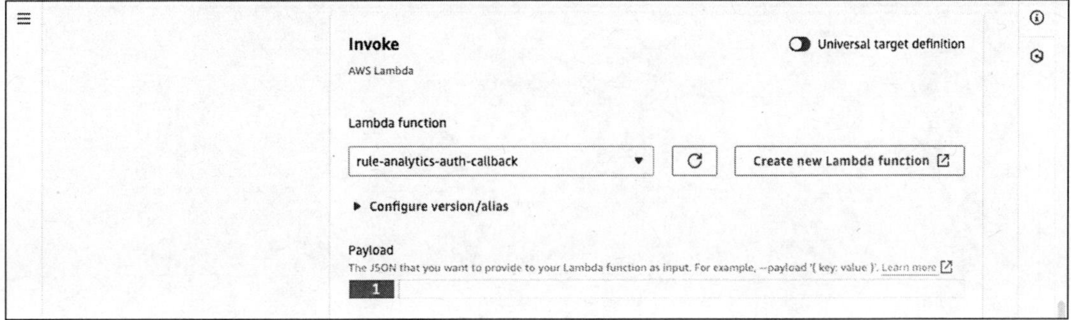

Figure 8.11: The target details

15. Click the **Next** button.
16. Check the **Enable** switch button.
17. Select **NONE** in the **Action after schedule completion** dropdown.
18. Uncheck the **Retry** switch button. See *Figure 8.12*:

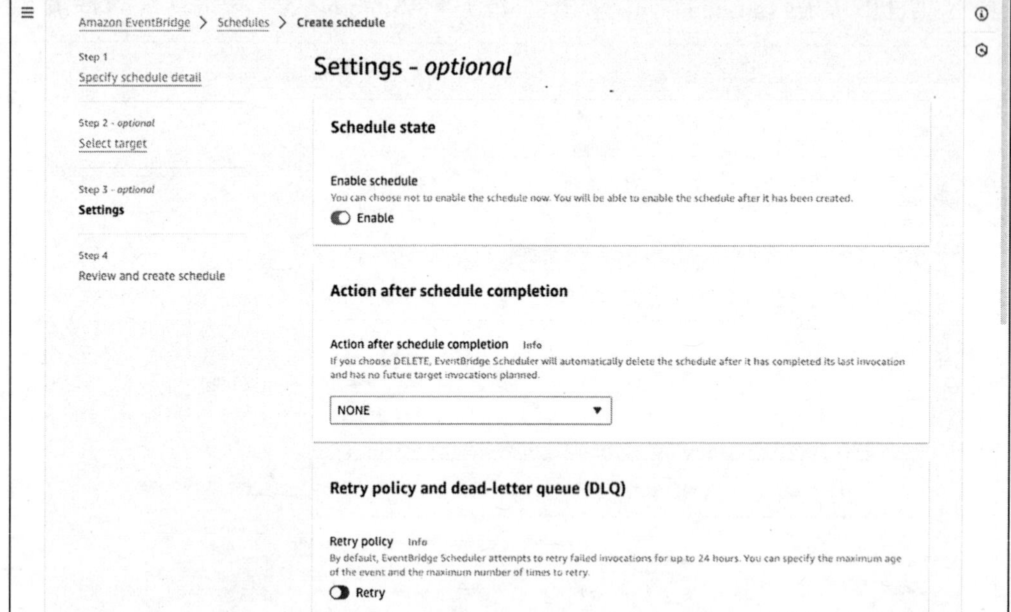

Figure 8.12: The schedule settings

19. Go to the **Permission** section.
20. Check the **Create new role for this schedule** radio button in the **Execution role** section.
21. Specify **`rule-analytics-auth-callback`** in the **Role name** field. See *Figure 8.13*:

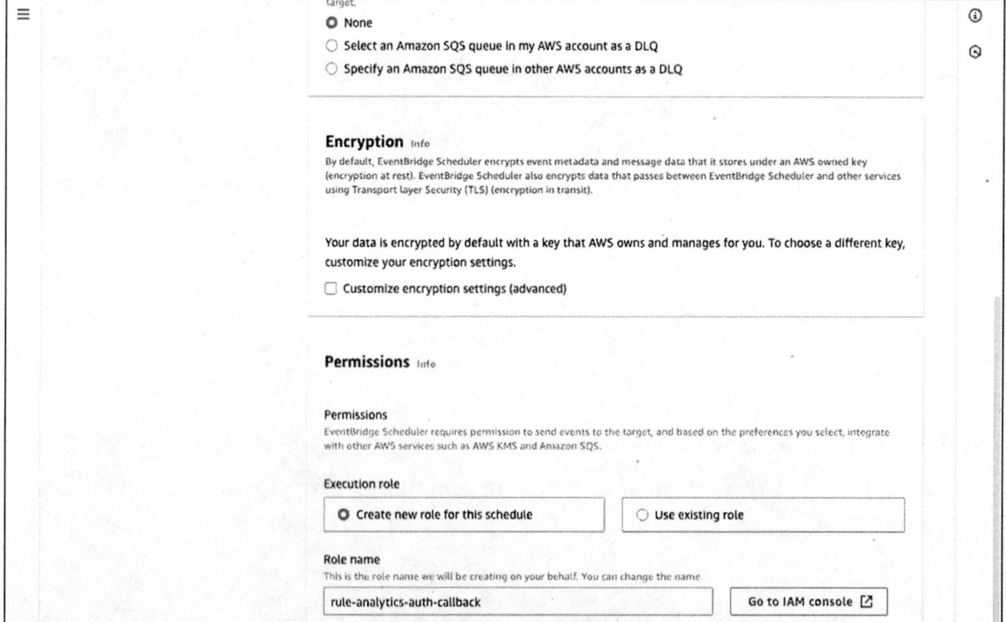

Figure 8.13: The schedule settings

22. Click the **Next** button.
23. Click the **Create schedule** button.

We have successfully created a schedule rule.

Checking the rule is working

We can check different places to make sure the rule is working. Follow the given steps:

1. If we check the `/aws/lambda/rule-analytics-auth-callback` CloudWatch log group, we should see new log entries over time.
2. If we check the `/function-rule-analytics-auth-callback/next-start-iso-timestamp` SSM parameter, we should see the value increment over time.
3. If we check the `masteringawsserverlessbook-data` bucket, we should see the `analytics/auth-callback.csv` object exists.
4. If we download the `analytics/auth-callback.csv` object, we should see the data grow over time.

We have successfully created a file we can use for machine learning.

Analyzing data using machine learning

Machine learning can be complex and takes time to master on its own. We will explore how to use serverless workflows to perform machine learning. The workflow consists of the following:

- Create an S3 event trigger for the `analytics/auth-callback.csv` object that sends a trigger to a Lambda function that performs training.
- Create an S3 event trigger for the `rcf/` object path that sends a trigger to a Lambda function that performs inference.
- The event notification triggers whenever the `analytics/auth-callback.csv` object is created or updated.
- The target Lambda function (that is, the training function) will receive the event and trigger the execution.
- The training function will create a SageMaker session, start the training and record the session information in SSM.
- When SageMaker finishes the training, it will write its output to the S3 bucket.
- The event notification triggers whenever an object is created or updated in the "rcf/" key prefix.
- The target Lambda function (that is, the inference function) will receive the event and trigger the execution.

- The inference function will use the session information from SSM to run the SageMaker inference and delete the SageMaker session when it completes.
- When SageMaker finishes the training, it will write its output to the S3 bucket `rcf/` key prefix.

The entire machine learning workflow is serverless and is based on an event-driven design.

We will explore the different parts of the workflow. We will use the Amazon SageMaker **Random Cut Forest** (**RCF**) machine learning algorithm to detect anomalies in the auth callback data. An anomaly might be an indicator of increased demand. We can use the anomaly information to attempt to determine its cause.

We will use the *An Introduction to SageMaker Random Cut Forests* article[1] in the *Amazon SageMaker Examples* website. The code and documentation on the website are licensed under Apache License 2.0. We will use parts of its code as inspiration to create our Lambda functions. The original code is meant to run on a server or a local computer. The adapted code for the Lambda functions uses the relevant parts of the code so it follows an event-driven design.

We will explore how to set up the different parts as examples instead of hands-on exercises. Machine learning can be costly, and performing the steps as hands-on exercises might be cost-prohibitive. We will be billed for the duration that SageMaker runs and the selected CPU size. The training and inference can each take several minutes to complete depending on the size of the data. As the amount of data grows, the training and inference will take longer. Over time, we would remove older data, and we can explore using longer time periods, such as one-hour periods, to reduce costs.

Creating IAM policies

We will create policies for the **`function-sagemaker-rcf-run-training`** function and **`function-sagemaker-rcf-run-inference`** function.

Example 1: Creating IAM policies

Let us create IAM policies using the given steps:

1. Go to the IAM service page.
2. Go to the **Access Management | Policies** menu option.
3. Click the **Create policy** button.
4. Click the **JSON** button.
5. Enter the following code in the **Policy editor** field.

1 "An Introduction to SageMaker Random Cut Forests." Amazon SageMaker Examples. Amazon Web Services. **https://sagemaker-examples.readthedocs.io/en/latest/introduction_to_amazon_algorithms/random_cut_forest/random_cut_forest.html**

Note: Replace the `{accountId}` with the desired AWS account ID.

```
{
  "Version": "2012-10-17",
  "Statement": [
    {
      "Sid": "VisualEditor0",
      "Effect": "Allow",
      "Action": [
        "iam:PassRole",
        "logs:DescribeLogStreams",
        "logs:GetLogEvents",
        "sagemaker:CreateModel",
        "sagemaker:CreateEndpointConfig",
        "sagemaker:DescribeTrainingJob",
        "sagemaker:CreateTrainingJob",
        "ssm:GetParameter",
        "ssm:PutParameter"
      ],
      "Resource": [
        "arn:aws:logs:us-east-1:{accountId}:log-group::log-stream:/
        aws/sagemaker/TrainingJobs:log-stream:*",
        "arn:aws:logs:us-east-1:{accountId}:log-group:/aws/
        sagemaker/TrainingJobs",
        "arn:aws:sagemaker:us-east-1:{accountId}:endpoint-config/*",
        "arn:aws:sagemaker:us-east-1:{accountId}:training-job/*",
        "arn:aws:sagemaker:us-east-1:{accountId}:model/*",
        "arn:aws:ssm:us-east-1:{accountId}:parameter/function-
        sagemaker-rcf/*"
      ]
    },
    {
      "Sid": "VisualEditor1",
      "Effect": "Allow",
      "Action": "s3:GetObject",
```

```
      "Resource": "arn:aws:s3:::masteringawsserverlessbook-data/
      analytics/auth-callback.csv"
    },
    {
      "Sid": "VisualEditor2",
      "Effect": "Allow",
      "Action": "s3:PutObject",
      "Resource": "arn:aws:s3:::masteringawsserverlessbook-data/rcf/*"
    }
  ]
}
```

6. Click the **Next** button.
7. Specify `function-sagemaker-rcf-run-training` in the **Policy name** section.
8. Click the **Create policy** button.

   We have successfully created the `function-sagemaker-rcf-run-training` policy.
9. Click the **Create policy** button.
10. Click the **JSON** button.
11. Enter the following code in the **Policy editor** field.

Note: Replace the `{accountId}` with the desired AWS account ID.

```
{
  "Version": "2012-10-17",
  "Statement": [
    {
      "Sid": "VisualEditor0",
      "Effect": "Allow",
      "Action": [
        "iam:PassRole",
        "logs:DescribeLogStreams",
        "logs:GetLogEvents",
        "sagemaker:CreateModel",
        "sagemaker:CreateEndpointConfig",
        "sagemaker:DescribeTrainingJob",
        "sagemaker:CreateTrainingJob",
```

```
        "ssm:PutParameter",
        "ssm:GetParameter"
      ],
      "Resource": [
        "arn:aws:logs:us-east-1:{accountId}:log-group::log-stream:/
        aws/sagemaker/TrainingJobs:log-stream:*",
        "arn:aws:logs:us-east-1:{accountId}:log-group:/aws/
        sagemaker/TrainingJobs",
        "arn:aws:sagemaker:us-east-1:{accountId}:endpoint-config/*",
        "arn:aws:sagemaker:us-east-1:{accountId}:training-job/*",
        "arn:aws:sagemaker:us-east-1:{accountId}:model/*",
        "arn:aws:ssm:us-east-1:{accountId}:parameter/function-
        sagemaker-rcf/*"
      ]
    },
    {
      "Sid": "VisualEditor1",
      "Effect": "Allow",
      "Action": [
          "s3:GetObject",
          "s3:PutObject"
        ],
      "Resource": "arn:aws:s3:::masteringawsserverlessbook-data/
      rcf/*"
    }
  ]
}
```

12. Click the **Next** button.
13. Specify `function-sagemaker-rcf-run-inference` in the **Policy name** section.
14. Click the **Create policy** button.

We have successfully created the `function-sagemaker-rcf-run-inference` policy.

Creating IAM roles

We will create roles for the `function-sagemaker-rcf-run-training` function, `function-sagemaker-rcf-run-inference` function and the SageMaker execution.

Example 2: Creating IAM roles

Let us create IAM roles:

1. Go to the IAM service page.
2. Go to the **Access Management | Roles** menu option.
3. Click the **Create role** button.
4. Select the **AWS service** radio button.
5. Select **Lambda** in the **Service or use case** dropdown.
6. Click the **Next** button.
7. Specify `function-sagemaker-rcf-run-training` in the search field.
8. Check the `function-sagemaker-rcf-run-training` checkbox.
9. Specify **AWSLambdaBasicExecutionRole** in the search field.
10. Check the **AWSLambdaBasicExecutionRole** checkbox.
11. Specify `function-sagemaker-rcf-run-training` in the **Role name** field.
12. Click the **Create role** button.

    We successfully created the `function-sagemaker-rcf-run-training` role.
13. Click the **Create role** button.
14. Select the **AWS service** radio button.
15. Select **Lambda** in the **Service or use case** dropdown.
16. Click the **Next** button.
17. Specify `function-sagemaker-rcf-run-inference` in the search field.
18. Check the `function-sagemaker-rcf-run-inference` checkbox.
19. Specify **AWSLambdaBasicExecutionRole** in the search field.
20. Check the **AWSLambdaBasicExecutionRole** checkbox.
21. Specify `function-sagemaker-rcf-run-inference` in the **Role name** field.
22. Click the **Create role** button.

    We have successfully created the `function-sagemaker-rcf-run-inference` role.
23. Click the **Create role** button.
24. Select the **AWS service** radio button.
25. Select **SageMaker** in the **Service or use case** dropdown.
26. Click the **Next** button.
27. Confirm **AmazonSageMakerFullAccess** is pre-populated.
28. Click the **Next** button.
29. Specify `sagemaker-full-access` in the **Role name** field.
30. Click the **Create role** button.

We have successfully created the **`sagemaker-full-access`** role.

Creating Lambda functions

We will create the **`function-sagemaker-rcf-run-training`** and **`function-sagemaker-rcf-run-inference`** functions.

Example 3: Creating Lambda functions

Let us create Lambda functions:

1. Go to the Lambda service page.
2. Click the **Create function** button.
3. Specify **`sagemaker-rcf-run-training`** in the **Function name** field.
4. Specify **Python** in the **Runtime** dropdown.
5. Check the **arm64** radio button in the **Architecture** section.
6. Expand the **Change default execution role**.
7. Check the **Use an existing role** radio button in the **Execution role** section.
8. Select **`function-sagemaker-rcf-run-training`** in the **Existing role** dropdown.
9. Click the **Create function** button.
10. Go to the **Configuration** tab.
11. Go to the **General configuration** menu option.
12. Click the **Edit** button in the **General configuration** section.
13. Specify **`1024`** MB in the **Memory** field.
14. Specify **`15`** min and **`0`** sec in the **Timeout** section.
15. Click the **Save** button.
16. Go to the **Code** tab.
17. Enter the following code in the **Code source** section:

```
#!/usr/bin/env python3
# Derived from https://github.com/aws/amazon-sagemaker-examples/blob/main/introduction_to_amazon_algorithms/random_cut_forest/random_cut_forest.ipynb
#
import boto3
import datetime
import numpy as np
import pandas as pd
```

```
import sagemaker
import tempfile


def handler(event, context):
    for record in event["Records"]:
        process_record(record)


def process_record(record):
    # input validation
    oldest_event_time = datetime.datetime.now() - datetime.
    timedelta(minutes=5)
    if (record["eventSource"] != "aws:s3"):
        print("incorrect eventSource")
        return
    if (record["eventName"] != "ObjectCreated:Put"):
        print("incorrect eventName")
        return
    if (record["eventTime"] < oldest_event_time.isoformat()):
        print("old eventTime:", record["eventTime"], " < ",
            oldest_event_time.isoformat())
        return
    bucket_name = record["s3"]["bucket"]["name"]
    object_key = record["s3"]["object"]["key"]
    object_key = object_key.replace("+", " ", len(object_key))
    if (bucket_name != "masteringawsserverlessbook-data"):
        print("incorrect bucket")
        return
    if (object_key != "analytics/auth-callback.csv"):
        print("incorrect file type")
        return
    # download data
    data_filename = tempfile.mkstemp(".csv")[1]
    s3 = boto3.client("s3")
    ssm = boto3.client("ssm")
```

```
    s3.download_file(bucket_name, object_key, data_filename)
    downloaded_data = pd.read_csv(data_filename, delimiter=",")
    # random cut forest
    training_data = downloaded_data.value.to_numpy().reshape(-1, 1)
    run_rcf_training(
        "training",
        training_data,
    )

def run_rcf_training(job_name, training_data):
    # vars
    bucket_name = "masteringawsserverlessbook-data"
    role_arn = "arn:aws:iam::{accountId}:role/sagemaker-full-access"
    ssm_prefix = "function-sagemaker-rcf"
    num_samples_per_tree = 365
    num_trees = 100
    data_name = "auth-callback"
    base_job_name = f"{data_name}-{job_name}"
    # specify general training job information
    print("Starting RandomCutForest for", job_name, "using role",
    role_arn)
    print("Using bucket", bucket_name, "and key prefix", job_name)
    rcf = sagemaker.RandomCutForest(
        base_job_name=base_job_name,
        role=role_arn,
        instance_count=1,
        instance_type="ml.m4.xlarge",
        data_location=f"s3://{bucket_name}/rcf/",
        output_path=f"s3://{bucket_name}/rcf/output",
        num_samples_per_tree=num_samples_per_tree,
        num_trees=num_trees,
    )
    # automatically upload the training data to S3 and run the training
    job
    rcf.fit(rcf.record_set(training_data))
```

```
ssm = boto3.client("ssm")
ssm.put_parameter(
    Name=f"{ssm_prefix}/{job_name}",
    Value=rcf.latest_training_job.name,
    Overwrite=True,
)
model_name = sagemaker.Session()
    .create_model_from_job(rcf.latest_training_job.name,
    role=role_arn)
config_name = sagemaker.Session()
    .create_endpoint_config(model_name, model_name, 1, "ml.
    m4.xlarge")
```

18. Click the "**Deploy**" button.

    We have successfully created the "**sagemaker-rcf-run-training**" function.
19. Click the "**Create function**" button.
20. Specify "**sagemaker-rcf-run-inference**" in the "**Function name**" field.
21. Specify "**Python**" in the "**Runtime**" dropdown.
22. Check the "**arm64**" radio button in the "**Architecture**" section.
23. Expand the "**Change default execution role**"
24. Check the "**Use an existing role**" radio button in the "**Execution role**" section.
25. Select "**function-sagemaker-rcf-run-inference**" in the "**Existing role**" dropdown.
26. Click the "**Create function**" button.
27. Go to the "**Configuration**" tab.
28. Go to the "**General configuration**" menu option.
29. Click the "**Edit**" button in the "**General configuration**" section.
30. Specify "**1024**" MB in the "**Memory**" field.
31. Specify "**15**" min and "**0**" sec in the **Timeout** section.
32. Click the "**Save**" button.
33. Go to the "**Code**" tab.
34. Enter the following code in the "**Code source**" section:

```
#!/usr/bin/env python3

# Derived from https://github.com/aws/amazon-sagemaker-examples/blob/
main/introduction_to_amazon_algorithms/random_cut_forest/random_cut_
forest.ipynb
```

```
#
import boto3
import datetime
import numpy as np
import pandas as pd
import sagemaker
from sagemaker.serializers import CSVSerializer
from sagemaker.deserializers import JSONDeserializer
import tempfile

def handler(event, context):
    print("event", event)
    print("context", context)

    for record in event["Records"]:
        process_record(record)

def process_record(record):
    # input validation
    oldest_event_time = datetime.datetime.now() - datetime.
    timedelta(minutes=5)
    if (record["eventSource"] != "aws:s3"):
        print("incorrect eventSource")
        return
    if (record["eventName"] != "ObjectCreated:Put"):
        print("incorrect eventName")
        return
    if (record["eventTime"] < oldest_event_time.isoformat()):
        print("old eventTime:", record["eventTime"], " < ",
            oldest_event_time.isoformat())
        return
    bucket_name = record["s3"]["bucket"]["name"]
    object_key = record["s3"]["object"]["key"]
    object_key = object_key.replace("+", " ", len(object_key))
```

```
    if (bucket_name != "masteringawsserverlessbook-data"):
        print("incorrect bucket")
        return
    if (not object_key.endswith(".csv")):
        print("incorrect file type")
        return
    # download data
    data_filename = tempfile.mkstemp(".csv")[1]
    s3 = boto3.client("s3")
    ssm = boto3.client("ssm")
    print("Downloading", object_key, "from", bucket_name, "to",
        data_filename)
    s3.download_file(bucket_name, object_key, data_filename)
    downloaded_data = pd.read_csv(data_filename, delimiter=",")
    # random cut forest
    inference_data = downloaded_data.value.to_numpy().reshape(-1, 1)
    run_rcf_inference(
        inference_data,
        downloaded_data,
    )

def run_rcf_inference(ssm_name, inference_data, downloaded_data):
    # vars
    bucket_name = "masteringawsserverlessbook-data"
    role_arn = "arn:aws:iam::{accountId}:role/sagemaker-full-access"
    ssm_prefix = "function-sagemaker-rcf"
    num_samples_per_tree = 365
    num_trees = 100
    max_std = 3
    # get training job
    ssm = boto3.client("ssm")
    endpoint_name = config_name = ssm.get_parameter(
        Name=f"{ssm_prefix}/training",
    )['Parameter']['Value']
```

```
# specify general training job information
print("Starting RandomCutForest for", endpoint_name)
print("Using role", role_arn)
print("Using bucket", bucket_name)
try:
    print("Try creating endpoint")
   sagemaker.Session().create_endpoint(endpoint_name, config_name)
except Exception as exc:
    # proceed, endpoint already exists
    print(exc)
try:
    print("Run inference")
    rcf_inference = sagemaker.RandomCutForestPredictor(
        endpoint_name,
        serializer=CSVSerializer(),
        deserializer=JSONDeserializer(),
    )
    results = rcf_inference.predict(inference_data)
except Exception as exc:
    # proceed, ignore error
    print(exc)
print("Try to deleting endpoint")
sagemaker.Session().delete_endpoint(endpoint_name)
if results:
    scores = [datum["score"] for datum in results["scores"]]
    downloaded_data["score"] = pd.Series(scores,
        index=downloaded_data.index)
    score_mean = downloaded_data["score"].mean()
    score_std = downloaded_data["score"].std()
    score_cutoff = score_mean + max_std * score_std
    anomalies = downloaded_data[
        downloaded_data["score"] > score_cutoff]
    print("anomalies\n", anomalies)
```

35. Click the **Deploy** button.

We have successfully created the `sagemaker-rcf-run-inference` function.

Creating S3 event triggers

We are going to create S3 event triggers that will trigger the Lambda functions when data is written to their respective object key prefix in the `masteringawsserverlessbook-data` bucket.

Example 4: Creating S3 event triggers

Let us create S3 event triggers.

1. Go to the Lambda service page.
2. Go to the **Functions** menu option.
3. Click the `sagemaker-rcf-run-training` function.
4. Go to the **Configuration** tab.
5. Go to the **Triggers** menu option.
6. Click the **Add trigger** button.
7. Select **S3** in the **Select a source** dropdown.
8. Select `masteringawsserverlessbook.com` in **Bucket** dropdown.
9. Check the **All object create events** checkbox in the **Event types** dropdown.
10. Specify `analytics/` in the **Prefix** field.
11. Specify `.csv` in the **Suffix** field.
12. Click the **Add** button.

    We have successfully added the S3 event trigger.
13. Go to the **Functions** menu option.
14. Click the `sagemaker-rcf-run-inference` function.
15. Go to the **Configuration** tab.
16. Go to the **Triggers** menu option.
17. Click the **Add trigger** button.
18. Select **S3** in the **Select a source** dropdown.
19. Select `masteringawsserverlessbook.com` in **Bucket** dropdown.
20. Check the **All object create events** checkbox in the **Event types** dropdown.
21. Specify `rcf/` in the **Prefix** field.

22. Specify **`.csv`** in the **Suffix** field.
23. Click the **Add** button.

We have successfully added the S3 event trigger.

Conclusion

In this chapter, we explored using an event-driven design to process data independently of user activity. We leveraged EventBridge schedule rules and S3 event triggers for processing data. The schedule rule triggered a Lambda function periodically to process data for a desired time window. The S3 event triggers were used to perform machine learning training and inference. We updated the authentication callback to provide us with analytics data.

Points to remember

- An API Gateway can write directly to a DynamoDB table without the need of a Lambda function by using an AWS service proxy integration.
- We used an EventBridge schedule rule that runs more periodically than expected in case there is a service outage. We could have created another schedule rule in a different AWS region to trigger the Lambda functions to create a backup if the primary region has an outage.
- The Lambda function triggered by the schedule rule should check whether it needs to exit depending on the state.
- Using the Systems Manager parameter store can be useful to track state needed by a Lambda function.
- Machine learning workflows can be performed using an event-driven serverless design. The two-step training and inference process in the machine learning workflow enabled us to use events to trigger each step.

Multiple choice questions

1. **Which data transformation technique was used in this chapter?**
   a. Extract, Load, Transform
   b. Extract, Transform, Load

   Answer: b

   Extract, Transform, Load was used because data was extracted from DynamoDB, transformed using a Lambda function and loaded into an S3 bucket.

2. **An EventBridge schedule rule could have been used instead of an S3 event trigger?**

   c. True

   d. False

   Answer: a

   True. Both Lambda functions were not designed to a specific event trigger. Also, a schedule rule might be more cost effective as it can be run once per day instead of whenever the S3 object was updated.

Join our book's Discord space

Join the book's Discord Workspace for Latest updates, Offers, Tech happenings around the world, New Release and Sessions with the Authors:

https://discord.bpbonline.com

CHAPTER 9
Sending Notifications

Introduction

This chapter will focus on sending notifications using email, text messaging, and mobile push notifications.

Structure

We will cover the following topics in this chapter:

- Overview of notifications
- Setting SES for emails
- Sending an email from a Lambda function
- Using an SNS topic to trigger a Lambda function
- Sending a topic message from a Lambda function
- Setting up SNS for text messages
- Sending a text message from a Lambda function
- Setting up SNS for push notifications

Objectives

By the end of this chapter, you will learn how to send notifications using the Amazon Simple Email Service and the Amazon Simple Notification Service.

Overview of notifications

In a previous chapter, we discussed how the Amazon **Simple Email Service** (**SES**), and **Simple Notification Service** (**SNS**) can be used to send notifications. SES is used to send email messages. SNS is used to send text messages, mobile push notifications, and messages to other AWS services (for example, a Lambda function or SQS queue).

We need to enable SES to send emails. We are first given a sandbox account when we active SES. The sandbox account limits how many emails we can send per day and per minute. Furthermore, we can only send emails to verified email addresses. This means we need to add the email address to the SES and the recipient needs to verify the email address by following the instructions sent by SES. We will need to create an AWS support ticket to request production access to SES. The production SES provides all the features and a much higher send limit.

We need to create a DNS record to be able to send emails from SES using our custom domain. Since we are using Route 53, the process to create the DNS record is simplified. Once we add the CNAME DNS record to our Route 53 hosted zone, SES will make a DNS request for the CNAME record. If the DNS returns the CNAME record and the matching value, the SES service will allow sending emails from our custom domain.

Next, we will want to set up SNS to send event notifications between AWS services and send text messages. Similar to SES, SNS is initially set up in a sandbox for sending text messages. The sandbox will limit sending text messages to 10 verified phone numbers. We will need to request to exit the sandbox mode to get the full text messaging functionality. SNS does not have a sandbox for sending event notifications to SNS topics. SNS topics allow HTTPS endpoints, email addresses, some AWS resources (such as a Lambda function), and mobile phone numbers (for text messaging) to subscribe to get the event notifications.

Setting SES for emails

We are going to set up SES so we can send emails.

Set up SES

We will register an email address and our custom domain. We will make a request to AWS Support to exit sandbox mode, but we will assume it was not approved or the request is still being processed.

Hands-on exercise 1: Setting up SES

Let us set up SES:

1. Search **ses** in the top search bar and click the **Amazon Simple Email Service** search result or enter **https://us-east-1.console.aws.amazon.com/ses/home** in the browser address bar.
2. Click the **Get started** button or the **Get set up** menu option.
3. Specify your email address in the **Email address** field.
4. Click the **Next** button. See *Figure 9.1*:

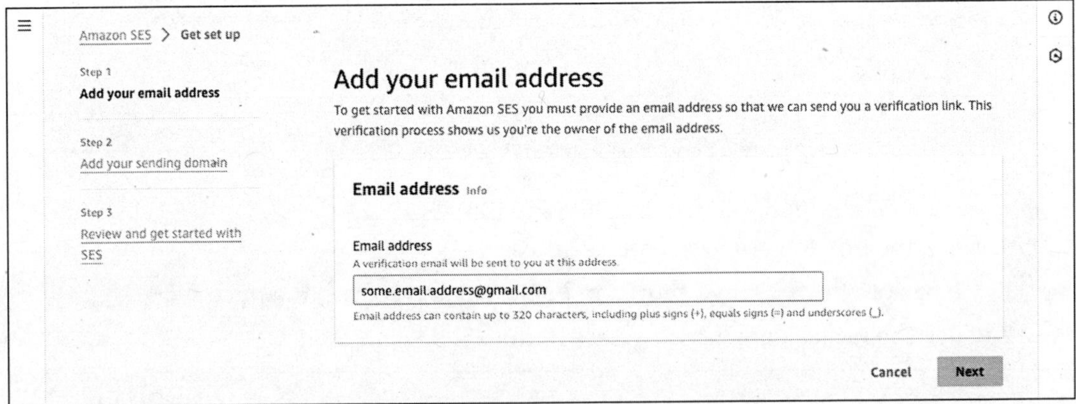

Figure 9.1: *Setting up SES*

5. Specify **masteringawsserverlessbook.com** in the **Sending domain** field.
6. Click the **Next** button. See *Figure 9.2*:

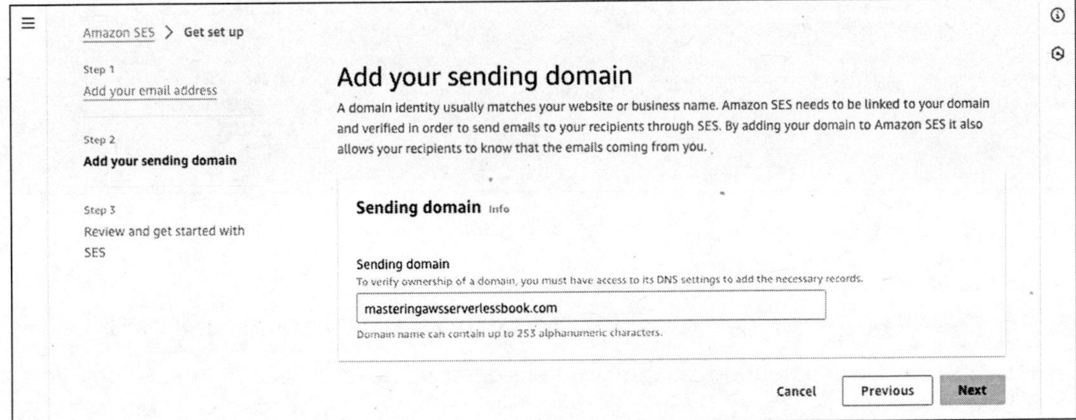

Figure 9.2: *Setting up SES*

7. Click the **Get started** button.
8. Observe we are in the SES sandbox. See *Figure 9.3*:

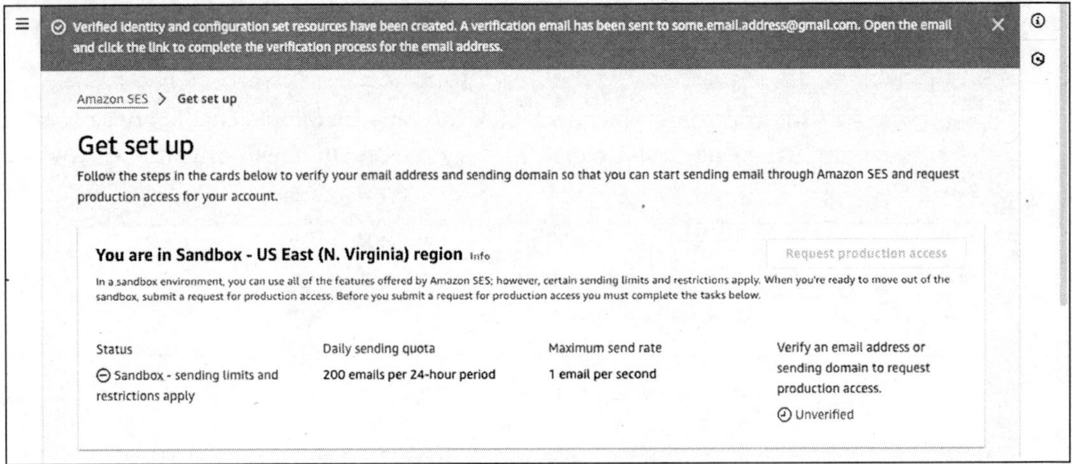

Figure 9.3: Setting up SES

9. Look for the email in the inbox or spam folder.
10. Click the link to verify the email address.
11. Go back to the SES page shown in *Figure 9.3* and refresh the page.
12. Click the **Request production access** button. See *Figure 9.4*:

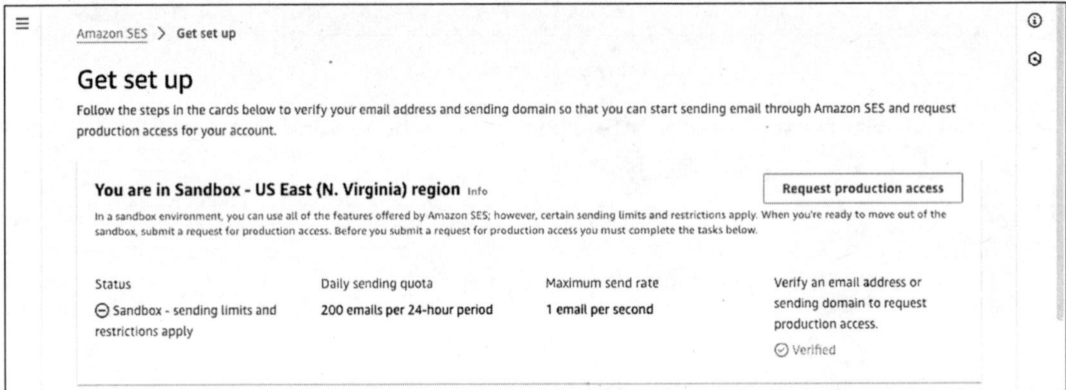

Figure 9.4: Setting up SES

13. Check the **Transaction** radio button in the **Mail type** section.
14. Specify **https://masteringawsserverlessbook.com** in the **Website URL** field.
15. Specify an explanation in the **Use case description** field. See *Figure 9.5* for your reference:

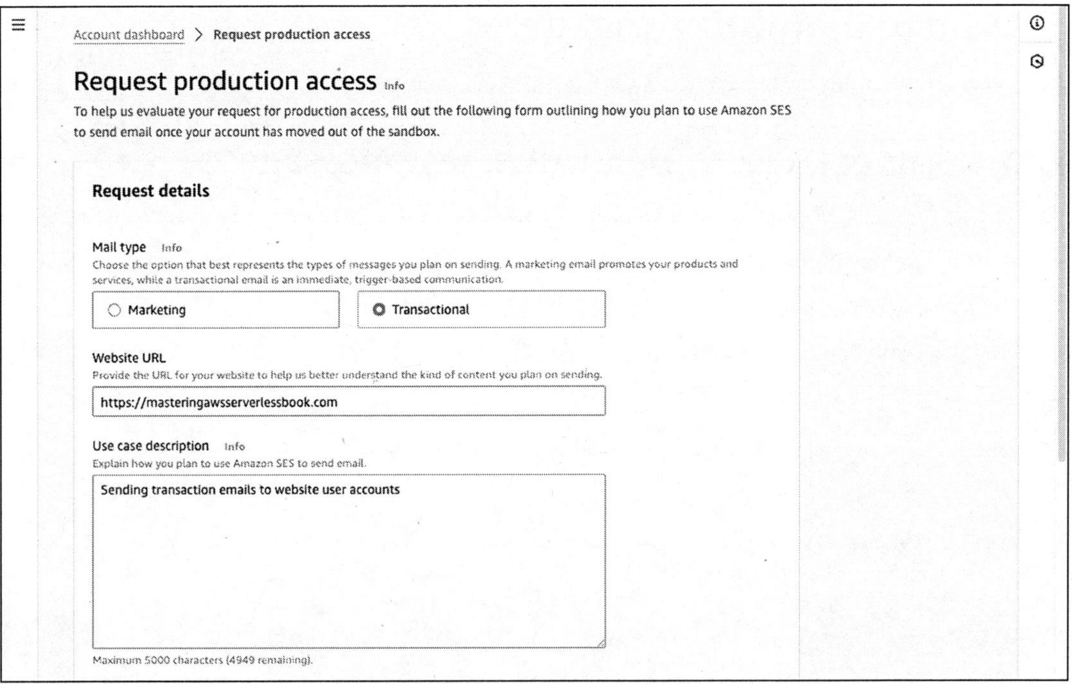

Figure 9.5: Requesting production access

16. Check the **Acknowledgement** checkbox.
17. Click the **Submit request** button. See *Figure 9.6*:

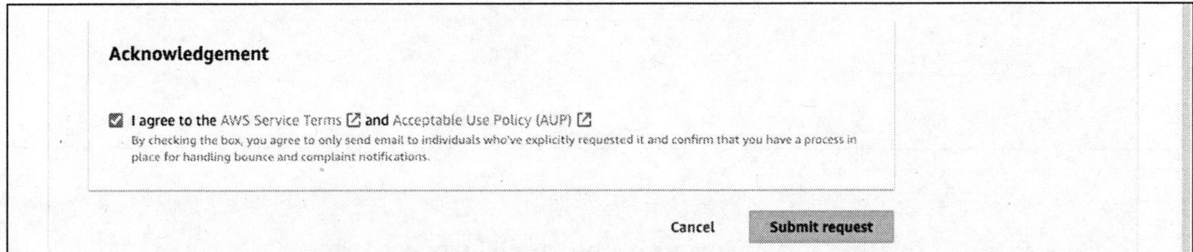

Figure 9.6: Requesting production access

The request was successfully submitted.

Note: It may take up to 24 hours for AWS to approve the request. Check the Get set up page periodically to check the status. If there is a More information needed status, click on the case link. Provide more information in the case to justify the need for production access.

We successfully set up the sandbox access. We will continue to use the sandbox access for the remainder of the chapter, assuming production access has not been granted.

Send a test email message

We are going to send a test message using the AWS console.

Hands-on exercise 2: Sending a test message

Let us send a test message using the given steps:

1. Go to the SES service page.
2. Go to the **Get set up** menu option.
3. Click the **Send test email** button. See *Figure 9.7*:

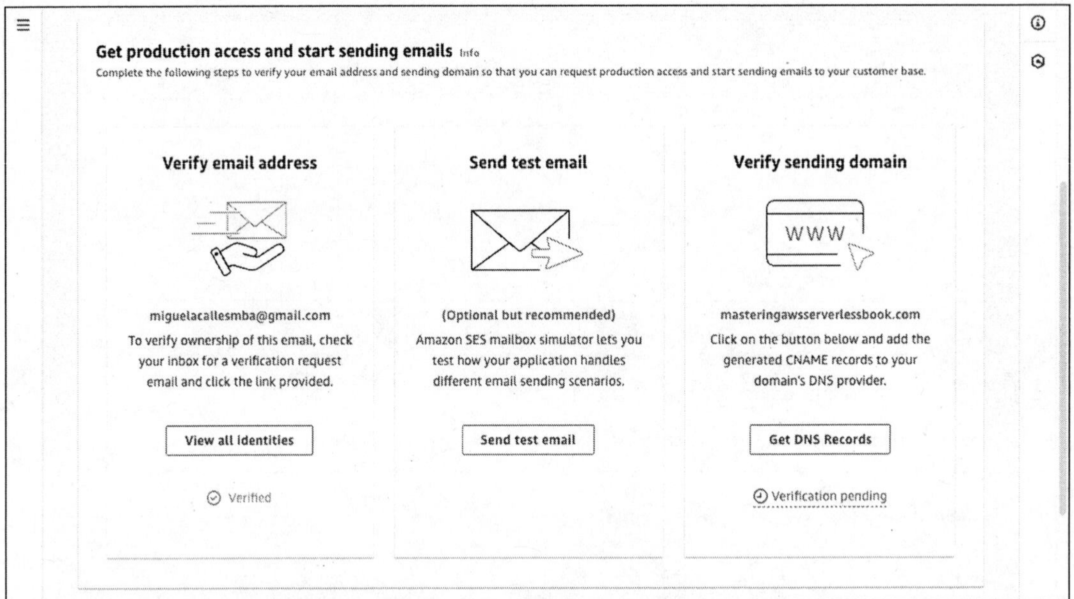

***Figure 9.7:** The get set up page*

4. Select the **Formatted** radio button in the **Email format** section.
5. Select **Successful delivery** in the **Scenario** dropdown.
6. Specify **Test email** in the **Subject** field.
7. Specify **Testing** in the **Body** field.
8. Click the **Send test email** button. See *Figure 9.8*:

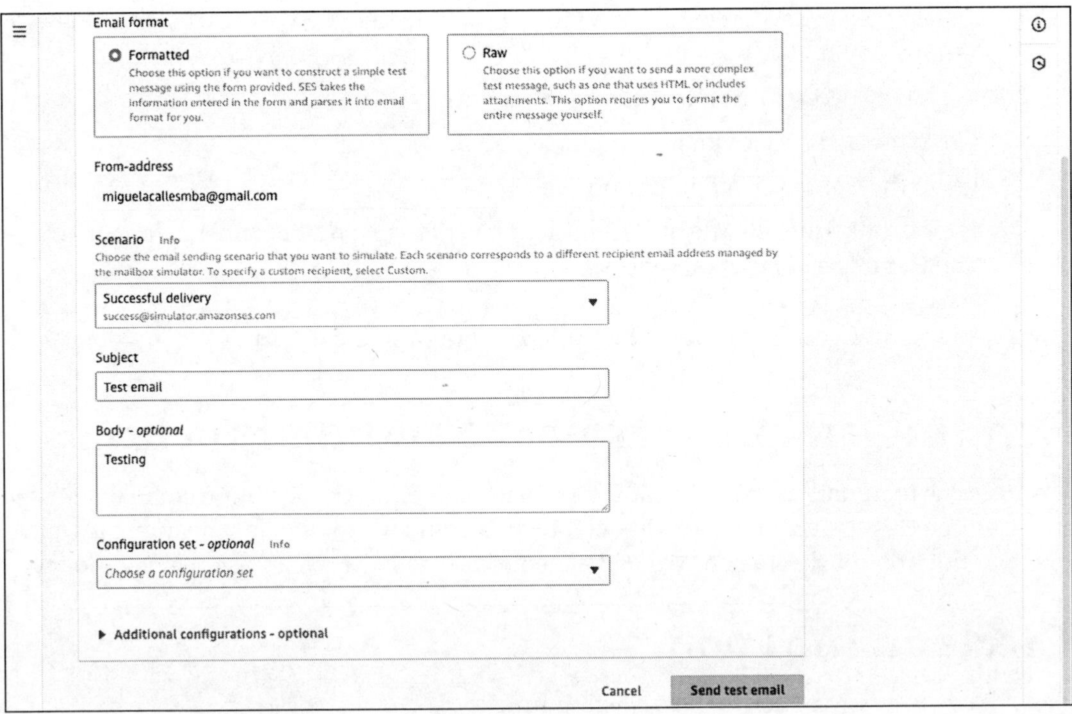

Figure 9.8: The test emails

We have successfully sent a test email.

Set up the DNS records

We will add the DNS records automatically created by SES into the Route 53 hosted zone.

Hands-on exercise 3: Setting up the DNS records

Let us set up the DNS records.

1. Go to the SES service page.
2. Go to the **Get set up** menu option.
3. Click the **Get DNS Records** button. See *Figure 9.7* for your reference.
4. Click the **Download .csv record set** button.
5. Open the downloaded CSV file.
6. Go to the Route 53 service page.
7. Go to the **Hosted zones** menu option.
8. Click the `masteringawsserverlessbook.com` hosted zone.

9. Create the CNAME records listed in the downloaded CSV file by using the **Create record** button.

   We have successfully set up the DNS records.

10. Go to the SES service page.
11. Go to the **Get set up** menu option.
12. Periodically refresh the page until the **Verify sending domain** no longer states **Verification pending** as the status.

Note: The sending domain may take up to 24 hours to be verified.

Sending an email from a Lambda function

We are going to update an existing Lambda function to send a confirmation email whenever the user updates their name. We will need to create an IAM policy for this function since one was not previously created. We will also update the IAM role to use the new policy.

Create an IAM policy

We will create a new policy for this existing function.

Hands-on exercise 4: Creating an IAM policy

Let us create an IAM policy using the given steps:

1. Go to the IAM service page.
2. Go to the **Access management | Policies** menu option.
3. Click the **Create policy** button.
4. Click the **Visual** button.
5. Select **SES v2** in the **Service** dropdown.
6. Search for **SendEmail** in the search field.
7. Check the **SendEmail** checkbox.
8. Click the **Add ARNs** link in the **configuration-set** section.
9. Select the **This account** radio button in the **Resource in** section.
10. Specify `us-east-1` in the **Resource region** field.
11. Check the **Any configuration set name** checkbox.
12. Click the **Add ARNs** button.
13. Click the **Add ARNs** link in the **identity** section.
14. Select the **This account** radio button in the **Resource in** section.
15. Specify `us-east-1` in the **Resource region** field.

16. Check the **Any identity name** checkbox.
17. Click the **Add ARNs** button.
18. Click the **Add ARNs** link in the **template** section.
19. Select the **This account** radio button in the **Resource in** section.
20. Specify `us-east-1` in the **Resource region** field.
21. Check the **Any template name** checkbox.
22. Click the **Add ARNs** button.
23. Click the **Next** button.
24. Specify `function-put-account-info` in the **Policy name** field.
25. Click the **Create policy** button.

We have successfully created the policy.

Update an IAM role

We will update the existing role to use the new policy.

Hands-on exercise 5: Updating an IAM role

Let us update an IAM role:

1. Go to the IAM service page.
2. Go to the **Access management | Roles** menu option.
3. Click the `function-put-account-info` role.
4. Go to the **Permissions** tab.
5. Click the **Add permission** button in the **Permissions policies** section.
6. Select **Attach policies** in the dropdown. See *Figure 9.9*:

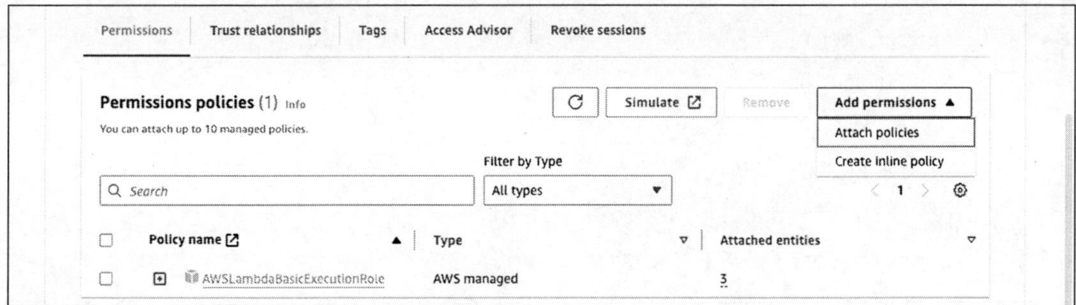

Figure 9.9: *The permissions policies section*

7. Select **Customer managed** in the **Filter by Type** dropdown.
8. Check the `function-put-account-info` policy.

9. Click the **Add permissions** button.
10. Observe the `function-put-account-info` policy was added to the **Permissions policies** section.

We have successfully updated the role.

Update a Lambda function

We will add code to the existing function to send a confirmation email to the user after the name was successfully updated.

Hands-on exercise 6: Updating a Lambda function

Let us update a Lambda function:

1. Go to the Lambda service page.
2. Go to the **Functions** menu option.
3. Click the `put-account-info` function.
4. Update the **Code source** to add the code changes noted as follows:

```
import {
  CognitoIdentityProviderClient,
  UpdateUserAttributesCommand,
/* !!!! START OF CHANGES !!!! */
  GetUserCommand,
/* !!!! END OF CHANGES !!!! */
} from "@aws-sdk/client-cognito-identity-provider";
/* !!!! START OF CHANGES !!!! */
import {
  SESv2Client,
  SendEmailCommand,
} from "@aws-sdk/client-sesv2";
/* !!!! END OF CHANGES !!!! */
export const handler = async (event) => {
  const response = {
    statusCode: 500,
    headers: {
      'Access-Control-Allow-Origin': '*',
      'Content-Type': 'application/json',
```

```
  },
  body: JSON.stringify({}),
};
try {
  if (!event.body) {
    throw new Error('Empty body');
  }
  const bodyObj = JSON.parse(event.body);
  if (!bodyObj.given_name) {
    throw new Error('No given_name');
  }
  const cognitoClient = new CognitoIdentityProviderClient({
    region: process.env.AWS_REGION,
  });
  const cognitoCommand = new UpdateUserAttributesCommand({
    AccessToken: event.headers.Authorization,
    UserAttributes: [
      {
        Name: 'given_name',
        Value: bodyObj.given_name,
      },
    ],
  });
  await cognitoClient.send(cognitoCommand);
  /* !!!! START OF CHANGES !!!! */
  const userInfo = await cognitoClient.send(
    new GetUserCommand({
      AccessToken: event.headers.Authorization,
    })
  );
  const userEmail = userInfo.UserAttributes.find(
    (x) => x.Name === 'email'
  ).Value;
  const fromEmail = 'Mastering AWS Serverless Book ' +
```

```
      '<no-reply@masteringawsserverlessbook.com>';
    const sesClient = new SESv2Client({
      region: process.env.AWS_REGION,
    });
    const sesCommand = new SendEmailCommand({
      FromEmailAddress: fromEmail,
      Destination: {
        ToAddresses: [userEmail],
      },
      ReplyToAddresses: [fromEmail],
      Content: {
        Simple: {
          Subject: {
            Data: 'Name was updated',
          },
          Body: {
            Text: {
              Data: 'You updated your name via the website.',
            },
            Html: {
              Data: 'You updated your name via the website.',
            },
          },
        },
      },
    });
    await sesClient.send(sesCommand);
    /* !!!! END OF CHANGES !!!! */
    response.statusCode = 200;
  } catch (e) {
    console.error(e);
  }
  return response;
};
```

5. Click the **Deploy** button.

We have successfully updated the Lambda function.

Test on the website

We will update our name in our website account to verify we get an email.

Hands-on exercise 7: Testing on the website

Let us test the website:

1. Go to **https://masteringawsserverlessbook.com**.
2. Click the **Log in** button.
3. Log in.
4. Click the **Update info** button.
5. Update the name.
6. Click the **Update** button.
7. Check the email inbox or spam folder for the email.

We have successfully sent an email message using SES.

Using an SNS topic to trigger a Lambda function

We are going to create an SNS topic that will send messages to a Lambda function.

Create an SNS topic

We will create an SNS topic in this section.

Hands-on exercise 8: Creating an SNS topic

Let us create an SNS topic.

1. Search `sns` in the top search bar and click the **Simple Notification Service** search result or enter **https://us-east-1.console.aws.amazon.com/sns/v3/home** in the browser address bar.
2. Go to the **Topics** menu option.
3. Click the **Create topic** button.
4. Select the **Standard** radio button in the **Type** section.
5. Specify `function-sns-send-email` in the **Name** field. See *Figure 9.10*:

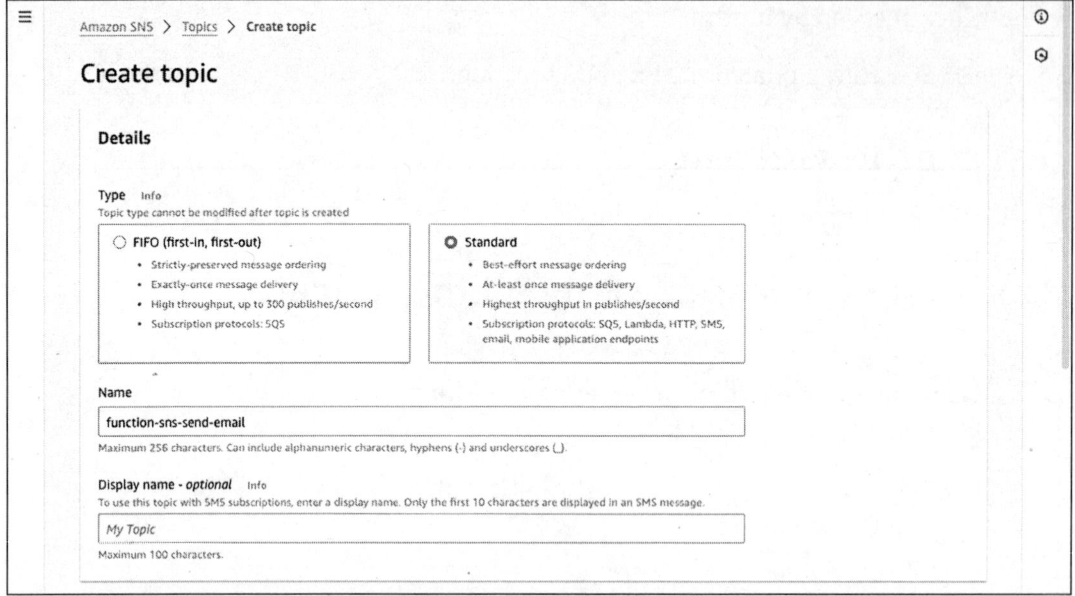

Figure 9.10: *The topic details*

6. Click the **Create topic** button.

We have successfully created the topic.

Create an IAM policy

We are going to create a policy for a new Lambda function.

Hands-on exercise 9: Creating an IAM policy

Let us create an IAM policy:

1. Go to the IAM service page.
2. Go to the **Access management** | **Policies** menu option.
3. Click the **Create policy** button.
4. Click the **Visual** button.
5. Select **SES v2** in the **Service** dropdown.
6. Search for **SendEmail** in the search field.
7. Check the **SendEmail** checkbox.
8. Click the **Add ARNs** link in the **configuration-set** section.
9. Select the **This account** radio button in the **Resource in** section.
10. Specify `us-east-1` in the **Resource region** field.

11. Check the **Any configuration set name** checkbox.
12. Click the **Add ARNs** button.
13. Click the **Add ARNs** link in the **identity** section.
14. Select the **This account** radio button in the **Resource in** section.
15. Specify `us-east-1` in the **Resource region** field.
16. Check the **Any identity name** checkbox.
17. Click the **Add ARNs** button.
18. Click the **Add ARNs** link in the **template** section.
19. Select the **This account** radio button in the **Resource in** section.
20. Specify `us-east-1` in the **Resource region** field.
21. Check the **Any template name** checkbox.
22. Click the **Add ARNs** button.
23. Click the **Next** button.
24. Specify `function-sns-send-email` in the **Policy name** field.
25. Click the **Create policy** button.

We have successfully created the policy.

Create an IAM role

We are going to create a role that uses the new policy.

Hands-on exercise 10: Creating an IAM role

Let us create an IAM role using the given steps:

1. Go to the IAM service page.
2. Go to the **Access management | Roles** menu option.
3. Click the **Create role** button.
4. Select the **AWS service** radio button in the **Trusted entity type** section.
5. Select **Lambda** in the **Service or use case** dropdown.
6. Specify `function-sns-send-email` in the search field.
7. Check the `function-sns-send-email` policy.
8. Specify **AWSLambdaBasicExecutionRole** in the search field.
9. Check the **AWSLambdaBasicExecutionRole** policy.
10. Click the **Next** button.
11. Specify `function-sns-send-email` in the **Role name** field.

12. Click the **Create role** button.

We have successfully created the role.

Create a Lambda function

We will create a Lambda function.

Hands-on exercise 11: Creating a Lambda function

Let us create a Lambda function:

1. Go to the Lambda service page.
2. Click the **Create function** button.
3. Specify `sns-send-email` in the **Function name** field.
4. Select **Node.js** in the **Runtime** dropdown.
5. Select the **arm64** radio button in the **Architecture** section.
6. Expand the **Change default execution role** section.
7. Select the **Use an existing role** radio button in the **Execution role** section.
8. Select `function sns-send-email` in the **Existing role** dropdown.
9. Click the **Create function** button.
10. Enter the following code in the **Code source** section:

```
import {
  CognitoIdentityProviderClient,
  GetUserCommand,
} from "@aws-sdk/client-cognito-identity-provider";
import {
  SESv2Client,
  SendEmailCommand,
} from "@aws-sdk/client-sesv2";
export const handler = async (event) => {
  try {
    const cognitoClient = new CognitoIdentityProviderClient({
      region: process.env.AWS_REGION,
    });
    const sesClient = new SESv2Client({
      region: process.env.AWS_REGION,
    });
```

```
for (let record of event.Records) {
  console.debug(record);
  if (!record.Sns || record.Sns.Type !== 'Notification') {
    console.warn('Record is not an SNS notification');
    continue;
  }
  const userInfo = await cognitoClient.send(
    new GetUserCommand({
      AccessToken: record.Sns.Message,
    })
  );
  const userEmail = userInfo.UserAttributes.find(
    (x) => x.Name === 'email'
  ).Value;
  const fromEmail = 'Mastering AWS Serverless Book ' +
    '<no-reply@masteringawsserverlessbook.com>';
  const sesCommand = new SendEmailCommand({
    FromEmailAddress: fromEmail,
    Destination: {
      ToAddresses: [userEmail],
    },
    ReplyToAddresses: [fromEmail],
    Content: {
      Simple: {
        Subject: {
          Data: 'Name was updated',
        },
        Body: {
          Text: {
            Data: 'You updated your name via the website.',
          },
          Html: {
            Data: 'You updated your name via the website.',
          },
```

```
                },
              },
            },
          });
          await sesClient.send(sesCommand);
        };
      } catch (e) {
        console.error(e);
      }
      return;
    };
```

11. Click the **Deploy** button.
12. Click the **Test** button.
13. Specify **TestEvent** in the **Event name** field.
14. Select **SNS Topic Notification** in the **Template** dropdown.
15. Click the **Save** button.
16. Click the **Test** button.
17. Go to the **Configuration** tab.
18. Go to the **Triggers** menu option.
19. Click the **Add trigger** button.
20. Select **SNS** in the **Select a source** dropdown.
21. Select **`function-sns-send-email`** in the **SNS topic** dropdown.
22. Click the **Add** button. See *Figure 9.11* for your reference:

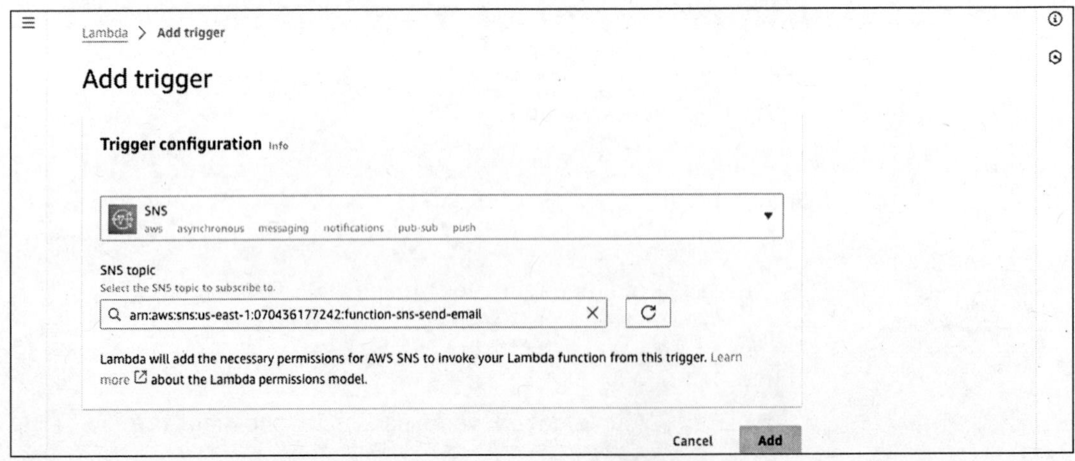

Figure 9.11: The trigger configuration

23. Observe that the SNS trigger is listed in the **Triggers** section.
24. Go to the **Permission** menu option.
25. Go to the **Resource-based policy statements** section.
26. Observe that an automatically-generated policy is listed for the **sns.amazon.com** principal.

We have successfully created a Lambda function triggered by the SNS topic.

Update the log group settings

We will update the log group retention settings to be one week.

Hands-on exercise 12: Updating the log group settings

Let us update the log group settings.

1. Go to the CloudWatch service page.
2. Go to the **Logs | Log groups** menu option.
3. Check the **/aws/lambda/sns-send-email** log group.
4. Click the **Actions** dropdown.
5. Select the **Edit retention setting(s)** dropdown option.
6. Select **1 week (7 days)** in the **Expire events after** dropdown.
7. Click the **Save** button.

We have successfully updated the log group retention settings.

Sending a topic message from a Lambda function

We will update the **put-account-info** Lambda function to send a message to the SNS topic. The SNS topic will trigger the **sns-send-email** Lambda function that will send the confirmation email. We will update the **put-account-info** function to remove the email functionality.

Updating the IAM policy

We will remove the SES permissions and add the SNS permissions to the policy.

Hands-on exercise 13: Updating the IAM policy

Let us update the IAM policy:

1. Go to the IAM service page.

2. Go to the **Access management | Policies** menu option.
3. Select **Customer managed** in the **Filter by Type** dropdown.
4. Click the `function-put-account-info` policy.
5. Click the **Edit** button in the **Permissions** tab.
6. Click the **Visual** button.
7. Delete the existing permissions.
8. Select **SNS** in the **Service** dropdown.
9. Search for **Publish** in the search field.
10. Check the **Publish** checkbox.
11. Click the **Add ARNs** link in the **topic** section.
12. Select the **This account** radio button in the **Resource in** section.
13. Specify `us-east-1` in the **Resource region** field.
14. Specify `function-sns-send-email` in the **Resource topic name** field.
15. Click the **Add ARNs** button.
16. Click the **Next** button.
17. Click the **Save changes** button.

We have successfully updated the policy.

Updating the Lambda function

We will update the function to remove the code we added earlier in the chapter and replace it with code to publish a message to the SNS topic.

Hands-on exercise 14: Updating the Lambda function

Let us update the Lambda function:

1. Go to the Lambda service page.
2. Go to the **Functions** menu option.
3. Click the `put-account-info` function.
4. Use the code below to update the code in the **Code source** section.

> **Note: Replace the entire code since some code lines were added while others were deleted:**
>
> **Note: Replace the `{accountId}` with the desired AWS account ID.**

```
import {
  CognitoIdentityProviderClient,
```

```
  UpdateUserAttributesCommand,
} from "@aws-sdk/client-cognito-identity-provider";
import {
  SNSClient,
  PublishCommand,
} from "@aws-sdk/client-sns";
export const handler = async (event) => {
  const response = {
    statusCode: 500,
    headers: {
      'Access-Control-Allow-Origin': '*',
      'Content-Type': 'application/json',
    },
    body: JSON.stringify({}),
  };
  try {
    if (!event.body) {
      throw new Error('Empty body');
    }
    const bodyObj = JSON.parse(event.body);
    if (!bodyObj.given_name) {
      throw new Error('No given_name');
    }
    const cognitoClient = new CognitoIdentityProviderClient({
      region: process.env.AWS_REGION,
    });
    const cognitoCommand = new UpdateUserAttributesCommand({
      AccessToken: event.headers.Authorization,
      UserAttributes: [
        {
          Name: 'given_name',
          Value: bodyObj.given_name,
        },
      ],
```

```
      });
      await cognitoClient.send(cognitoCommand);
      const snsClient = new SNSClient({
        region: process.env.AWS_REGION,
      });
      const publishCommand = new PublishCommand({
        TopicArn: 'arn:aws:sns:us-east-1:{accountId}:' +
          'function-sns-send-email',
        Message: event.headers.Authorization,
      });
      await snsClient.send(publishCommand);
      response.statusCode = 200;
    } catch (e) {
      console.error(e);
    }
    return response;
  };
```

5. Click the **Deploy** button.

We have successfully updated the function.

Testing on the website

We will update our name in our website account to verify we get an email.

Hands-on exercise 15: Testing on the website

Let us test the website:

1. Go to **https://masteringawsserverlessbook.com**.
2. Click the **Log in** button.
3. Log in.
4. Click the **Update info** button.
5. Update the name.
6. Click the **Update** button.
7. Check the email inbox or spam folder for the email.

We have successfully sent an email message using SES via an SNS topic.

Setting up SNS for text messages

Sending text messages (**SMS**) is more expensive than sending email messages. Furthermore, SNS has a free tier for event notifications but not for SMS.

We will explore how to add the ability to SMS messages with examples. Sending SMS messages might be costly, and performing the steps as hands-on exercises might be cost-prohibitive.

Exiting the SMS sandbox

We will make a request to exit the SMS sandbox.

Example 1: Exiting the SMS sandbox

Let us apply to exit the SMS sandbox using the given steps:

1. Go to the SNS service page.
2. Go to the **Mobile | Text messaging (SMS)** menu option.
3. Go to the **Account information** section.
4. Click the **Exit SMS Sandbox** button.
5. Complete the questionnaire.
6. Click the **Submit** button.

Note: It may take up to 24 hours for AWS to approve the request.

We have successfully requested to exit the SMS sandbox. We will continue to use the sandbox access in the remainder of the chapter, assuming exiting the SMS sandbox was not granted or is still pending.

Create an SNS topic

We will create an SNS topic for sending text messages.

Example 2: Creating an SNS topic

Let us create an SNS topic:

1. Go to the SNS service page.
2. Go to the **Topics** menu option.
3. Click the **Create topic** button.
4. Select the **Standard** radio button in the **Type** section.
5. Specify **`send-sms`** in the **Name** field.

6. Specify **Book site** in the **Display name** field.
7. Click the **Create topic** button.

We have successfully created the topic.

Request an originating number

We will be requesting an originating number. This request has a monthly fee.

Example 3: Requesting an originating number

Let us request an originating number:

1. Go to the SNS service page.
2. Go to the **Mobile | Origination numbers** menu option.
3. Click the **Provision numbers in Pinpoint** button.
4. Click the **Request phone number** button.
5. Choose **United States** in the **Country** dropdown.
6. Check the **Toll-free** radio button in the **Number type** section.
7. Check **SMS** and uncheck **Voice** in the **Capabilities** section.
8. Check the **Transaction** radio button in the **Default message type** section.
9. Click the **Next** button.
10. Click the **Request** button.

We have successfully requested a phone number.

Adding a Sandbox destination phone number

Until AWS approves exiting the SMS sandbox, we can add Sandbox destination phone numbers.

Example 4: Adding a Sandbox destination phone number

Let us add a sandbox destination phone number using the given steps:

1. Go to the SNS service page.
2. Go to the **Mobile | Text message (SMS)** menu option.
3. Click the **Add phone number** button in the **Sandbox destination phone numbers** section.
4. Specify the desired mobile phone number in the **Phone number** field.
5. Specify **English (United States)** in the **Verification message language** dropdown.

6. Click the **Add phone number** button.
7. Specify the one-time password received on the mobile phone in the **Verification code** field.
8. Click the **Verify phone number** button.

We have successfully verified the phone number.

Sending a text message from a Lambda function

We will continue with examples and independent exercises to discuss how to use the setup done in the previous section.

Update the Cognito user pool

We can update the user pool to add a new attribute for the mobile phone number.

Example 5: Updating the Cognito user pool

Let us update the Cognito user pool:

1. Go to the Cognito user pool.
2. Click the `masteringawsserverlessbook.com` user pool.
3. Go to the **Sign-up experience** tab.
4. Click the **Add custom attributes** button in the **Custom attributes** section.
5. Specify `mobile_number` in the **Name** field.
6. Select **String** in the **Type** dropdown.
7. Click the **Save changes** button.

Update the website

We will discuss updating the website to allow the user to enter their mobile phone number.

Independent exercise 1: Updating the website

Attempt to do this exercise independently. Use the following guidance.

We should update the `account/info.html` page to include a section to enter a mobile phone number. The JavaScript code should verify that the entered information is a valid phone number. When the user clicks the **Update** button, it should include the phone number of the existing API request.

The webpage should show a verification code field if the user specifies a new phone number. We are duplicating the SMS sandbox phone number process since we assume

AWS will not approve the existing SMS sandbox. We will use a new **/account/sandbox-code** POST API endpoint to send the verification code.

Updating an existing Lambda function

We will discuss updating the **put-account-info** Lambda function.

Independent exercise 2: Updating an existing Lambda function

Attempt to do this exercise independently. Use the following guidance.

We will update the **put-account-information** function to send a message to the **send-sms** topic with the phone number. The user will get a text message whenever the name is changed. We should consider updating the JavaScript code to check whether the name has changed.

We will update the JavaScript code to get the phone number from the event body. We will check whether the phone number differs from the value in the Cognito user profile. If it is different, we will use the **DeleteSMSSandboxPhoneNumberCommand** function in the **@aws-sdk/client-sns** library to delete the existing number. We will update the Cognito user profile. We will use the **CreateSMSSandboxPhoneNumberCommand** function in the **@aws-sdk/client-sns** library to start the SMS sandbox verification process. We will not send a message to the **send-sms** topic until the number is verified.

We will need to update the **put-account-information** policy to allow the **SNS:Publish** action for the **send-sms** topic resource. We will update the JavaScript code to use the **PublishCommand** function in the **@aws-sdk/client-sns** library to send a message to the **send-sms** topic for the destination number and a desired message.

Creating new API endpoint and related resources

We will create a new API endpoint, Lambda functions and the related resources.

Independent exercise 3: Creating a new Lambda function and related resources

Attempt to do this exercise independently. Use the following guidance.

We will create a **post-account-sandbox-code** function. It will accept the verification code from the event body and send it to the **VerifySMSSandboxPhoneNumberCommand** function in the **@aws-sdk/client-sns** library. If successful, it will subscribe the phone number to the **send-sms** topic using the **Subscribe** command.

We will create a **post-account-sandbox-code** policy that will allow the **Subscribe** and **VerifySMSSandboxPhoneNumber** actions for the **send-sms** topic resource. We will create a **`post-account-sandbox-code`** role that uses the **`post-account-sandbox-code`** and **`AWSLambdaBasicExecutionRole`** policies.

We will create a **`/account/sandbox-code`** API endpoint with CORS enabled and a **`POST`** method. The **`POST`** method will use the Lambda proxy integration for the **`post-account-sandbox-code`** function.

We will update the CloudWatch log group retention settings after having invoked the function.

Setting up SNS for push notifications

As mentioned earlier in the book, we are focusing on a website for our serverless application, but it would be good to discuss using push notifications since the website might become so popular that we might decide to launch a mobile app.

We will create a **`send-mobile-push`** SNS topic. When we send messages on this topic, SNS will send the messages as push notifications to the subscribed smartphones.

We will need to sign up for developer accounts on the app stores. Some app stores may require a yearly subscription to publish apps, whereas others do not. Each of these app stores has its own process to allow sending push notifications. They will provide secret keys, certificates, or unique identifiers. These pieces of information need to be protected to ensure only we can send push notifications to the mobile app users. We will provide these pieces of information to SNS.

On the SNS service page, we will create a new platform application for each app store. We will select the desired app store and specify the information the app store provides. Once created, we can create subscriptions to the platform application.

When the mobile app enables the push notifications in the app settings, the respective app store push messaging service creates a unique identifier or token for that device. The mobile app code will use that token to create a platform endpoint using the AWS SDK. When the subscription is successful, we use the **`Subscribe`** command in the AWS SDK to subscribe the endpoint to the **`send-mobile-push`** topic. We should store the platform endpoint in the user's profile in the Cognito user pool user account or a DynamoDB table. We will need that endpoint when we want to send a message to a selected user.

We will use a Lambda function to send the push notification. The JavaScript code will use the **`PublishCommand`** in the AWS SDK to send a message to the specific endpoint. We will specify the platform endpoint we saved in the **`TargetArn`** property and the **`send-mobile-push`** topic ARN in the **`TopicArn`** property.

Conclusion

In this chapter, we set up SES to send emails using our custom domain. We assumed AWS had not yet approved or rejected us having SES production access. We updated an existing Lambda function to send an email when a user updates their name via the website.

We created an SNS topic that would trigger a new Lambda function that will send an email when a user updates their name via the website. The existing Lambda function was updated again to send a message to the SNS topic instead of sending the email.

We discussed using SNS to SMS and push notifications. Much like the SES sandbox, SNS also has a sandbox for SMS. We assumed AWS had not yet approved or rejected exiting the SMS sandbox. We discussed how to verify a mobile phone number in the SMS sandbox and how to send a text message via the SNS topic.

We quickly reviewed the process for setting up and sending push notifications. We would need to sign up for the app stores, obtain secret information for sending push notifications, and specify that information in the SNS platform application.

Points to remember

- Every AWS account starts with a sandbox mode for SES that limits sending emails and SNS that limits sending text messages.
- An AWS Support request is needed to exist the sandbox modes.
- We can use a Lambda function to send emails using SES.
- SNS can send messages to Lambda functions, mobile phone numbers, push notifications, and other services.

Multiple choice questions

1. **The custom domain does not work in SES. What might be the issue(s)? (Select one or more.)**
   a. The SES DNS records were not added to the Route 53 hosted zone.
   b. There was a typo in the custom domain when setting up SES.
   c. AWS rejected sandbox mode.

   Answer: a and b

   The sandbox mode still supports the custom domain but with a limited number of messages that can be sent.

2. **The Lambda function does not show available SNS topics when creating an SNS topic. What might be the issue(s)? (Select one or more.)**
   a. No SNS topic was created.
   b. There is a missing statement in the IAM policy.
   c. A FIFO SNS topic was created.

   Answer: a and c

   The IAM policy statements have no effect on creating an SNS trigger for a Lambda function.

CHAPTER 10
Additional Automation Topics

Introduction

This chapter will focus on additional automation tasks that a serverless architecture can support.

Structure

We will cover the following topics in this chapter:

- Overview of automation
- Setting up backups
- Analyzing text using Amazon Comprehend
- Performing text-to-speech using Amazon Polly
- Analyzing images using Amazon Rekognition
- Auditing security settings using AWS Config

Objectives

By the end of this chapter, you will learn how to set up automated backups, image resizing and analysis, text analysis, text-to-speech and security audits.

Overview of automation

In a previous chapter, we discussed data processing using automation. This chapter will focus on other types of automation. Some of these tasks include data, but automation is not specific to data. It can include images, audio, video and cybersecurity. It is important to automate as many parts of our application and AWS account setup to ensure we reduce errors and omissions from manual tasks. Let us explore some of these other types of automation.

Backups

Backing up data is an important maintenance task for any application. Although AWS has high availability and reliability, they recommend backing up data to different regions. We discussed high availability and fault tolerance in a previous chapter. The discussion focused on creating replicas if there was an outage. However, backups focus on keeping a copy of the data somewhere else *just in case*. We can use serverless to help with backing up data.

There are some ways we can use serverless:

- Create a backup plan.
- Set up point-in-time recovery for DynamoDB.
- Set up an S3 bucket to replicate to another S3 bucket hosted in a different AWS region.
- Use a Lambda function triggered by an EventBridge schedule rule to write DynamoDB data to an S3 bucket.

We can consider these as serverless because no server is needed to orchestrate these backups. They are managed services. We will explore these later in the chapter.

Text analysis

We can use the Amazon Comprehend service for text analysis. This service provides text analysis and natural language processing. These features can be helpful in understanding what our users are saying. This assumes we have a way for users to submit feedback (for example, a comments feature for each page or blog post). It might give us insights into parts of the website that need improvement or additional information and services our users are seeking.

We will explore how to perform text analysis later in the chapter.

Text-to-speech

We could add a blog to our website. We might want each blog post to have a *listen* option that reads the blog post. This feature will play an audio file. We can use Amazon Polly to convert our blog post text to audio files.

We will explore how to perform text-to-speech later in the chapter.

Image resizing

We might want to add pictures to our blog posts. We will upload large resolution images to the **masteringawsserverlessbook.com** bucket. Having large file sizes reduces speed and performance when loading the website. We want to have different versions of the image file at different image sizes. Different sizes allow us to use the optimal size for thumbnails, header images, and social media sharing.

We can create a Lambda function that will do the following:

- List all object keys for the original larger size files.
- Check whether there are object keys for the different sizes of an image.
- If different sizes exist, then that image file is done processing.
- If it does not exist, the function will create the different sizes and put them into the bucket.

We will create an IAM policy that will allow the following:

- The **ListBucket** and **PutObject** actions for the **masteringawsserverlessbook.com/images/*** object key prefix resource.
- We will create an IAM role that uses the policy and **AWSLambdaBasicExecutionRole** policies.

- We will then create an EventBridge schedule rule to trigger the Lambda function every 15 minutes.
- We will update the CloudWatch log group retention settings after invoking the function.

Image analysis

We might want to allow users to upload their pictures. Suppose we created a contest for users to submit funny or creative pictures of their favorite AWS or serverless book. The users upload the pictures to the website. We want to analyze the pictures to gain some insight into the user community. We can use Amazon Rekognition to help with the image analysis.

Amazon Rekognition can detect objects, persons, and text within the image. We will explore how to perform image analysis later in the chapter.

Security

Keeping our AWS account, resources and data secure is important. We can use the AWS Config service to automatically audit our AWS account for security risks. Config comes with multiple managed rules that will check for common security issues. For example, Config can check whether MFA is enabled for the root account and IAM users and whether public access is disabled for S3 buckets. We will explore how to use Config later in the chapter.

We can do the same with Lambda functions. We can set up Lambda functions triggered by an EventBridge schedule rule. The Lambda function can check that desired resources meet security settings. If the security settings fail, we can have the function make the corrections using the AWS SDK. Furthermore, we can write the results to a DynamoDB table to have an audit record.

By automating security tasks, we can continuously monitor compliance with security requirements set by the business, industry, customers, laws, and regulations. Furthermore, in some cases, we can automatically remediate a security finding, which reduces our risk. The faster we know about a misconfiguration or vulnerability and fix it, the less chance and smaller time window there is for a malicious actor to take advantage of it.

Setting up backups

We will back up our data stored in S3 buckets and DynamoDB tables. We will be using the AWS Backup plan, DynamoDB point in time recovery, and S3 bucket replication features to automatically back up the data.

Enable versioning in the S3 buckets

We need to enable versioning in buckets to leverage the AWS backup service and enable S3 replication.

Hands-on exercise 1: Enabling versioning in the S3 buckets

Let us enable versioning in the S3 buckets:

1. Go to the S3 service page.
2. Go to the **Buckets** menu option.
3. Click the `masteringawsserverlessbook-data` bucket.
4. Go to the **Properties** tab.
5. Click the **Edit** button in the **Bucket Versioning** section.
6. Select the **Enable** radio button in the **Bucket Versioning** section.
7. Click the **Save changes** button.
8. Go to the **Buckets** menu option.
9. Click the `masteringawsserverlessbook.com` bucket.
10. Go to the **Properties** tab.
11. Click the **Edit** button in the **Bucket Versioning** section.
12. Select the **Enable** radio button in the **Bucket Versioning** section.
13. Click the **Save changes** button.

Create an AWS Backup plan

We will create a backup plan to create backups on a schedule.

Hands-on exercise 2: Creating an AWS Backup plan

Let us create an AWS Backup plan. Follow the given steps:

1. Search **backup** in the top search bar and click the **AWS Backup** search result or enter **https://us-east-1.console.aws.amazon.com/backup/home** in the browser address bar.
2. Click the **Create backup plan** button.
3. Select the **Start with a template** radio button in the **Backup plan options** section.
4. Select **Daily-35day-Retention** in the **Templates** dropdown.
5. Specify `daily-backup` in the **Backup plan name** field. See *Figure 10.1*:

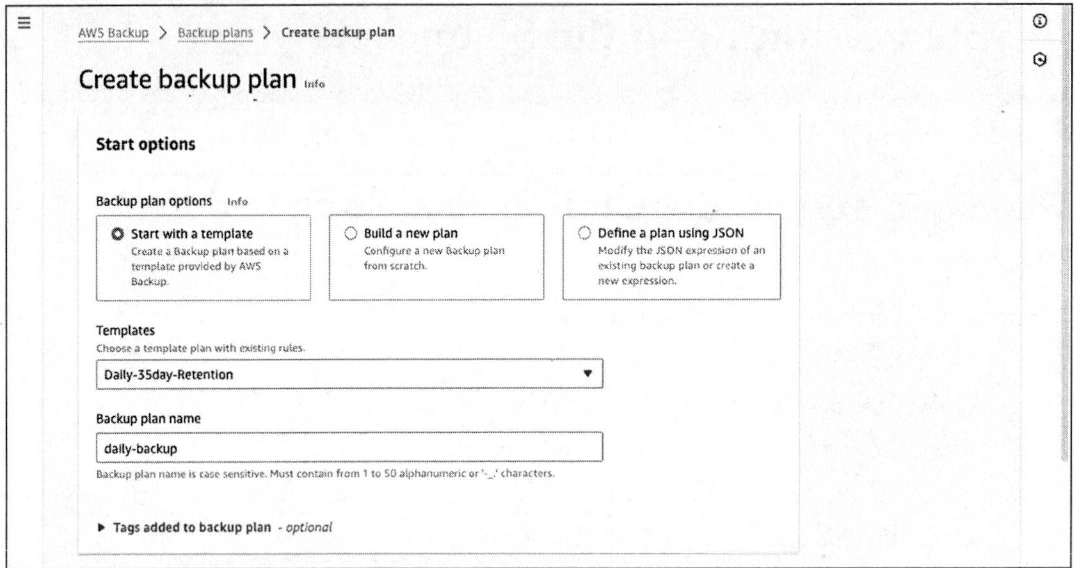

Figure 10.1: Creating a backup plan

6. Click the **Create plan** button.
7. Specify **dynamodb-s3-resources** in the **Resource assignment name** field.
8. Select the **Default role** radio button in the **IAM role** section. See *Figure 10.2*:

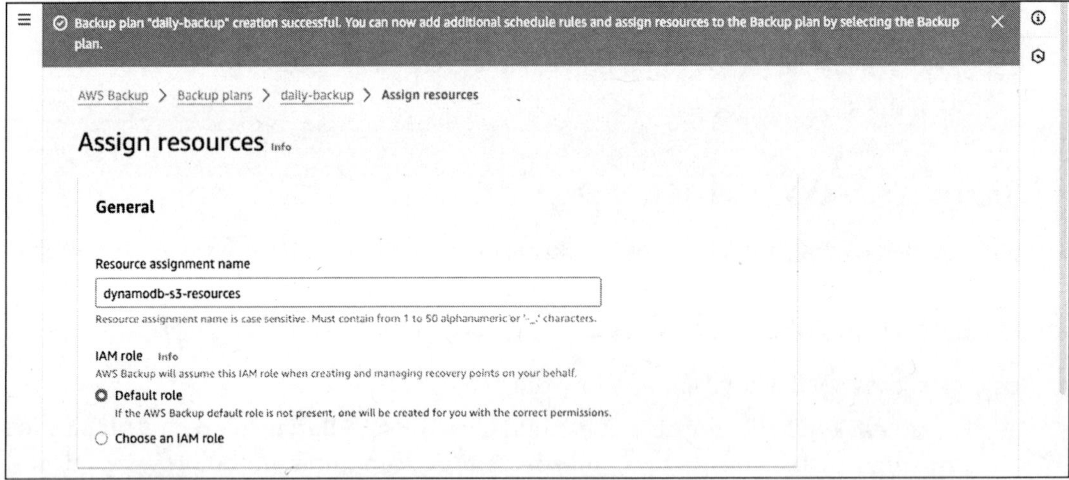

Figure 10.2: Creating a backup plan

9. Select the **Include specific resource types** radio button in the **Define resource selection** section.
10. Select the **DynamoDB** and **S3** checkboxes in the **Select specific resource types** dropdown.

11. Delete the preselected **All tables** in the DynamoDB and S3 resource types.
12. Check the **`analytics`** and **`chapters`** tables in the **Table names** dropdown.
13. Check the **`masteringawsserverlessbook-data`** and **`masteringawsserverlessbook.com`** buckets in the **Bucket names** dropdown. See *Figure 10.3* for your reference:

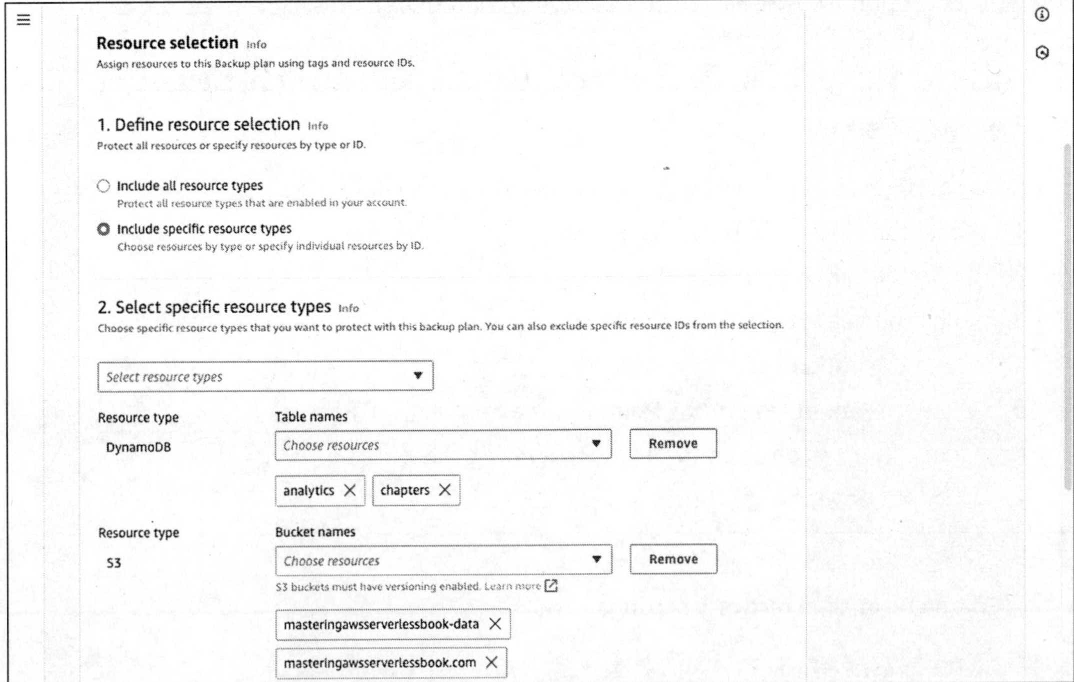

Figure 10.3: Creating a backup plan

14. Click the **Assign resources** button.
15. We successfully created the backup plan.
16. Go to the **Backup rules** section.
17. Click the **DailyBackups** rule.
18. Click the **Edit** button.
19. Go to the **Copy to destination** section.
20. Select **US East (Ohio)** in the **Region** dropdown. See *Figure 10.4*:

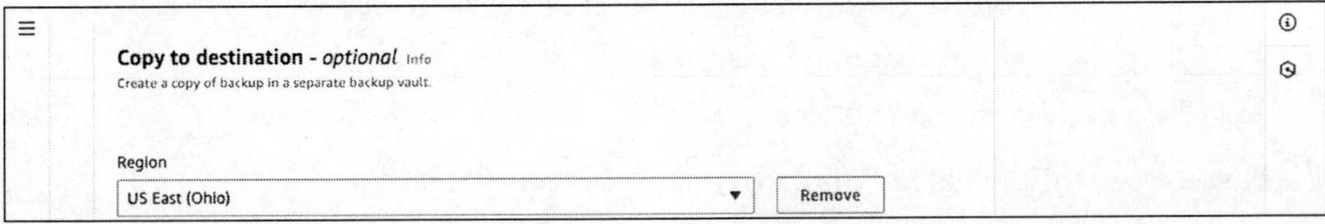

Figure 10.4: Creating a backup plan

21. Click the **Save** button.

We have successfully updated the backup rule.

Set up DynamoDB point-in-time recovery

We will set up point-in-time recovery for our DynamoDB tables.

Hands-on exercise 3: Setting up DynamoDB point in time recovery

Let us set up DynamoDB point in time recovery using the given steps:

1. Go to the DynamoDB service page.
2. Go to the **Tables** menu option.
3. Click the `analytics` table.
4. Go to the **Backups** tab.
5. Click the **Edit** button in the **Point-in-time recovery (PITR)** section.
6. Check the **Turn on point-in-time recovery** checkbox.
7. Click the **Save changes** button. See *Figure 10.5*:

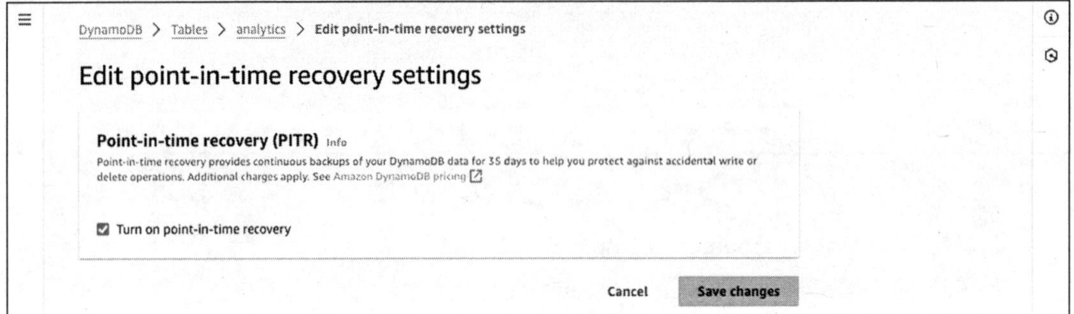

***Figure 10.5:** Turning on point-in-time recovery*

8. We successfully enabled PITR.
9. Click the `chapters` table.
10. Go to the **Backups** tab.
11. Click the **Edit** button in the **Point-in-time recovery (PITR)** section.
12. Check the **Turn on point-in-time recovery** checkbox.
13. Click the **Save changes** button.

We have successfully enabled **Point-In-Time Recovery (PITR)**.

Set up S3 bucket replication

We will set up bucket replication for our S3 buckets.

Hands-on exercise 4: Setting up S3 bucket replication

Let us set up S3 bucket replication:

1. Go to the S3 service page.
2. Go to the **Buckets** menu option.
3. Click the **Create bucket** button.
4. Specify **US East (Ohio) us-east-2** in the **AWS Region** section.
5. Specify `masteringawsserverlessbook-data-replication` in the **Bucket name** field.
6. Select the **Enable** radio button in the **Bucket Versioning** section.
7. Click the **Create bucket** button.
8. Click the **Create bucket** button.
9. Specify **US East (Ohio) us-east-2** in the **AWS Region** section.
10. Specify `masteringawsserverlessbook.com-replication` in the **Bucket name** field.
11. Select the **Enable** radio button in the **Bucket Versioning** section.
12. Click the **Create bucket** button.
13. Click the `masteringawsserverlessbook-data` bucket.
14. Go to the **Management** tab.
15. Click the **Create replication rule** button in the **Replication rules** section.
16. Specify `masteringawsserverlessbook-data` in the **Replication rule name** field.
17. Select the **Enabled** radio button in the **Status** section. See *Figure 10.6*:

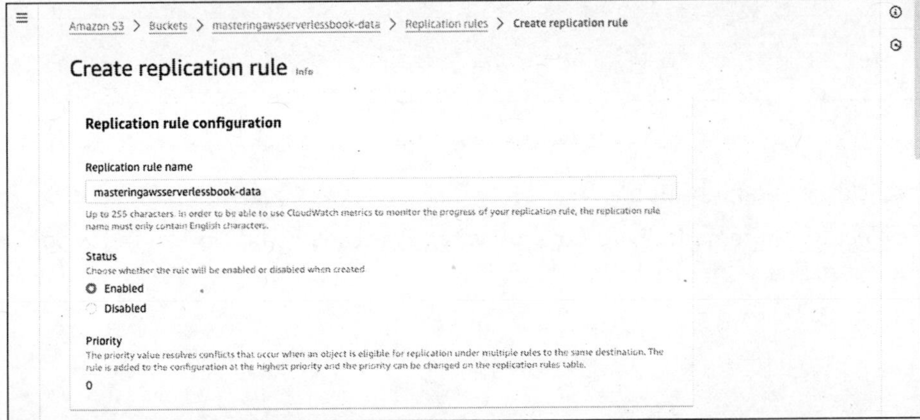

***Figure 10.6:** Creating a replication rule*

18. Select the **Apply to all objects in the bucket** in the **Choose a rule scope** section. See *Figure 10.7* for your reference:

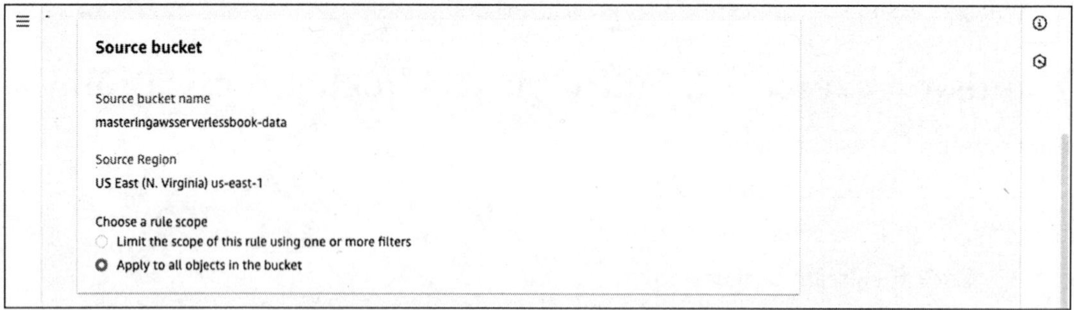

Figure 10.7: Creating a replication rule

19. Select the **Choose a bucket in this account** radio button in the **Destination** section.
20. Click the **Browse S3** button.
21. Select the **`masteringawsserverlessbook-data-replication`** radio button.
22. Click the **Choose path** button.
23. Select **Create new role** in the **IAM role** dropdown.
24. Click the **Save** button.
25. Select the **Yes, replicate existing objects** radio button in the **Replicate existing objects?** dialog. See *Figure 10.8*:

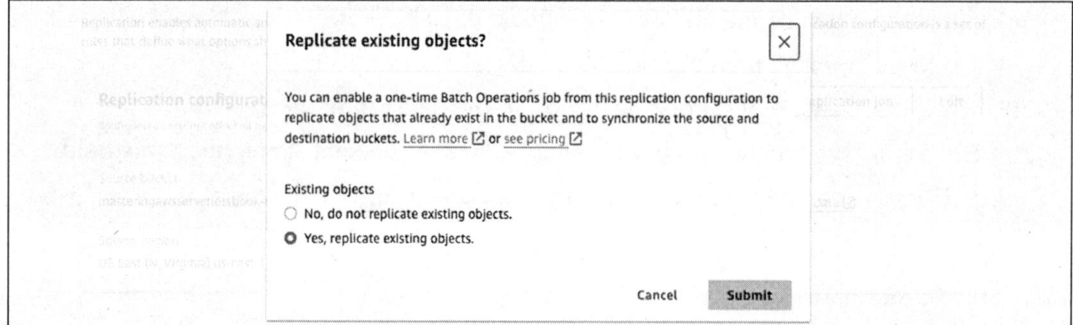

Figure 10.8: Creating a replication rule

26. Click the **Submit** button.
27. Select the **Automatically run the job when it's ready** radio button in the **Job settings** section. See *Figure 10.9*:

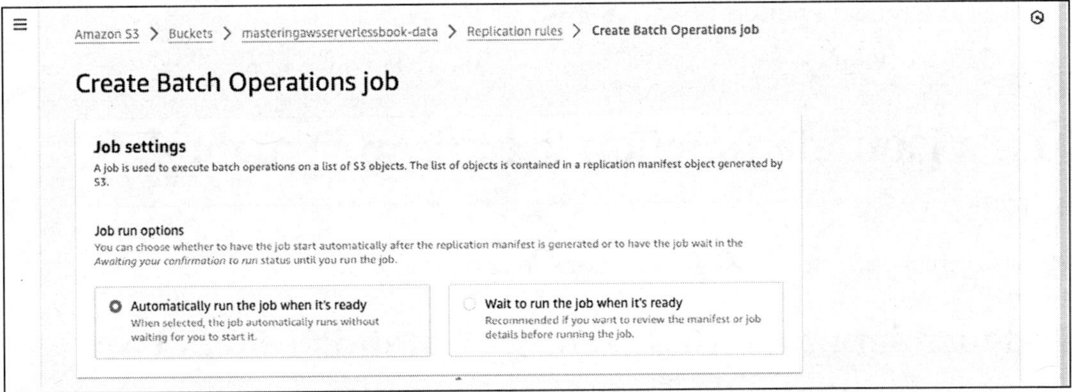

Figure 10.9: Creating a replication rule

28. Uncheck the **Generate completion report** checkbox.
29. Select **Create new role** in the **IAM role** dropdown.
30. Click the **Save** button.

We have successfully created the replication rule and batch operation.

31. Go to the **Buckets** menu option.
32. Click the `masteringawsserverlessbook.com` bucket.
33. Go to the **Management** tab.
34. Click the **Create replication rule** button in the **Replication rules** section.
35. Specify `masteringawsserverlessbook.com` in the **Replication rule name** field.
36. Select the **Enabled** radio button in the **Status** section.
37. Select the **Apply to all objects in the bucket** in the **Choose a rule scope** section.
38. Select the **Choose a bucket in this account** radio button in the **Destination** section.
39. Click the **Browse S3** button.
40. Select the `masteringawsserverlessbook.com-replication` radio button.
41. Click the **Choose path** button.
42. Select **Create new role** in the **IAM role** dropdown.
43. Click the **Save** button.
44. Select the **Yes, replicate existing objects** radio button in the **Replicate existing objects?** dialog.
45. Click the **Submit** button.
46. Select the **Automatically run the job when it's ready** radio button in the **Job settings** section.
47. Uncheck the **Generate completion report** checkbox.
48. Select **Create new role** in the **IAM role** dropdown.

49. Click the **Save** button.

We have successfully created the replication rule and batch operation.

Use a Lambda function to backup DynamoDB data

We will discuss how to use a Lambda function to backup data.

Independent exercise 1: Using a Lambda function to backup DynamoDB data

Attempt to do this exercise independently. Use the following guidance.

We will create an SSM parameter to keep track of the next start and query time window. For example, `2024-01-01T00:00:00.000Z` and `3600000` milliseconds (which is one hour).

We will create an IAM policy that will allow the following:

- The `ssm:GetParametersByPath` and `ssm:PutParameter` actions for the SSM parameter resource.
- The `dynamodb:Query` action for the DynamoDB tables resources.
- The `s3:PutObject` action for the `masteringawsserverlessbook.com/dynamodb-backups/` bucket key prefix resource.

We will create an IAM role that uses the policy and `AWSLambdaBasicExecutionRole` policies.

We will create a Lambda function that uses the following:

- The `GetParametersByPathCommand`, `PutParameterCommand` functions in the `@aws-sdk/client-ssm` library.
- The `QueryCommand` function in the `@aws-sdk/client-dynamodb` library.
- The `PutObjectCommand` function in the `@aws-sdk/client-s3` library.

The JavaScript code will read the SSM parameters and determine whether the current time has passed the one-hour query time window. If it is, it will query the DynamoDB. It will then transform the data to either JSON or CSV format. It will write that text data to the `masteringawsserverlessbook.com/dynamodb-backups/` object key prefix with a suffix containing the timestamp and the correct file extension (for example, `.json` or `.csv`). It will update the SSM parameter to have the next start time after successfully writing the object.

We will then create an EventBridge schedule rule to trigger the Lambda function every 15 minutes.

We will update the CloudWatch log group retention settings after having invoked the function.

Analyzing text using Amazon Comprehend

We will discuss how we can use Amazon Comprehend for text analysis.

Using Amazon Comprehend

We will observe a text analysis example in this section.

Hands-on exercise 5: Using Amazon Comprehend

Let us use Amazon Comprehend. Follow the given steps:

1. Search **comprehend** in the top search bar and click the **Amazon Comprehend** search result or enter **https://us-east-1.console.aws.amazon.com/comprehend/home** in the browser address bar.
2. Click the **Launch Amazon Comprehend** button or go to the **Real-time analysis** menu option. See *Figure 10.10*:

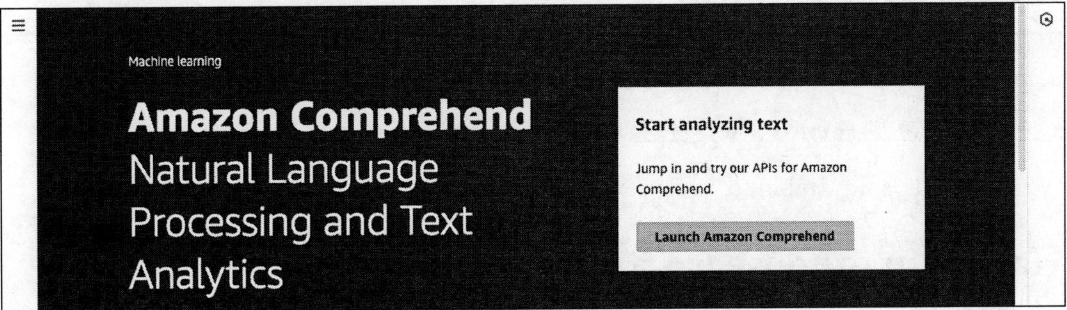

Figure 10.10: *Launching Amazon Comprehend*

3. Observe the pre-populated text in the **Input data** section and the pre-populated responses in the **Insights** section, and the example API calls and responses in the **Application integration** section. See *Figure 10.11* for your reference:

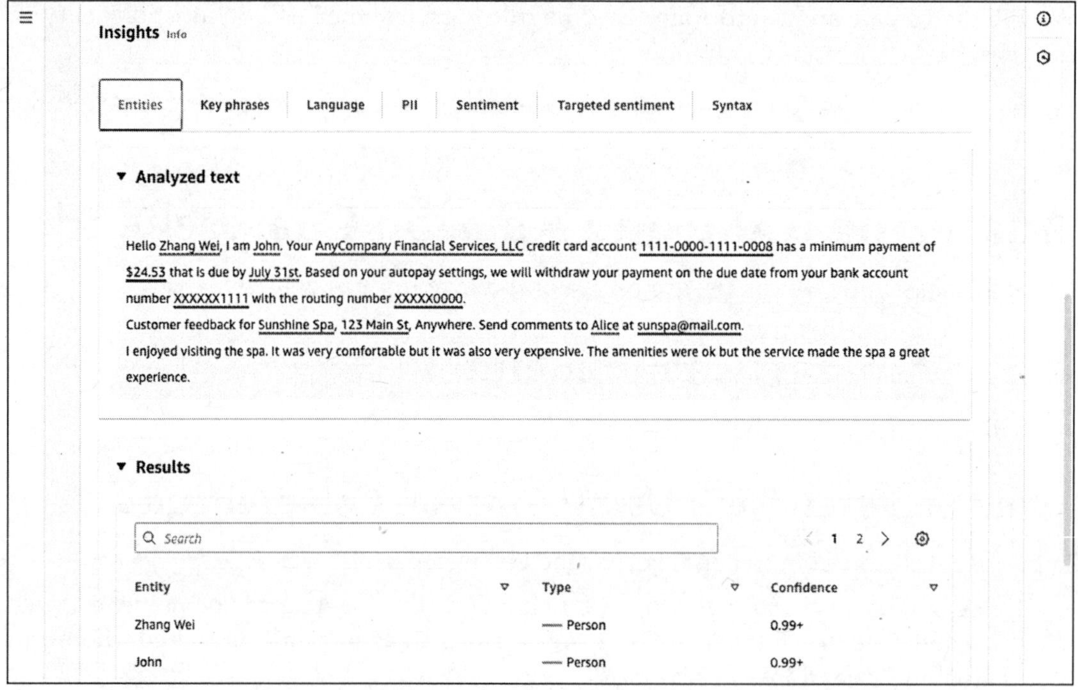

Figure 10.11: Sample Comprehend responses

4. Change the text and observe the updated results.

We have successfully used Amazon Comprehend.

Create a new DynamoDB table

We will create a new table for user comments.

Hands-on exercise 6: Creating a new DynamoDB table

Let us create a new DynamoDB table:

1. Go to the DynamoDB service page.
2. Click the **Create table** button.
3. Specify **`comments`** in the **Table name** field.
4. Specify **`dataType`** in the **Partition key** field.
5. Select **String** in the dropdown in the **Partition key** section.
6. Specify **`timestamp`** in the **Sort key** field.
7. Select **Number** in the dropdown in the **Sort key** section.
8. Select the **Customize settings** radio button in the **Table settings** section.

9. Select the **DynamoDB Standard** radio button in the **Table class** section.
10. Select the **On-demand** radio button in the **Capacity mode** section.
11. Select **Owned by Amazon DynamoDB** radio button in the **Encryption key management** section.
12. Click the **Create table** button.

We have successfully created the table.

Update the website

We will update the website to add a webpage to allow users to submit comments.

Independent exercise 2: Updating the website

Attempt to do this exercise independently. Use the following guidance:

1. Open the `/account/index.html` file.
2. Add the HTML code to display a form where a user can leave comments.
3. Add the JavaScript code for the page to send a `POST` request to a `/account/comments` API endpoint.

Create new API endpoint and related resources

We will create a new API endpoint, a Lambda function, and the related resources.

Independent exercise 3: Creating an API endpoint and related resources

Attempt to do this exercise independently. Use the following guidance:

- We will create a `post-account-comments` function. It will accept the comment text from the event body. It will create a record in the `comments`DynamoDB table by setting the `dataType` to `comments-form`, `timestamp` to the current value, and adding a `commentText` property with the comment text.
- We will create a `function-post-account-comments` policy that will allow the `ddb:PutItem` for the `comments` table resource. We will create a `function-post-account-comments` role that uses the `function-post-account-comments` and `AWSLambdaBasicExecutionRole` policies.
- We will create a `/account/comments` API endpoint with CORS enabled and a `POST` method. The `POST` method will use the Lambda proxy integration for the `post-account-comments` function.
- We will update the CloudWatch log group retention settings after having invoked the function.

Use a Lambda function to analyze the comments

We will discuss how to use a Lambda function to analyze the comments.

Independent exercise 4: Using a Lambda function to analyze the comments

Attempt to do this exercise independently. Use the following guidance.

We will create an SSM parameter to keep track of the next start and query time window. For example, **`2024-01-01T00:00:00.000Z`** and **`3600000`** milliseconds (which is one hour).

We will create an IAM policy that will allow the following:

- The **`ssm:GetParametersByPath`** and **`ssm:PutParameter`** actions for the SSM parameter resource.
- The **`dynamodb:Query`** action for the **`comments`** table resource.
- The **`dynamodb:BatchWriteItem`** action for the **`analytics`** table resource.
- The **`comprehend:DetectKeyPhrases`** and **`comprehend:DetectSentiment`** actions for all resources.

We will create an IAM role that uses the policy and **`AWSLambdaBasicExecutionRole`** policies. We will create a Lambda function that uses the following:

- The **`GetParametersByPathCommand`**, **`PutParameterCommand`** functions in the **`@aws-sdk/client-ssm`** library.
- The **`QueryCommand`** and **`BatchWriteItem`** functions in the **`@aws-sdk/client-dynamodb`** library.
- The **`DetectKeyPhrasesCommand`** and **`DetectSentimentCommand`** functions in the **`@aws-sdk/client-comprehend`** library.

The JavaScript code will read the SSM parameters and determine whether the current time has passed the one-hour query time window. If it is, it will query the DynamoDB table.

It will use Comprehend to detect each comment text's key phrases and sentiment. It will write the results to the **`analytics`** table with the **`comprehend-key-phrases`** and **`comprehend-sentiment`** as the **`dataTypes`** values, respectively.

We will then create an EventBridge schedule rule to trigger the Lambda function every 15 minutes.

We will update the CloudWatch log group retention settings after having invoked the function.

Performing text-to-speech using Amazon Polly

We will discuss how we can use Amazon Polly for text-to-speech.

Using Amazon Polly

We will try the Polly demo in this section.

Hands-on exercise 8: Using Amazon Polly

Let us use Amazon Polly:

1. Search **polly** in the top search bar and click the **Amazon Polly** search result or enter **https://us-east-1.console.aws.amazon.com/polly/home** in the browser address bar.
2. Click the **Try Polly** button or go to the **Text-to-Speech** menu option. See *Figure 10.12*:

***Figure 10.12:** Trying Amazon Polly*

3. Select one of the radio buttons in the **Engine** section.
4. Select a language from the **Language** dropdown.
5. Select a voice from the **Voice** dropdown.
6. Enter text in the **Input text** section.
7. Click the **Listen** button and listen to the playback. See *Figure 10.13*:

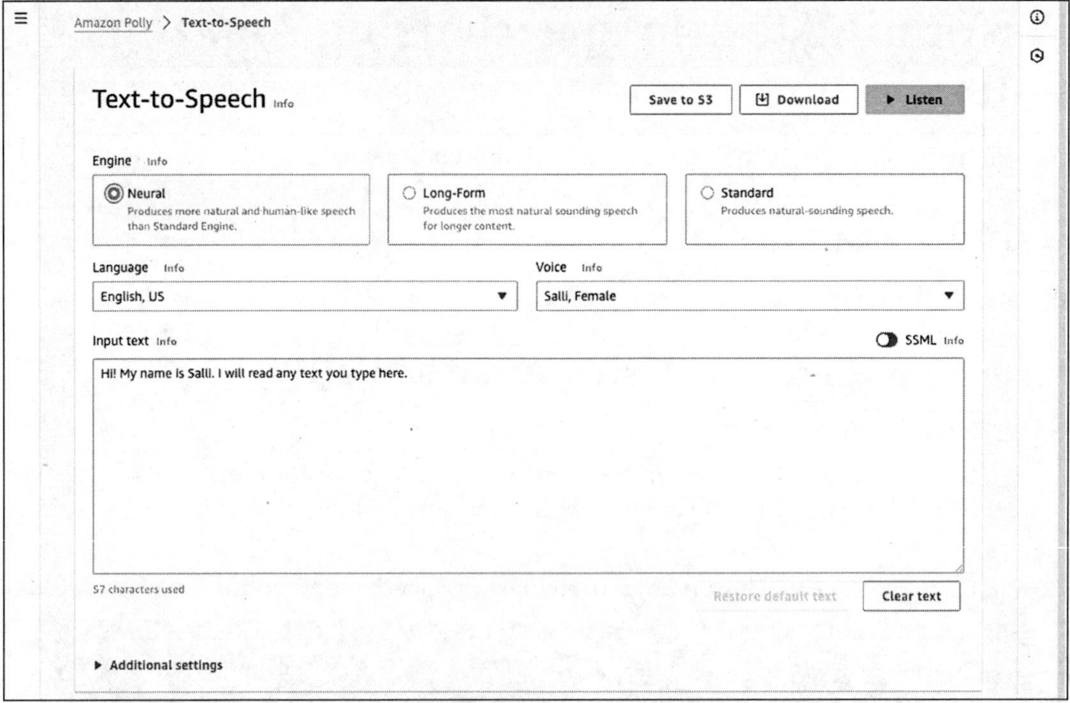

Figure 10.13: Trying Amazon Polly

8. Click the **Save to S3** button.
9. Specify **`masteringawsserverlessbook-data`** in **S3 output bucket** field.
10. Specify **`polly/test`** in the **S3 key prefix** field.
11. Click the **Save to S3** button. See *Figure 10.14*:

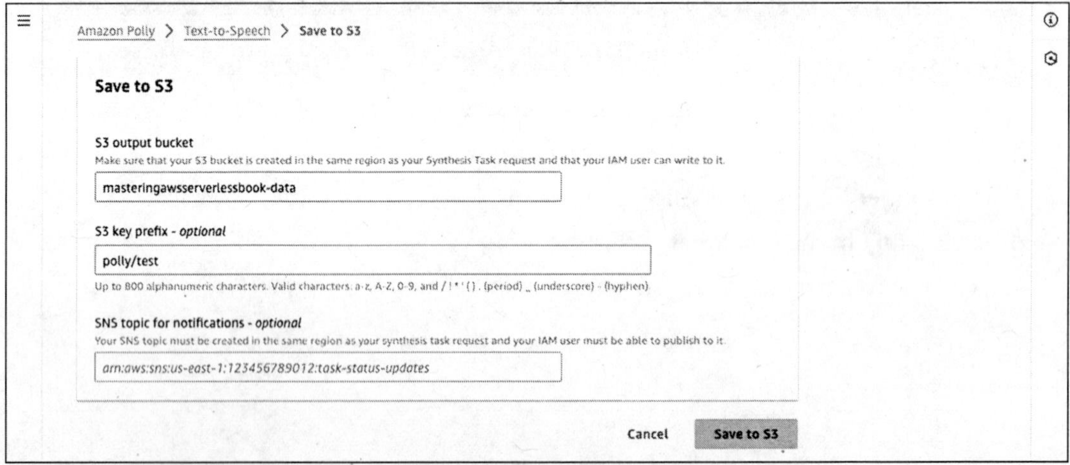

Figure 10.14: Saving Polly data

12. Go to the S3 synthesis tasks menu option.
13. Observe the completed task. See *Figure 10.15* for your reference:

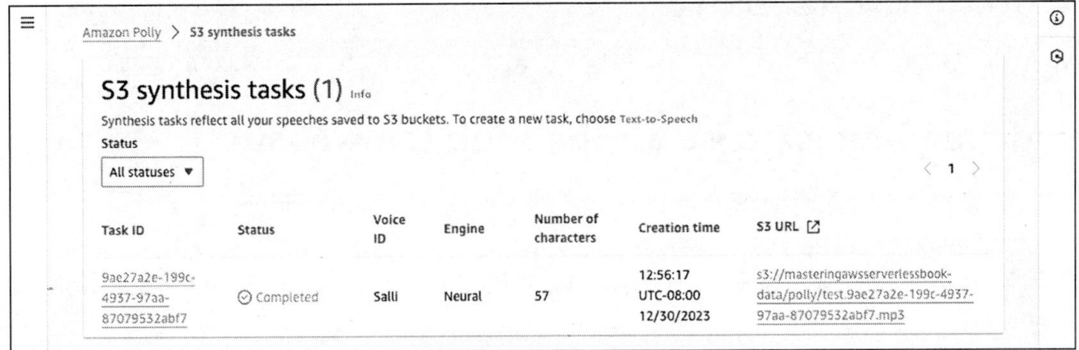

Figure 10.15: Polly synthesis tasks

14. Click the S3 URL link.
15. Click the **Download** button.

We have successfully created a text-to-speech audio file in S3.

Create a new DynamoDB table

We will create a new table for blog posts.

Hands-on exercise 9: Creating a new DynamoDB table

Let us create a new DynamoDB table using the given steps:

1. Go to the DynamoDB service page.
2. Click the **Create table** button.
3. Specify **`blog-posts`** in the **Table name** field.
4. Specify **`slug`** in the **Partition key** field.
5. Select **String** in the dropdown in the **Partition key** section.
6. Specify **`timestamp`** in the **Sort key** field.
7. Select **Number** in the dropdown in the **Sort key** section.
8. Select the **Customize settings** radio button in the **Table settings** section.
9. Select the **DynamoDB Standard** radio button in the **Table class** section.
10. Select the **On-demand** radio button in the **Capacity mode** section.
11. Select **Owned by Amazon DynamoDB** radio button in the **Encryption key management** section.
12. Click the **Create table** button.

We have successfully created the table.

Update the website

We will update the website to add a webpage to allow users to submit comments.

Independent exercise 5: Updating the website

Attempt to do this exercise independently. Use the following guidance:

1. Create the **`blog.html`** file.
2. Add the HTML code to display a list of blog posts based on the response from an API request.
3. Add the JavaScript code for the page to send a **`GET`** request to a **`/blog-posts`** API endpoint.
4. Create the **`blog-post.html`** file.
5. Add the HTML code to display the text and audio file link for a single blog post. The blog post information is obtained from the response to an API request. The AP request will send the slug value obtained from the **`/blog-post.html?slug=value`** in the URL.
6. Add the JavaScript code for the page to send a **`GET`** request to a **`/blog-posts/{slug}`** API endpoint.

Create new API endpoint and related resources

We will create a new API endpoint, a Lambda function, and the related resources.

Independent exercise 6: Creating API endpoints and related resources

Attempt to do this exercise independently. Use the following guidance:

1. We will create a **`get-blog-posts`** function. It will list all the blog posts.
2. We will create a **`function-get-blog-posts`** policy that will allow the **`ddb:Scan`** for the **`blog-posts`** table resource. We will create a **`function-get-blog-posts`** role that uses the **`function-get-blog-posts`** and **`AWSLambdaBasicExecutionRole`** policies.
3. We will create a **`/blog-posts`** API endpoint with CORS enabled and a **`GET`** method. The **`GET`** method will use the Lambda proxy integration for the **`get-blog-posts`** function.
4. We will update the CloudWatch log group retention settings after having invoked the function.

5. We will create a **`get-blog-post`** function. It will get the information for one blog post.
6. We will create a **`function-get-blog-post`** policy that will allow the **`ddb:Query`** for the **`blog-posts`** table resource. We will create a **`function-get-blog-post`** role that uses the **`function-get-blog-post`** and **`AWSLambdaBasicExecutionRole`** policies.
7. We will create a **`/blog-posts/{slug}`** API endpoint with CORS enabled and a **`GET`** method. The **`GET`** method will use the Lambda proxy integration for the **`get-blog-post`** function.
8. We will update the CloudWatch log group retention settings after having invoked the function.

Use a Lambda function to create the audio files

We will discuss how to use a Lambda function to create the audio files.

Independent exercise 7: Using a Lambda function to create the audio files

Attempt to do this exercise independently. Use the following guidance.

We will create an SSM parameter to keep track of the next start and query time window. For example, **`2024-01-01T00:00:00.000Z`** and **`3600000`** milliseconds (which is one hour).

We will create an IAM policy that will allow the following:

- The **`ssm:GetParametersByPath`** and **`ssm:PutParameter`** actions for the SSM parameter resource.
- The **`dynamodb:Query`** and **`dynamodb:BatchWriteItem`** actions for the **`blog-posts`** table resource.
- The **`StartSpeechSynthesisTask`** and **`ListSpeechSynthesisTasks`** actions for all lexicon resources.
- The **`PutObject`** action for the **`masteringawsserverlessbook-data/polly/*`** object key prefix resource.

We will create an IAM role that uses the policy and **`AWSLambdaBasicExecutionRole`** policies. We will create a Lambda function that uses the following:

- The **`GetParametersByPathCommand`**, **`PutParameterCommand`** functions in the **`@aws-sdk/client-ssm`** library.
- The **`QueryCommand`** and **`BatchWriteItem`** functions in the **`@aws-sdk/client-dynamodb`** library.
- The **`StartSpeechSynthesisTaskCommand`** function in the **`@aws-sdk/client-comprehend`** library.

The JavaScript code will read the SSM parameters and determine whether the current time has passed the one-hour query time window. If it is, it will query the DynamoDB table.

It will use Polly to start speech synthesis tasks for any new blog posts. When done, the tasks will write the audio file to the **`masteringawsserverlessbook.com/audio/`** S3 object key prefix. This will likely happen after the function finishes the execution.

It will also get the list of speech synthesis tasks. It will use the information of the completed tasks to update the **`blog-posts`** table to add the location of the audio file.

We will then create an EventBridge schedule rule to trigger the Lambda function every 15 minutes. We will update the CloudWatch log group retention settings after having invoked the function.

Analyzing images using Amazon Rekognition

We will discuss how we can use Amazon Rekognition for image analysis.

Using Amazon Rekognition

We will try the Rekognition demo in this section.

Hands-on exercise 10: Using Amazon Rekognition

Let us use Amazon Rekognition:

1. Search **`Rekognition`** in the top search bar and click the **Amazon Rekognition** search result or enter **https://us-east-1.console.aws.amazon.com/rekognition/home in** the browser address bar.
2. Click the **Try Demo** button or go to the **Label detection** menu option. See *Figure 10.16*:

Figure 10.16: Trying Amazon Rekognition

3. Observe the demo images and the results. See *Figure 10.17*:

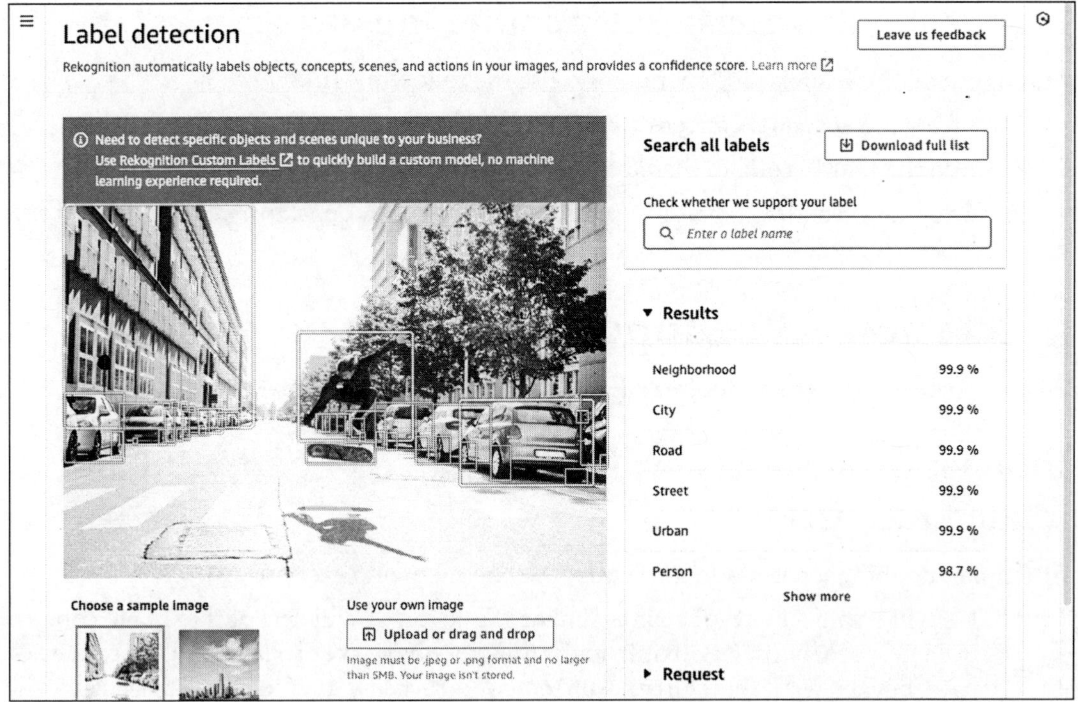

Figure 10.17: Trying Amazon Rekognition

4. Click the **Upload or drag and drop** button to analyze another image.
5. Observe the results.
6. Go to the **Text in image** menu option.
7. Observe the demo images and the results.
8. Click the **Upload or drag and drop** button to analyze another image.
9. Observe the results.
10. Click through the various demos in the **Demos** and **Video demos** menu options.

We have successfully used Amazon Rekognition.

Update the website

We will update the website to add a webpage to allow users to submit comments.

Independent exercise 8: Updating the website

Attempt to do this exercise independently. Use the following guidance:

1. Create the **account/contest.html** file.
2. Add the HTML code to display a form where a user can upload pictures.
3. Add the JavaScript code for the page to send a **POST** request to a **/account/contest** API endpoint.

Create new API endpoint and related resources

We will create a new API endpoint, a Lambda function, and the related resources.

Independent exercise 9: Creating an API endpoint and related resources

Attempt to do this exercise independently. Use the following guidance:

1. We will create a **post-account-contest** function. It will accept the image content from the event body. It will upload the image to the **masteringawsserverlessbook-data** bucket with the **contest-uploads/** object key prefix. The object key will contain the timestamp so we can search based on time.
2. We will create a **function-post-account-contest** policy that will allow the **s3:PutObject** for the **masteringawsserverlessbook-data/contest-uploads/*** object key prefix resource. We will create a **function-post-account-contest** role that uses the **function-post-account-contest** and **AWSLambdaBasicExecutionRole** policies.
3. We will create a **/account/contest** API endpoint with CORS enabled and a **POST** method. The **POST** method will use the Lambda proxy integration for the **post-account-contest** function.
4. We will update the CloudWatch log group retention settings after having invoked the function.

Use a Lambda function to analyze the images

We will discuss how to use a Lambda function to analyze the images.

Independent exercise 10: Using a Lambda function to analyze the images

Attempt to do this exercise independently. Use the following guidance.

We will create an SSM parameter to keep track of the next start and query time window. For example, **`2024-01-01T00:00:00.000Z`** and **`3600000`** milliseconds (which is one hour).

We will create an IAM policy that will allow the following:

- The **`ssm:GetParametersByPath`** and **`ssm:PutParameter`** actions for the SSM parameter resource.
- The **`s3:ListBucket`** action for the **`masteringawsserverlessbook-data/contest-uploads/*`** bucket object key prefix resource.
- The **`dynamodb:BatchWriteItem`** action for the **`analytics`** table resource.
- The **`rekognition:DetectLabels`** and **`rekognition:DetectText`** actions for all resources.

We will create an IAM role that uses the policy and **`AWSLambdaBasicExecutionRole`** policies.

We will create a Lambda function that uses the following:

- The **`GetParametersByPathCommand`**, **`PutParameterCommand`** functions in the **`@aws-sdk/client-ssm`** library.
- The **`ListBucketCommand`** functions in the **`@aws-sdk/client-s3`** library.
- The **`BatchWriteItem`** functions in the **`@aws-sdk/client-dynamodb`** library.
- The **`DetectLabelsCommand`** and **`DetectTextCommand`** functions in the **`@aws-sdk/client-rekognition`** library.

The JavaScript code will read the SSM parameters and determine whether the current time has passed the one-hour query time window. If it is, it lists the bucket object and filters the uploaded image object keys based on the timestamp.

It will use Comprehend to detect each comment text's key phrases and sentiment. It will write the results to the **`analytics`** table with the **`comprehend-key-phrases`** and **`comprehend-sentiment`** as the **`dataTypes`** values, respectively. It will write the results to the **`analytics`** table with **`rekognition-labels`** and **`rekognition-text`** as the **`dataType`** values.

We will then create an EventBridge schedule rule to trigger the Lambda function every 15 minutes. We will update the CloudWatch log group retention settings after having invoked the function.

Auditing security settings using AWS Config

We will be discussing how we can use AWS Config for security in this section. AWS Config can be cost prohibitive depending on the number of rules and whether there is continuous or daily recording. As a result, we will discuss how to use Config instead of doing hands-on exercises.

Set up AWS Config

We will set up Config.

Example 1: Setting up AWS Config

Let us set up AWS Config:

1. Search **config** in the top search bar and click the **Config** search result or enter **https://us-east-1.console.aws.amazon.com/config/home** in the browser address bar.
2. Click the **Get started** button or go to the **Set up AWS Config** menu option. See *Figure 10.18* for your reference:

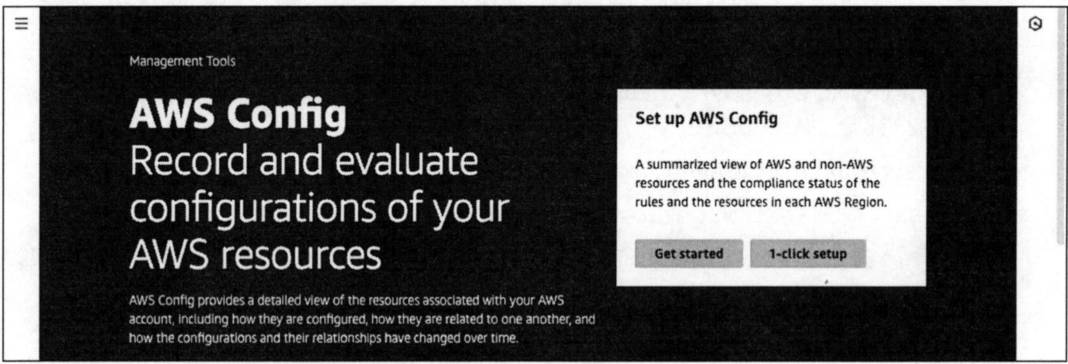

Figure 10.18: *Getting started with AWS Config*

3. Select the **All resource types with customizable overrides** radio button in the **Recording strategy** section.
4. Select the **Daily recording** radio button in the **Recording frequency** section.

Note: The Continuous recording option provides the most security and the highest cost.

See *Figure 10.19*:

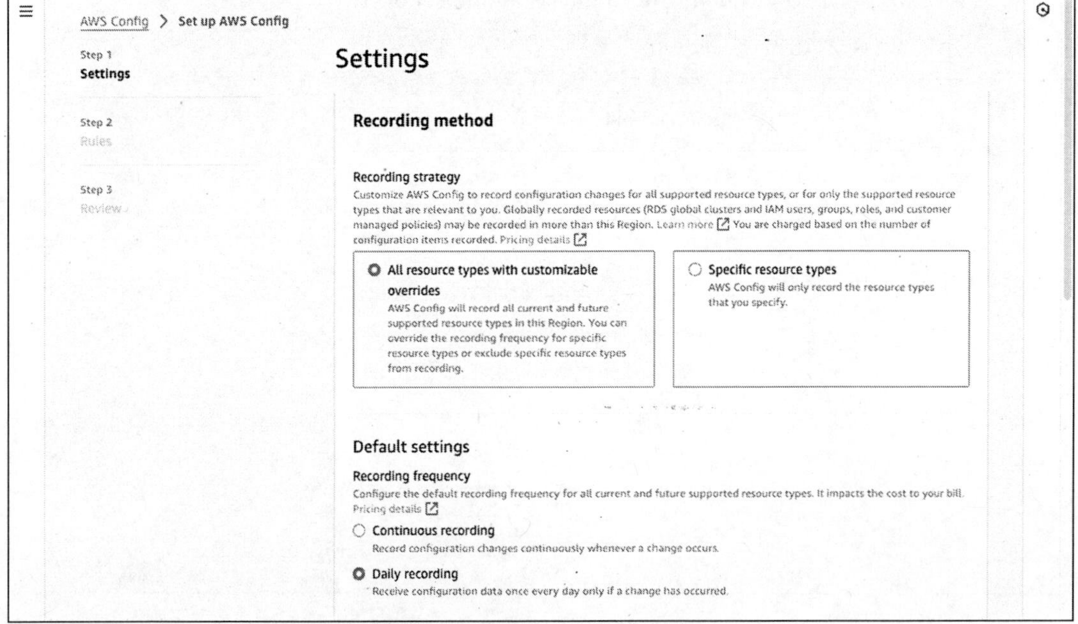

Figure 10.19: *AWS Config settings*

5. Click the **Remove** button in the **Override settings** section. See *Figure 10.20*:

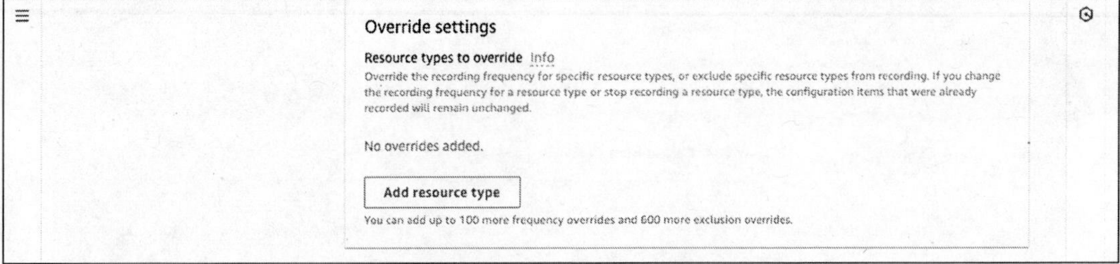

Figure 10.20: *AWS Config settings*

6. Select the **Create AWS Config service-linked role** radio button in the **IAM role for AWS Config** section. See *Figure 10.21*:

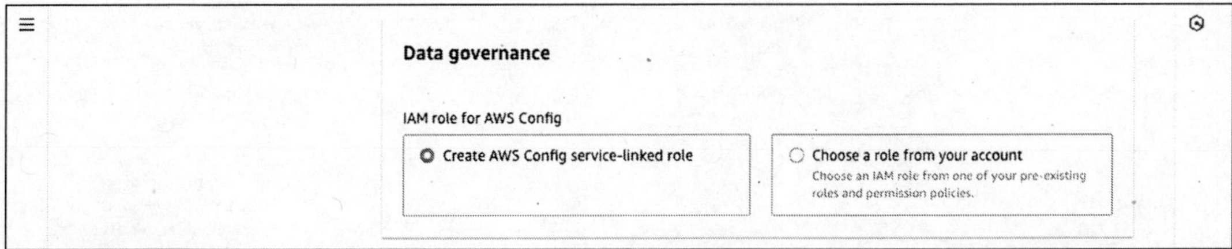

Figure 10.21: *AWS Config settings*

7. Select the **Create a bucket** radio button in the **Amazon S3 bucket** section.
8. Use the prefilled value in the **S3 Bucket name** section.
9. Click the **Next** button. See *Figure 10.22*:

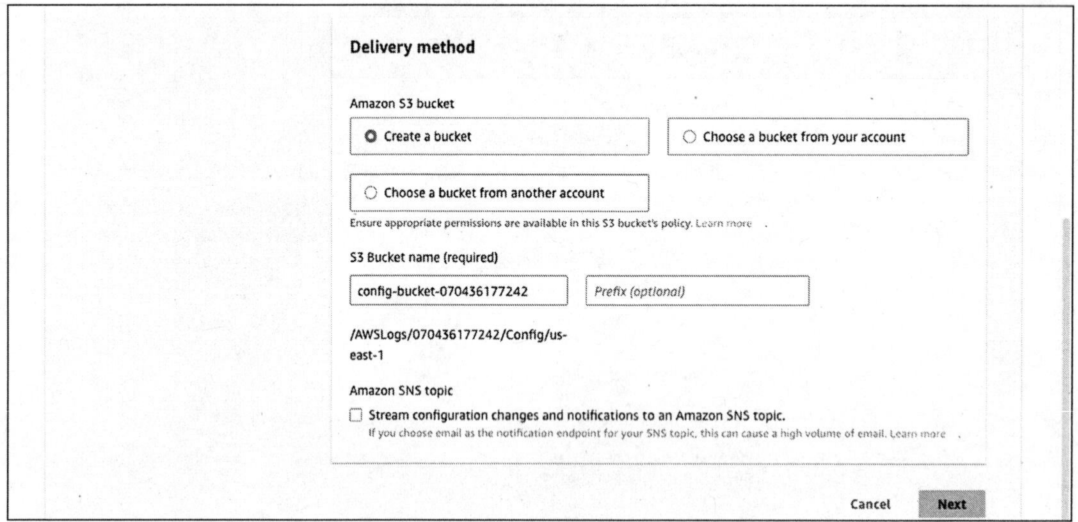

Figure 10.22: AWS Config settings

10. Search `mfa` in the **Find Rules** search field.
11. Check all the checkboxes. See *Figure 10.23*:

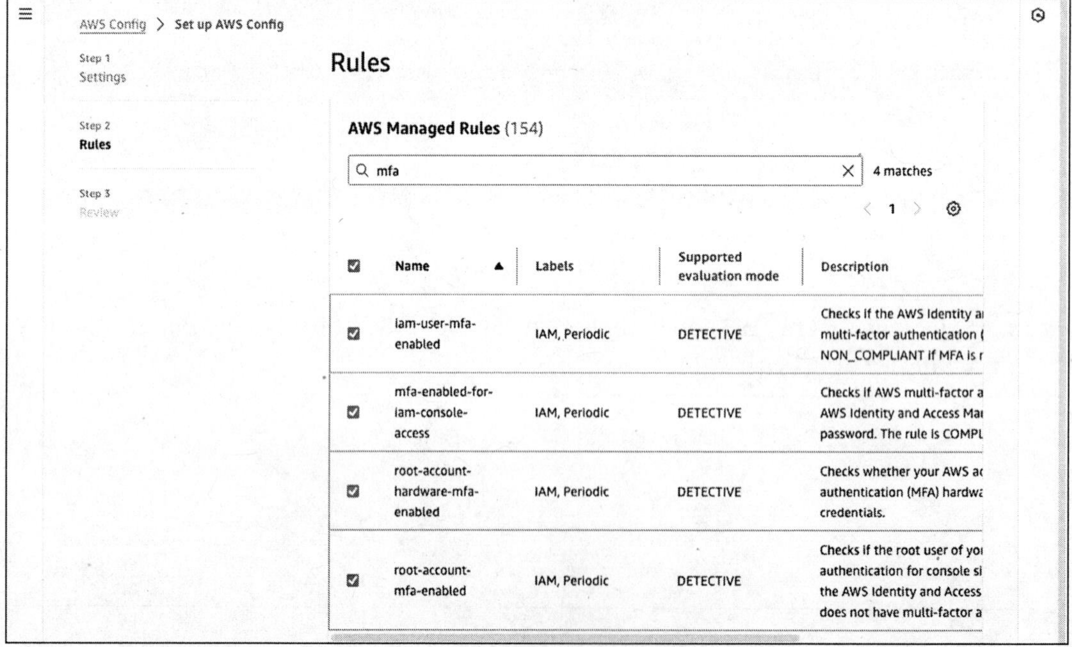

Figure 10.23: AWS Config rules

12. Search **`s3-bucket-level`** in the **Find Rules** search field.
13. Check all the checkboxes. See *Figure 10.24*:

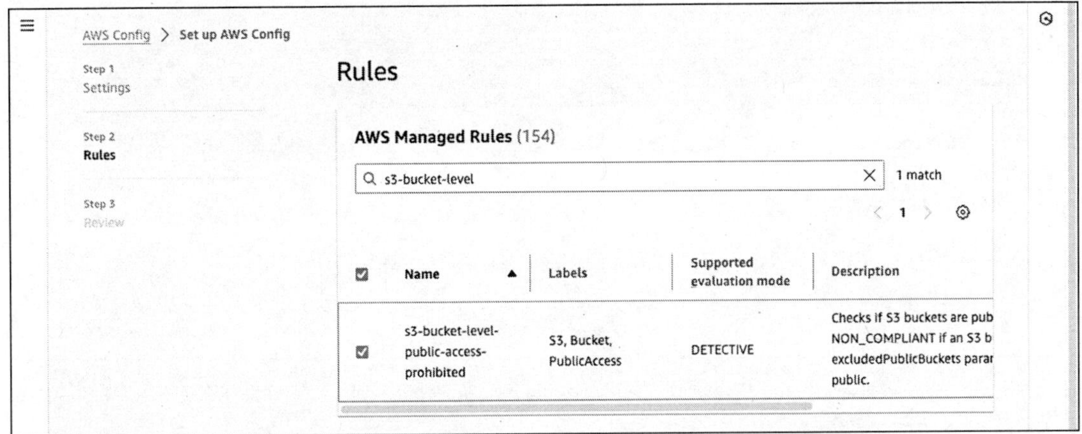

Figure 10.24: *AWS Config rules*

14. Click the **Next** button.
15. Click the **Confirm** button.
16. The page automatically refreshes to show the dashboard.

We have successfully set up Config.

Deploying conformance packs

We will explore how to deploy a conformance pack. These conformance packs have various rule checks and may be cost prohibitive. As a result, this will not be a hands-on exercise.

Example 2: Deploying conformance packs

Let us deploy a conformance pack:

1. Go to the Config service page.
2. Go to the **Conformance packs** menu option.
3. Click the **Deploy conformance pack** button. See *Figure 10.25* for your reference:

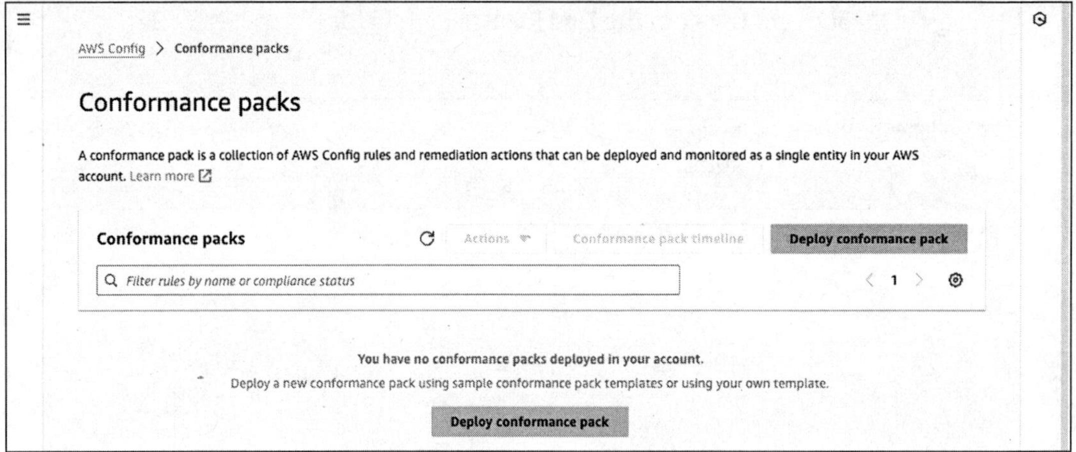

Figure 10.25: Deploying a conformance pack

4. Select the **Use sample template** radio button in the **Conformance pack template** section.
5. Select the **Operational Best Practices for Serverless** from the **Select a sample template** dropdown.
6. Select the **Next** button. See *Figure 10.26*:

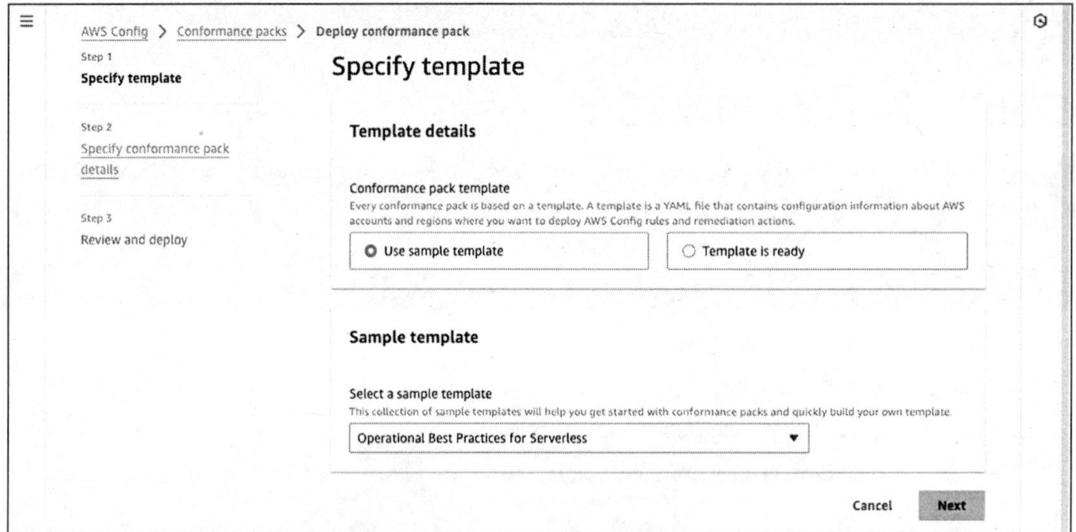

Figure 10.26: Deploying a conformance pack

7. Specify **`serverless-conformance-pack`** in the **Conformance pack name** field.
8. Click the **Next** button. See Figure 10.27:

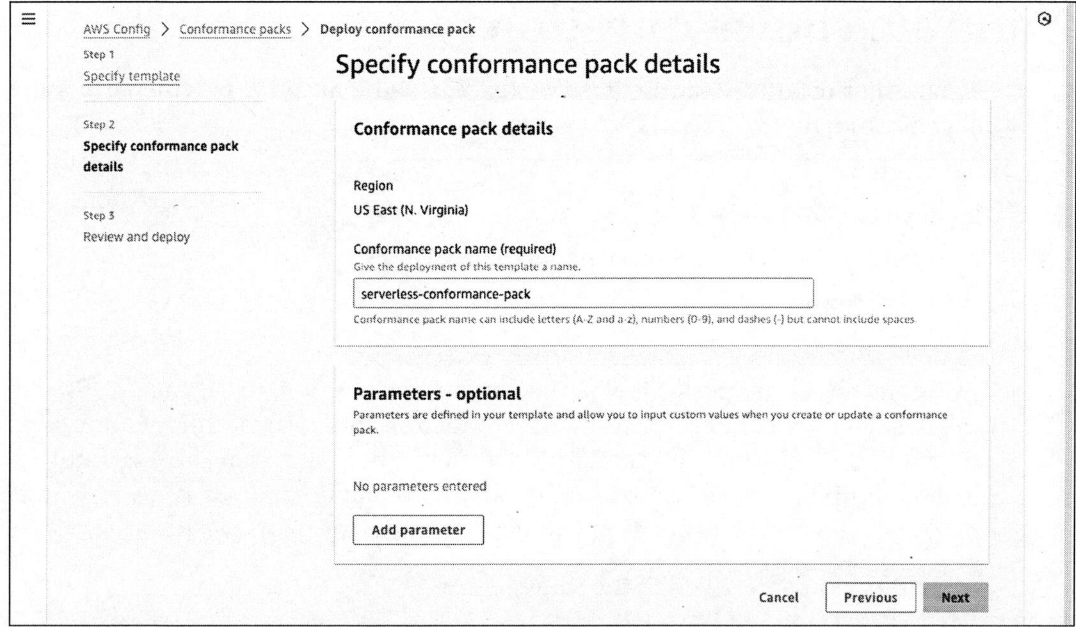

Figure 10.27: Deploying a conformance pack

9. Click the **Deploy conformance pack** button.

We have successfully deployed a conformance pack.

Conclusion

In this chapter, we discussed additional types of automation. We discussed how we can back up our data using AWS Backup, DynamoDB point in time recovery, S3 bucket replication and a Lambda function. We can perform text analysis using Amazon Comprehend, text-to-speech using Polly and image analysis using Rekognition. We discussed a workflow for using Lambda functions, API endpoints, and our website for using Comprehend, Polly, and Rekognition. We concluded by using Config to perform automated security audits.

Points to remember

- Using API Gateway API endpoints, Lambda function, SSM parameters, and EventBridge schedule rules is a common design pattern for automation tasks.
- Some AWS services provide automation tasks without having to create a Lambda function.
- Not all automation tasks require using AWS services but can be done independently, such as the image resizing example.

Multiple choice questions

1. **What other resources can be used instead of using an SSM parameter to store state information?**

   a. S3 object

   b. DynamoDB table

   c. Lambda function environment variables

   d. All of the above

   Answer: d

   All of the above are possible. Reading from the S3 bucket and DynamoDB table might have higher or lower costs than reading from SSM, depending on the number of invocations. Reading from DynamoDB might be faster than reading from S3. Although updating the Lambda function environment variables is possible, this might be risky since the function will need permissions to update itself.

2. **Should backups be saved to the same region?**

   a. Yes

   b. No

   c. It depends

   Answer: c

   It depends. In general, backing up data in a different region is a good practice, but the decision will depend on the architecture and the business requirements.

CHAPTER 11
Architecture Best Practices

Introduction

This chapter will focus on architecture best practices when using serverless computing.

Structure

We will cover the following topics in this chapter:

- The AWS Well-Architected Framework
- Using the Serverless Applications Lens framework extension

Objectives

By the end of this chapter, you will be exposed to best practices in serverless computing with regard to state, events, service outages, and more.

The AWS Well-Architected Framework

There are several best practices for serverless computing and AWS cloud computing. AWS has documented the AWS Well-Architected Framework, which has best practices for creating applications in the AWS cloud.

The framework[1] consists of the following pillars:

- **Operational excellence** focuses on running and monitoring systems and continually improving processes and procedures.
- **Security** focuses on protecting information and systems.
- **Reliability** focuses on workloads performing their intended functions and how to recover quickly from failure to meet demands.
- **Performance efficiency** focuses on structured and streamlined allocation of IT and computing resources.
- **Cost optimization** focuses on avoiding unnecessary costs.
- **Sustainability** focuses on minimizing the environmental impacts of running cloud workloads.

The framework also has lenses (or extensions) that focus on specific domains. There is a Serverless Applications Lens[2] we can use.

Using the Serverless Applications Lens

We will explore the design principles and pillars for the Serverless Applications Lens.

Design principles

This lens has seven key design principles.[3] They include:

- Speedy, simple, singular.
- Think of concurrent requests, not total requests.
- Share nothing.
- Assume no hardware affinity.
- Orchestrate your application with state machines, not functions.
- Use events to trigger transactions.
- Design for failures and duplicates.

Let us explore these design principles in more depth.

---

1 "AWS Well-Architected." Amazon Web Services. **https://aws.amazon.com/architecture/well-architected/**

2 "Serverless Applications Lens - AWS Well-Architected Framework." AWS Well-Architected Framework. Amazon Web Services. **https://docs.aws.amazon.com/wellarchitected/latest/serverless-applications-lens/welcome.html**

3 "Design principles." Serverless Applications Lens. AWS Well-Architected Framework. Amazon Web Services. **https://docs.aws.amazon.com/wellarchitected/latest/serverless-applications-lens/general-design-principles.html**

Speedy, simple, singular

Lambda functions are billed by memory, milliseconds, and CPU architecture. The memory is the amount of RAM allocated. Milliseconds is the execution time of the function. The CPU architecture can be either x86 or Arm. For example, we created a function in a previous chapter where we set the memory to 1024 MB from the default 128 MB and used the Arm architecture. If the function takes 10 seconds to execute, we will bill for 10 seconds at the 1024 MB rate for the Arm architecture. Typically, the higher the memory usage, the more costly the execution per millisecond. The Arm architecture is typically less costly than x86.

We might be tempted to think that we will use the lowest memory size and Arm architecture to get the lowest price. That might not be the case necessarily. Some JavaScript and Python libraries use more CPU and memory than others. In some cases, it makes sense to use more memory to save costs. Giving more memory to memory-hungry libraries will improve the execution time. Let us explore an example.

Suppose we use the faux MemoryHungry library. Here is what might happen in this hypothetical scenario:

- We configure our Lambda function to use 128 MB memory and it takes 10 seconds for the execution.
- We update the memory to 512 MB, and it takes two seconds for the execution.
- At the time of this writing, the 512 MB memory is approximately 3.95 times more expensive than the 128 MB.
- The execution time is 5 times faster.

We used more expensive memory to save money.

This concept is also true for the DynamoDB tables. In a previous chapter, we discussed the potential cost savings of using the on-demand capacity mode compared to the provisioned capacity mode. Here are some things to consider:

- The on-demand capacity mode is billed per million read and write request units.
- Provisioned capacity mode is billed by the hour per the read and write capacity units.
- If the read/write requests are unpredictable or have low volume, it may make sense to use the on-demand capacity mode.

Determining how many kilobytes are read and written and the number of requests per hour will help determine which mode is more cost-effective.

Going back to the function execution discussion, keeping the purpose of the function as simple as possible is a good practice. In our previous function examples, the functions were typically less than 100 lines of code, and they used five or fewer AWS SDK commands. We could use Step Functions or SNS to simplify functions. Rather than having longer functions with more logic, they can be broken up into smaller functions and orchestrated to run in a specific order. This approach works well when the functions are generic and reusable by multiple logic flows.

Another approach is to consider a different programming language. For example, the faux MemoryHungry library in JavaScript has a similar library in Python. It is possible that switching from JavaScript to Python using a similar library might result in faster execution times with less memory, which would result in cost savings.

We can leverage CloudWatch metrics for Lambda function executions and memory usage. The metrics will show their usage over time and could help us size our Lambda functions to the most cost effective memory usage.

Think concurrent requests, not total requests

We can design our application to take advantage of concurrent requests. This means we can tune our API Gateway and Lambda function settings to accept a number of requests made at the same time. By default, API Gateway has 10,000 requests per second with an additional burst capacity of 5,000 requests, and Lambda has 1,000 concurrent executions.

A new application will likely have low traffic, and concurrency limits may not be an issue. As the application grows in popularity, there will be more requests. We should monitor the API Gateway requests per second and the Lambda concurrent executions to see whether they are hitting the limits.

Suppose there is a burst in traffic, such as 10,000 API requests in one second. The first 1,000 requests will be processed immediately by the instances of a Lambda function. The remaining 9,000 requests will be throttled until a Lambda function instance becomes available. If 30 seconds pass and a Lambda function instance is unavailable, the API Gateway will timeout the request. If this happens periodically, we should increase the Lambda concurrency to meet the demand. We can manually increase the concurrency or configure the concurrency scaling rate. We can leverage CloudWatch metrics to monitor the Lambda concurrency to help us determine the optimal concurrency limits and scaling rate.

Share nothing

Traditional server applications use temporary storage, in-memory storage, and permanent file system storage. This might work well for a single server design, but Lambda functions are not persistent. Lambda functions are inherently stateless.

The Lambda function will create an instance when it is invoked, and an instance does not exist. The instance will stay active while the function continues to be triggered. It will destroy itself if there are no triggers after a period of time.

If we try to store information in the Lambda function instance filesystem, we are likely to lose it. Furthermore, since Lambda uses concurrency, there is no guarantee that the next invocation will use the same function instance. Therefore, we should not assume anything we write to the file system will be available during the next invocation.

In our previous examples, we have used SSM parameter store as a way to store state. The Lambda function can get the state information from the SSM parameter, which is persistent. We could store the state in a DynamoDB table or an S3 bucket object. Step Functions can store state information too.

Assume no hardware affinity

The Lambda function runtimes (for example, Python, Node.js, and so on) allow tuning their performance. For example, a server that runs Node.js can be configured to modify the default Node.js settings. In a server-based environment, we want to configure Node.js to perform as efficiently as possible. We can do this because we likely know the server hardware, and we can take advantage of its features.

For the AWS-managed Lambda function instances, AWS may change the configuration without notice. Furthermore, we do not know what type of hardware the Lambda function instance will run on. It may run on one type of hardware for one invocation but a different piece of hardware in a different invocation.

We do have the choice of selecting x86 or Arm architectures in the Lambda function settings. Many runtime libraries work with x86 or Arm architectures. Yet, there might be some libraries that are designed for x86 architecture and will not work with Arm architectures. In this case, we choose the x86 architecture as the hardware affinity.

Orchestrate your application with state machines, not functions

This principle encourages the use of AWS Step Functions. Step Functions allow us to create a flow diagram where we can define which Lambda function to use for each step. Furthermore, it can keep track of state information and pass it through the flow.

Using Step Functions is not mandatory. The intent of this design principle discourages having a function invoke another function. Having functions invoke functions has the following drawbacks:

- Increased complexity in the main function.
- Double billing since the main function is incurring execution time while it waits for the other function.
- Inefficient use of concurrency since two invocations are used when the main function executes.
- More complex IAM policies.
- Difficulty troubleshooting.

- The approach resembles a monolithic design which is contrary to the intent of event-driven and microservices designs inherent in serverless computing.

We could use SNS and SQS to orchestrate functions instead of using Step Functions. When we need one function to trigger another function, it could send a message to a topic or queue. We used this approach in a previous chapter.

Deciding whether SNS, SQS, and Step Functions will vary on the desired workflow, and whether they can integrate with each other. We will typically use an SNS topic to send an event to multiple recipients. We will typically use an SQS queue when we want to ensure an event is processed by the intended recipient. We will use Step Functions when we need to process more complex business logic. We might want to receive an event in an SNS topic which will forward it to an SQS queue where the recipient will process it. There is a risk that an SNS topic will send an event to a recipient who may be unavailable to process it, and the event is lost. Whereas the queue will keep the event until the recipient can process it or the event expires. Step Functions could send events to an SNS topic or SQS queue, depending on the business logic. These are some examples of orchestration.

Using events to trigger transactions

This principle suggests changing S3 objects or DynamoDB tables to trigger an event. By using this approach, we can process data changes right when they happen. This faster data processing approach may be beneficial for more time-sensitive data. We discussed this type of approach in a previous chapter.

These are some factors to consider for this approach:

- We should be selective about which S3 objects and DynamoDB tables to trigger an event. Not all types of data need to be processed right away.
- We could use EventBridge schedule rules to process data on a periodic basis for less time-sensitive data. This is a cron-based design.
- We also want to be cautious about vicious loops. For example, a bucket will trigger a Lambda function when an object is created or updated. The Lambda function will process the event and write its output to the same bucket. The S3 bucket will send another event.

In principle, using events to trigger transactions lines up well with event-driven design but should not be limited to S3 objects and DynamoDB table changes to trigger them.

Design for failures and duplicates

We should consider failures in our design. These are the types of failures we might experience:

- Service outages.
- Degraded service performance.

- Unexpected errors or bugs in the Lambda function code.
- Misconfiguration issues in the Lambda function settings or IAM policies.

Furthermore, we might get duplicate messages, or old events are sent again. We can do the following to help address these:

- Design the function code to be idempotent such that sending the same input results in the same output.
- Check whether the event has been previously processed by checking state information.
- Checking the age of the event to discard old events that were sent again.

We can write unit tests and negative path tests to help test these scenarios during development.

Next, we will explore the six pillars in Serverless Applications Lens.

Pillar 1: Operational excellence

This pillar has the following design principles:

- Perform operations as code.
- Make frequent, small, reversible changes.
- Refine operations procedures frequently.
- Anticipate failure.
- Learn from all operational failures.
- Use managed services.
- Implement observability for actionable insights.

This pillar focuses on the following best practices:

- Organization
- Prepare
- Operate
- Evolve

We will explore each concept mentioned above.

Performing operations as code

This Serverless Applications Lens design principle encourages automating how we create our infrastructure in AWS. This means using scripts or tools that we can use to create and modify our serverless resources instead of doing it manually.

This book has focused on using the AWS management console to create all the infrastructure. We did this to help you build the fundamental knowledge and experience to master AWS serverless. If we started with scripting and tools right away, you might have missed all the steps and pieces required to deploy a resource. Furthermore, we might need to troubleshoot bugs when we start building an application using tools,. If the tool has an issue, we could fall back to creating it manually and comparing the tool output to it.

There are many tools we can use to help us with automation.

- Using the **AWS command line interface (CLI)** tools in a terminal.
- Using the **AWS SDK** in a script.
- Using the **AWS Serverless Application Model** tool to write deployment scripts.
- Using the **AWS Cloud Development Kit (CDK)** tool to write deployment scripts.
- Using the **Terraform**[4] **by HashiCorp** to write deployment scripts.
- Using **AWS CloudFormation** to write deployment templates.
- Using **AWS CodeBuild** and **AWS CodePipeline** to run the deployment commands, scripts and templates.

We will explore some of these tools in the next chapter.

Another benefit of using a code-based approach is being able to track changes in a configuration management tool. Some tools or their counterpart services provide code review features where reviewers can submit comments and approve the changes. Being able to see and approve changes improves the quality of the changes and reduces the risk of accidental errors being introduced.

Making frequent, small, reversible changes

This Serverless Applications Lens design principle encourages making changes more often but having them be of smaller magnitude. Instead of making a big deployment with several updates, we can make several deployments with the less updates.

Using this approach makes it easier to back out of a change if something goes wrong. For example, we might introduce a Lambda function with a 15-minute timeout that gets stuck in an endless loop. That Lambda function would execute for 15 minutes for every invocation until it is caught and fixed. If this change was deployed among several changes, it is possible that it might take a while for us to notice this bug. Furthermore, if other resources depend on this Lambda function's output, we might need to blackout all its dependencies. If we had only deployed this Lambda function and tested it before deploying its dependencies, we could have backed out of the change and fixed it much more easily.

In this book, we have followed this principle inherently. By creating everything in the AWS management console, we are deploying small changes. When the author was testing

4 Terraform is a registered trademark of HashiCorp.

the code changes shared in this book, there were some changes that resulted in bugs. One bug was the endless loop for a function with a 15-minute timeout. The author was able to test the function code and catch the mistake quickly. The IAM policy and role, and function were deleted to terminate the execution within minutes to avoid a costly 15-minute invocation.

This design principle becomes more relevant when we adopt automated deployments, as previously discussed.

Refining operations procedures frequently

This Serverless Applications Lens principle encourages us to review our operations to look for ways to improve their procedures and identify any gaps. To ensure success, this principle encourages communicating with stakeholders and introducing gamification.

When we review our operations, we should review our testing processes, deployment procedures, and the system design. When we are adding or modifying our application, we should conduct tests while we are developing them. Tests can include:

- **Unit tests** to validate the parts of the code return expected outputs for given inputs.
- **Integration tests** to test parts of code that use the services. Ideally, these tests should use the real service, but that might become cost-prohibitive. We can instead choose to mock or simulate these services if they are stable or if there are mock libraries to leverage.
- **End-to-end tests** to validate that the new feature works from the start of the process all the way to the end.
- **Sandbox testing,** where we make the changes in a non-production version of our application where issues will not affect actual users and data.
- **Post-deployment testing,** where we test the change shortly after deploying it. We can test with a test user account or test data.

When we review our deployment procedures, we should consider these topics:

- **Manual vs. automated**: In some cases, a manual deployment might be simpler and safer. This is true when we need to modify existing resources that require multi-part changes, and the deployment tools do not support this scenario.
- **Roles and responsibilities**: If we are working in a team, we might designate certain people with the role to be responsible for deployments. We can set up our AWS privileges to limit deployment permissions to those persons. This discourages others from making unwanted changes to our applications without following a formal process.
- **Post-deployment reviews**: After deploying a change, conduct a quick review of the deployment. Document any lessons learned and suggestions for future deployments.

When we review our system design, we should consider these topics:

- **Deployment complexity**: Did we find part of the system more difficult to deploy? This might be an opportunity to improve.
- **Design complexity**: Did a new team member find it difficult to understand how part of the system was designed? This might be an opportunity to improve.
- **Troubleshooting**: Did we find it difficult to trace a bug in part of the system? This might be an opportunity to add more logging and simplify processes.
- **Unused or less used resources**: Are some resources no longer being used or have little traffic or have they not been updated in a long time? This might be an opportunity to clean up the system design.
- **Lack of knowledge**: Are there parts of the system where no one remembers how they work or understands how and why they are used? This might be an opportunity to improve documents or clean up the system design.

We should consider discussing any of the changes above with others to get feedback and approval. If we are a single person team, we can discuss with our trusted advisors for feedback if needed.

Anticipating failure

This Serverless Applications Lens principle encourages testing for failures before they happen. We can conduct the following types of exercises:

- **Tabletop exercises** where we discuss a failure or data loss scenario, how it might affect our system, and what we would do to resolve it.
- **Pre-mortem exercises** that anticipate failures or issues before they happen. Rather than waiting and reacting to issues, the pre-mortem is a proactive approach to prevent issues.
- **Fuzzing,** so we intentionally send inputs out of range or invalid inputs to see how the function code and system resources will respond.
- **Sending duplicate events** to test whether the application is idempotent.

We can use the findings from these exercises and improve our code and system design. Performing these reviews regularly can help keep our application resilient and improve our incident response procedures.

Learning from all operational failures

No matter how much we try to prevent a failure, it is inevitable that one will happen. The goal is to keep the magnitude of the failure's impact to a minimum. Regardless of the magnitude, we can always learn and improve our system.

We should conduct a post-mortem review. We should understand the following:

- The **conditions** that triggered the failure.
- The **system response** to the failure.
- The **impact** of the failure (for example, data loss or denial of service).
- The **repeatability** of the failure.
- The **likelihood** that failure will happen again.
- The **mitigations** to implement to eliminate the failure or reduce its impacts in the future.

Any lessons learned should be used to improve the system design.

Using managed services

This Serverless Applications Lens design principle encourages us to use AWS managed services. The idea is that AWS takes the responsibility to maintain high availability and reliability for their services. By leveraging AWS managed services, we can improve our system rather than having to invest the time and cost to implement higher availability and reliability.

By adopting serverless, we are inherently adopting this principle. The AWS serverless services are managed services.

We should consider expanding this principle to managed services in general. For example, we might choose to use a different identity provider than Cognito. Identity providers are managed services outside of AWS.

Implementing observability for actionable insights

This Serverless Applications Lens design principle encourages monitoring our system using **key performance indicators** (**KPIs**). By measuring KPIs, we can understand the following:

- **Performance**: Is our system performing as efficiently as we expected? How can we make it faster and reduce latency?
- **Cost**: Are our system costs as low as possible, and can they be improved? What are the costliest services, and is there a way to reduce the cost or choose an alternative solution?
- **Health**: Are we observing an increased number of failures? Are logs showing increased warnings or errors? Are we seeing an increased number of HTTP codes in the 300s, 400s and 500s?

We cannot know how well our system is working without monitoring. We would have difficulty improving our system or fixing issues without having data.

We can use Amazon CloudWatch for monitoring. CloudWatch provides out-of-the-box metrics (or KPIs) for various services. We can also create a custom metric that our application will write to. We can create a dashboard that visualizes these metrics to help us with our review. Furthermore, we can set up alarms to send us an alert when a metric exceeds or falls below a threshold value.

Organization

This Serverless Applications Lens practice encourages aligning our system and development team to meet the goals or missions of the team, organization or business. This practice is not unique to serverless. As a result, we will review the questions from the AWS Well-Architected Framework without using the Serverless Applications Lens.

This AWS Well-Architected Framework practice asks the following questions:[5]

- How do you determine what your priorities are?
- How do you structure your organization to support your business outcomes?
- How does your organizational culture support your business outcomes?

We briefly discussed roles and responsibilities earlier and that is related to this best practice. We should step back and understand what we are trying to achieve. Even with a one-person team or organization, we created this system with a goal in mind. Our AWS serverless development should support these goals, and that means system design, time invested, and costs.

Prepare

This Serverless Applications Lens best practice encourages thinking ahead. This practice is not unique to serverless. As a result, we will review the questions from the AWS Well-Architected Framework without using the Serverless Applications Lens.

This AWS Well-Architected Framework practice asks the following questions:[6]

- How do you implement observability in your workload?
- How do you reduce defects, ease remediation, and improve flow into production?
- How do you mitigate deployment risks?
- How do you know that you are ready to support a workload?

We can answer some of these questions by refining our operations procedures and using monitoring to anticipate failures as discussed earlier.

5 "Organization." AWS Well-Architected Framework. Amazon Web Services. **https://docs.aws.amazon.com/wellarchitected/latest/framework/oe-organization.html**

6 "Prepare." AWS Well-Architected Framework. Amazon Web Services. **https://docs.aws.amazon.com/wellarchitected/latest/framework/oe-prepare.html**

Operate

This Serverless Applications Lens best practice asks the following question:[7]

- **OPS 1**: How do you understand the health of your serverless application?

We have discussed some of these topics earlier, but we will discuss them in more detail.

This practice has some topics that are beneficial to serverless architectures and applications. These topics include:

- **Metrics and alerts**: As mentioned previously, we can use CloudWatch to monitor out-of-the-box metric and custom metrics. We can also set up alerts when the metrics fall out of range. We can also set up alerts for billing costs. These alerts can be sent to an email address or an SNS topic that can distribute the alert to various destinations.
- **Centralized and structured logging**: Our Lambda functions use CloudWatch logs by default and the log group is automatically created when a function is invoked. We can include `console.log` (JavaScript) or `print` (Python) statements in our code to help us troubleshoot issues. We omitted them in our sample code to keep the line count lower. We can search and analyze logs using CloudWatch. This can help us get insights from the logging that might not be obvious from the metrics.
- **Distributed tracing**: We can track a system operation from start to finish with distributed tracing. This approach adds a tracing identifier to each part so the entire flow can be analyzed. For example, an HTTP request to an API endpoint would be the start of the flow. The tracing ID would be added to the API endpoint request. The tracing ID is passed to the Lambda function. The function will include the tracing ID when it makes a request to DynamoDB. The function response will have the tracing ID. We can use the AWS X-Ray service to help add the tracking ID.
- **Prototyping**: Earlier, we discussed testing changes in a sandbox environment. The prototype is doing similar testing but at an earlier stage. We can prove out a concept or idea in a sandbox environment (ideally a separate AWS account). We can experiment with different designs to see which would be the best to implement. Furthermore, we test our failure scenarios in our prototypes. We can add the best prototype to the system design.
- **Configuration**: There are different aspects to this:
    - o **SSM parameter store**: We have explored tracking the state in the SSM parameter store. We also captured some configuration information when we stored the query time window as a configuration value in an SSM parameter. We can store similar configuration data in SSM parameters for various resources in our system.

7 "Operate." AWS Well-Architected Framework. Amazon Web Services. **https://docs.aws.amazon.com/wellarchitected/latest/serverless-applications-lens/operate.html**

- o **AWS AppConfig**: This service is part of SSM and intended to store feature flags and application configuration information. We can use the AWS AppConfig Agent Lambda extension so our Lambda functions can get the configuration information instead of having to use the AWS SDK to request information from AppConfig or Parameter Store.
- o **AWS Secrets Manager**: Sometimes we need to use secret information. So far, we have avoided using secrets in our application. We can store secrets in Secrets Manager since they are encrypted. When a Lambda function requests the secret value using the AWS SDK, the secret will be decrypted in real time. We could use the Parameter Store with SecureString values as an alternative.
- o **DynamoDB**: As previously mentioned, we can use DynamoDB to store configuration and state information.
- o **Lambda extensions**: We can use other extensions from AWS Lambda Partners or create a custom extension.

- **Testing**: We discussed testing earlier.
- **Deploying**: To add to the previous discussion, it is best to use different AWS accounts for the different stages: prototyping, development and production.

These topics also apply to non-serverless architectures on AWS and should be considered if we propose moving parts of a monolithic or server-based application to use serverless services.

Evolve

This Serverless Applications Lens practice focuses on continuously evolving and improving our operations. This practice is not unique to serverless. As a result, we will review the question from the AWS Well-Architected Framework without using the Serverless Applications Lens.

This AWS Well-Architected Framework practice asks the following question:[8]

- How do you evolve operations?

We discussed earlier how refining operation procedures frequently, anticipating failure and learning from operational failures can help us evolve operations. To add to this discussion, we can consider scheduling a recurring meeting to review operations. Having a quarterly review seems to be a good cadence for many organizations.

8 "Evolve." AWS Well-Architected Framework. Amazon Web Services. **https://docs.aws.amazon.com/wellarchitected/latest/framework/oe-evolve.html**

Useful services and tools

The following service and tools can help achieve operational excellence:

- AWS CLI
- AWS SDK
- AWS CDK
- AWS Systems Manager Parameter Store
- AWS AppConfig
- AWS Serverless Application Model
- Amazon CloudWatch
- AWS CodeBuild
- AWS CodePipeline
- AWS X-Ray
- Amazon Lambda
- Amazon Lambda extensions
- Amazon API Gateway
- Amazon DynamoDB

We have reviewed some of these services earlier in this book.

Pillar 2: Security

This pillar has the following design principles:

- Implement a strong identity foundation.
- Maintain traceability.
- Apply security at all layers.
- Automate security best practices.
- Protect data in transit and at rest.
- Keep people away from data.
- Prepare for security events.

This pillar focuses on the following best practices:

- Identity and access management
- Detective controls
- Infrastructure protection

- Data protection
- Incident response

We will explore each concept mentioned above.

Implementing a strong identity foundation

This Serverless Applications Lens design principle focuses on ensuring that our identity access management is secure from the start. We can achieve a strong identity foundation by doing the following:

- **Using principle of least privilege**: We should grant a service or resource with only the privileges it needs to perform its desired operation. For example, in a previous chapter we created a Lambda function and assigned it a custom IAM role. The role used the **`AWSLambdaBasicExecutionRole`** policy, but we did not create a custom IAM policy. This function used the user's access token to authorize a request to Cognito. The function did not need to use its own privileges to interact with Cognito. As a result, we did not give the function any access to Cognito. We gave the function the least privileges which included writing logs to a CloudWatch log group.
- **Enforcing separation of duties**: We should consider having different roles for different job roles by using IAM users. For a single-person team, we should have administrator, developer, and read-only IAM users with their respective roles. We should use the role with the least privileges needed to perform the desired task. For a multi-person team, we should assign team members the privileges of the roles appropriate for their job description. For example, not every team member needs administrator privileges. Enforcing separation of duties uses the concept of role-based access control.
- **Setting up role-based access control**: We can create an IAM user group for each type of role. For example, we can have a user group for administrators with a policy that has admin privileges. We can set up a developer's user group with a policy that allows creating and updating relevant resources but denies modifying IAM users and user groups.
- **Having one role per resource**: We should use one role per Lambda function and other services that support assigning a role per resource. We might be tempted to create a role that includes a catch-all IAM policy and assign it to all Lambda functions, for example, because it takes less effort. This makes our application vulnerable. Suppose a Lambda function was exploited, and a malicious actor was able to send AWS CLI or SDK commands to modify our AWS account. If the function has a lot of permissions, the adversary might be successful in accessing a desired resource. However, if it only had permission to read data from a specific DynamoDB table, for example, the adversary would be unsuccessful when trying to access any other resource.

- **Centralizing identity**: The IAM service provides us with a centralized identity for our AWS account. We should have a centralized identity for our application users. We can use an identity provider to achieve this. In previous chapters, we used Cognito as the identity provider to allow users to sign up and sign in. We can use the AWS IAM Identity Center instead of IAM users. IAM Identity Center provides an identity provider solution to the AWS management console.
- **Enforcing MFA**: We also enforced MFA in Cognito. The AWS root account and IAM service do not enforce MFA by default. We discussed enabling MFA for the root account in a previous chapter. We can create an IAM policy to limit what the IAM users can do until they enable MFA though. If we use the IAM Identity Center, it can enforce MFA.

Failure to follow these principles can lead to severe consequences. For example, if MFA is not enforced, we risk a malicious actor guessing a username and password and taking over an account. In another example, a Lambda function using an IAM role and policy that does not follow the principle of least privilege might result in a maliciously crafted payload that returns data from a sensitive DynamoDB table that the Lambda function was not meant to read. Following these principles reduces our security risk.

Maintaining traceability

This Serverless Applications Lens design principle is similar to monitoring but more focused on security. We should monitor changes in our infrastructure and check for misconfigurations. This type of monitoring is typically referred to as auditing.

We can enable AWS CloudTrail to record event history whenever a user, role or AWS service takes an action via the AWS management console, CLI, SDK or APIs. Having these events can help us look for suspicious activity.

Applying security at all layers

This Serverless Applications Lens principle focuses on the defense in depth approach. This approach encourages implementing security from the lowest level to the highest level. These are examples of security at different layers:

- **Software libraries**: We should periodically check any software libraries we use in our code for vulnerabilities. Malicious actors look for opportunities to exploit applications that use older versions of libraries that have known vulnerabilities.
- **Lambda function code**: We should write our function code using secure principles. This includes validating all inputs, validating software libraries, avoiding writing secrets into the code, safely deserializing data, handling errors, enabling logging, etc.

- **Authentication and authorization**: We want to verify that users are who they claim to be (authentication) and allow them to perform by the operations they are allowed (authorization).
- **Security benchmarks**: We can use security benchmarks that provide recommendations on the best practices to securely configure AWS resources.
- **Rate limiting**: We can enable rate limiting at the API Gateway to discourage denial of service attacks.
- **Web application firewalls**: We can add a WAF to protect our API and website from HTTP-based and web-based exploits.

We should evaluate every aspect of our system to review the security settings.

Automating security best practices

This Serverless Applications Lens design principle focuses on using automation to make sure we follow security best practices. We can use AWS Config and Lambda functions to perform automated checks as discussed in a previous chapter.

Protecting data in transit and at rest

This Serverless Applications Lens principle focuses on using encryption to protect data when in transit (for example, an HTTPS request) or at rest (for example, data being stored in an S3 bucket or DynamoDB table with encryption enabled). API Gateway, CloudFront, DynamoDB and S3 use encryption at rest and in transit by default. We need to ensure our web application uses HTTPS and not HTTP when sending request to our API. CloudFront will upgrade HTTP requests to our website to HTTPS. The AWS SDK we use in the Lambda function code automatically uses HTTPS.

Some data needs to be restricted. For example, user data should only be accessible by that one user. We can use authentication to determine who is the user and use authorization to check whether the user can access that data.

Keeping people away from data

This Serverless Applications Lens design principle encourages limiting access to data and relying on automated data processing instead of manually processing data. We discussed automated data processing in a previous chapter.

Preparing for security events

This Serverless Applications Lens design principle encourages us to plan for an incident. We should develop procedures for how we would respond when a security incident happens and how we investigate what happened. Earlier we discussed conducting tabletop exercises for failures. We should consider doing the same for security incidents.

We can use AWS Config to help detect security incidents related to misconfiguration. We can use Lambda functions to automatically remediate security misconfigurations when the Config rules only support detection. We can use CloudTrail events to help determine how the security incident occurred.

Amazon offers additional security services which include:

- AWS Security Hub
- Amazon GuardDuty
- Amazon Inspector
- Amazon Detective
- AWS Audit Manager

We can consider using generative artificial intelligence to write procedures before an incident happens and get guidance on how to respond to a security incident after it has happened.

Identity and access management

This Serverless Applications Lens practice asks the following questions:[9]

- **SEC 1**: How do you control access to your serverless API?
- **SEC 2**: How are you managing the security boundaries of your serverless application?

This practice reviews the following authorization techniques available in API Gateway:

- **AWS_IAM authorization**: This approach uses IAM temporary credentials which the API Gateway authorization will verify. If the credentials are valid, it will attempt to perform the action. The IAM credential should be tied to a least privileged policy. We did not use this approach in this book.
- **Amazon Cognito user pools**: This approach focuses on a Cognito user pool providing the user an access token that the API Gateway authorization will verify. We used this approach in this book.
- **API Gateway Lambda authorizer**: This approach on creating a custom Lambda authorizer that will verify an access token before authorizing the request. We could have written a custom authorizer to validate the Cognito user pool access token instead of using the built-in authorizer. This approach is useful when we use a third-party identity provider or create our own authorization solution.
- **Resource policies**: This approach uses a resource policy that is similar to the IAM policies we used for our Lambda function. We can add restrictions to limit access. For example, we can restrict access to the API Gateway to a specific IP address.

9 "Identity and access management." AWS Well-Architected Framework. Amazon Web Services. **https://docs.aws.amazon.com/wellarchitected/latest/serverless-applications-lens/identity-and-access-management.html**

This approach is useful if we only want users from a corporate network with a single external IP address to access the API Gateway.

- **Mutual TLS authentication**: We configure API Gateway to verify a TLS certificate in an API request. The requester will include the certificate in the API request. If the certificate is valid, the API request is authorized. This approach is useful for application-to-application authentication or Internet of Things devices.

Furthermore, this best practice encourages the following for Lambda functions:

- Granting least-privileged access.
- Assigning one IAM role to each function.

We discussed these earlier.

Detective controls or detection

This Serverless Applications Lens best practice focuses on detecting security events and vulnerabilities. This practice is not unique to serverless. As a result, we will review the question from the AWS Well-Architected Framework without using the Serverless Applications Lens.

This AWS Well-Architected Framework practice asks the following question:[10]

- How do you detect and investigate security events?

The Serverless Applications Lens focuses on the following techniques:

- **Log management**: Both the Serverless Applications Lens and the AWS Well-Architected Framework focus on log management. Having logs in CloudWatch and CloudTrail helps with identifying security event, performing forensics and support complying with legal and regulatory requirements.
- **Application dependencies**: When we use software libraries, we are using someone else's code in ours. Our code becomes dependent on theirs. We should use vulnerability databases to check for known vulnerabilities in our application dependencies and respond by updating to a newer version if available, changing to a different library is possible, or updating our code and WAF to mitigate the risk of an exploit.
- **Vulnerability scans**: We can use various tools to look for vulnerabilities. Software composition analysis tools help us stay up-to-date on vulnerabilities in our dependencies. Static code analysis tools can check our code follows secure coding principles. Dynamic application security testing tools can help find vulnerabilities in deployed Lambda functions, API Gateway configurations and WAF rules. Web application security testing tools can check for common security vulnerabilities in our JavaScript code and business logic.

10 "Detection." AWS Well-Architected Framework. Amazon Web Services. **https://docs.aws.amazon.com/wellarchitected/latest/framework/sec-detection.html**

We should consider leveraging AWS services, open-source tools and third-party services and tools to help us detect security issues and events.

Infrastructure protection

This Serverless Applications Lens practice focuses on protecting our resources by leveraging the Amazon **Virtual Private Cloud** (**VPC**). This practice is not unique to serverless. As a result, we will review the questions from the AWS Well-Architected Framework without using the Serverless Applications Lens.

This AWS Well-Architected Framework practice asks the following questions:[11]

- How do you protect your network resources?
- How do you protect your computing resources?

Lambda function instances natively run in private VPCs that we cannot access or configure. We can, however, assign a function to run inside our VPC. We can configure an API Gateway to be private and reside in a VPC. DynamoDB and S3 are public services and cannot be put in a VPC. We can, however, configure the resources within a VPC to access DynamoDB and S3 using a VPC endpoint.

The default VPC that comes with our AWS account has Internet access. If we want to protect some resources to not have Internet access, we can create another VPC that will be private by default. We can allocate protected resources to that VPC. This approach is useful when we have servers in our architecture that are not meant to have Internet access. Another reason to use a private VPC is to protect a VPN integration to an on-premises network. Our Lambda function might need to get data from an on-premises database, for example, to perform ETL to put the data in a DynamoDB table. The Lambda function would need to attach to the private VPC to be able to access the on-premises network.

Data protection

This Serverless Applications Lens practice asks the following question:[12]

- **SEC 3**: How do you implement application security in your workload?

The Serverless Applications Lens focuses on the following techniques:

- **Enabling API Gateway access logs**: We can enable access logs for our APIs so we can have a request history similar to web server access logs. We can use this information to look for security events.
- **Secure requests from the client**: Clients (for example, our serverless website) should use HTTPS and encrypt sensitive payloads. Sensitive information should

11 "Infrastructure protection." AWS Well-Architected Framework. Amazon Web Services. **https://docs.aws.amazon.com/wellarchitected/latest/framework/sec-infrastructure.html**

12 "Data protection." AWS Well-Architected Framework. Amazon Web Services. **https://docs.aws.amazon.com/wellarchitected/latest/serverless-applications-lens/data-protection.html**

not be sent using the HTTP query string parameters or the request path since this information is not encrypted.

- **Using encryption in transit and at rest**: We discussed this earlier.
- **Cautiously logging information**: We should be careful what we log. Logs are stored in plain text and logging secret information could expose it.
- **Validating and sanitizing inputs**: We should not trust inputs are valid even if they originate from another AWS resource. It is possible the input or event has a malicious payload or may fail to conform with input types and ranges our application is accepting. Input validation should be done in the web application code and in Lambda function code.
- **Signing Lambda function code**: We can use AWS Signer to sign our application code. Lambda will check whether the code was modified by checking against the signature and stop the execution if it fails.
- **Safely storing secrets**: We can use AWS Secrets Manager to store our secrets.

The AWS Well-Architected Framework has additional techniques:

- **Leveraging S3**: S3 provides *99.999999999% durability of objects over a given year*, which means it has a very high reliability.
- **Versioning**: We can enable versioning in S3, so we have an older copy of an object in the event it is accidentally overwritten.
- **Logging**: We can enable S3 access logs, so we have records when S3 objects are accessed.

There are additional techniques we can consider:

- **CloudFront logging**: We can enable standard logs to provide us access records for our distribution.
- **Keep buckets private**: There have been several data breaches due to misconfigurations of S3 buckets where they were made public when they were meant to be private. Buckets should only be public when the data is not sensitive and using CloudFront distributions and S3 pre-signed URLs are not an option.

Using these techniques will help us protect our data.

Incident response

This Serverless Applications Lens best practice encourages planning and preparing for security incidents. This practice is not unique to serverless. As a result, we will review the question from the AWS Well-Architected Framework without using the Serverless Applications Lens.

This AWS Well-Architected Framework practice asks the following question:[13]

- How do you anticipate, respond to, and recover from incidents?

We discussed preparing for security incidents earlier.

Useful services and tools

The following services can help achieve the security pillar:

- Amazon Cognito
- IAM
- IAM Identity Center
- Lambda
- CloudWatch Logs
- AWS CloudTrail
- Amazon S3
- DynamoDB
- AWS Config
- AWS Security Hub
- Amazon GuardDuty
- Amazon Inspector
- Amazon Detective
- AWS Audit Manager
- AWS SDK
- AWS Signer
- AWS CloudFormation

We have reviewed some of these services earlier in this book.

Pillar 3: Reliability

This pillar has the following design principles:

- Automatically recover from failure.
- Test recovery procedures.
- Scale horizontally to increase aggregate workload availability.
- Stop guessing capacity.
- Manage change in automation.

13 "Incident response." AWS Well-Architected Framework. Amazon Web Services. **https://docs.aws.amazon.com/wellarchitected/latest/framework/sec-incresp.html**

This pillar focuses on the following best practices:

- Foundations
- Change management
- Failure management

We will explore each concept mentioned above.

Automatically recover from failure

This Serverless Applications Lens design principle encourages using KPIs and monitoring to determine failures. The KPIs should track business value. For example, a deployment time KPI might be 15 minutes or less because any longer results in a service disruption to users. By tracking this KPI, we can observe whether deployment times increase over time. We can proactively take measures to speed up a long deployment time before it disrupts the service to the users.

Furthermore, we can automatically track failures and recover from them. When we use CloudFormation, it has a built-in feature that will rollback a change if it detects a deployment issue during the deployment. We can use Amazon CloudWatch Synthetics to create canaries that can monitor API endpoints to detect possible issues that end users might experience.

Testing recovery procedures

This Serverless Applications Lens principle encourages simulating failures and testing recovery procedures. We can use a sandbox AWS account to experiment with failure scenarios and attempt to recover data. It is best to do this in a separate AWS account to avoid accidentally disrupting the production system and affecting the users.

Scaling horizontally

To scale horizontally means adding more instances of a resource while scaling vertically means growing the size of the resource. For example, we can increase our Lambda function concurrency limit instead of increasing the function memory size to meet demand. Another approach is to increase the memory size to try to speed up the execution time. If it does, there is a point of diminishing returns where adding more memory will not result in significant improvements to execution time. At this point, it becomes cost prohibitive because more memory becomes more expensive with little return. Adding more concurrency so more function instances can execute will likely have more impact.

Stop guessing capacity

We should consider using CloudWatch metrics to observe how much capacity we are using. For example, we might find we need a higher rate limit for our API Gateway. We might learn our Lambda functions are using memory than needed. We might discover our DynamoDB reads and writes have a consistent pattern, and moving to provisioned capacity might be more cost-effective. By having these metrics data, we can tune our resources.

Managing change in automation

This Serverless Applications Lens design principle encourages us to use automation (for example, CloudFormation) to change our infrastructure. Furthermore, using automated approaches allows us to review changes before and after they happen because we can use a compare tool to see what changes were made to the CloudFormation templates.

Foundations

This Serverless Applications Lens practice asks the following questions:[14]

- **REL 1**: How are you regulating inbound request rates?
- **REL 2**: How are you building resiliency into your serverless application?

The Serverless Applications Lens focuses on the following techniques:

- **Using throttling**: Implementing throttling allows us to reduce the risk of overwhelming our application and giving a malicious actor the ability to attempt an exploit numerous times. We can configure API Gateway to throttle requests.
- **Using API keys**: We can protect API endpoints to require API keys. Only requests including the valid API key will be allowed.
- **Concurrency controls**: We can limit the concurrency per function. For example, a function that is meant to run on a schedule only needs to have a concurrency limit of one. A function getting events from an API Gateway will need a large concurrency limit based on the expected traffic.
- **Managing failures**: We should assume there might be failures in function code, business logic, and AWS services with degraded performance. We should design our system to handle those scenarios.
- **Managing duplicate or unwanted events**: We previously discussed idempotence and validating inputs which includes events.
- **Orchestrating long-running transactions**: We can use Step Functions to break up long-running transactions. This reduces the risk of having a Lambda function with a long execution timeout running a large bill if there is a bug.
- **Evaluating bursts**: We should assess what might happen if there is a burst in traffic. We should determine whether the Lambda functions will be able process the throttled API requests before the API Gateway times them out. We should understand the impacts if a burst in traffic cannot be processed.

14 "Foundations." AWS Well-Architected Framework. Amazon Web Services. **https://docs.aws.amazon.com/wellarchitected/latest/serverless-applications-lens/rel-foundations.html**

Limiting the number of requests to an expected quantity and planning for failures, idempotence, and bursts will help improve our system reliability.

Managing changes

This Serverless Applications Lens practice focuses on monitoring resources, changing them based on demand and controlling how changes are made. This practice is not unique to serverless. As a result, we will review the questions from the AWS Well-Architected Framework without using the Serverless Applications Lens.

This AWS Well-Architected Framework practice asks the following questions:[15]

- How do you monitor workload resources?
- How do you design your workload to adapt to changes in demand?
- How do you implement change?

We can use CloudWatch to monitor KPIs. They will tell us how well our resources are performing and whether traffic patterns and demand are changing over time. We can use this information to improve our system design. When we change our system design, we should follow a change process before, during and after making the changes. Change processes allow us to take the time to review what changed and why they changed. Taking the time to review the changes may help us find potential issues or improvements before making them in the production system.

Failure management

This Serverless Applications Lens practice focuses on the automated processes followed when failures occur. This practice is not unique to serverless. As a result, we will review the questions from the AWS Well-Architected Framework in addition to using the Serverless Applications Lens.

This AWS Well-Architected Framework practice asks the following questions:[16]

- How do you back up data?
- How do you use fault isolation to protect your workload?
- How do you design your workload to withstand component failures?
- How do you test reliability?
- How do you plan for **Disaster Recovery** (**DR**)?

15 "Change management." AWS Well-Architected Framework. Amazon Web Services. **https://docs.aws.amazon.com/wellarchitected/latest/framework/rel-chg-mgmt.html**

16 "Failure management." AWS Well-Architected Framework. Amazon Web Services. **https://docs.aws.amazon.com/wellarchitected/latest/framework/rel-failmgmt.html**

The Serverless Applications Lens focuses on the following techniques:

- **Retry attempts**: We can configure Lambda functions to retry executing the function again when it returns an error. It will retry until the maximum number of retries is reached. When working with DynamoDB batches, we should retry processing the failed batch items.
- **Record ages**: We can configure a maximum age for an event record. This is useful when the data has an expected lifetime. It also helps prevent an unexpected event trigger for an old record that might no longer be relevant and would overwrite meaningful data.
- **Failure destinations**: When the maximum retry attempt has exceeded, we would lose that data. We can send the failed to a dead letter queue to an SQS queue that can save the event information for later investigation.

The AWS Well-Architected Framework also discussed the following techniques:

- **Backing up data**: In addition to backing up data, we should evaluate how we can meet recovery time objectives and recovery point objectives when recovering data.
- **Isolating faults**: A failure in one part of the system should not affect the rest of the system. A failure in a Lambda function will typically not affect another function unless a function is invoking another. A failure in a Lambda function might prevent the downstream resources that would follow from running though. In this scenario, the failure should be isolated, so it does not cause undesired effects in the remainder of the workflow.
- **Disaster recovery plans**: We should have a strategy for recovering from a disaster.

Following these techniques will help our systems and team best respond to failures.

Useful services

The following services can help achieve the reliability pillar:

- AWS Marketplace
- Trusted Advisor
- CloudFormation
- CloudWatch Logs
- CloudWatch
- CloudWatch Synthetics
- API Gateway
- Lambda
- X-Ray

- Step Functions
- Amazon SQS
- Amazon SNS

We have discussed some of these services in this book.

Pillar 4: Performance efficiency

This pillar has the following design principles:

- Democratize advanced technologies.
- Go global in minutes.
- Use serverless architectures.
- Experiment more often.
- Consider mechanical sympathy.

This pillar focuses on the following best practices:

- Architecture selection
- Review
- Monitoring
- Tradeoffs

We will explore each concept mentioned above.

Democratizing advanced technologies

This Serverless Applications Lens design principle encourages us to use a cloud provider or service provider when adopting new technology. For example, artificial intelligence has been a big interest in the 2020s with the mass adoption of generative AI. We could set up our own servers, databases, data stores, APIs, and so on. That might be difficult and costly to do for an organization or a small team. Instead, we could use the following AWS AI services:[17]

- Amazon Bedrock
- Amazon SageMaker
- GPU-powered Amazon EC2 instances
- Amazon EC2 UltraClusters
- AWS Trainium
- AWS Inferential

17 "How to build and scale generative AI applications on AWS." Amazon Web Services. **https://aws.amazon.com/generative-ai/technology/**

We discussed a serverless AI workflow in *Chapter 8: Processing Data using Automation and Machine Learning*.

Going global in minutes

We can deploy services in different parts of the world by using the various AWS regions. The physically closer the resources are to the end user, the lower latency the end user will experience which typically results in a better user experience since there is less delay while data loads.

Although this book uses the North Virginia (`us-east-1`) region in our example, we could have chosen any region. For example, we were able to replicate and backup our data to the Ohio (`us-east-2`) region with ease.

Using serverless architectures

This Serverless Applications Lens design principle encourages serverless architectures because it removes the burden of managing servers and our application can scale more easily since we leverage managed services.

Experimenting more often

This Serverless Applications Lens design principle encourages us to experiment when we are designing. Earlier, we discussed prototyping and using a different AWS account for prototyping.

Considering mechanical sympathy

This Serverless Applications Lens principle encourages us to choose the best service for what we are trying to accomplish. For example, using an S3 bucket might be a more appropriate storage location for image files than using a DynamoDB table to store the image file content.

Architecture selection

This Serverless Applications Lens practice asks the following question:[18]

- **PER 1**: How have you optimized the performance of your serverless application?

The Serverless Applications Lens focuses on the following techniques:

- **Performance testing**: We should test our workflows using the expected traffic patterns and bursts of traffic. These tests will help identify limitations, bugs and cost spikes.

18 "Architecture selection." AWS Well-Architected Framework. Amazon Web Services. **https://docs.aws.amazon.com/wellarchitected/latest/serverless-applications-lens/selection.html**

- **Amazon API Gateway endpoint selection**: We should use either edge endpoints or regional endpoints depending on our use case. Edge endpoints are useful when we host an API endpoint in one region, but our users are dispersed geographically. Regional endpoints are useful when the related resources are in the same region. If our users are close to the region, we can use regional endpoints. We could consider having the same API endpoint in different regions and have our application client select the regional endpoint that is closest to the user.
- **AWS Lambda tuning**: We should test the execution time using different memory sizes and CPU architectures. When we introduce dependencies in our code that are not the AWS SDK, we should optimize the cold start. The cold start time is the time it takes for the function instance to become operational. We should also consider provisioned concurrency as discussed earlier.
- **Amazon DynamoDB capacity mode**: We should use the on-demand mode for unpredictable traffic and the provisioned mode for consistent traffic as previously discussed.

This lens also discussed Step Functions and Kinesis. We did not cover these services in detail or with hands-on exercises, and thus were omitted.

Optimizing

This Serverless Applications Lens best practice focuses on optimizing our serverless architecture with performance testing and design tradeoffs. It focuses on the following services:

- **Amazon API Gateway**: We can enable API caching when the response content is relatively static; this minimizes Lambda function invocations. We can use global secondary indices and local secondary indices to conduct queries instead of querying with the primary index and filtering out data or scanning the entire table and filtering out data. We can enable content encoding to reduce the response payload size. Smaller payloads typically transmit more quickly over the Internet. The application client will need to decode the response to get the data.
- **AWS Lambda**: We should set the execution timeout to be as close to the expected execution time. If it is set too long, we might have a costly invocation when we have a bug. We should minimize the function code size by packaging dependencies. We should avoid monolithic designs or long workflows in a single Lambda function. We should have a different Lambda function for each API endpoint.

This lens also discussed Step Functions and AppSync. We did not cover these services in detail or with hands-on exercises, and thus were omitted.

Review, monitoring, and tradeoffs

We reviewed these Serverless Applications Lens best practices earlier in the chapter.

Useful services

The following services can help achieve performance efficiency pillar:

- Amazon DynamoDB Accelerator
- Amazon API Gateway
- AWS AppSync
- AWS Step Functions
- Amazon VPC
- NAT gateway
- AWS Lambda

We have discussed some of these services in this book.

Pillar 5: Cost optimization

This pillar has the following design principles:

- Implement cloud financial management.
- Adopt a consumption model.
- Measure overall efficiency.
- Stop spending money on undifferentiated heavy lifting.
- Analyze and attribute expenditure.

This pillar focuses on the following best practices:

- Cost-effective resources
- Matching supply and demand
- Expenditure and usage awareness
- Optimizing over time

We will explore each concept mentioned above.

Implementing cloud financial management

This Serverless Applications Lens design principle encourages us to understand our cloud costs and look for opportunities to optimize costs. We can use AWS Cost Explorer to review costs. We can view daily and monthly costs. We can group them by service, region and AWS API operation. Changing the views could help us identify costly resources.

Let us walk through an example of how we can use the Cost Explorer. Suppose we notice that our bill is $15 more expensive than expected. The monthly view shows a spike in a particular month. We change the view to the daily view. We see a cost spike on a specific date. We change the view to group by service. We find the cost spike is from Route

53. We change the grouping to API service and find the cost spike was caused by the **`DomainRegistration`** API operation. We determine the root cause as a domain name being purchased. In this case, this would be an expected charge if the team meant to buy a new domain name.

We can use AWS Budgets to set up alerts when our costs exceed an expected budget.

Adopting a consumption model

This Serverless Applications Lens principle encourages us to think about what resources for which we want to pay and how much. We pay-per-usage with serverless services. For example, we will pay for how much S3 bucket storage and DynamoDB storage. We can choose to pay for S3 storage over DynamoDB storage since S3 storage is typically less expensive. If we are storing test data, we can choose to delete the data at the end of business day and upload it the next time we need to run a test. For production data, we can enable lifecycle rules to delete data when it is no longer needed.

For Lambda, we will pay for the number of function execution milliseconds based on the memory size. We can choose to disable EventBridge scheduled events for test resources.

Measuring overall efficiency

This Serverless Applications Lens design principle encourages us to measure the output we get from using the AWS cloud and calculating its efficiency. We may choose to stop using the AWS cloud for some processes since they are inefficient and costly, or we can choose to optimize them.

Stop spending money on undifferentiated heavy lifting

This Serverless Applications Lens design principle encourages us to use AWS since they take care of the data center operations, setting up the server racks, managing power consumption, configuring server operating systems, and creating managed services. By using serverless, we inherently adopt this principle.

Analyzing and attributing expenditure

This Serverless Applications Lens design principle encourages us to consider the return on investment by using the AWS cloud compared to the IT costs of us doing everything ourselves. This ROI can be up to *priceless* since it would be costly and time consuming to replicate the AWS serverless managed services.

Cost-effective resources

This Serverless Applications Lens practice asks the following question:[19]

- **COST 1**: How do you optimize your costs?

The Serverless Applications Lens focuses on the following:

- **Pay-per-use**: As mentioned earlier, we pay for what we use in our serverless resources.
- **Lambda billing**: The more memory we allocate to a function, the better its initiation time and potentially the shorter its execution time. Earlier, we discussed how optimizing memory and execution time can help with optimizing costs.

We should continually review costs and how they can be optimized.

Matching supply and demand

This Serverless Applications Lens practice encourages us to match our resources to manage demand. For example, we should avoid using DynamoDB provisioned capacity mode if we have inconsistent traffic. We can consider using infrequent access storage classes in S3 and DynamoDB for data that is retrieved less often since these classes have different pricing tiers.

Expenditure and usage awareness

This Serverless Applications Lens practice suggests we monitor usage and categorize costs by tagging resources and decommissioning resources when their lifespan ends. We can also use different AWS accounts for different projects to help with categorization and decommissioning. We can manage all our AWS accounts with AWS Organizations.

Optimizing over time

This Serverless Applications Lens best practice provides guidance on the following services:

- **Lambda cost and performance optimization**: We have discussed this concept earlier. We can use AWS Compute Optimizer to help us optimize the memory size for our Lambda functions.
- **Logging ingestion and storage**: In previous chapters, we configured the CloudWatch logs retention period, so we do not pay for log storage longer than needed. We can choose what to log instead of logging excessively. If we need excessive logs, we can set up a workflow to copy CloudWatch logs to an S3 bucket and keep the log group retention period short. This practice also suggests using

19 "Cost-effective resources." AWS Well-Architected Framework. Amazon Web Services. **https://docs.aws.amazon.com/wellarchitected/latest/serverless-applications-lens/cost-effective-resources.html**

CloudWatch Embedded Metric Format instead of the CloudWatch `PutMetricData` API when recording metrics to CloudWatch.

- **Leverage VPC endpoints**: This practice suggests we use VPC endpoints to access resources within a VPN instead of setting up an internet gateway or NAT within the VPC.
- **DynamoDB on-demand and provisioned capacity**: We have previously discussed that on-demand capacity is best for unpredictable traffic whereas provisioned capacity is best for predictable traffic.
- **Direct integrations**: This practice encourages us to use direct integrations instead of using a Lambda function to perform it. In *Chapter 8: Processing Data using Automation and Machine Learning*, we set up a direct integration from API Gateway to DynamoDB instead of using a Lambda function to write to DynamoDB. We omitted the Lambda function execution cost. The Serverless Applications Lens documentation provides an example of an API Gateway integrating to an Amazon Kineses Data Firehose and the Firehose writes the data to an S3 bucket.
- **Code optimization**: We can write our function code more efficiently to save on costs. The Serverless Applications Lens documentation provides an example of the code for two Lambda functions. One function used the S3 `GetObjectCommand` and parsing the object content to get the desired data. This function took 200 seconds to execute. The other function uses the S3 `SelectObjectCommand`, which uses a query expression to get the desired data. The second function took 95 seconds to execute.

This lens also discussed AWS Step Functions Express Workflows. We did not cover these services in detail or with exercises, and thus, it was omitted.

Useful services

The following services can help achieve the cost optimization pillar:

- Amazon CloudWatch alarms
- AWS Cost Explorer
- AWS Budgets
- AWS Compute Optimizer
- AWS Organizations

We have discussed some of these services in this book.

Pillar 6: Sustainability

This pillar has the following design principles:

- Understand your impact.
- Establish sustainability goals.

- Maximize utilization.
- Anticipate and adopt new, more efficient hardware and software offerings.
- Use managed services.
- Reduce the downstream impact of your cloud workloads.

We will explore each concept mentioned above.

This pillar has no practices unique to serverless. As a result, we will focus on the following practices from the AWS Well-Architected Framework without using the Serverless Applications Lens:

- Region selection
- Alignment to demand
- Data

We will explore each concept mentioned above.

Understanding your impact

This Serverless Applications Lens design principle encourages us to consider the environmental impact of our workloads from start to decommissioning and retirement. By using serverless, we inherently have less impact on the environment. As we continue to optimize our workloads to make them more efficient and less costly, we will improve our environmental impact.

Establishing sustainability goals

This Serverless Applications Lens principle encourages us to have goals for the environmental impact for each transaction. We can choose to limit how much data we store in an S3 bucket and DynamoDB tables. We can keep Lambda function executions short and reduce how many times they need to execute.

Maximizing utilization

This Serverless Applications Lens principle encourages us to size our workloads to minimize the environmental impact. We can size our Lambda function memory size to the optimal size. We can choose a different storage class for S3 buckets and DynamoDB tables.

Adopting new hardware and software offerings

We should review updates to our serverless services to look for ways to reduce impact. For example, provisioning capacity mode was the only option for DynamoDB initially. AWS later introduced the on-demand capacity which reduces impact for unpredictable traffic patterns. In another example, Lambda offered the x86 CPU architecture for its functions. AWS later introduced the Arm architecture which uses AWS Graviton processors. The

Arm architecture was less expensive and could improve execution times for many pieces of code.

Using managed services

This Serverless Applications Lens principle suggests using managed services since they typically reduce impact compared to self-managed resources and data centers. By using AWS serverless, we embrace this principle.

Reducing the downstream impact of your cloud workloads

This Serverless Applications Lens principle encourages us to reduce the energy used by downstream resources and reduce the needs for our end users to have to upgrade to use our application. We should consider evaluating ways to optimize our workflows. For example, we could periodically review SNS subscribers and remove outdated subscribers to avoid sending unnecessary notifications.

Region selection

This Serverless Applications Lens best practice encourages us to use the region that best improves performance, cost and carbon footprint. This practice is not unique to serverless. As a result, we will review the question from the AWS Well-Architected Framework without using the Serverless Applications Lens.

This AWS Well-Architected Framework practice asks the following question:[20]

- **SUS 1**: How do you select Regions for your workload?

In this book, we used the North Virginia (**`us-east-1`**) region for consistency. For our next project, we should choose a region that is closer to our user base and best supports our KPIs.

Alignment to demand

This Serverless Applications Lens practice encourages us to scale our resources based on demand while using the least amount of resources. This practice is not unique to serverless. As a result, we will review the question from the AWS Well-Architected Framework without using the Serverless Applications Lens.

20 "Region selection." AWS Well-Architected Framework. Amazon Web Services. **https://docs.aws.amazon.com/wellarchitected/latest/framework/sus-region-selection.html**

This AWS Well-Architected Framework practice asks the following question:[21]

- **SUS 2**: How do you align cloud resources to your demand?

By using serverless, our application has built in scaling to meet demand. We should review the DynamoDB capacity modes, the API Gateway limits, Lambda function provisioned concurrency and the storage classes for DynamoDB and S3.

Data

This Serverless Applications Lens practice encourages us to review our data access and storage patterns. This practice is not unique to serverless. As a result, we will review the question from the AWS Well-Architected Framework without using the Serverless Applications Lens.

This AWS Well-Architected Framework practice asks the following question:[22]

- **SUS 4**: How do you take advantage of data management policies and patterns to support your sustainability goals?

We can use S3 lifecycle rules to delete old data or move it to colder storage. Data that is in colder storage is put on hardware that uses less resources since the data does not need to be readily available.

We can enable the DynamoDB **Time-To-Live** (**TTL**) feature to automatically delete table records that have a timestamp set in the TTL attribute. The smaller we keep the DynamoDB table, the less compute and electricity is used to find data in the tables.

Conclusion

In this chapter, we reviewed the AWS Well-Architected Framework with the Serverless Applications Lens for architecture best practices. We discussed some of the suggestions they provided and added additional suggestions. We can review these documents for every serverless architecture and cloud architecture we create and update.

Points to remember

- The AWS Well-Architected Framework has six pillars.
- Each pillar has design principles and best practices.
- The framework has different lenses that help focus it to a specific use case, for example, the Serverless Applications Lens.

---

21 "Alignment to demand." AWS Well-Architected Framework. Amazon Web Services. **https://docs.aws.amazon.com/wellarchitected/latest/framework/sus-user-behavior-patterns.html**

22 "Data." AWS Well-Architected Framework. Amazon Web Services. **https://docs.aws.amazon.com/wellarchitected/latest/framework/sus-data-patterns.html**

Multiple choice questions

1. **Reading only the Serverless Applications Lens document provides all the best practices and design principles.**

   a. True

   b. False

   Answer: b

   False. This document provides a subset of the best practices and design principles documented in the AWS Well-Architected Framework document.

2. **The AWS Well-Architected Framework dictates or prescribes how an architecture should be created.**

   a. True

   b. False

   Answer: b

   False. The framework shares best practices and design principles AWS has gathered over the years. Ultimately, the framework is a set of questions for us to consider and answer. The answers to the questions should influence our architecture and design.

Join our book's Discord space

Join the book's Discord Workspace for Latest updates, Offers, Tech happenings around the world, New Release and Sessions with the Authors:

https://discord.bpbonline.com

CHAPTER 12
Next Steps

Introduction

This chapter will focus on the next steps you can explore to continue mastering AWS serverless. There were many topics we did not cover in-depth, but we explored them since it was important to gain exposure to them. Some of the next steps will include advanced topics such attaching layers to Lambda functions, orchestrating function execution, automatically creating resources using infrastructure as code, creating repeatable deployment processes, and testing.

Structure

We will cover the following topics in this chapter:

- AWS Lambda layers
- AWS Step Functions
- AWS CloudFormation
- AWS Serverless Application Model
- AWS Cloud Development Kit (CDK)
- AWS CodeBuild
- AWS CodePipeline
- Testing Serverless Applications

Objectives

By the end of this chapter, you will be exposed to other AWS services and development approaches that can be used when creating serverless applications.

AWS Lambda layers

Lambda layers allow us to extend our Lambda functions by including additional files without affecting the main zip file that contains our code.

AWS recommends using layers for the following reasons:[1]

- To reduce the size of your deployment packages.
- To separate core function logic from dependencies.
- To share dependencies across multiple functions.
- To use the Lambda console code editor.

We will walk through creating and using a Lambda layer.

Packaging the layer

The layer package should have specific directories if we plan to add dependencies for our runtime.[2]

Since we are using Node.js, our package must have the **`nodejs/node_module`** folder.

Example 1: Packaging the layer

We will create a **`nodejs`** folder on our computer. We will use a terminal to enter the terminal. The following example command assumes the terminal is inside the **`nodejs`** folder:

```
npm init -y

npm i lodash
```

We will use an archiving tool to compress the **`nodejs`** folder. We have successfully created our layer package that has the **`lodash`** library.

Creating a layer

We are going to use our compressed file to create a layer.

1 "Working with Lambda layers." AWS Lambda Developer Guide. Amazon Web Services. **https://docs.aws.amazon.com/lambda/latest/dg/chapter-layers.html**

2 "Packaging your layer content." AWS Lambda Developer Guide. Amazon Web Services. **https://docs.aws.amazon.com/lambda/latest/dg/packaging-layers.html**

Example 2: Creating a layer

Let us create a layer using the given steps:

1. Go to the Lambda service page.
2. Go to the **Additional resources | Layers** menu option.
3. Click the **Create layer** button.
4. Specify **nodejs** in the **Name** field.
5. Select the **Upload a .zip file** radio button.
6. Click the **Upload** button.
7. Select the compressed file.
8. Select all the **Node.js** checkboxes in the **Compatible runtimes** dropdown. See *Figure 12.1*:

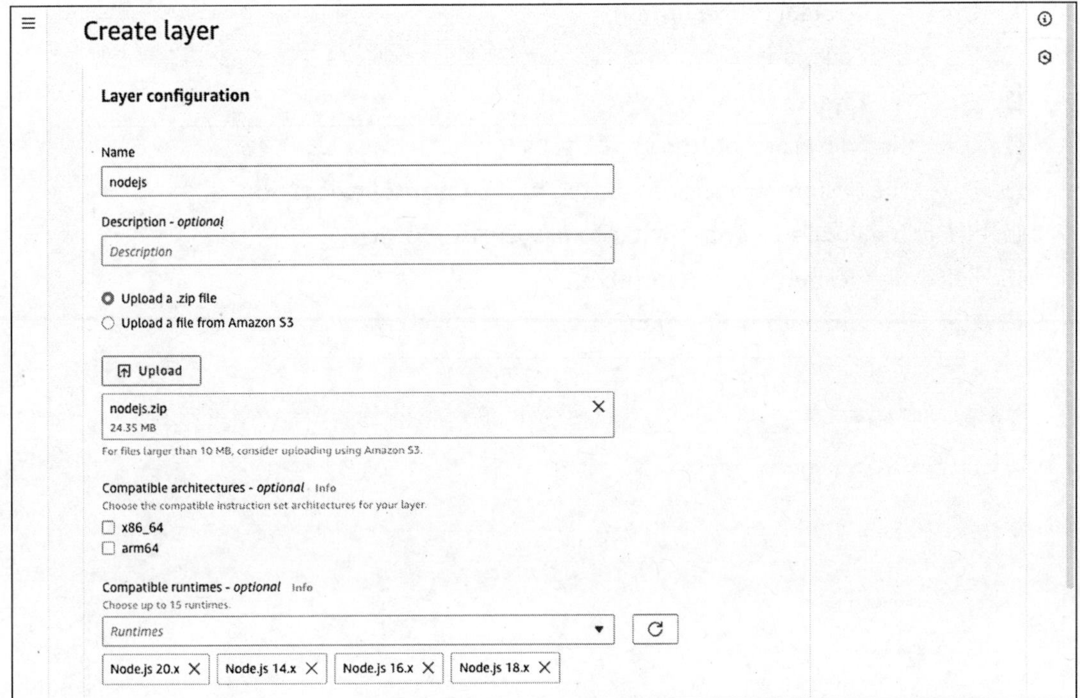

***Figure 12.1:** Creating a layer*

9. Click the **Create** button.

We have successfully created the layer.

Using the layer

We will use the layer in a new Lambda function.

Example 3: Using the layer

Let us use the layer in a Lambda function:

1. Go to the Lambda service page.
2. Go to the **Functions** menu option.
3. Click the **Create function** button.
4. Select the **Author from scratch** radio button.
5. Specify **`layer-example`** in the **Function name** field.
6. Select **Node.js** in the **Runtime** dropdown.
7. Expand the **Change default execution role** section.
8. Select the **Create a new role with basic Lambda permissions** radio button in the **Execution role** section.
9. Click the **Create function** button.
10. Go to the **Code** tab.
11. Go to the **Layers** section.
12. Click the **Add a layer** button.
13. Select the **Custom layers** radio button in the **Layer source** section.
14. Select the **nodejs** layer in the **Custom layers** dropdown.
15. Select the desired version number.
16. Click the **Add** button. See *Figure 12.2*:

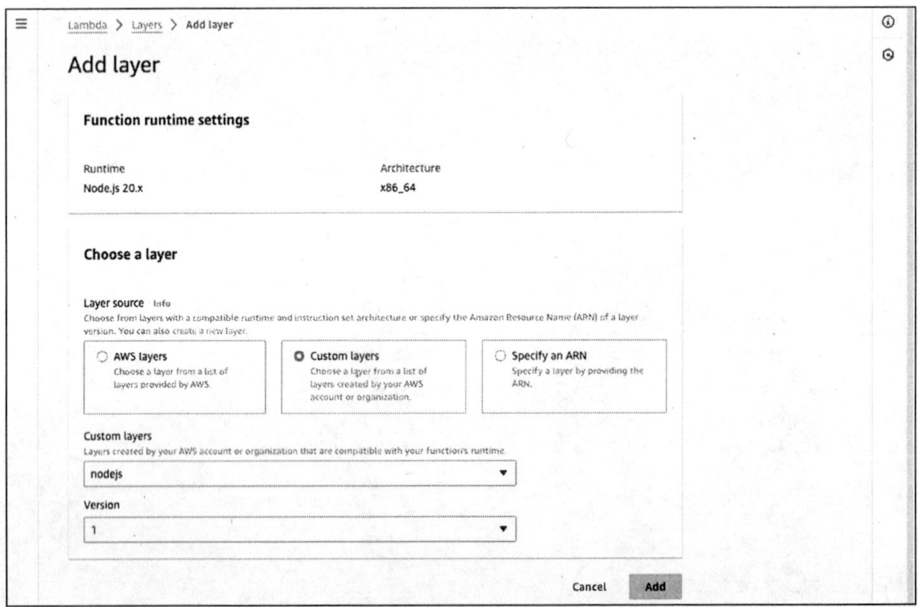

Figure 12.2: Adding a layer

We have successfully added the layer to the function.

17. Specify the following code in the **Code source** section:

```
import _ from "lodash";
export const handler = async (event) => {
  console.log(_.now());
  const response = {
    statusCode: 200,
    body: JSON.stringify(_.now()),
  };
  return response;
};
```

18. Click the **Deploy** button.
19. Click the **Test** button.
20. Select the **Create new event** radio button in the **Test event action** section.
21. Specify **TestEvent** in the "" field.
22. Click the **Save** button.
23. Click the **Test** button. See *Figure 12.3* for your reference:

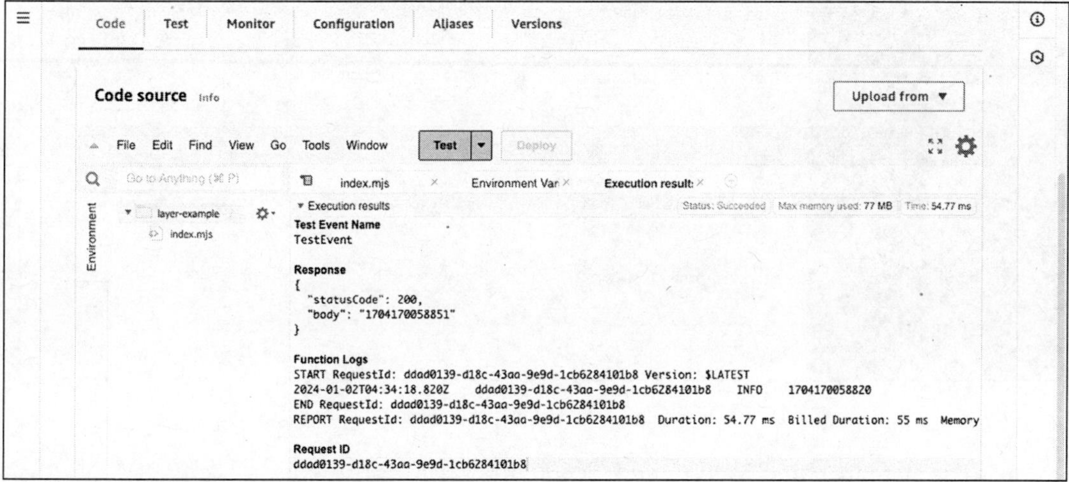

***Figure 12.3:** The execution results*

We have successfully used the **lodash** library from the layer. Remember to update the CloudWatch logs retention settings.

AWS step functions

Step functions allow us to create state machines. We will use a visual flow diagram editor to define the tasks and pass the state to the tasks.

Creating an example state machine

We are going to create the example Hello World workflow as a state machine.

Example 4: Creating an example state machine

Let us create an example state machine using step functions:

1. Search for `step functions` in the top search bar and select the **Step Functions** service or enter **https://us-east-1.console.aws.amazon.com/states/home** in the browser address bar.
2. Click the **Get started** button.
3. Click the **Run Hello World** button. See *Figure 12.4*:

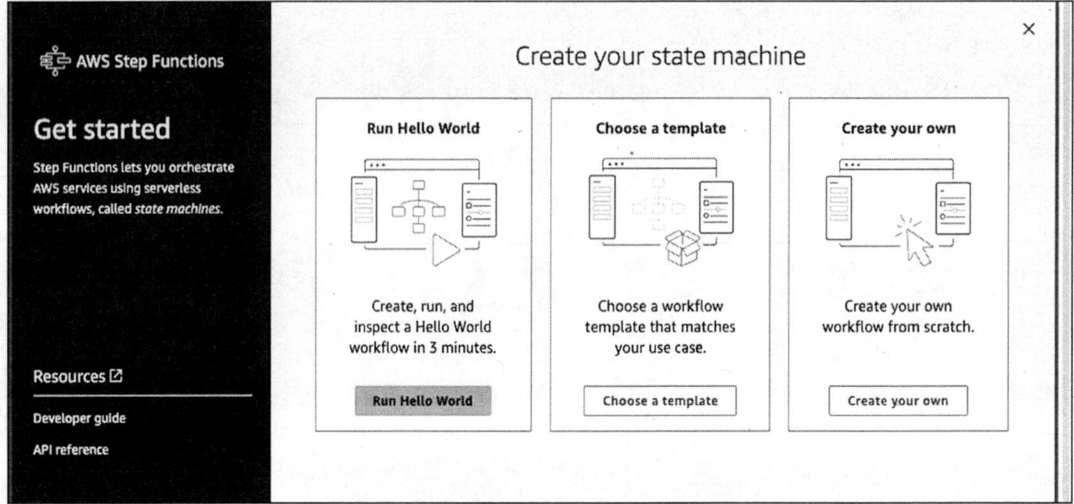

Figure 12.4: *Creating a state machine*

4. The state machine was created. See *Figure 12.5*:

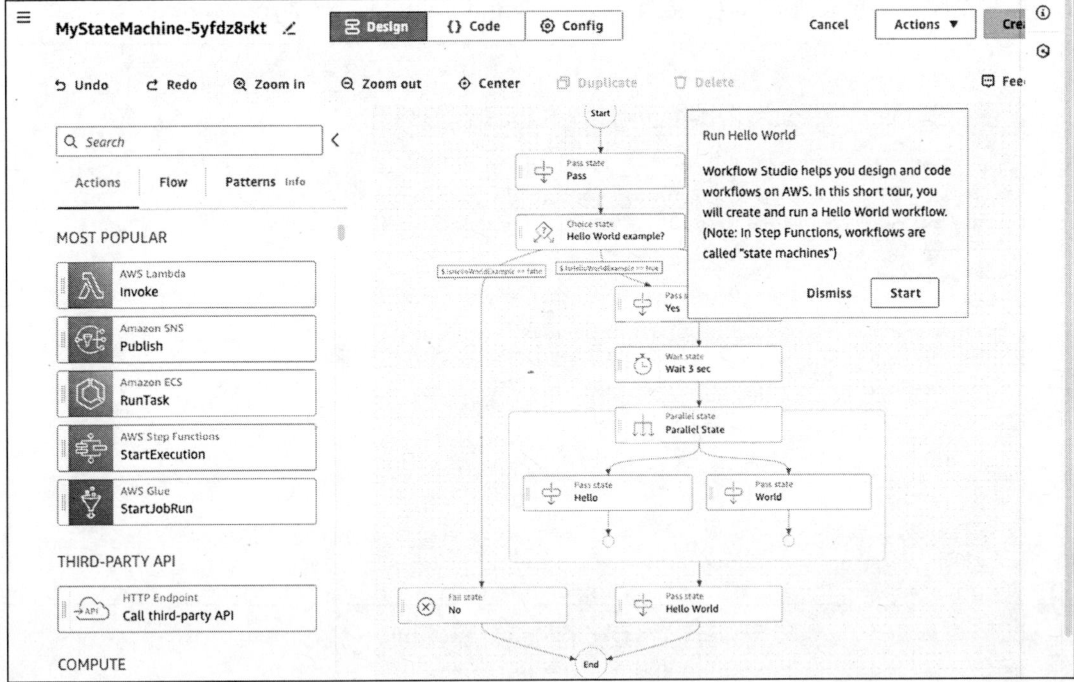

Figure 12.5: The state machines

5. Click the **Create** button.
6. Leave the pre-populate value in the **Name** field.
7. Click the **Start execution** button in the **Start execution** dialog. See *Figure 12.6*:

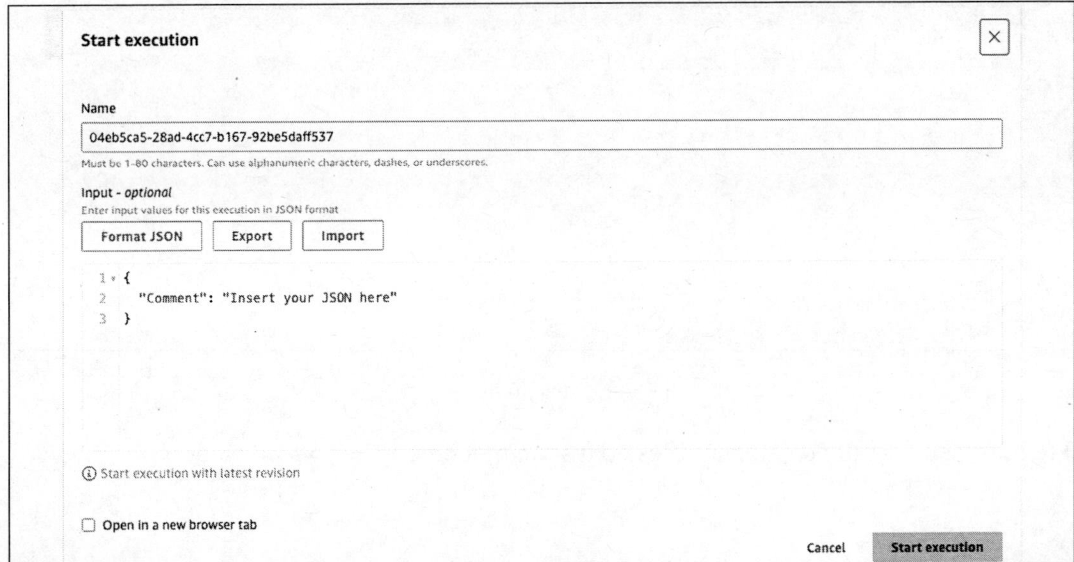

Figure 12.6: Starting the execution

8. Observe the test results. See *Figure 12.7* and *Figure 12.8* for your reference:

Figure 12.7: The execution results

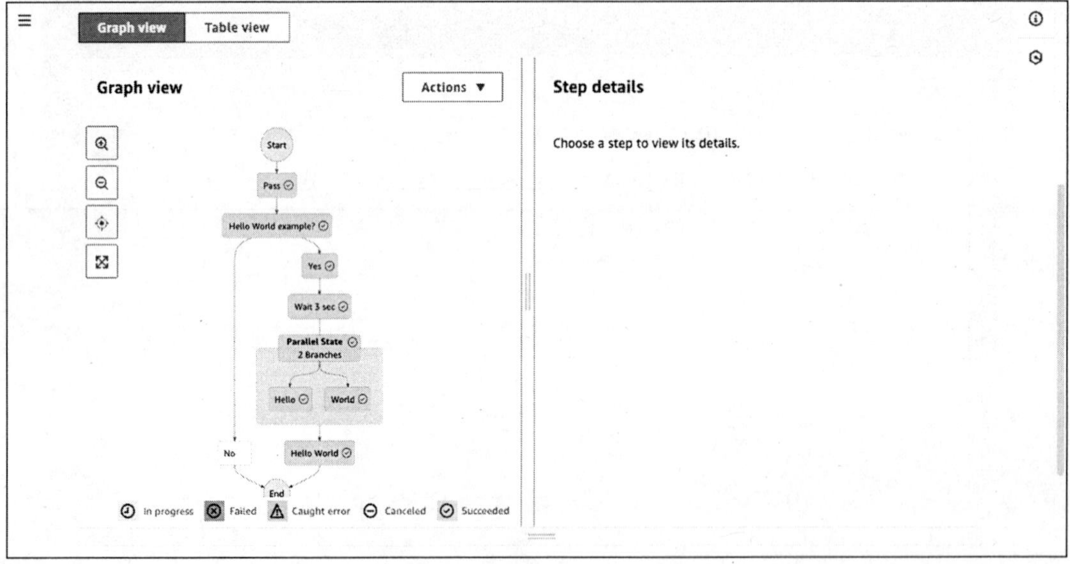

Figure 12.8: The execution results

We have successfully created and tested a state machine.

Integrating a Step Function with API Gateway

We can integrate a state machine with API Gateway so that it is executed when there is an HTTP request to a specific API endpoint. This integration is similar to how we integrated DynamoDB to API Gateway in a previous chapter.

Example 5: Integrating a step function with API Gateway

Let us integrate a state machine with an API endpoint:

1. Go to the IAM service page.
2. Go to the **Access Management | Roles** menu option.
3. Click the **Create role** button.
4. Select the **Custom trust policy** radio button in the **Trusted entity type** section.
5. Specify the following code in the **Custom trust policy** section:

```
{
  "Version": "2012-10-17",
  "Statement": [
    {
      "Sid": "Statement1",
      "Effect": "Allow",
      "Principal": {
        "Service": "apigateway.amazonaws.com"
      },
      "Action": "sts:AssumeRole"
    }
  ]
}
```

6. Click the **Next** button.
7. Specify `AmazonAPIGatewayPushToCloudWatchLogs` in the **Search** field.
8. Check the `AmazonAPIGatewayPushToCloudWatchLogs` checkbox.
9. Specify `AWSStepFunctionsFullAccess` in the **Search** field.
10. Check the `AWSStepFunctionsFullAccess` checkbox.
11. Click the **Next** button.
12. Specify `apigateway-step-function-hello-world` in the **Role name** field.
13. Click the **Create role** button.

We have successfully created the role.

14. Click the **`apigateway-step-function-hello-world`** role.
15. Copy the value in the **ARN** section.
16. Go to the API Gateway service page.
17. Click the **website** API.
18. Create a **`hello-world`** API resource.
19. Click the **Create method** button.
20. Select **POST** in the **Method type** dropdown.
21. Select the **AWS service** radio button in the **Integration type** section.
22. Select **`us-east-1`** in the **AWS Region** dropdown.
23. Select **Step Functions** in the **AWS service** dropdown.
24. Select **POST** in the **HTTP method** dropdown.
25. Select the **Use action name** radio button in the **Action type** section.
26. Specify **`StartExecution`** in the **Action name** field.
27. Paste the **`arn:aws:iam::{accountId}:role/apigateway-step-function-hello-world`** ARN value copied earlier in the **Execution role** field.

Note: The `{accountId}` is the AWS account ID.

28. Click the **Create method** button.

    We have successfully created the API endpoint.

29. Go to the **Test** tab.
30. Use the following code in the **Request body** section.

Note: Update the account ID and state machine name.

```
{
    "input": "{}",
    "name": "TestExecution",
    "stateMachineArn": "arn:aws:states:us-east-1:{accountID}:stateMachine:{stateMachineName}"
}
```

31. Click the **Test** button.

    We have successfully invoked the step function from the API Gateway.

32. Click the **Deploy** button.

    We have successfully deployed the API.

This was a basic example. It can be improved to avoid having the website client send the state machine ARN in the API request.[3]

Infrastructure as Code

Infrastructure as Code (**IaC**) is a concept where we can define our cloud infrastructure and create resources using code. We touched on this in the previous chapter. There are various IaC tools. Some are provided by AWS, and others are third-party.

We will focus on the following AWS IaC tools:

- **CloudFormation**: This is an AWS service where we upload a CloudFormation template specification to configure and update our AWS cloud resources. We can use the AWS management console or the AWS CLI to use CloudFormation.
- **AWS Serverless Application Model (SAM)**: This is a CLI tool that uses a SAM template specification to create serverless resources.
- **AWS Cloud Development Kit (CDK)**: This is a framework where we can specify Cloud resources using JavaScript, Python, and other languages.

We will explore each in the following sections.

AWS CloudFormation

In the previous chapter, we discussed automating the deployment of our serverless resources in the AWS cloud. We will explore using CloudFormation to create resources.

Creating a new IAM policy and role

We will create an IAM policy that gives full privileges to CloudFormation for the services it will modify. We will create an IAM role that uses that policy.

Example 6: Creating a new IAM policy and role

Let us create a new IAM policy and role using the given steps:

1. Go to the IAM service page.
2. Go to the **Access management | Policies** menu option.
3. Click the **Create policy** button.
4. Select **S3** in the **Service** dropdown.
5. Check the **All S3 actions (s3:*)** checkbox in the **Actions allowed** section.
6. Select the **All** radio button in the **Resources** section.

3 "Creating a Step Functions API using API Gateway." AWS Step Functions Developer Guide. Amazon Web Services. **https://docs.aws.amazon.com/step-functions/latest/dg/tutorial-api-gateway.html**

7. Click the **Next** button.
8. Specify **`cloudformation-deploy`** in the **Policy name** field.
9. Click the **Create policy** button.

   We have successfully created the policy.
10. Go to the **Access management | Roles** menu option.
11. Click the **Create role** button.
12. Select the **AWS service** radio button in the **Trusted entity type** section.
13. Select **CloudFormation** in the **Service or use case** section.
14. Click the **Next** button.
15. Specify **`cloudformation-deploy`** in the search field.
16. Check the **`cloudformation-deploy`** policy.
17. Click the **Next** button.
18. Specify **`cloudformation-deploy`** in the **Role name** field.
19. Click the **Create role** button.

We have successfully created the role.

Creating a stack

We will use a CloudFormation template to create a stack with an S3 bucket.[4] CloudFormation supports both YAML and JSON formats. We will use YAML for improved readability.

Example 7: Creating a stack

Let us create a stack:

1. Create a **`stack.yaml`** file on our computer.
2. Paste the following YAML code in file:

```
Resources:
  TestBucket:
    Type: AWS::S3::Bucket
    Properties:
      BucketName: masteringawsserverlessbook-created-by-cf
      VersioningConfiguration:
        Status: Enabled
```

   We have successfully saved the CloudFormation template file.

4 "AWS::S3::Bucket." AWS CloudFormation User Guide. Amazon Web Services. **https://docs.aws.amazon.com/AWSCloudFormation/latest/UserGuide/aws-resource-s3-bucket.html**

3. Search **`cloudformation`** in the top search bar, select the **CloudFormation** service, or enter **https://us-east-1.console.aws.amazon.com/cloudformation/home** in the browser address bar.
4. Go to the **Stacks** menu option.
5. Click the **Create stack** button.
6. Click the **Template is ready** radio button in the **Prepare template** section.
7. Select the **Upload a template file** radio button in the **Template source** section.
8. Click the **Choose file** button.
9. Select the **`stack.yaml`** file. See *Figure 12.9*:

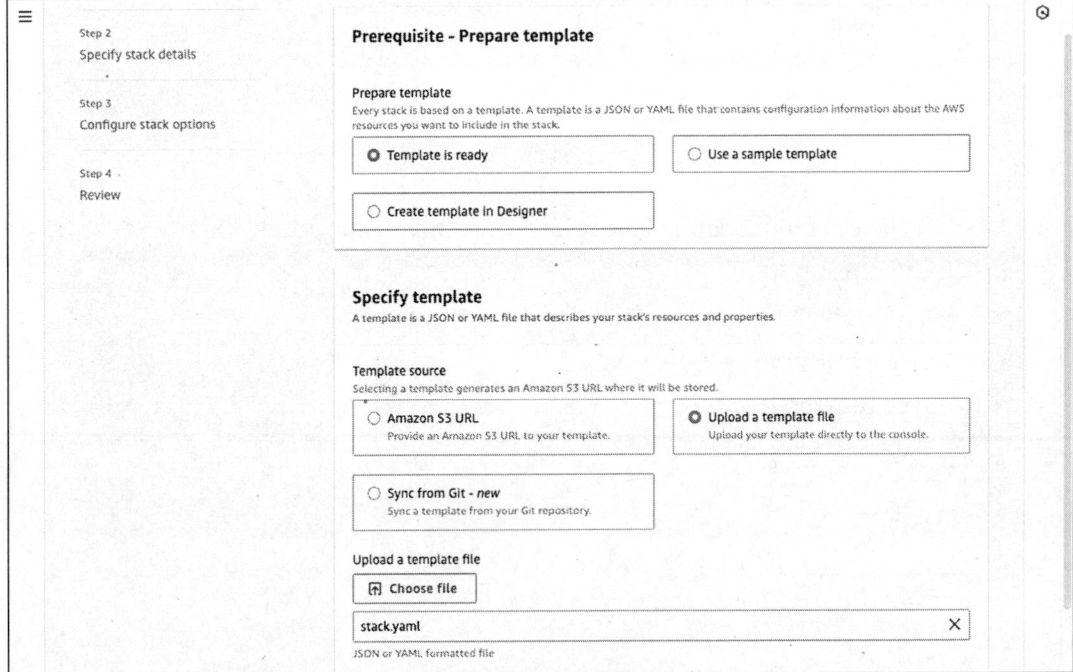

Figure 12.9: Creating a stack

10. Click the **Next** button.
11. Specify **`test-stack`** in the **Stack name** field.
12. Click the **Next** button. See *Figure 12.10*:

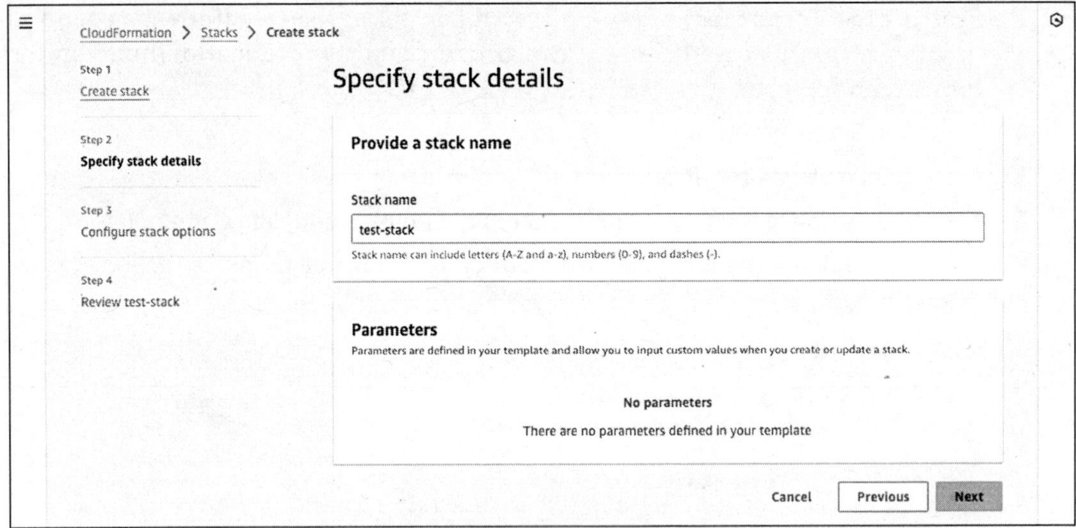

Figure 12.10: Creating a stack

13. Select the **cloudformation-deploy** role in the **IAM role** dropdown.
14. Click the **Next** button.
15. Click the **Submit** button.
16. We successfully created the stack.
17. Observe that the stack is being created. See *Figure 12.11*:

Figure 12.11: Creating a stack

The status changes from **`CREATE_IN_PROGRESS`** to **`CREATE_COMPLETED`** when it finishes deploying.

We have successfully created an S3 bucket using CloudFormation.

Updating a stack

We will update our stack to add a Lambda function[5] with simple code and its related IAM role[6].

Example 8: Updating a stack

Let us update a stack, as shown:

1. Go to the IAM service page.
2. Go to the **Access management | Policies** menu option.
3. Click the **`cloudformation-deploy`** policies.
4. Click the **Edit** button.
5. Click the **Visual** button.
6. Click the **Add more permissions** button.
7. Select **Lambda** in the **Service** dropdown.
8. Check the **All Lambda actions (lambda:*)** checkbox in the **Actions allowed** section.
9. Select the **All** radio button in the **Resources** section.
10. Click the **Add more permissions** button.
11. Select **IAM** in the **Service** dropdown.
12. Search **Role** in the **Filter Actions** search field.
13. Check the following checkboxes:
    a. **`GetRole`**
    b. **`PassRole`**
    c. **`CreateRole`**
    d. **`DeleteRole`**
    e. **`UpdateRole`**
    f. **`GetRolePolicy`**
    g. **`AttachRolePolicy`**
    h. **`DeleteRolePolicy`**

---

5 "AWS::Lambda::Function." AWS CloudFormation User Guide. Amazon Web Services. **https://docs.aws.amazon.com/AWSCloudFormation/latest/UserGuide/aws-resource-lambda-function.html**

6 "AWS::IAM::Role." AWS CloudFormation User Guide. Amazon Web Services. **https://docs.aws.amazon.com/AWSCloudFormation/latest/UserGuide/aws-resource-iam-role.html**

   i. **`DetachRolePolicy`**
   j. **`PutRolePolicy`**

14. Select the **Specific** radio button in the **Resources** section.
15. Click the **Add ARNs** link in the **role** section.
16. Click the **Visual** button.
17. Select the **This account** radio button in the **Resource in** section.
18. Specify **`function-*`** in the **Resource role name with path** field.
19. Click the **Add ARNs** button.
20. Click the **Next** button.
21. Click the **Save** changes button.

    We have successfully updated the policy.
22. Open the **`stack.yaml`** file on our computer.
23. Append the YAML code below to the end of the file.

Note: We are going to reuse the automatically created `layer-example-role` role since it has.

```
HelloWorldRole:
  Type: AWS::IAM::Role
  Properties:
    AssumeRolePolicyDocument:
      Version: "2012-10-17"
      Statement:
        - Effect: Allow
          Principal:
            Service:
              - lambda.amazonaws.com
          Action:
            - 'sts:AssumeRole'
    Description: String
    ManagedPolicyArns:
      - arn:aws:iam::aws:policy/service-role/
      AWSLambdaBasicExecutionRole
    RoleName: function-hello-world
```

```
HelloWorldFunction:
  Type: AWS::Lambda::Function
  Properties:
    Architectures:
      - arm64
    Code:
      ZipFile: |
        export const handler = async (event) => {
          const response = {
            statusCode: 200,
            body: JSON.stringify(
              'Hello world'
            ),
          };
          return response;
        };
    FunctionName: hello-world
    Handler: handler
    MemorySize: 128
    Role: !GetAtt HelloWorldRole.Arn
    Runtime: nodejs20.x
    Timeout: 3
```

We have successfully updated the CloudFormation template file.

24. Go to the CloudFormation service page.
25. Go to the **Stacks** menu option.
26. Click the **`test-stack`** stack.
27. Click the **Update** button.
28. Select the **Replace current template** radio button in the **Prepare template** section.
29. Select the **Upload a template file** radio button in the **Template source** section.
30. Click the **Choose file** button.
31. Select the **`stack.yaml`** file. See *Figure 12.12*:

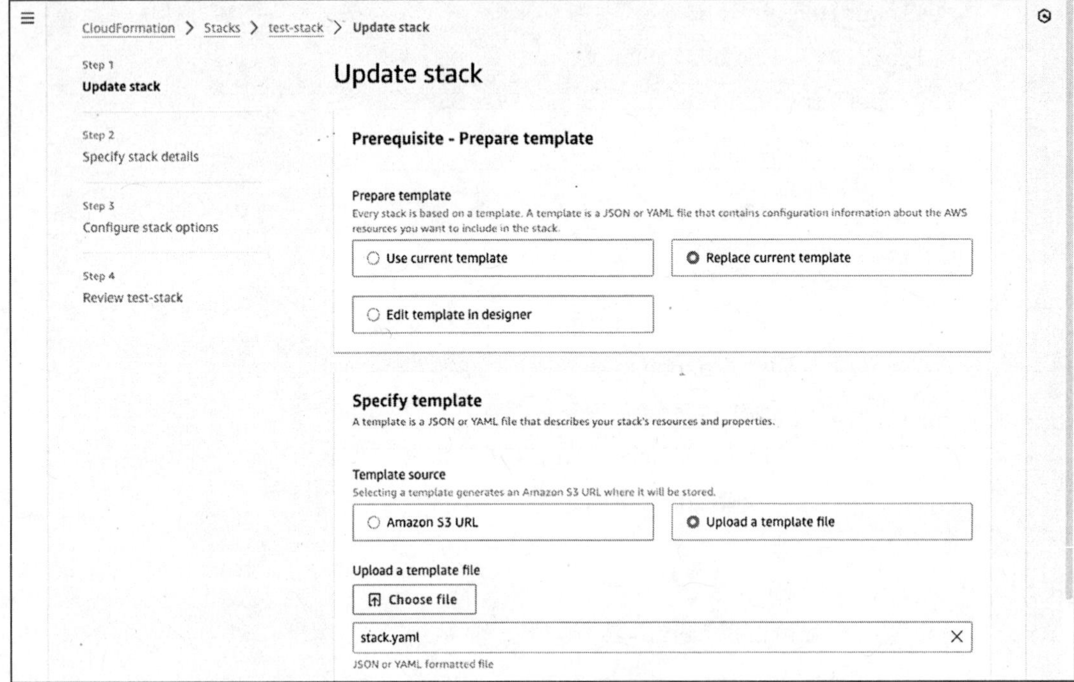

Figure 12.12: Updating a stack

32. Click the **Next** button.
33. Click the **Next** button in the **Specify stack details** page.
34. Click the **Next** button in the **Configure stack options** page.
35. Click the **Submit** button.

We have successfully submitted the update. The status changes from **UPDATE_PROGRESS** to **CREATE_COMPLETED** when it finishes deploying.

We have successfully updated the stack to create a Lambda function and its IAM role.

AWS serverless application model

We will explore creating serverless sources using the **Serverless Application Model (SAM)**.

We will explore the example commands below. We will use a Linux terminal in all our examples. Other than the installation package, the Linux commands can be used on other operating systems when using the correct terminal application.

Creating an IAM group and IAM user

We will need privileges to deploy our SAM application using the CLI. We will use the CloudFormation deploy privileges we created earlier. Ideally, we would use the IAM Identity Center to create the user, but that will require an in-depth discussion that is not specific to serverless. As a result, we will create an IAM user assigned to an IAM group that has certain privileges.

Example 9: Creating an IAM group and IAM user

Let us create an IAM group and user:

1. Go to the IAM service page.
2. Go to the **Access Management | Groups** menu option.
3. Click the **Create group** button.
4. Specify `iac-cli-tools` in the **User group name** field. See Figure *12.13*:

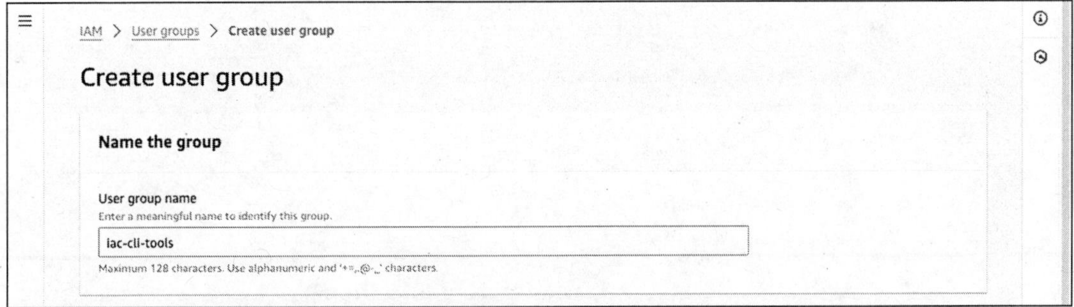

Figure 12.13: *Creating an IAM group*

5. Specify **AmazonAPIGatewayAdministrator** in the search field.
6. Check the **AmazonAPIGatewayAdministrator** policy.
7. Specify **AmazonS3FullAccess** in the search field.
8. Check the **AmazonS3FullAccess** policy.
9. Specify **AWSCloudFormationFullAccess** in the search field.
10. Check the **AWSCloudFormationFullAccess** policy.
11. Specify **AWSLambda_FullAccess** in the search field.
12. Check the **AWSLambda_FullAccess** policy.
13. Specify **IAMFullAccess** in the search field.

14. Check the **IAMFullAccess** policy.
15. Click the **Create group** button.

Note: We could have used AdministratorAccess since we would have all the necessary privileges, but this violates the principle of least privilege.

We have successfully created the group.

16. Go the **Access management** | **Users** menu option.
17. Click the **Create user** button.
18. Specify a username.

Note: Consider including CLI in the username to clarify that the user only has CLI access.

19. Click the **Next** button. See *Figure 12.14*:

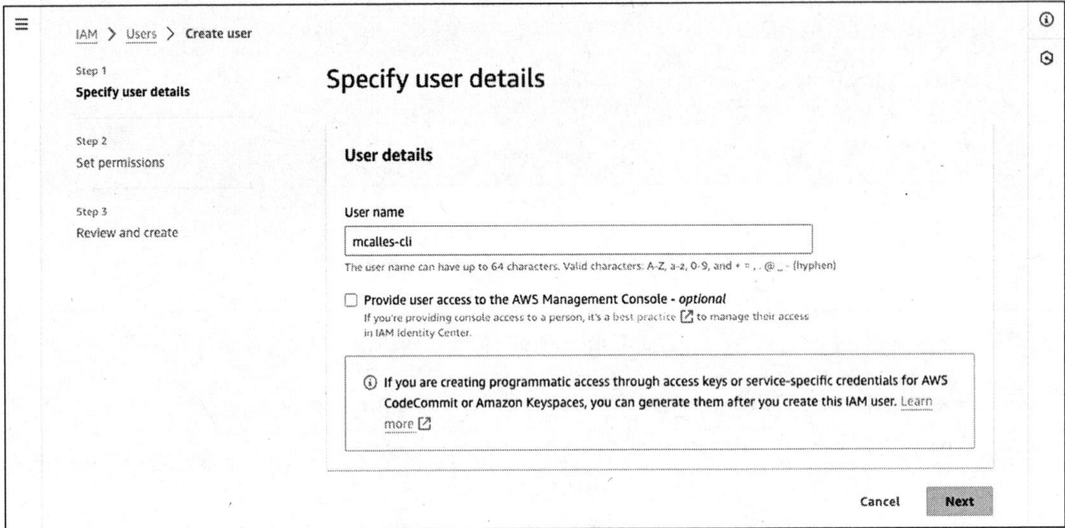

***Figure 12.14:** Creating an IAM user*

20. Select the **Add user to group** radio button in the **Permissions options** section.
21. Check the **iac-cli-tools** group. See *Figure 12.15*:

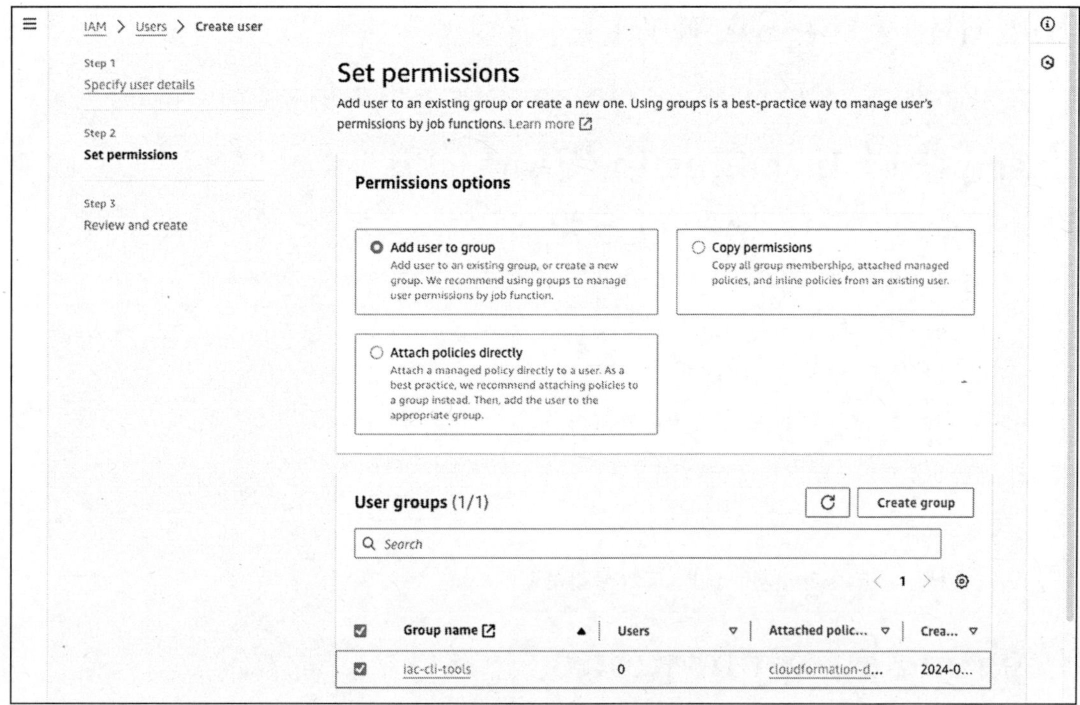

Figure 12.15: Creating an IAM user

22. Click the **Next** button.
23. Click the **Create user** button.

    We have successfully created the user.
24. Click the **mcalles-cli** user.
25. Go to the **Security credentials** tab.
26. Click the **Create access key** button.
27. Select the **Command Line Interface (CLI)** radio button in the **Use case** section.
28. Click the **Next** button.
29. Click the **Create access key** button.
30. Click the **Download .csv file** button.

Note: Make sure to protect this file on your computer.

31. Click the **Done** button.

We have successfully downloaded the access key.

Installing the SAM CLI

We will install the SAM CLI.[7]

Example 10: Installing the SAM CLI

We will use the following Linux commands:

```
# use wget to download the file or download using a web browser

wget https://github.com/aws/aws-sam-cli/releases/latest/download/aws-sam-cli-linux-x86_64.zip

unzip aws-sam-cli-linux-x86_64.zip -d sam-installation

sudo ./sam-installation/install

sam -version
```

We have successfully installed the SAM CLI.

Creating an application

We will create a serverless application using the SAM CLI.

Example 11: Creating an application

We will use the following Linux command:

```
sam init
```

Follow the on-screen instructions to do the following:

1. Select the **AWS Quick Start Templates** template source.
2. Select the **Hello World Example** template.
3. Specify **N** for the most popular runtime and package type.
4. Select the desired run time.
5. Select **Zip** as the package type.
6. Specify **N** for enabling X-Ray tracing on the function(s).
7. Specify **N** for enabling monitoring using CloudWatch Application Insights.
8. Specify **N** for setting Structured Logging in JSON format.
9. Specify **sam-app** as the project name.

---

7 "Installing the AWS SAM CLI." AWS Serverless Application Model Developer Guide. Amazon Web Services. **https://docs.aws.amazon.com/serverless-application-model/latest/developerguide/install-sam-cli.html**

We will use the following Linux commands:

```
cd sam-app
```

```
ls
```

We have successfully created our app.

Building the app

We will build the new app using the SAM CLI.

Example 12: Build the app

We will use the following Linux commands:

```
sam validate
```

```
sam build
```

We have successfully built the app.

Deploying the app

We will deploy the new app using the SAM CLI.

Example 13: Deploying the app

We will use the following Linux commands:

```
export AWS_ACCESS_KEY_ID="the value from the CSV file"
```

```
export AWS_SECRET_ACCESS_KEY="the value from the CSV file"
```

```
export AWS_DEFAULT_REGION="us-east-1"
```

```
sam deploy --guided
```

Follow the on-screen instructions to do the following:

1. Press the *Enter* key to accept the default **Stack Name** value.
2. Press the *Enter* key to accept the default **AWS Region** value.
3. Press the *Enter* key to accept the default **Confirm changes before deploy** value.
4. Press the *Enter* key to accept the default **Allow SAM CLI IAM role creation** value.
5. Press the *Enter* key to accept the default **Disable rollback** value.
6. Specify *y* in the **`HelloWorldFunction`** warning.
7. Press the *Enter* key to accept the default **Save arguments to configuration file** value.

8. Press the *Enter* key to accept the default **SAM configuration file** value.
9. Press the *Enter* key to accept the default **SAM configuration environment** value.
10. Specify **y** in the **Deploy this changeset?** option.

    We have successfully deployed the app.
11. Go to the CloudFormation service page.
12. Go to the **Stacks** menu option.
13. Click the **sam-app** stack.
14. Go to the **Resources** tab.
15. Observe the created resources.

AWS Cloud Development Kit

We will explore creating serverless sources using the **Cloud Development Kit** (**CDK**).

Updating the IAM group

We will update the IAM group to add the permissions needed by CDK.

Example 14: Updating the IAM group

Let us update the IAM group.

1. Go to the IAM service page.
2. Go the **Access management** | **Groups** menu option.
3. Click the **iac-cli-tools** group.
4. Go to the **Permissions** tab.
5. Select **Attach policies** in the **Add permission** dropdown.
6. Specify **AmazonEC2ContainerRegistryFullAccess** in the search field.
7. Check the **AmazonEC2ContainerRegistryFullAccess** policy.
8. Specify **AmazonSNSFullAccess** in the search field.
9. Check the **AmazonSNSFullAccess** policy.
10. Specify **AmazonSQSFullAccess** in the search field.
11. Check the **AmazonSQSFullAccess** policy.
12. Specify **AmazonSSMFullAccess** in the search field.
13. Check the **AmazonSSMFullAccess** policy.
14. Click the **Attach policies** button.

We have successfully updated the group.

Installing CDK

We will install CDK.

Example 15: Installing CDK

We will use the following Linux commands:

```
npm install -g aws-cdk

# or use sudo depending on the user OS privileges

sudo npm install -g aws-cdk

cdk --version
```

We have successfully installed CDK.

Creating an application

We will create a CDK application.

Example 16: Creating an application

We will use the following Linux commands:

```
mkdir cdk-app

cd cdk-app

cdk init sample-app --language=javascript

ls
```

We have successfully created an application.

Bootstrapping CDK

We need to prepare our AWS account to use CDK.

Example 17: Bootstrapping CDK

We will use the following Linux commands:

```
cdk bootstrap
```

We have successfully bootstrapped CDK.

Deploying an application

We will deploy the CDK application.

Example 18: Deploying an application

We will use the following Linux commands:

```
cdk synth

# observe the cloudformation template in the output

cdk deploy

# specify "y" when prompted to deploy the changes
```

We have successfully created an application and deployed the app. Let us observe the new stack in the CloudFormation service page:

1. Go to the CloudFormation service page.
2. Go to the **Stacks** menu option
3. Click the **CdkAppStack** stack.
4. Go to the **Resources** tab.
5. Observe the created resources.

Updating the application

We will update the CDK application to create an S3 bucket and a Lambda function. We will allow the function to have read privileges to the bucket. CDK will automatically create the function role and permissions for us.

Example 19: Updating an application

Let us update the CDK application using the given steps:

1. We are going to update the **`cdk-app/lib/cdk-app-stack.js`** file with the following code is highlighted in bold:

   ```
   const cdk = require('aws-cdk-lib');

   const sns = require('aws-cdk-lib/aws-sns');

   const subs = require('aws-cdk-lib/aws-sns-subscriptions');

   const sqs = require('aws-cdk-lib/aws-sqs');

   const s3 = require('aws-cdk-lib/aws-s3');

   const lambda = require('aws-cdk-lib/aws-lambda');

   const fs = require('fs');
   ```

```
const path = require('path');

class CdkAppStack extends cdk.Stack {
  /**
   * @param {cdk.App} scope
   * @param {string} id
   * @param {cdk.StackProps=} props
   */
  constructor(scope, id, props) {
    super(scope, id, props);

    const queue = new sqs.Queue(this, 'CdkAppQueue', {
      visibilityTimeout: cdk.Duration.seconds(300)
    });

    const topic = new sns.Topic(this, 'CdkAppTopic');

    topic.addSubscription(new subs.SqsSubscription(queue));

    const bucket = new s3.Bucket(this, 'CdkAppBucket', {
      bucketName: 'masteringawsserverlessbook-created-by-cdk',
    });

    const fn = new lambda.Function(this, 'CdkAppFunction', {
      runtime: lambda.Runtime.NODEJS_LATEST,
      memorySize: 128,
      architecture: lambda.Architecture.ARM_64,
      handler: 'handler',
      code: lambda.Code.fromInline(
        fs.readFileSync(
          path.resolve(__dirname, '..', 'src', 'hello-world.mjs')
        ).toString()
      ),
      timeout: cdk.Duration.seconds(3),
   });
```

```
        bucket.grantRead(fn);
    }
}

module.exports = { CdkAppStack }
```

2. Next, we will create the **cdk-app/src/hello-world.mjs** file for our Lambda function with the code shown below:

```
export const handler = async (event) => {
  const response = {
    statusCode: 200,
    body: JSON.stringify(
      'Hello world'
    ),
  };
  return response;
};
```

Finally, we will deploy the updates.

```
cdk synth
cdk deploy
```

We have successfully created the S3 bucket, Lambda function and its IAM role.

AWS CodeBuild

1. We can use CodeBuild to automatically deploy our serverless application when using a git-provider such as AWS CodeStart.
2. We will create a **buildspec.yml** file and included it in our git repository. See the following example file:

```
version: 0.2
phases:
  install:
    runtime-versions:
      nodejs: latest
    commands:
      - npm i -g cdk
      - cd cdk-app
```

```
        - npm i
  build:
    commands:
      cdk deploy --require-approval never
```

When we commit a change to git, CodeBuild can automatically start and run through the commands in the **`buildspec.yml`** file. The command execution will install CDK, the npm dependencies in the **`cdk-app`** folder and perform a CDK **`deploy`** command.

AWS CodePipeline

We could use CodePipeline with CodeBuild to deploy. We can create a workflow whenever a git commit happens:

1. The **first stage** would be to collect the files from all the code repositories. We would connect a GitHub or Bitbucket account to our AWS account so that CodePipeline can check out the code repository.
2. The **second stage** would be to run a test and build any source code. The tests should consist of unit tests, integration tests and end-to-end tests to verify the source code meets the application requirements and any bugs are caught in this stage rather than the production application.
3. The **third stage** would be an approval step that requires someone to approve or reject the changes. Having an approval step helps prevent an unintended release to the production application.
4. If approved, the **fourth stage** would be running the deployment.

This type of workflows provides us with a consistent and repeatable process to deploy our application.

Testing serverless applications

AWS SAM has local testing capabilities. AWS recommends using SAM to test CDK applications locally, too.[8]

With SAM, we can do the following:[9]

- Invoking Lambda functions locally.
- Running API Gateway locally.

8 "Locally testing AWS CDK applications." AWS Serverless Application Model Developer Guide. Amazon Web Services. **https://docs.aws.amazon.com/serverless-application-model/latest/developerguide/serverless-cdk-testing.html**

9 "Testing and debugging serverless applications." AWS Serverless Application Model Developer Guide. Amazon Web Services. **https://docs.aws.amazon.com/serverless-application-model/latest/developerguide/serverless-test-and-debug.html**

- Integrating with automated tests.
- Generating sample event payloads.
- Debugging Lambda functions locally.

We will use the `sam local` command.

Next steps

The following are some ideas about steps now that we are at the conclusion of this book:

- **Create a new website**: We only used HTML and JavaScript on the website to eliminate the confusion of using single-page application frameworks. We did use Bootstrap to help give our website a nice look and feel. There are other design frameworks that only use HTML and JavaScript. Try creating a new website without using the code provided in this book.
- **Updating Cognito to use SES**: We set up Cognito to use the AWS-provided sender email address. We had not set up SES prior to that. Consider updating the Cognito user pool to use SES to send emails from the custom domain.
- **Independent exercises and examples**: We reviewed independent exercises and examples. Consider working through them.
- **Adding serverless to an existing architecture**: If you are working on an existing architecture that does not use serverless, consider looking for an opportunity to introduce it to the smallest existing feature or a new upcoming feature.
- **Cloud migration**: If you are running on-premises, consider looking for an opportunity to migrate the smallest pieces of your architecture to the AWS cloud.
- **Deconstructing monolithic architectures**: Similar to adding serverless to an existing architecture, look for an opportunity to introduce serverless and start the process of breaking moving away from a monolithic architecture if it makes sense to the business goals.
- **Porting server-based designs**: Consider looking for a way to introduce serverless to an existing server-based design. If a new API endpoint is needed, propose using API Gateway to host it.
- **Mailing list sign-up form:** Consider creating a mailing list sign-up page for the website. This page will have a form where someone can enter their email address and sign up for a mailing list. When a user submits the form, the email address is saved to a DynamoDB table, and a confirmation email is sent to the email address.
- **Automated security check**: Create a Lambda function that automatically checks that the root account MFA is enabled rather than using the AWS Config service.

- **Use a frontend web framework**: We use HTML, JavaScript and CSS to create the serverless website. Consider using a frontend framework, such as React and Vue, to improve the developer experience and add authentication and authorization libraries.

Conclusion

In this chapter, we touched on using AWS Lambda Layers and Step Functions. We also discussed infrastructure as code with CloudFormation, SAM, and CDK. We introduced the concept of automated deployments with CodeBuild and CodePipeline and local testing with SAM.

We covered many topics in this book. We performed several hands-on exercises to build a serverless website and its backend. Many people learn best with hands-on exercises, and we made sure to do as many as we practically could.

Go use an AWS account and continue building. Wishing you much success on your serverless journey!

Points to remember

- Lambda layers are useful for packaging dependencies and custom runtimes.
- Step Functions allow us to create state machine workflows.
- CloudFormation is the AWS service that provides infrastructure as code for automated infrastructure deployments.
- SAM and CDK provide an abstraction layer to CloudFormation.
- SAM provides local testing features.
- CodeBuild and CodePipeline allow us to automate deployments by specifying the Linux commands in a file.

Multiple choice questions

1. **Should we create an IAM role with administrator access?**

   a. Yes

   b. No

   Answer: b

   No. This violates the principle of least privilege and gives a malicious actor full privilege if they get access to those permissions.

2. **CDK provides more functionality than SAM?**

   a. True

   b. False

   Answer: a

   True. SAM focuses on serverless applications whereas CDK supports most AWS services.

Join our book's Discord space

Join the book's Discord Workspace for Latest updates, Offers, Tech happenings around the world, New Release and Sessions with the Authors:

https://discord.bpbonline.com

Index

A

E

F

G

H

I

J

K

L

M

N

O

P

R

S